DIARY OF A JOURNEY

THROUGH

MONGOLIA AND TIBET

IN

1891 AND 1892

DIARY OF A JOURNEY

THROUGH

MONGOLIA AND TIBET

IN

1891 AND 1892

WILLIAM WOODVILLE ROCKHILL

GYAN

Published by

Gyan Publishing House
5, Ansari Road
Daryaganj, New Delhi-110002
Phone: 011-47034999, 9811692060
E-mail: books@gyanbooks.com

Distribution Network
gyanbooks.com
India, USA, Canada, UK, Australia, France

ISBN: 978-81-212-9368-6 (PB)
First Published, 1894

2nd Impression 2023

Printed at: Gyan Press, Delhi.

DIARY OF A JOURNEY THROUGH MONGOLIA AND TIBET IN 1891 AND 1892

AUTHOR:WILLIAM WOODVILLE ROCKHILL

DIARY OF A JOURNEY

THROUGH

MONGOLIA AND TIBET

IN

1891 AND 1892

BY

WILLIAM WOODVILLE ROCKHILL

Gold Medalist of the Royal Geographical Society

CITY OF WASHINGTON
PUBLISHED BY THE SMITHSONIAN INSTITUTION
1894

ADVERTISEMENT.

The journey described in this volume was undertaken by Mr. Rockhill partly under the auspices of the Smithsonian Institution, and the work is issued as a special publication of the Institution, with the general object of "increasing and diffusing knowledge" in regard to the little known countries traversed by the explorer.

S. P. LANGLEY,
Secretary of the Smithsonian Institution.

TABLE OF CONTENTS.

ILLUSTRATIONS—PLATES.

ILLUSTRATIONS IN THE TEXT.

INTRODUCTORY NOTICE.

As far as my knowledge goes, the first European traveler who entered Tibet was Friar Odoric, who, coming from Northwestern China, traversed Central Tibet on his way to India in or about 1325, and sojourned some time in its capital, Lh'asa. The information he has left us of this country in his "Eastern Parts of the World Described,"* is, however, very meager and of no geographical value.

Three centuries elapsed before another Western traveler visited this country. In 1624 the Jesuit Antonio Andrada went from Agra to the sources of the Ganges and Sutlej, and thence through Western Tibet, to Kiria probably, whence he journeyed along the northern base of the Kun-lun to the Koko nor country, or Tangut, ultimately reaching China.†

The next journey through Tibet was performed by Fathers Grueber and Dorville in 1661. They left Hsi-ning Fu in Kan-su and followed the highroad to Lh'asa by Nya-ch'uk'a and Réting gomba. After staying two months in Lh'asa, they pushed on to Nepaul by way of the Kuti la. Grueber's narrative contains much valuable information on Tibet, its people, their customs and religion.‡

In 1716 the Jesuit Fathers Desideri and Freyre reached Lh'asa, coming from Sikkim, and remained there until 1729. In 1719

---

* Published in Col. H. Yule's *Cathay and the Way Thither*, I, pp. 1–162.

† See Péron et Billecocq, *Recueil de Voyages du Tibet.*

‡ Published in Thévenot's *Relations*, II, part iv. See also Clem. R. Markham, *Narrative of the Mission of George Bogle and of the Journey of Thomas Manning*, 295 et seq. This latter work has been constantly before me in writing these notes.

the Capuchin Francisco della Penna and twelve other members of his order also reached the capital of Tibet, and established a mission there which flourished until about 1760. While most of the information collected by Desideri still remains in manuscript, the letters of Orazio della Penna have been published several times and are of great value.*

Of the journey to Tibet of the Dutchman Samuel van de Putte, in or about 1730, we know but little. He went to Lh'asa from India, and then traveled by the Hsi-ning road to Peking, returning again to Lh'asa and to India, and dying in Batavia in 1745.†

In 1774 George Bogle was sent by Warren Hastings to Shigatsé to try and open commercial relations with Tibet. The account of his journey has been published in 1879 by Mr. Clements R. Markham.

In 1783 Captain Samuel Turner also visited Shigatsé, and on his return published a valuable account of his journey.‡

I pass over the work of Brian H. Hodgson, Dr. Campbell, Dr. Hooker, Alexander Cunningham, Wilson, Ashley Eden and others in Sikkim, Bhutan and the adjacent countries, as the field of their labors was in those parts of Tibet which are under British rule or influence.

The next foreigner to visit Tibet and Lh'asa was the Englishman Thomas Manning, who traveled there *viâ* Pari djong and Gyantsé djong in 1811 returning to India by the same road in the early part of the following year. His fragmentary journal, published by Mr. Markham‖ adds but little to our knowledge of the country

*See Clem. R. Markham, *op. sup. cit.*, pp. lviii, 302 et seq., and for Orazio della Penna's *Breve Notizia del Regno del Tibet*, the same work, p. 309 et seq. Much valuable information derived from notes and letters written by the Jesuit and Capuchin fathers in Tibet may be found in Georgi's *Alphabetum Tibetanum*, published at Rome in 1762, 1 vol., 4°.

†See Clem. R. Markham, *op. cit.*, p. lxii et seq. Also the letter of Père Gaubil in *Lettres édifiantes et curieuses* (Pantheon littéraire edit.), IV, 60.

‡*An Account of an Embassy to the Court of the Teshoo Lama*, 1 vol., 4°, 1800.

‖ *Op. sup. cit.*, 213–294.

he traversed, but it is nevertheless of considerable value. In 1844 the Lazarist fathers Huc and Gabet traversed the Ordos, Alashan, the Koko nor and the Ts'aidam, and following the highroad which passes by Nya-ch'uk'a, reached Lh'asa in 1846. Here they stayed a few months when they were expelled by the Chinese Amban and conducted to Ta-chien-lu in Ssŭ-ch'uan by the highroad which goes through Ch'amdo, Draya, Bat'ang, and Ho-k'ou.* On their way to Lh'asa they followed the road which in 1661 had been gone over by Father Grueber, and which more recently has been explored by the Russian traveler Nicholas Prjevalsky, as far at least as the frontier post of Nya-ch'uk'a.

Between the time of Huc's adventuresome journey and that of Col. Prjevalsky in 1870–'71, no foreigners, as far as I am aware, entered Tibet. After exploring the Tibetan country around the Koko nor, Prjevalsky pushed on along the highroad to Lh'asa as far as the Dré ch'u, a point which may be considered as in Tibet proper, though politically speaking it is in a no-man's-land.†

In 1879 the indefatigable Prjevalsky undertook a second expedition into Tibet with the avowed object of reaching Lh'asa. Coming from the Ts'aidam he followed the highroad to Lh'asa, and got as near the capital as Nya-ch'uk'a. Here he was stopped and forced to retrace his steps. In this expedition he also explored considerable country south of the Koko nor, an unknown region inhabited by the predatory Tibetan Kamb'a and Golok.‡ During Prjevalsky's fourth and last expedition into Central Asia he visited in 1887 a small section of Tibetan country between southern Ts'aidam and the Dré ch'u and inhabited by K'amba pastoral tribes.‖ In 1889 I followed this route myself, and coming to the Dré ch'u a little below where Prjevalsky reached that river, I crossed it and after-

* See *Souvenirs d'un voyage dans la Tartarie et le Thibet*, 2 vol. 12°.

† See *Mongolia, the Tangut Country*, 2 vols., 8°, 1876.

‡ See his *Tretye puteshestvie v Centralnoi Asii*, 4°, 1883.

‖ See his *Ot Kiachtii na istoki joltoi reki, etc.*, 4°, 1888.

wards traversed a considerable section of Eastern Tibet, ultimately re-entering China at Ta-chien-lu in the summer of the same year.*

Ta-chien-lu in Ssŭ-ch'uan is the frontier town on the highroad connecting Western China with Central Tibet, and through it pass nearly all the caravans going to or coming from Lh'asa.† Explorers have repeatedly endeavored to enter Tibet from this point, and it has been the basis of the operation of the Catholic missionaries in Tibet ever since about 1858.

In 1868 the Englishman T. T. Cooper entered Tibet from Ta-chien-lu in an attempt to reach India, and pushed on as far as Bat'ang where he was stopped and obliged ultimately to retrace his steps, after traveling some distance southward.‡ In 1877 Capt. Wm. Gill, R. E., also reached Bat'ang from Ta-chien-lu, but he also was turned southward at that point, and so went to Yün-nan and Burmah.‖ The same fate overtook in 1880 the Hungarian Count Bela Szechenyi and his well-organized expedition, with which he wanted to go to Lh'asa.§

The French missionaries operating in the Tibetan borderland have been fairly successful since they opened their mission at Bonga in 1854. On one occasion they reached Ch'amdo, and at Gart'ok they were allowed by the Lh'asan authorities to open a station for a short time, while in Bat'ang and the country south of it, they have maintained themselves with varying fortunes down to the present day.¶

The attempts made by Wilcox in 1826, by Dr. Griffiths in 1836, by l'Abbé Krick in 1852, by T. T. Cooper in 1870, and by Mr.

* See *Land of the Lamas*, 8°, 1891.

† The much older and easier road between China and Lh'asa is the Hsi-ning—Ts'aidam one, but since the breaking out of the Dzungan rebellion in the sixties, the Chinese government have kept it closed as much as they could. Nearly every year the Lh'asa or Trashilhunpo people ask to be allowed to send their tribute missions over it, but they are invariably refused.

‡ *Travels of a Pioneer of Commerce*, 8°, 1871.

‖ See *The River of Golden Sands*, 2 vols., 8°, 1880.

§ See Lieut. Kreitner's *Im fernen Osten*, 8°, 1882.

¶ See *Le Thibet d'après la correspondence des missionnaries*, par C. H. Desgodins, 8°, 1885.

Needham in 1885, to enter Tibet from the south, all met with failure, and the country between the Assam frontier and the Lh'asa—Ta-chien-lu highroad is still the least known of all Tibet, though perhaps the most interesting.

The last three explorations into Tibet, all of which have met with comparative success, have been undertaken from the north and northwest. In 1889 the French traveler Bonvalot, following a trail sometimes used by the Torgot Mongols, coming from the Lob nor, managed to reach the Tengri nor. There he was stopped and forced to go eastward by a route parallel to the Lh'asa—Ta-chien-lu highroad as far as Gart'ok, from which town to Ta-chien-lu he followed the highroad itself.* The country traversed by this explorer between the Lob nor basin and the Tengri nor was absolutely unknown to us, as was also that part lying between the Tengri nor and Gart'ok, and his journey has added very considerably to our knowledge concerning one of the least known portions of Tibet.

In 1890–'91 Capt. Henry Bower, of the 17th Bengal Cavalry, traversed the whole of Tibet from west to east, his road, as far as north of the Tengri nor lying over the nearly desert plateau known as the "Northern plateau" or *Chang t'ang*, another portion of which had been explored the year before by Bonvalot.† Bower like Bonvalot was stopped near the Tengri nor, and forced to follow practically the same trail that traveler had taken all the way to China.

The diary published in the present volume was kept during my second journey in Tibet in the years 1891–'92. It will, I hope, help to extend our knowledge of the country previously explored by Bonvalot and Bower, my route in many places running parallel to theirs, and for a considerable distance being the same as the one they followed. It also contains my researches in other sections of the country until then entirely unexplored.

*See *De Paris au Tonkin à travers le Tibet inconnu*, 1 vol., 8°, 1892.

†See *Diary of a Journey Across Tibet*, 8°, 1893.

Summarizing what has been said in the preceding remarks we see that the highroad between Hsi-ning and Lh'asa has been followed, over a portion or the whole of its length, by Odoric de Pordenone, by Fathers Grueber and Dorville, by Samuel van de Putte, by Huc and Gabet and by Prjevalsky.

The Lh'asa—Ta-chien-lu road has been gone over by Huc and Gabet, and along a portion of its length by a number of the French missionaries since 1861, also by Cooper, Gill, Szechenyi, Bonvalot, Bower and myself.

The various roads between Nepaul, or Sikkim and Central Tibet have been traveled over by the Franciscan monk Odoric in the 14th century, by the Jesuit and Capuchin fathers in the 17th and 18th, and also by Bogle, Turner and Manning.

The high plateau (*Chang t'ang*) of Northern Tibet has been traversed along four lines: by Prjevalsky and myself at its eastern extremity; by Prjevalsky and the other travelers who have gone over the Hsi-ning—Lh'asa road, at about four degrees of longitude west of the preceding line; by Bonvalot and myself in its greatest width from north to south; and finally by Bower in its greatest length from west to east.

The above embraces practically all the explorations made by foreigners in Great Tibet down to the present day.

In the preceding remarks I have made no mention of one of our most valuable sources of information concerning Tibet, I refer to the work of the native explorers sent to Tibet and other trans-Himalayan countries by the Great Trigonometrical Survey of India. The plan of training natives for scientific geographical work and sending them beyond the Indian frontier to countries closed to Europeans was inaugurated by Col. T. G. Montgomerie some twenty-five or thirty years ago. By this means those portions of Tibet which lie to the north of Nepaul and Sikkim, and to the east of Kashmir, and also, to a less extent, Bhutan, have been carefully surveyed. Some of these explorers, especially Nain Singh (Pundit A——), Kishen Singh or A——

K——, and Lama Ugyen jyats'o, have traversed the whole of Tibet from south to north and from west to east. Lh'asa, Shigatsê and most of the important towns and all the adjacent country of Central and Western Tibet have been carefully surveyed, and of Lh'asa especially, we now know through them the most minute topographical detail.* But while these native explorers are most admirable surveyors, they are not well-trained observers, and details of great value, both ethnological and even geographical, often escape their attention, while the most puerile and unimportant story or legend is often recorded by them in the most careful and prolix way.

The roads leading from Lh'asa to Hsi-ning and to Ta-chien-lu have been gone over by Kishen Singh, Nain Singh has traversed the Ch'ang t'ang from west to east along a line a little to the south of Bower's, the road I followed in 1889 through Eastern Tibet had been previously explored, in 1881, by Kishen Singh, and what little we know of Southern Tibet is from native explorers' travels and reports. Notwithstanding this, the work of the European travelers who have explored these same routes has not been lost, the information they have collected would have escaped the attention of Asiatic explorers, no matter how many had gone over the road before them.

Another valuable source of information concerning Tibet which must not be overlooked, is Chinese literature. Since the middle of the seventeenth century, when Chinese intercourse with Tibet took a sudden and wide expansion, travelers of that nation have composed a number of guide-books, mostly concerned with the

* See especially on this work *Report on the Explorations made in Sikkim, Bhutan and Tibet from 1856 to 1886. Report on the Explorations in Great Tibet and Mongolia, made by A—— K—— in 1879-'82. Narrative of a Journey to Lh'asa in 1881-'82*, by Sarat Chandra Das. *Narrative of a Journey Round Lake Yamdo (Palti) in 1882*, by the same; and also *A Memoir on the Indian Surveys*, by Clements R. Markham, 148 et seq., and *A Memoir on the India Surveys, 1875-1890*, by Charles E. D. Black, 151-165. A—— K—— has made a map of the city of Lh'asa on a scale of four inches to the mile.

highroads through Tibet, though some of them give valuable information relating to little-known trails. Not a few of these books contain much valuable information bearing on the trade, climate, history, products, industries and other resources of the various districts to which they refer.* Besides these works, each of the various Chinese dynastic histories contains chapters on the history, geography and ethnography of Tibet during the different periods to which each relates.

A large portion of the information contained in these two classes of Chinese works I have translated or condensed and published in the "Journal of the Royal Asiatic Society." The data they supplied me were found of the greatest value during my several journeys in Tibet, even when, as in the case of the road between Ch'amdo and Nya-ch'uk'a followed by Bonvalot, Bower and myself, and which is given in these translations (p. 86), only a very few of the names were known in the country at the present day.

The journey which I undertook in 1888–'89, some of the results of which I have published in "The Land of the Lamas," encouraged me to believe that I could, if I undertook a second journey into Tibet, add considerably to our knowledge of that remote region; and so, when I had worked up the results of my first journey, I determined upon once more visiting Mongolia and Tibet, and endeavoring to traverse the latter country from northeast to southwest, or in other words to try and reach Nepaul or Sikkim from the Chinese province of Kan-su.

I had learned during my first journey that in that portion of Tibet which is under the rule of Lh'asa, opposition to foreigners was much more violent than elsewhere, so I endeavored in this journey to steer clear of Lh'asa, but various circumstances, which will be found related in my Diary, and over which I had no control, turned me from the path I had intended to follow, and so, when not over thirty or forty miles from the Tengri nor, and less

* For a list of the most important of this class of works on Tibet, see *Journal Royal Asiatic Society*, new series, XXIII, pp. 3 and 4.

than a month's travel from British India, and when at very nearly the same spot at which Bonvalot and Bower had been stopped, my further progress southward was arrested by the Tibetans, and I was forced to turn my face eastward.

The remainder of my journey was not through country absolutely unknown, for my route frequently crossed and sometimes coincided with those of Bonvalot and Bower, and from Ch'amdo to Ta-chien-lu I followed the route taken in 1861 by Monseigneur Thomine Desmazures, and more recently by Captain Bower, but notwithstanding this, I believe that I have been able to collect, even during this portion of my journey, thanks to my knowledge of the Tibetan and Chinese languages, not a few data which will prove of interest and of possible value to future explorers.

Of Southern Mongolia and Western Kan-su, through which the first part of my journey took me, we really know less than of Tibet, for our sources of information on this section of Mongolia are confined to the letters and other writings of the Jesuits who resided in Peking in the 17th and 18th centuries, to Huc's charming but rather romantic "Souvenirs," and to Prjevalsky's first journey, and, as regards the Koko-nor country and Western Kan-su, to Prjevalsky's works and to what little has been so far published of Potanin's papers.

Regarding the method followed in preparing the sketch route-map accompanying this volume, the original was made on a scale of four statute miles to the inch, and the instruments used were a prismatic compass, an aneroid and a six-inch sextant. In the first part of the survey, between Kalgan and Kuei-tê in Kan-su, I passed through several localities whose positions had been determined, with more or less exactitude, by the Jesuits in the 17th century, and more recently by Prjevalsky, and my observations agree fairly well with theirs. In the second and less known half of my journey my traverse, wherever it crosses that made by Bower, shows a close agreement with his in latitude for points situated along it, and a fairly good one for longitude. On the whole I consider the results of this long and hasty survey of over 3,400 miles as satisfactory and fairly accurate, but it is nothing more than its name implies—a rough preliminary sketch of a nearly unknown region. Numerous observations for time and latitude, and for altitude, by the boiling point of water and from aneroid readings, were taken during the whole length of the journey. The instruments with which these latter observations were made were corrected before and after the journey at the United States Weather Bureau at Washington, and the altitudes deduced have also, through the kindness of Professor Mark W. Harrington, Chief of the Bureau, been calculated there. They show, wherever comparisons are possible, a fairly close agreement with those taken by my predecessors, as an examination of the table in the appendix will demonstrate.

Meteorological observations for temperature, pressure, cloudiness, wind, etc., etc., were taken three times daily, at 7 A.M., 2 P.M. and 7 P.M.; I have given in an appendix a table showing the mean monthly temperature at these three hours from January 1st, 1892, to October 1st of the same year, the date at which I reached Ta-chien-lu in Ssŭ-ch'uan.

The illustrations accompanying this volume are either reproductions of photographs taken during the journey, or drawings of objects brought back by me, most of which now belong to the United States National Museum.

As to the transcription of Chinese words, I have followed the system of Sir Thomas Wade, in which the sounds are given according to the Peking pronunciation. In transcribing Tibetan I have, as in my previous work, applied as nearly as possible Wade's system, while adhering to the native spelling and the Lh'asa pronunciation, as far as phonetic spelling would admit. The only sound to which I need call attention is that of *ö*, which is the French *eu*, as in "peu," thus Pönbo is to be pronounced as if written Peunbo, Bönbo as if it were Beunbo, etc.; in the written language of Tibet all these words are written with an o, Dpon-po, Bon-po. The acute accent is used, in accordance with the suggestion made in that invaluable book, "Hints to Travellers," to show the emphasized syllable, not to change the sound of the vowel over which it is placed. In transcribing Mongol, I have followed a purely phonetic system, giving, as a general thing, the sound of the words according to the western or Kalmuk pronunciation with which alone I am at all familiar.

The reader's indulgence is asked for some apparent inconsistencies in my transcription of foreign words; they result either from negligence on my part or from over-anxiousness to make the correct pronunciation perfectly clear without lengthy explanations.

The form in which I now publish the results of my journey was only adopted after much hesitation, as I feared it might prove tedious to even the enthusiastic reader of books of travel—if such happily there still be. But a journal, kept from day to day, and often under great difficulties shows better, I think, than any other form of reçord the true impressions of the writer, his moods, his hopes, his anxieties, even when they concern nothing more important than his next meal, of which I am, however, assured the public likes to be informed. In such a Diary as is here given numerous glaring errors in style—if nothing worse—tedious detail and monotonous repetition cannot fail to confront the too critical reader, but let him be charitable—dirt, cold, starvation and a thousand minor discomforts which beset the explorer in Mongolia and Tibet who lives and travels like the barbarous inhabitants of those wild regions, are not conducive to sustained or successful literary work, as he may find out for himself if he will but try it.

It gives me great pleasure to acknowledge here my high appreciation of the deep interest which my friend General James H. Wilson has always taken in my explorations in Tibet since the days when we first talked over my plans in China, and of the many services which he has rendered me in connection with them. My acknowledgments are also due to Mr. Charles E. Dana, Mr.

E. R. Bacon, Mr. J. B. Houston and Mr. J. H. Schiff, all of New York, who assisted and encouraged me in my undertaking.

To Mr. S. P. Langley, Secretary of the Smithsonian Institution, without whose generous interest in my work this volume would probably never have been published, and to my numerous friends in the Smithsonian and the United States National Museum, I am under lasting obligations which I can never forget nor adequately acknowledge.

William Woodville Rockhill.

Department of State,
Washington, December 14, 1894.

JOURNEY
THROUGH MONGOLIA AND TIBET

MONGOLIA AND TIBET

DIARY OF A JOURNEY
1891–92.

BY WILLIAM WOODVILLE ROCKHILL.

PART I.

FROM PEKING THROUGH MONGOLIA TO KUMBUM.

PEKING.—*November 30, 1891.*—I received to-day my passport from the Tsung-li Yamen. It is what we would call at home a "special passport," authorizing me as former Secretary of the United States Legation to visit Kan-su, Ssŭ-ch'uan, Yün-nan, Hsin-chiang (the New Dominion), and the Ching-hai, or the Mongol and Tibetan country under the administrative control of the Hsi-ning Amban. This opens the road to Lh'asa for me as far as Dréch'u rabden and consequently Nagch'uk'a, for there are no inhabitants, only an occasional band of roaming K'amba before reaching the latter point.

I have two drafts on a Shan-hsi bank at Kuei-hua Ch'eng for 1103.31 taels, and I carry 172.56 taels in sycee. I will draw an additional 700 taels on reaching Lan-chou Fu in Kan-su. This and the goods I carry with me will have to do for the journey—a year or more.

We hear many rumors about the rebels up Jehol way. It is said here that they have crossed the Great Wall and are marching on Peking. There is no doubt that five hundred desperate men, willing to sacrifice their lives, could capture Peking by a *coup de main*, for there is only the Peking field force (*Shen-ch'i ying*) to defend it, which, as a Chinese general remarked a few years ago to the Seventh Prince, who is the chief of this body, is more expert with the opium pipe (*yen chiang*) than with the musket (*yang chiang*). This little rebellion is a specimen of what frequently occurs on the northern and southwestern frontiers of China. One day a chief of a band of highwaymen (*ma-tsei*) gave in his submission to the government and made himself so agreeable that he was after awhile given official preferment. His band, for the sake of economy probably, retained his name on their banners and kept to the road. This caused the Jehol officials to believe that the ex-chief, Li, I think he was named, was still connected with the profession, so he was arrested, tried, and beheaded. His son, to avenge his sire, joined the band, dubbed himself Ping Ch'ing Wang ("The Prince leveler of the Ch'ing dynasty"), and announced on his banners that his platform was "First, right (*li*), then reason (*tao*), to put an end to the Catholic (*t'ien chu*) faith, to bring down the reigning dynasty, and to destroy the hairy foreigners." A pretty pretentious scheme for a few hundred men. They are more or less connected with a secret society called the Tsai huei, a kind of northern Ko-lao huei, and some people here tell me they are called Hung mao-tzŭ ("red haired") because they put on false beards of red hair in their secret conclaves. At all events they are very probably well armed, with Winchester rifles, I believe, supplied them by an enterprising foreign firm at Newchwang. Li Hung-chang is said to be sending troops from around Tientsin to the disturbed district, and soon the rebel band will disperse and the imperial forces will announce a glorious victory and the condign punishment of the guilty ones.*

December 1.—I hired two carts to take me and my boy to Kuei-hua Ch'eng, *via* Kalgan and the *Ts'ao-ti*, they were to be at the house by daylight to-day, but it was eight o'clock before we

* This revolt was naturally crushed with enormous loss of life to the rebels, if we are to believe the memorial of the military commissioner for Manchuria, Ting An, published in the Peking Gazette of December 11, 1891. According to this document the rebels must have numbered from four to five thousand. See Imperial decrees, December 6 and 12, 1891, in *For. Rel. of the United States*, 1892, pp. 77 and 80. Kuo Wan-chang appears to be the name of the rebel leader and Chi Yao-shih that of the person made Prince by the rebel bands.

got off, and ten before we left the inn outside the Tê-shih men where the cart office (*ch'e hang*) is located. The carts are drawn by played-out ponies and bare-boned mules, three, in one, two in the other. I expostulated on the miserable condition of the teams, but the *chang-kuei-ti* insisted that they were wonderfully strong animals though perhaps a bit rough looking. The drivers are good natured Shan-hsi men from Ta-t'ung and do not know what hurry means, and it is for this reason that Shan-hsi teams are not in favor with the Pekinese public.

We jogged along very leisurely to Ching ho (18 *li* from the Tê-shih men), and towards nightfall reached Chang-ping Chou, where I witnessed a magistrate coming to a man's domicile (the inn in which I was stopping) to administer justice (in the form of a volley of smacks on the face) to a tradesman who had tried to cheat the inn-keeper. And we want to teach the Chinese our methods of procedure! Can anything be more expeditious and inexpensive than this?

December 2.—We left in the middle of the night and made Nan-k'ou by 9 A. M., passing endless strings of camels, the big bells around their necks sounding very dismally in the stillness of the night. They were coming down by thousands from the pasturages north of Kalgan to be used in the Peking coal trade and the Kalgan—Tung-chou tea-carrying business; some also were loaded with wool, hides, camel's hair, and led by Mongols now on their annual visit to the Capital.

The road up the pass has, since last I saw it in 1888, been wonderfully improved, and is now in really excellent order for cart travel and I don't begrudge the little toll I have to pay at Chü-yung kuan. At this latter place I noticed that the inscriptions in the famous gateway are no longer as distinct as when last I examined them. Proclamations and advertisements have been pasted over them for such a long time and in such quantities that the surface of the stone on the inscribed portions has at last become considerably defaced. Why have so few studied these curious inscriptions? The Kitan and Niu-chih versions are priceless. I heard Dr. Bushell* say once that he had devoted

*Dr. Bushell has been for the last twenty-seven years physician to H. B. M.'s Legation at Peking. His thorough knowledge of things Chinese is too well known to necessitate any further reference to it here.

considerable study to them. It's a thousand pities he does not give us the results of his researches, they would certainly be very valuable—all he has ever done is so very good. The bas-reliefs on the faces of the gateway also merit careful study. We reached Ch'a-tao by 5 P. M. in a violent northwesterly gale. Ever since leaving Peking the sky has been getting redder, a sure forerunner of the present storm which will probably last three days.

December 3.—We left Ch'a-tao in a fearful northwest gale; it was bitterly cold, and so dusty that we several times strayed from the road. The gravel was blown with such violence that it cut our faces like the lash of a whip, and the cold made the tears course down our cheeks. We stopped for lunch at Huai-lai Hsien, and reached by dark Tu-mu where we found a good inn and a well heated *k'ang*. The night was beautifully clear but the wind continued blowing with such fury that I could not take any sextant observations. The inn-keeper told me that about thirty thousand camel loads of tea are taken up every year over this road to Kalgan from Tung-chou. A camel load is paid 17 taels from Tung-chou to Ta-kuren (Urga).

December 4.—Got off late as we had the first casualty of the journey in our party. The black mule is dead! The kicker and most disorderly member of the party is no more. Before he had breathed his last, his carcass was sold for $2, his tail cut off to show the owner on the carter's arrival at home, and his body carried off by the natives who were licking their chops over the anticipated feast. Our loss did not effect our rate of speed, except perhaps that it was slightly better, for we made twenty miles to Ch'i-ming-i. The day was pleasant but the road horribly stony, limestone pebbles, and such jolting as I never experienced. If ever I go over this road again I will take mule litters, they are much more convenient, and one travels just as rapidly as in a cart.

December 5.—We jogged on leisurely to Hsüan-hua Fu, passing around the base of the famous Ch'i-ming shan on the top of which is a large temple said to have been transported there in the days of old by Liu-pan from Ch'ü-yung kuan where it had originally been built. A good deal of rather poor coal is dug out of this mountain, which appears to be mostly of friable sandstone and porphyritic rocks. The Hun ho, along whose right bank the road to Kalgan runs, is frozen so deep that we crossed it with the carts.

At Hsüan-hua Fu we noticed the first signs of our proximity to the Jehol rebel bands. Little banners were stuck out of numerous houses to indicate the places of refuge for the inhabitants of the neighboring houses; and this is all that is done to protect a town of probably fifty thousand inhabitants against the brigands!

December 6.—From Hsüan-hua Fu to near Kalgan the road is covered with drifted sand and loess, the walls of Hsüan-hua are half buried in it. Farmers with their carts are seen everywhere, even in the streets of the towns shovelling up the drifted dirt and carting it back to where it belongs—on their fields. Just outside the west gate of the city of Hsüan-hua we passed through a grove of gnarled poplars. Here in the fifth moon is celebrated the Liang-chuo-huei, "airing-the-feet-festival," when the women walk up and down dressed in their best and the men admire, criticise or condemn the shape and size of each one's feet. I have never heard of this feast being celebrated elsewhere in China. The Shan-hsi women (and Hsüan-hua is populated mostly by people from that province) are not over modest; they wear in summer a single upper garment or waistcoat (*kan-chien*) which leaves the breasts exposed to the view, another custom I have not met with elsewhere in China.

We passed a great many camels carrying soda (*chien*) to Peking, in large blocks, about two and a half feet long. They probably came from the Ta-t'ung plain, as a great deal of soda is obtained by a very simple process there, some ten or fifteen miles south of the city, which I visited in 1888.

The weather remains hazy. A clear day is a rarity in these parts in the dry season. The mountains at a few miles distance are lost in the haze. The first part of the night is hazy and the atmosphere is only really clear just before and after dawn, the dust which constitutes the haze being precipitated by the moisture in the air, for there is a good deal of moisture in suspension even at this season of the year.

December 7.—We reached Kalgan towards three o'clock and put up in an inn on the market street and facing the shrine of the god of wine, the pet deity of the place. I have numerous purchases to make here, among others a supply of mongol felt socks, Halha Russian leather boots, rugs in which to wrap up my boxes, buckskin breeches, etc., etc.; as to my tents I will purchase them at Kuei-hua Ch'eng. I found ponies dearer here than at the Tê-shih men of Peking, for Mongols can easily take those they bring here back to their pasture lands, if they cannot get good prices, while at Peking they have to sell at any price. The people who came in the inn yard and saw me busy observing first the sun then the stars, inquired of the boy in subdued tones if any calamity was impending, if the rebels were about to attack the town. Ma Chih-pao reassured them and told them I was a worshiper of the *pei-t'ou* (Ursa Major) and busy making out what my luck would be on my journey.

December 8.—My boy says he is not afraid to accompany me anywhere, but I see that he has invested in an enormous sword marked with the ominous *pei-t'ou*, a dragon and several soul-stirring mottoes, in lieu of the big cudgel he started out with.

December 9.—On the 20th of the eighth moon at the *miao huei* or "temple fair" held here, several hundred ponies run, not races but to show their gait and speed. A Mongol refused this year 180 taels for a pony. Mongol ponies are branded as are ours in America. Lama miao is unquestionably the best place at which to buy ponies; west of that section of Mongolia they lose in size and speed, but possibly gain in staying powers.

The name Kalgan is but a poor transcription of the Mongol word *halha*;* it means a "frontier mart." The people hereabout call Kuei-hua Ch'eng the Ch'eng, Hsüan-hua Fu they call Fu, just as those of Ta-chien-lu in Ssŭ-ch'uan call it Lu or Lu Ch'eng. This at all events has the merit, a considerable one in our estimation, of brevity.

The people say no day is perfect here unless it blows hard during a part of it. The climate, they add, is equable, which means, I fancy, that it blows every day in the year. Mr. Roberts, one of the American missionaries here, tells me he has seen (especially among the Manchus living here) quite a number of albinos. Persons with supplementary thumbs are also frequently met with here as

* I transcribe this and all Mongol words phonetically and according to the Kalmuk pronunciation, the only one with which I am at all familiar.

in Peking. These are the most common abnormalities. There are three Mohammedan theological schools in Kalgan and they have a high standing in northern China, young men being sent here from remote quarters to study. The Mohammedans here do not seem however, to be as strict, in the usual observances prescribed to all believers, as those in western Kan-su. Thus some smoke opium, and it is commonly said that they are not averse to eating pork—if sold them under the name of mutton. The population of Kalgan is roughly estimated at between 75,000 and 100,000.

December 10.—We left for Kuei-hua Ch'eng at seven o'clock, and followed up the river bed, which serves in the dry season as the principal street of the city, passing, just before leaving town, two small cages tied to the ends of poles and containing the heads of two lately executed highwaymen. The road was without interest, rocky and deep in loess dust. It is curious that loess even when, as here, it is not a subaerial deposit but has been brought down by the rains from higher levels, retains its characteristic vertical cleavage.

Crossing a low range of hills west of the city, we passed by little Wan-chüan Hsien the prefectural city in whose district is Kalgan, and shortly after entered the valley of the Yang ho or Hsi ("West") yang ho (the stream flowing by Wan-chüan Hsien being the Tung or "Eastern" Yang ho). Every mile or so we passed through villages around which were groves of willows, their long, crooked stems with only a tuft of small branches at the tops, adding little to the beauty of the surroundings. Basket making is one of the chief industries of this district and the river is probably called Yang ho or "Willow River," from these numerous groves.

December 11.—We lost our way; this is usual with Chinese carters and especially those of the Shan-hsi breed, who are proverbially stupid, and so we had to put up for the night at a village called Su-chia tsui a good deal to the north of the road. There was no inn, but we found lodgings in a farm house; the rooms were of the arched loess-cave-dwelling style common in north China, and are called hereabout *shen-hsien t'ung* or "fairy caves," for these, like their prototypes, are warm in winter and cool in summer. The road followed up the river course in a due westerly direction. A violent west wind began to blow at 11 A. M. and so dense was the dust during the rest of the day's travel that, as the way was long and we only reached an inn far in the night, we had to guide ourselves by the stars, for we could not make out the road under our feet. We tried to reach Hsin-ping k'ou (or Hsi-feng k'ou as it is called at Peking), a gate in the Great Wall, but had to stop a couple of miles east of it in a wayside inn, which class of houses are, by the way, usually larger and cleaner than those in towns or villages.

December 12.—All the way up the Yang ho I noticed on the hill slopes on either side of the valley, truncated cone-shaped towers about thirty feet high with an encircling wall some ten feet in height. The people call them *pao-tai* or "gun towers" and say they were once used by the inhabitants to defend themselves against Mongol and Tartar raiders. They are too regularly separated and built with too little regard to neighboring villages, to have been solely for the purpose now claimed for them; they are on the other hand too near each other to have been watch towers, unless signals other than fire signals were used by the sentries. The explanation given me of their use is possible, though I have not seen any mention of such a system in China.* The Great Wall at Hsin-ping K'ou is entirely of earth, without any trace of brick or stone facing. The village at the gate is tolerably large, but much the worse for wear and sadly in lack of some repairs.

Continuing up the valley to where it takes a southerly bend, we crossed a range of hills, and then by a very gradual descent, reached Ch'ang-k'ou, a big village of over six hundred families of Shan-hsi people and with a large number of inns. Coal is brought here from near Ta-t'ung Fu by way of Fu-ming Fu (or Feng Ch'eng as it is also called). The coal used at Kalgan comes also from the same locality by this apparently round-about way—probably to escape *likin* at some point or other along the road.

At Ch'ang-k'ou the Lung wang ("the rain god") had been prayed to in vain; first by the men, then the women, then the children. Even the Lao-yeh, the local official, had kotowed and

* Conf. the remarks on these watch towers in the History of the Embassy of Shahrokh to the Emperor of China in 1419. (Thevenot, *Relations* II, Part xviii, 3.) These towers, it says, are of two kinds, the larger called *Kidifous*, the smaller *Cargous*.

burnt incense with much firing of crackers and beating of gong, but to no avail. The people told me they knew long ago the year would be disastrous for the sand grouse* had been more numerous of late than for years, and the saying goes, *Sha-ch'i kuo, mai lao-po*, "when the sand grouse fly by, wives will be for sale."

Ch'ang-k'ou is a place of considerable importance, as two roads from Kuei-hua meet here (or rather two miles west of here). One is called the "inner road," and passes by Lung-sheng chuang, Hou-tao-sha, Ge-ho-wa (pronounced in Pekinese Ai-ho-wa), Yung-shan chuang, Feng Ch'eng (or Fu-ming Fu), Ma-chao ling, Ma-Wang miao, Tien-ch'eng ts'un, Han-ching ling, Ma-ka-tu, Sa-tei-go, Hsaio pa-tzŭ, Eu-ling-trin (in Pekinese O-ling tan), Chahar (or Tsahan?) bolan, Ta-yu-shu, Shui-mo, Ku-lüeh, Shih-rung-wa, Me-tar, Tieh-mung, To-ko-lang (in Mongol Tak-lang) and thence to Kuei-hua. The road I will follow crosses this one at Chahar polang, and falls into it at To-ko-lang. The first is 100 *li* (thirty-three miles) longer than that I have chosen, which is 780 *li*.

I find that all the people hereabout, and even those of Kalgan, use the term *Mantzŭ* to designate the Chinese, in contradistinction to the Mongols. I had thought its use in this acceptation was confined to west Ssŭ-ch'uan and the Tibetan language, but I now find it has a much wider range.

December 13. We only made a half day's march as I was anxious to make some solar observations for time. We stopped at a village on the border of the Chahar Mongol's pasture lands called Tsahan (or Chahan) obo, "the white obo," thus called from a large pile of stones (*obo*) on a hill near the village. Since leaving the Yang ho valley, tufa is the principal rock seen along the road.

Around every village in this region willows are planted; the Shan-hsi people are harder workers than the Chih-li Chinese, and they are much more agreeable to be thrown with, gay, polite, and not by any means as hot-headed as the latter. Physically they are very different, shorter of stature, with rounder faces and approaching more closely the southern Chinese type.

---

*Huc, *Souvenirs d'un voyage dans la Tartarie*, I, 245, says these birds are called *Lung chuo* "Dragon's feet," I for my part have never heard any other name than *sha-ch'i* "sand fowl," given them. This name is used however, for a variety of birds, among others the partridge,

The year now ending has been a very bad one for all this border region, one small rainfall in the sixth moon; but these people bear their troubles with perfect composure.

My boy is a great doctor, he carries a large supply of medicine —one a sovereign remedy for eye diseases, cataract disappearing rapidly by its use, and he has also a wonderful balm, curing not only wounds but every pain and ill to which poor humanity is subject. I have amused myself to-day watching him doctoring the people in the inn. It is lucky we are leaving early to-morrow, for should the medicine not have the desired effect, he and I might have the whole village down on us, though I must do the boy the justice to say he asks nothing for his drugs, he only wants "to do good" (*tso haoshih*).

December 14.—A few miles west of Tsahan obo we crossed a low pass marked by eight *obo* (three large and five small ones) and descended into the plain occupied by the yellow banner of the Chahar Mongols.* It is a circular depression of some thirty miles in diameter encircled by hills a few hundred feet high, and has been at no remote period a lake with an outlet to the northeast. A remnant of the lake remains in a pool called "Black Lake" (*Hiré-nor*) near the village of the No. 2 Ta-jen or Erh Ta-jen ying-tzŭ. The soil is partly alkaline, but good water is abundant in wells only a few feet deep.

These Mongols live more like Chinese than any tribe I have visited, though I believe that around Jehol, and to the east of it, they are nearly indistinguishable from them. Many of the Chahar have small houses of Chinese style, and all the men wear the Chinese dress, as do many of the women, with the exception of the mode of dressing the hair which is of the national type—a long tress hanging down on either side of the face. They have also taken to smoking opium and have retained their national fondness for drink.

We stopped for the night at a Mongol hamlet, near which was the residence of a chief and also a small lamasery, and put up in an inn with one small room in which were two big k'angs. My party had one of them as the other was already occupied by the inn-keeper, a tailoring lama, his face eaten up by some cancerous

* On the Chahar (or Chakhar) Mongols, see H. H. Howorth, *History of the Mongols*, I, 384 et seq.

disease, and a couple of little Mongol chiefs smoking opium. I paid for the use of the whole room and finally after a great deal of persuasion got the unpleasant neighbors out of it. Fortunately the night was very cold and the house but poorly heated so the vile odors which would have offended our nostrils in warmer weather were frozen up.

December 15.—To-day has been bitterly cold, with a violent west wind blowing the dust down our throats. The road ascended gently and we passed now and then a solitary tree—probably Chinese enterprise had planted it. Crossing a low, stony pass we descended to Hu-lu-shih-tai,* consisting of a couple of inns kept by very Chinesified Mongols. Thence we went to Shih-pa-erh-tai, another post station with four or five inns and as many dwelling houses. The rooms in the former consist mainly of two huge k'angs on each of which fifteen or twenty people can find accommodation, and between these k'angs, and on the level of the ground, is a big cooking stove on which two or three very large cast iron pans fit—one for water, the other for cooking food in. The fire is fed with dried manure and straw, and a big box-bellows keeps up the flame. The stench in such a room, well filled with travelers—mostly carters—all eating, drinking, smoking opium, covered with the dirt of years and raising with each movement the dust of ages and the microbes of cycles, is beyond description.

The Mongols, I hear, begin shaving the heads of their male children at the age of three.†

December 16.—The country we are now in is a tableland cut by low ranges of hills a few hundred feet high, but we see no running water anywhere. Tufa is the chief rocky formation visible. We stop for lunch at Kuei-yueh-t'u, consisting of two small, bleak inns kept by Mongols, who, like most of these Chahar, speak Chinese fluently. Some twelve miles west of this place we crossed higher hills, and after a sharp descent reached a broad valley dotted over with Chinese villages. Between us and the villages a low earth wall cut the valley—it marks the boundary of the lands ceded by the Chahar to the Chinese for agricultural purposes.

* Probably the place called Houstai by Father Gerbillon, Duhalde, *Description de l'Empire de la Chine*, IV, 347.

† See also on other Mongol usages concerning mode of hair dressing, under date of *April 25, 1892*.

Just before reaching Wu-li-pa ("5 li hill") I got a shot at a big wolf standing quietly near a cottage. At Wu-li-pa we found a very neat, large roomed inn where I was most hospitably treated. The Shan-hsi people are very kindly disposed, though not over bright, very inquisitive, with no manners, and confirmed opium smokers. The Shan-hsi women of all classes are remarkable among northern Chinese for the smallness and perfect forms (according to native standards) of their feet.

December 17.—Crossing a low *col* a mile west of Wu-li-pa we came to Tsahan bolan ("White Stick"), the first large Chinese village we have seen since leaving Ch'ang-k'ou, but it looked unkempt, like all these places, with houses half dug in the loess cliffs and entirely made of mud and adobe bricks.

The people all say that the land outside the border (*k'ou wai*) is much richer than any inside the Wall (*k'ou nei*), hence the rapidity with which these pasture lands are being taken up by farmers.

Freight is scarce, although we are now traveling on a high road —the Fu-ming Fu road joining the one we are following at Tsahan bolan; a few loads of goat skins, hides, camel's wool, and the like, is all we have seen going eastward. We passed several carts for Kalgan coming from Kuei-hua. They were flying the hang flags of Wilson & Co., of Tien-tsin, of Butterfield & Swire and a Russian firm of Kalgan, the name of which I could not make out.

The hills on either side of the broad valley in which we traveled to-day were slightly steeper than those to the east, and were of igneous rock covered with loess. Before reaching Shih-jen-wan, where we stopped for the night, we passed through several miles of deep cuts in the loess. From Tsahan bolan to Shih-jen-wan we followed the course of a good sized stream, the headwaters of the Heiho or Hsiao Hei ho which flows by Kuei-hua Ch'eng, and empties into the Yellow River at Ho-k'ou.

December 18.—The valley broadened beyond Shih-jen-wan, and after a few miles we saw the Ch'ing shan, a high and rugged range of mountains running nearly due west as far as the eye could reach. Between this range and the southern side of the valley—in places some three or four miles—the country was dotted over with villages, each in a little willow grove, and by each a rivulet flowed sluggishly along towards the Heiho, or a canal which carried a meagre supply of water from the river to remote sections of the plain. We saw large flocks of sheep and droves of camels pasturing about, all destined to supply the Peking and southern markets. We lunched at Taklang ("a crook, or bend in a river"), a small hamlet some ten miles from Kuei-hua, which latter place, or rather the New or Manchu town some 5 *li* east of it, came here in view.

At three o'clock we made our entry into Kuei-hua, where we were led by inn-runners to a house said by them to be the best in the city, but which proved to be little better than a tumble down pig sty. Abbé Huc* relates in his delightful style a similar adventure which befell him on arriving at this famous place.

In the New Town (Hsin Ch'eng) live some five thousand Manchu bannermen who are in receipt of a small monthly stipend from the government—the foot soldiers (*pu-ping*) 3.0 taels a month, the mounted men (*ma ping*) 9 taels. They do nothing but smoke opium, gamble, hawk, and raise a few greyhounds, and are of no conceivable use.

After driving about the town for quite a while in search of decent, quiet quarters, I chose at last a small inn where, at all events, I will get clean food, for it is kept by a Mohammedan who, however, has a bad reputation for "eating" people, in other words, making large commissions on all the purchases made by his guests.

I called on Dr. Stewart of the China Inland Mission. The Mission's medical work has been of incalculable value to China generally. The Chinese admire this philanthropic work, though it is quite beyond them to believe it disinterested; they think the missionaries have some personal motive impelling them to do this work, and in a certain sense they are right, for is it not said of those who go forth to preach the Word that surely they shall have their reward? It matters little if it is in this world or another.

December 20.—A Mohammedan from Ta-t'ung Fu called on me. He was a man of some literary pretentions among his people, and said that all Mohammedans in China are taught to read Arabic (*ching tzŭ*), but that he himself could only understand a few words of it. He spoke of the country in which is Mekka and

*Huc, *op. cit.*, I, 166 et seq.

Medina as *Farsi* or *Rum*, and stated that the capital of that Empire was Ta-erh-ko-erh (*i. e.*, Stamboul). These Huei-huei hold themselves to be quite a distinct race from the ordinary Chinese. Their ancestors, this man said, had first come to China in the T'ang period and had married Chinese women. This foreign origin explained, he proudly remarked, their well known courage and characteristic pugnaciousness. They keep up some intercourse with the rest of Islam, though they have hardly any with the great Mohammedan section of the Empire (Turkestan). Thus last year some Indian Mohammedans came here from Kashgar and went on to Kalgan and Peking.* They had been sent by the Church of India, to report on the state of the faith in China. There is hardly any direct trade between this place and Hami or Kashgar. Every year two or three traders from that country (Ch'an-t'ou, the Chinese call them) come here with raisins, dried melons and a few other products of no great value. What trade Turkestan has with China reaches Hsi-an Fu *via* Hsia-yü kuan and Hsi-ning or else by Pao-tu and across the Ordos country south of the Yellow River, but it is insignificant.

Dr. Stewart, who called on me to-day, said syphylis is terribly prevalent here. The population he said is a floating one, and belongs to the dregs of society. The Chinese women here are quite as inveterate opium smokers as the men, and the whole population (some 100,000 to 120,000) is about as depraved a lot as can be found in China; it is entirely Chinese, the ground being, however, rented from the Tumed Mongols who are paid annually sums varying from ten to fifty cash a *mou* (1/6 acre).

There is a Tao-t'ai here, also a Chiang-chün or General, and a Tu-t'ung who rules the Yo-mu or Herdmen tribes of Mongols, comprising all the Chahar, Bargu and Tumed tribes of the adjacent regions.†

* In 1688 when Père Gerbillon was at Kuei-hua in the suite of the Emperor K'ang-hsi he saw there "cinq vagabonds Indiens . . . ils se disoient de l'Indoustan et Gentils: ils étoient habillêz à peu près comme des Hermites, avec un grand manteau de toile de couleur isabelle déjà vieille, et un capuchon qui s'élevoit un peu au dessus de leur tete." Duhalde, *op. cit.*, *IV*, 105. Later on, in 1697, when he visited Ning-hia with the same Emperor he records that dried currants and raisins are brought there, also different colored serges, brought there by "les Marchands Mores que viennent du côté des Yusbeks, pour trafiquer à la Chine." Ibid, p. 372. The raisins and currants came, of course, from Hami.

† See on this subject W. F. Mayers, *The Chinese Government* (2d edit.), 86.

1. TIBETAN BOOT. Red and black leather. (U. S. N. M. 167303.)
3. HALHA MONGOL BOOT. Black, russian leather. (U. S. N. M. 167178.)
5. LAMA BOOT. Red russian leather, stitching in coloured silks. (U. S. N. M. 167179.)

2. TIBETAN BOOT. Cotton vamp, pulo leg. (U S. N. M. 131045.)
4. KOKO NOR LEATHER BOOT. (U. S. N. M. 131012.)
6. CH'AMDO BOOT. Black buckskin. (U. S. N. M. 167177.)

December 21.—I went out with Dr. Stewart to buy two tents and some camping utensils. Most of the day was spent haggling over prices, and I finally bought two blue cotton tents for 7.5 taels a piece. I also visited the big lama temple or Ta chao, a fine specimen of Sinico-tibetan work, and which has just been restored.*

There is a Hsiao-chao here but I did not have time to visit it. The word *chao* is used on the Chinese frontier for "temple," though it is only the Tibetan word *jo* meaning "Lord," and refers to the images of the Buddha said to have been made during the life time of the Buddha by sculptors who had seen his divine person.† There are three in existence, but wherever there are copies of the originals, as here, they are also called *Jo* or *chao*.

Camels are quite cheap here ranging from 16 to 40 taels a head. A curious custom obtains here in buying these animals, which consists in counting 8.5 as 10 taels; thus a camel sold for 20 taels only costs in reality 17 taels.‡ This custom is called at Kuei-hua *erh-pa-yin* and at Peking *pao ch'iao*. The trade of this place consists in camels, sheep, sheepskin goods, goatskins and tallow. The quantity of the last article shipped to Peking for making candles is very great. I was told that some 3,000 or 4,000 sheep are killed here daily (in winter I suppose) principally for their tallow.

There is no direct trade between here and Ning-hsia, and I can find no carters willing to take me there, for, they say, they will have to return with empty carts. They hardly ever go westward beyond Pao-tu. Lan-chou tobacco and other Kan-su products used here come from Hsi-an Fu *via* T'ai-yüan and Ta-t'ung or even *via* Peking.

The name given on most of our maps to the range of mountains north of this place, In shan, is unknown here, everyone calls it Ch'ing (or Ta-ch'ing) shan, and I fancy that *In* is but a poor transcription of the sound Ch'ing. This name of Ch'ing shan applies to the range as far west as Pao-tu, beyond which place it is known as Wu-la shan for fifty miles or so, then as Lang-shan,

* Gerbillon in 1688 and Huc in 1844 refer to the lamaries of Kuei-hua as the only remarkable edifices in the town. See Duhalde, *op. cit.*, IV, 103 and Huc, *op. cit.*, I, 185.

† See my *Land of the Lamas*, 104-105.

‡ See also *February 10, 1892*, and *April 28, 1892*.

and finally as Ala shan.* The coal used here at Kuei-hua comes from Pao-tu or the neighborhood; it is very impure but burns freely and is used in every house.

December 22.—After a great deal of trouble I engaged to-day two carts to take me to Ning-hsia Fu *via* the route south of the Yellow River which passes through T'eng-kou and Shih-tsui-tzŭ;† I have paid 55 taels for them, the drivers to provide themselves with provisions and feed for their mules. It is probably a good deal more than I should have paid, but I had no choice, no one else would go.

Dr. Stewart told me (he has been living here four years) that the climate of Kuei-hua is good. The mountains naturally protect it from the prevailing northwest wind; the snow fall is very slight, in fact many winters there is none. The rainy season is from June to September. Grapes, apples, apricots and peaches are raised here, the grapes being specially fine.

The peculiar haze seen throughout these regions has, during the few days I have been here, resolved itself every morning, when the sun was about two hours high, into thin, ragged clouds, which ascending have become a veil-like film, finally vanishing. Hence dust is not always the cause of this haze, though it unquestionably frequently is. The cause of the haze is a question requiring time and long series of observations, which I can never hope to make; some of the European residents here should take it up.

December 23.—The carters (not I) have decided that we will leave here the day after to-morrow. I have had to engage another servant to take the place of the one who had come with me from Peking and who has now worked himself ill through his anxiety to get out of the job of accompanying me. I have taken the cook of the inn, a bright young Mohammedan, a good cook but possibly a rascal. He is to receive as wages 7 taels a month. He is the only Arabic scholar I have seen in China, quotes whole *surats* of the Koran, though his accent, I am fain to admit, is peculiar; he is willing apparently to discuss every subject con-

* Timkowski, *Voyage à Peking*, II, 265, 267, calls this range Khadjar Khosho or Onghin oola, and Prjevalsky calls the Wula shan the Munni ula.

† The route followed for most of the way by Huc and Gabet in 1844.

nected with his religion *et quibusdam aliis*, and is decidedly entertaining—when taken in small doses.

The work of the missionaries here and elsewhere in China, for that matter, seems to me hopeless. Gratitude is, I believe, an unknown virtue among most Chinese, and the other Christian virtues have small room in their compositions. Dr. Stewart told me that frequently while administering medicine (gratuitously of course) to them, they have stolen bottles, books, and anything they could lay their hands on in his dispensary. The Chinese may admire the disinterestedness of the missionaries, but that does not convince them of the beauty of the faith which inspires such deeds.

December 24.—Chinese business methods at Kuei-hua Ch'eng are beautifully illustrated by what the inn-keeper has to-day undertaken to do. I engaged his cook to go with me on my wanderings and promised him fairly good wages. The Chang-kuei-ti saw at once a good chance to squeeze the man, so he announced that the said cook was short in his accounts with him, and that he would not allow him to leave, and would have him arrested if he tried to. This meant the payment of a sum of money to the magistrate to clear himself, a probable delay of three or four days and, as I am going to leave to-morrow, he would lose a good job. As a matter of fact the inn-keeper owes Kao his wages for nearly a year, this he refused to pay him, and not satisfied with this, forced the cook to pay him 10 taels to escape the criminal prosecution with which he had threatened him, all of which, and a great deal more, my new *compagnon de voyage* will make out of me before we reach the journey's end.

December 25.—All the guests at the inn and the friends I have made while stopping here escorted me to the west end of the town and there wished me *I lu ping-an* "a prosperous journey." The road we followed took a west-southwesterly direction, receding considerably from the northern mountain range. The soil was but slightly cultivated, most of it being used as pasture lands for the innumerable flocks and herds waiting here to be sold. As we advanced the soil became more and more alkaline, but villages, as dirty as usual, were still numerous, with willow groves, around each one. We passed a few primitive carts, in which not a bit of iron is used, drawn by miserable little cows, carrying soda to Kuei-hua, or "big beans" (*ta t'ou*), or willow twigs for making baskets.

We reached Shih-erh-t'eng by 6.30 P. M. and made ourselves pretty comfortable in the inn, thanks to the presence in my party of an old cart driver called Li who had driven me in '88 from Peking to Hsi-an Fu, and whom I had met at Kuei-hua where he was buying tallow to send to Peking. He had insisted on escorting me as far as Ho-k'ou and knew how to "hustle about" and get all he wanted from the apparently meagre supplies in the inns, every one dreading his tongue, irrefutable logic, and endless profanity.

December 26.—The road bent a little more to the south than yesterday, the soil was whiter with alkaline efflorescence, and the hamlets smaller and not so numerous. Away to the south some fifteen to eighteen miles we saw low hills, of loess apparently. The sand grouse flew here and there in vast flocks, and boys and men were trapping them, using for that purpose a hair noose tied to a lump of clay or a little stick, a number of little clay decoys being placed around each trap. The birds get their clumsy parrot-like feet firmly entangled in the noose and fall an easy prey to the trappers, who hawked them about boiled in the inn yards; the meat is very dry and flavorless, but if roasted would probably be quite palatable.

We passed through Tou Ch'eng, the Togto of the Mongols and possibly Marco Polo's Tenduc, and 5 *li* south of it reached Ho-k'ou on the Yellow River.* On the loess hill behind this place are the ruins of a large camp or ch'eng, in all likelihood the site of the old town. The Yellow River is on this side embanked, with fine willows growing along the dykes. Ho-k'ou, called Dugus or Dugei by the Mongols, carries on an important trade in soda; it is made into large blocks about a foot square and three feet long, and

* Père Gerbillon, in the account of his sixth voyage in Tartary (Duhalde, *op. cit.*, IV, 345) speaks of the city of Toto as follows: "Cette Ville est quarrée comme celles de la Chine; ses murailles ne sont que de terre, mais d'une terre ni bien battue, qu' elle ne s'est éboulée nulle part depuis trois ou quartre cens ans et plus, qu' elle est bâtie." Col. Yule, *The Book of Ser Marco Polo* (2d edit.) I, 277, thinks that Kuei-hua Ch'eng was Tenduc, the capital of Prester John, but I cannot but think that he overlooked the existence of Togto when he made the identification. Huc (*op. cit.*, I, 215) calls Ho-k'ou by its Mongol name of Tchagan Kouren, meaning, I presume, "the white camp."

in this shape sent to Peking and other cities of northern China. There is also a good deal of business done here with the Ordos Mongols who live across the river.

December 27.—The people hereabout make clumsy flat boats in which they descend the river in summer to T'ung-kuan* in three or four days; there the boats are usually sold for lumber, as it is too hard work to get them up to Ho-k'ou again. I noticed moored to the bank a number of these typical mud-scows made of willow planks. They are some forty feet long with about fifteen feet beam; they are the only craft made along this part of the river, and do little credit to the ship-building skill of the people. The rafts from Kan-su (Lan-chou and Ning-hsia) do not come this far, but stop at Pao-tu, as do the ox-hide rafts from Hsi-ning which bring down oil.

Having to stop over here to-day to make some purchases, I went across the river to some Mongol houses to buy butter. These Mongols are of the Djungar branch of the Ordos tribe, and are very Chinesefied, though the women have retained the Mongol fashion of braiding the hair and their peculiar ornaments, especially the big earrings; the men, however, dress in purely Chinese style. These Djungars are very thrifty and much less demoralized than the Chahar. At the house in which I called, milk-tea was served and parched millet, instead of the *tsamba* eaten by the western tribes, eaten soaked in it. They eat, however, cheese and sour milk as do the western tribes. Unlike the western Mongols who do not object to being called Ta-tzŭ, these Djungar and all eastern Mongols resent the use of the term, and always speak of themselves as Meng-gu.

These Djungars have entirely given up the use of tents and live in Chinese style, observing only a few of the customs of their people; the most carefully adhered to is that of exchanging snuff-bottles for a whiff with each guest as he arrives, though neither the host nor the guest takes any snuff, but only partially withdraws the stopper and raising the bottle to the nose, then returns it, holding it in both hands and making a profound bow to the owner.

December 28.—The Djungar Mongols enjoy the honor of having at present the supremacy among the tribes forming the Iké chao

* T'ung-kuan is an important barrier on the highroads between Peking, Hsi-an, Ssŭ-ch'uan, Han-k'ou, etc. See *Land of the Lamas*, 17 et seq.

league, their chief being known as the Djungar (in Chinese Chung-kou-erh) t'a or "Generalissimo." This title was formerly borne by the Prince of Wushun, but on his demise the Djungars managed by a liberal distribution of presents to the Mongol superintendency at Peking (*Li-fan yüan*), with whom the appointment rests, to secure the honor to their Wang.

I left Ho-k'ou at 10 A. M., and after crossing the Hsiao Hei ho, which flows through the town and empties into the Yellow River two and a half miles south of it, we traversed the latter river (here some four hundred yards wide) on the ice, and ascended the Shen-hsi plateau which is about one hundred yards higher than the river. The Yellow River, at this point of its course, does not appear to spread much beyond its present bed, for villages are built on the river bottom, though the embankment at Ho-k'ou shows that it occasionally threatens the town.*

Leaving the river behind, we found ourselves on an undulating plateau of sand and loess with little farms of Chinese and Mongols scattered here and there in sheltered nooks. Wherever possible (*i. e.*, where protected from the winds) the soil is cultivated, but water is scarce, though wells of very inconsiderable depth are numerous and might be used to irrigate the fields from. A few willow trees around each mud house relieve, in a measure, the monotony of the view.

We traveled some fifteen miles and stopped for the night at Lien-pi yao-tzŭ, a hamlet of Shan-hsi farmers where we found sleeping room only.† Fortunately I had laid in a supply of provisions at Ho-k'ou, enough to last me until we reach Ning-hsia. Among other articles I had prepared about ten catties of mutton *chiao-tzŭ* or pâtés, which had been frozen so as to stand the roughest handling, ten catties of *chao-mien*, or parched meal, in which a little greese and hashed mutton is added, and which mixed with boiling water, forms an excellent and filling mush. I had also fifteen catties of vermicelli (*kua-mien*), a boiled sheep cut in pieces

---

*I am not aware that severe inundations occur along this portion of the Yellow River valley or higher up it. Below T'ung-kuan, near which point the river receives three large affluents, terrible inundations are of frequent occurrence.

†The owner and his son got very mad with me because I whistled, and insisted that I should not do so in the house, as it would bring them bad luck. The same superstition is found in parts of Turkestan, Eugene Schuyler, *Turkestan*, II, 29 (3rd Amer. edit.).

of about a pound each, a brick of tea, plenty of good butter packed in a sheep's paunch, and a bag of small loaves of wheaten bread. I had also bought at Kuei-hua a kettle, a copper tea-pot, a grate in which to burn argols and a few other indispensable articles for camp life, so I felt absolutely independent and fared sumptuously.

I notice hereabout, as also on the left bank of the river, that the potash-impregnated soil in all the little hollows has been carried away to Ho-k'ou, where it is put on a reed seive and water poured on it. The water that drains off is evaporated and the soda (or potash, *chien*) made into the large cakes previously referred to, shipped to Peking by way of Kuei-hua Ch'eng. Sand grouse fly about in vast flocks, especially at dawn and late at night, during the day we see but few; except when they have been disturbed, they move about but little.

December 29.—The country does not differ from that traversed yesterday. No Mongols live along our road, but now and then we pass one riding along on a miserable little rough and lank pony. The road for part of the way to-day led along the base of a range of low hillocks of sand, with no habitations or cultivation to be seen anywhere. Towards three o'clock we stopped to drink a cup of tea at a little Chinese hamlet, near a temple called by the Chinese Hato Lohé jo,* on a hillock near by.

We lost our road repeatedly to-day in the drifting sands, but kept in the right direction and finally pulled up for the night at a little village called Chang-kai Ying-tzŭ, about 7 *li* from Hsin chao (the "New Temple," Kolinjo the Mongols call it) where the Djungar Wang resides. The village is on the Husetan River, a good sized stream (for this region) flowing southwest by west and emptying into the Yellow River below Ho-k'ou.

The man to whom the house in which we have stopped belongs told me it had not snowed for two years, and that the people were in dire distress. Weeds are the only fuel the country affords—they are even carried to Ho-k'ou—there is very little cattle in this district, the Mongols living quite a distance to the south, so the usual Mongol fuel, dry dung or *argal*, is totally wanting, and now the soil has been so baked for the last year that no weeds have grown on it.

* Hato Lohé jo represents a Mongol name, or possibly a half Mongol, half Chinese one.

December 30.—We left with a strong west wind blowing. Our road led west, northwest, first through sand hillocks, then over firmer soil strongly impregnated with alkali. The low range, which we have seen yesterday and to-day to the south, is evidently the former bank of the Yellow River. One may notice here and there all the way from Ho-k'ou to where we now are what appear to be old channels of the river.

SPINDLE OF ORDOS MONGOLS.

We reached towards dusk Hsiao nor, a station of the Belgian Catholic Mission. I found the father in the school room lecturing to his flock. He could not at first make out who I was, whether Chinese or foreigner, nor could he speak, the words would not come. Finally he broke forth in French, addressing both me and his Chinese in that language. After a while he got his speech under control, and we passed a most agreeable evening smoking and talking over our experiences in China and Mongolia.

This station was founded five years ago, the ground having been leased from the Talat Princess. The Mission has erected substantial buildings and small cottages in which dwell about one hundred families of Chinese converts. The station farms several hundred acres and is practically self-supporting. The Father acts as a spiritual and temporal ruler, the people having no intercourse with the Chinese officials beyond paying their taxes to them. It is doubtful whether this system of keeping the converts in tutelage is a good one, though it is a sure means of getting proselytes when required, especially if a famine is (as is now the case) raging in the country. Father Lehmanns told me that "the pagans" are far more careful of their clothing and belongings than the Christians, for they have no one but themselves on whom to count. As to the latter, they trust blindly to the Mission for clothing, shelter, and all the necessaries and comforts of life. While talking on the subject to the Father a man came in who told him there were two villages of some forty families each which wanted to become neophytes to escape starving to death. Should the Mission be able, which is not probable, to accept them, nine-tenths will, in all probability, revert to their so-called "paganism" as soon as the famine is at an end.

I have had to change my plans here as I find it impossible to get a guide to take me directly to Teng-k'ou by the route south of the river. The Chinese hereabout do not go that way and there are no Mongols living here. It would require, furthermore, to hire camels to carry fodder for the mules, as none is to be had west of here; all this would require more time than I want to give it, so I will cross to the right bank of the river and travel by way of San-tao ho-tzŭ, the residence of Monseigneur Hamer of the Belgian Mission.

From this point the Wula shan, some of whose peaks are sprinkled with snow, appears quite close to us, though the Yellow River, which separates us from it, is eight miles away, and Pao-tu at its base is thirteen. The portion of the Ordos country along the banks of the Yellow River has only been settled by Chinese within the last thirty years. When Huc traversed this region there were no Chinese in it, but twenty years later when the Mohammedan rebellion broke out at Hua Hsien in Shen-hsi, many of the more peacefully inclined Chinese found a refuge here, just as others have found it in the *ts'ao-ti* outside the Great Wall to the north of the province of Chih-li and Shan-hsi.

December 31.—Father Lehmanns escorted me three or four miles on my way. We managed to keep in the right direction to-day, though there is hardly any trail visible and my head driver deserves his name of "Mule Colt" (Lo chŭ-tzŭ) for he will never listen to any suggestion from me about the road, or anything else, but follows the even tenor of his way, which is nine times out of ten the wrong one. Ch'iang-pan, where we have stopped for the night, is one of the usually-met-with tumble-down hamlets, no better, no worse than any other we have seen west of Kuei-hua.

Among the Djungars (and probably the other Mongols of the Ordos) grain is not ground on a quern but crushed in a large stone mortar with a stone armed trip-hammer similar to that which the Chinese use for husking rice. It consists of a trunk of a tree about ten feet long, with a stone some eight inches in diameter fixed in a hole at one end. This trunk is pivoted near one end on a wooden axle, and on the short end a woman presses with her foot, letting the hammer fall a height of about eighteen inches on the grain. It is a very clumsy contrivance, but answers its purpose well.

I noticed to-day the first scythe I have seen in China. It was used to cut the long grass which supplies the fuel (and at present part of the food of the people), and consisted of a short, broad knife with a concave surface and a socket handle—the blade about ten inches long and four broad, fixed in a six-foot handle. The curve in the surface of the blade was near the back. The Chinese generally use a sickle, the blade of which is nearly at right angle with the handle, but scythes I had thought unknown to them, and really I do not know whether the instrument seen to-day ought not rather be termed a long-handled sickle.

January 1, 1892.—The ordinary Chinese house of this country can be built, the people tell me, for about three dollars. It consists usually of two small rooms, in one of which is a *k'ang* or stove-bed and a cooking-stove with one large hole for a cast-iron saucepan. Then there is a cup board, a few bed clothes and a heterogeneous mass of dirty rags and odds and ends which would disgrace the dust heap of any other country in the world but China. When a person wants to move, he takes what little wood-work there is about his house, rafters, doors, etc., packs them on a roughly made cart, in which not a piece of iron enters, and hitching to it his cow or donkey goes his way.

The road to-day led us along the base of low hills, probably marking the former south bank of the Yellow River, and also for several miles along the dry bed of one of its present branches.

We stopped at Tan-kai mao-to which boasts of being quite a place, with five or six inns and some thirty houses. In my room in the inn, among many mottoes written on slips of red paper and pasted around the domestic shrine, I noticed one "*Fu, shui*" ("happiness and water"), a truly pathetic and, I fear, unheard appeal.

The existing maps of this section of country are far from satisfactory. Thus on many, some seventeen miles west of Pao-tu, there appears a town called Pilchetai on the left bank of the Yellow River near the mouth of what would appear to be an important stream. The stream exists, it is called Kundulung, but of the city no one living knoweth. Then again Ho lai liu is given as the name of another locality, but it only means "River Willow," the ground near the river being everywhere hereabout covered with scrubby willows.

The mountains to the north of the river are now called Pao (t'u) shan, and two days farther west they take the name of Wula shan from the Orat (in Chinese Wula) Mongols who live near by.

January 2.—There is a little irrigation carried on hereabout, but, taken all together, the irrigated lands (*ch'iu ti*) are of small extent. I do not understand why the people do not irrigate their fields from wells, for water, and good at that, is found nearly everywhere a few feet below the surface of the ground.

At Sumutu, where we stopped to eat our lunch of *chiao-tzŭ* and tea, the people were threshing the seed out of the briars and grass they had cut to feed their cattle with. This they boiled, then dried, finally grinding it and making bread in which they mixed a very little wheat flour which they had to go to Pao-t'u to buy. The distress among the people is so great that they have taken to pillaging each other to get the wherewithal to eke out their miserable existence.

We stopped for the night at quite a respectable village called Ta hua-erh, the best looking place we have seen since leaving Ho-k'ou. Before reaching it we had to cross the river on the ice. It is at this point about one-third of a mile wide and apparently very shallow; the ice was, however, so thickly covered with dust it was difficult to make out where the river began and ended. All the country west of Pao-t'u as far as this place belongs to the Hsi Kung or Western Duke of the Orat Mongols. The Orat Mongols are divided into three branches under the rule of a Western (*Hsi*), Eastern (*Tung*), and Middle (*Tumta*) Duke (*Kung*). The Chinese living in the Ordos country are, I believe, under the jurisdiction of Yü-lin Fu in Shen-hsi, but they pay rent to the Mongol princes for the land they occupy. The Chinese here tell me that the Yellow River flows under ground at Pao-t'u, by which I suppose is to be understood that a second stream flows under that which is seen passing at that locality. It is curious in this connection to recall that Chinese authors say that the Yellow River has its source in the Lob nor and thence flows under the mountains to the north and south of the Ts'aidam to reappear in the Odontala, where we know that its true sources are located.

January 3.—Our route led us along the base of the Wula shan and past the residence of the Hsi Kung of the Orats, a Chinese-looking place, quite recently built and with a very substantial appearance. A couple of miles to the west of it is a handsome lamasery of the Tibetan style of architecture, also recently built or restored. It is called Baron gomba ("Eastern lamasery") by Mongols, and Kung miao or "the Duke's monastery" by the Chinese.

A stream, a real one and the only one worthy the name we have seen since leaving Ho-k'ou, flows by the Kung's residence; it is probably the Ho lai liu river of our maps, for it is about from this point that the river willow (*ho lai liu*) grows thick all over the river bottom, and affords an inexhaustible supply of fuel to the inhabitants. It seems to me to be the same as the *sha liu* ("sand willow") of the Ts'aidam. I am informed, however, that such is not the case, for the sha liu is called *borgaso* in Eastern Mongol and in the Ts'aidam *balro*, while the ho liu (or *ho lai liu*) is the *ulan borgaso* or "red willow." I am also told that there is a third variety called *hung liu* ("red willow") known to Eastern Mongols as *ulan moto* ("red wood") and in the Ts'aidam called *ulasun moto*.*

We passed now and then one or two small Mongol tents surrounded with brushwood fences to protect them from the wind and wolves. The people who inhabit them have neither flocks nor herds, probably they are farther south for there is absolutely no grazing along our line of march. We saw to-day a few loads of wool and hides being carried eastward on camels and in Chinese carts; this is the first freight we have met since leaving Kuei-hua.

Since crossing the Huang ho yesterday I have seen quite a number of pheasants, a few partridges, some geese, but no more

*On the flora of this section of the Yellow River valley, see Prjevalsky, *Mongolia*, I, 189 et seq.

Hsi Kung Miao. Lamasery in the Ordos Country.

T'a-Erh Ssu or Kumbum Lamasery.

sand grouse. Antelope (*Huang yang* or *Antilope gutturosa* of Prjevalsky) are very numerous on both sides of the river.

The Wula shan range* is certainly not more than from twelve hundred to eighteen hundred feet high, but the country is so flat that even when miles away it does not lose a foot of its height, and appears quite imposing.

There is a very little snow on the ground to-day, it fell last night. A little fell on leaving Tsahan obo (December 14), and that is all we have had so far on the journey.

We stopped for the night at a little inn at a point where the mountains take a northwest bend; it is called Hsiao miao-tzŭ ("the little temple"). The water is abominably brackish and as a result our tea is undrinkable—and it has to be bad for that! The mountain slopes hereabout are covered with a stunted juniper (*pai shu* the Chinese call it); the predominating rocks are gneiss and granite.

Since passing the Hsi Kung's residence we have seen no Chinese villages or farms and. I learn that that potentate only allows a very few farmers to cultivate land. He is a wise man in his generation, but the Chinese will some day own his domains for all that.

January 4.—Two or three miles beyond Hsiao miao-tzŭ the Wula shan takes a sudden bend north-northeast, and connects by a line of low hills with another range to the west which in turn trends west-southwest, some ten or twelve miles from our route. We can now and then see the Yellow River a few miles on our left, its course nearly parallel to our route which passes through interminable thickets of *liu shu* (willow) and spear grass. Occasionally we see a few head of cattle and ponies and conclude that there are inhabitants to be found somewhere, but we see none. I notice once more large flocks of sand grouse, a few pheasants, some antelopes and a wolf. We stopped for lunch at a miserable cabin inhabited by some Chinese; near it are a few Mongol tents, this is Hamar hosho. The water is terribly brackish, and that is all there is to be said of this desolate spot.

---

* Prjevalsky calls this range Munni ula. All the country between the meridian of Pao-t'u and that of San-tao ho-tzŭ, on the south side of the Yellow River, he calls the Kuzupchi sands. Kuzupchi, he says, means "collar" in Mongol and is a very appropriate name "on account of the distinct fringe which they (these sands) form along the valley." *Mongolia*, I, 93.

We passed quite a number of camels going eastward and carrying goat-skins, camel's hair and wool, but the traffic is on the whole very small, and judging by the accommodations in inns along the road, and by their small number, it is probably never large at any season of the year.

We put up for the night at Shelakang (Ta-pu ho of the Chinese), a solitary inn where I took up my abode in a miserable out-house so dirty that it would not have been used with us for a pig sty, and so low I could not stand upright in it; but I escaped the opium smokers in the *huo fang;* and was left in quiet to do my evening's work. It snowed off and on during the day, about two and one-half inches fell, but hardly any wind blew the while, and the cold was not severe.

January 5.—The route to-day still led us through dense brush-wood—hardly any habitations were visible, but Mongol boys herding sheep and an occasional passing horseman showed that the country was inhabited. The few Chinese dens we saw were occupied by miserable wretches, opium fiends of the purest type, thin and of the color of clay.

It is seventeen miles from Shelakang to Ashan, where we stopped for the night, and from which place the people count 300 *li* to San-tao ho-tzŭ. The soil along the route to-day was alkaline and devoid of vegetation, where irrigated, brush grows; the size and length of the irrigation ditches is astonishing, especially when one considers the sparse agricultural population of this region, and that the ever drifting sands oblige the farmers to be forever cleaning the canals which would otherwise be rapidly choked.

Ashan has a few dismal inns and a theater, that is to say the usual covered stage seen in most villages in North China in front of the local temple, where strolling actors perform, or amateurs give a play once a year. It is the first one we have seen since passing Tan-kai mao-to, and so Ashan must rank with that place in importance.

The mountain range to our north is now called Lang shan, as to the country round-about Ashan it belongs to the Hangkin Mongols, and in Chinese it is called Hang-kai ti. West of Ashan we will reënter the Orat Mongols' district.

January 6.—Of the country between Ashan and Ho-k'ou-ti, at which place or farm we arrived late this evening after losing ourselves, as usual, a dozen times on the way, little can be said. The road led all the way through brush and sand. Now and then we crossed a big irrigation ditch or a ploughed field, showing that somewhere, far from the road, were Chinese settlers. These irrigation canals are the bane of a traveler's existence as we have often to make enormous detours to get around or even across them.

We stopped for lunch at Tsahan (or Chahan) nor ("White Lake"), but saw no sign of a lake. Some Mongols live, we are told, near here, but we only saw two Chinese hovels.

Ho-k'ou-ti consists of a very small and dirty hovel (unless the name applies to the cluster of four or five hovels scattered over a radius of a mile or so near it). The owner let us have the use of a large and dirty empty room; the roof over it only covered a portion of the room, enough to let in the piercing wind but not to let out the smoke of our fire of brush which nearly suffocated us, as we had to build it in a sheltered corner to keep it from being blown about by the wind, which swept in eddying gusts into the house, bringing down clouds of dust and soot from the mud roof.

The Ordos Mongols comprise seven clans: the Djungar (Chungkor in Chinese), Talat, Wang, Ottok, Djassak, Wushun and Hangkin.* At present the head of the league is the Djungar Wang or Djungar Ta. His predecessor was the Wushun Wang. This prince receives a patent from the Colonial Office of Peking (Li-Fan Yüan), which is, it is rumored, greatly influenced in its selection by the value of the presents the rival candidates make it.

The Orat Mongols, of whom I have spoken previously, are, I hear, divided into three clans: Hsi kung, Tung kung and Tomta

* We are told by Ssanang Setzen that the Ordos Mongols had the special duty of protecting the camp (*Ordu*) of Jingis Khan and the other great Mongol Khans, and it is conjectured, very reasonably, that it was from this office that the tribe received its name. See H. H. Howorth, *History of the Mongols*, I, 401; also I. J. Schmidt, *Geschichte der ost Mongolen von Ssanang Setzen*, 191 and 408. Timkowski, *op. cit.*, II, 268, gives also some details concerning this tribe. Prjevalsky calls the Talat Taldi, and has by so doing introduced considerable confusion in not only the study of this section of country but also into that of a corner of northwest Kan-su where he makes mention of a tribe which he likewise calls Taldy or Daldy, but which are, in all likelihood, of Turkish descent.

kung.* Hangkin is the westernmost of the Ordos clans. It confines on the territory of the Prince of Alashan, who is colloquially designated by Chinese as the Hsi Wang or "Western Prince."

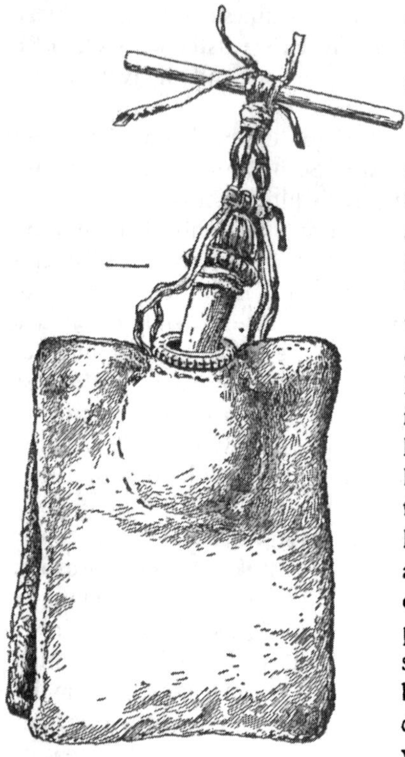

WATER BOTTLE AND CLOTH COVER.
Used by lamas to moisten their lips from during the forenoon (Kumbum).

January 7.—Twenty miles through willow brush, spear grass and sand hillocks. We saw a few Mongol habitations, tents and houses, and a small lamasery, called by the Chinese Ch'ang chi miao, probably meaning "Long good luck lamasery," and built in half-Tibetan half-Chinese style. The whole face of the country was cut up by irrigation canals, the length and size of which astonished me. We stopped for lunch at Wei-yang-chi ti, a hamlet of four or five substantial houses. That in which we lunched was especially fine, and the old Shen-hsi man who owned it was the most prosperous looking being we had seen for a long time. A goodly bunch of sheep of his were drinking from troughs in the yard around which were huge piles of brushwood neatly arranged, and carts and farming implements nearly filled the remaining space. We left this place

* Meaning "West Duke," "East Duke" and "Middle Duke." These Orat Mongols are probably Kalmucks. See H. H. Howorth, *op. cit.*, I, 497, et seq. I am unable, however, to account for their presence among the Ordos Mongols; possibly they came there at the time when the Eleuts first occupied Alashan, in 1686, according to Timkowski, *op. cit.*, II, 279. This same author (II, 265), quoting probably Chinese geographical works of the 18th century, says, however, that three Orat banners were living in the valley of Khadamal, which begins about a mile to the west of Kuei-hua Ch'eng and extends westward about seventy miles, in other words, they lived in the lower Hsi-ho valley.

towards two o'clock and wandered about till after dark trying to find Wu-ta-ku, where we had been told we would find lodgings and fodder.

It was dark when we reached this place, but we were refused admittance—a party of travelers had the only room in the inn—so we went on further, and the mules led us of themselves to a farm house. Again we were turned away, but pushing my way into the *huo fang*, I found that the *chang-kuei-ti* was an asthmatic old woman of rather kindly and decidedly inquisitive nature who, on the promise of a little medicine and the hope of making something out of the party, persuaded the most ragged of her motley and disreputable band of retainers, a blind and opium smoking beggar, to cede me his hovel for the night. He, his wife and two bairns and a few lambs turned out of their twelve-feet square cabin, and I tried to make myself comfortable for the night, for it was bitter cold outside and I had rather stifle than freeze. It was warm in the hut, but it was also the vilest, dirtiest hole it had ever been my bad fortune to put up in. Later on in the evening the beggar asked permission to sing a song for me, he being, it appeared, a noted minstrel among his people. In an evil hour I consented. He strummed on an antiquated *san-hsien*, and then with much wheezing, snorting and horrible grimacing he sang, or rather yelled, an interminable ditty about an honest official and the great rewards the Emperor conferred on him for his astonishing virtues. It was long, very long, and painful for us who understood but a word here and there of his jargon, but I thanked him, and then—he wanted to sing again. I bribed him to desist, and he went and charmed our neighbors far into the night.

We saw a few pheasants to-day, some partridges and sand grouse. We are still in Hangkin, but Alashan begins a little to the west of this place before one reaches San-tao ho-tzŭ, which is now but a stage off.

January 8.—The day's march was through dense brush, and the detours to get over irrigating canals, long and numerous, and, to add to our trouble, we did not reach San-tao ho-tzŭ, but only Ta-chung-t'an, some six miles away from it. To add to our misery and the discomfort of cart travel—never agreeable under the most favorable circumstances—the soil had been turned up by licorice diggers, making pitfalls two and three feet deep and as many across all over the face of the country. Licorice is exported from here in large quantities to Tien-tsin; it is the most valuable, in fact the only natural product of the soil. The Chinese call it *kan ts'ao*, the Mongols *shiker ebuso*, both meaning "sweet grass or plant."*

A few miles before reaching Ta-chung-t'an we crossed the Wula ho flowing southeast. This stream marks the boundary of Alashan. Ta-chung-t'an is a fortified village and resembles an Arab *borj*, or rather it is a big farm house with a large number of out houses, the whole surrounded by a fifteen-foot wall in which there is but one heavy gate. The people had to resort to fortifying themselves in this way during the Mohammedan rebellion in the sixties. The rebels devastated the whole country, and it has not even yet recovered from their ravages.

The carts we see here at Ta-chung-t'an are of a new type, well suited to sandy soil. The wheels are five feet six inches in diameter and about four inches broad.† The body of the cart is quite light, and it is drawn by one bullock yoked between the shafts; the yoke is attached to the shafts and consists of a bent piece of wood resting on the animal's back, or rather against its neck, and is held firmly in place by a rope passing around the oxen's neck.

I hear that when the crops are good, a large quantity of hemp seed oil (*ma yu*) is exported from here, but at present there is nothing to export, nothing to sell, and hardly anything to eat. It is pitiable to hear the poor people talk. They speak of nothing but the price of flour, and their only question is whether in my country it ever happens that for two years no rain falls.

January 9.—Although we were only a few miles from San-tao ho-tzŭ it took us until three o'clock to reach that place, and we traveled about sixteen miles, so stupid and obstinate were the cart drivers. It was with no little pleasure that I at last saw a cross on top of a foreign-looking building, rising amidst a number of smaller ones looking too neat to be Chinese houses, and a few

* In Tibetan of the Koko now it is called *sha-nyar*. It is also very abundant in western Kan-su, near Lusar, and in western Ts'aidam, but there is no market for it. Prjevalsky calls it *Glycyrrhiza Uralensis*, and says the Chinese name for it is *so* or *soho*. *Mongolia*, I, 191. *So* and *soho* probably represent the sound *ts'ao*.

† Huc, *op. cit.*, II, 5, referring to these high wheeled carts of northeast Kan-su says that even in ancient times this portion of Kan-su was inhabited by Tartars called by the Chinese Kao-che or "High carts."

minutes after I was shaking hands with my good friend Bishop Hamer and the jolly, kind-hearted fathers of the Belgian Catholic Mission. My boy, the carters, the mules, were all provided for, and the fathers and I sat down in the refectory over a glass of schnapps and a pipe and talked till late in the evening.

As I expressed some doubt as to the possibility of converting Mongols, the Bishop told me that at Boro balgasun ("Grey Town"), eight days southwest of here in the Ottok Mongol country, he had some thirty families of Christian Mongols. Between here and Shih-tsui-tzŭ, at Kang-tzŭ-tien or Fu-erh-tien there live a few families of Mohammedan Mongols.

I heard that in the Ordos and in Alashan there grows a kind of currant, used by the Chinese as a medicine, or to make a medicine of: it is known to them as *hung kuo-tzŭ* ("red fruit") and to Mongols as *kéré innuto*. The fruit-bearing thorn (*pei-tzŭ* in Chinese, *bota* or *kéré innudun* in Mongol) is also found here. Its fruit is called *hamorok*, probably the same word as the Ts'aidam Mongol's *harmak*, the Chinese *hara-ma-ku*.*

January 10.—I had not intended stopping at San-tao ho-tzŭ, or San sheng-kung ("the Trinity's palace") as the fathers call it, but the Bishop insisted that, as it was Sunday, I must pass it with him. I consented with pleasure. I have cut out for myself a little more work than I can manage single-handed without a very great tax on my strength, and an occasional day of rest is very enjoyable.

The Bishop has built this last year over fifty new houses for famine converts, and altogether he has here, or in the villages in the immediate neighborhood some three hundred odd Christian families. Many of them are absolutely dependent on him; he gives a peck (*tou*) of flour to each family every month, enough for one meal of *mien* a day—sufficient to support life, and the lazy beggars ask nothing else, and do not a hand's turn to help themselves or assist the fathers in any way.

In the church I saw the tomb of Monseigneur de Voos, the first Catholic bishop of the Ordos; he died about two years ago and was succeeded by Monseigneur Hamer, who was then Bishop of western Kan-su, living at Liang-chou. One of the peculiar

* The *Nitraria schoberii* of Prjevalsky, who transcribes the Mongol name *Karmyk*. See also under May 4th, 1892.

changes which Christianity everywhere effects in Chinese women is curing them of the silly bashfulness of the so-called "heathens." This results, it would appear, from the fact that they receive the same religious instruction as the men and attend church with them. It is no easy matter to get them to the church for the first time, but, this ordeal over, they feel raised in the social scale and are decidedly improved by the change (at least in Europeans' eyes). Often native Christian women have paid me visits, sitting down in my room and talking as freely as did the men. On the whole, the salutary effects of Christianity are more visible in the women than in the men, in this country as in others.

San-tao ho-tzŭ is about two miles from the Yellow River, which is visible from the church steeple. There is a range of hills along the right (south) bank of the river, which gradually increases in height to the southwest till it appears to culminate in a flat topped mountain called Orondeshi.

January 11.—We left at about 1:30 P. M., after having photographed the Bishop, the fathers and the mission houses. The latter are wonderfully well built, when one considers the difficulties of every sort with which the builders have had to contend. The broad, well-irrigated fields, the rows of willows lining the roads and surrounding the various hamlets, are all their work, the result of their energy during the last sixteen years.

Between San-tao ho-tzŭ and Kang-tzŭ tien, where we stopped for the night, we saw nothing but sand hillocks, willow brush and sand flats, and everywhere were innumerable big holes, dug by licorice hunters, over which we had to bump our way. Just before reaching Kang-tzŭ tien we came to the bank of the Yellow River, here some three hundred to four hundred yards wide. To our southwest we saw the northern extremity of the Chua-tzŭ shan, the Orondeshi or "Anvil peak" of the Mongols.* This name is of common use among Mongols who frequently apply it to mountains with flat tops, which we would call small *mésas*. We passed several Mongol shepherds

* Orondeshi is properly the name of a peak in this short range, with a flat, mésa-shaped top of rock, but by extension its name is given to the whole of it. According to Col. Prjevalsky (*Mongolia*, I, 221), it is called Arbus-ula. "According to a Mongol tradition, he also says, one of the rocky peaks of the Arbus-ula, which has the shape of a table, served as a forge for Chinghiz Khan's smithy." There is another Orondeshi near the source of the Yellow River.

carrying about on the end of a stick a smouldering bit of dry dung. now and then when their hands and feet were numbed with the cold they used it to light a bunch of grass, and warm themselves by the blaze.

January 12.—Shortly after starting this morning our route turned due south and followed the bank of the Yellow River, here between four hundred and eight hundred yards wide. The bottom lands were covered everywhere with different varieties of the *liu* willow, bunch grass and a few shrubs and briars on which sheep were feeding, *faute de mieux*. The sand dunes were larger and more numerous, to our west they stretched for miles in parallel lines till they reached the base of the Alashan Mountains, here some ten to fifteen miles from the river.

Of Mongol life one sees nothing along this road, and of Chinese only the very lowest form. A filthier, more good-for-nothing, shiftless lot I never saw anywhere in China, and yet, when I look at the irrigation ditches these people have dug and keep clean, I must fain admit that they can not be quite what they look. Winter is a bad time to see them in, they must bloom out in summer.

One of the Fathers at San-tao ho-tzŭ told me that he had frequently seen letter carriers traveling for some private post-office, and having to reach their destination in a given time, which only permitted them to take a little sleep now and then, tie, when about to take a nap, a bit of joss-stick to their thumb, light it and sleep on till the stick had burned down to the thumb, when the pain of the burn awakened them and they resumed their journey. The people of Shen-hsi also use a joss-stick to time the noon-day rest of the workmen in the fields, letting them rest while a given length of it burns.

We stopped for the night in a solitary inn called Kuan-ti, about half a mile from the bank of the river. The two big *k'ang*, which nearly filled the only room, were occupied by some twenty travelers, but we squeezed into a corner and made ourselves tolerably comfortable. Fortunately I have long ago ceased to mind bad smells ; were it otherwise, the odor of this house would have stifled me.

January 13.—We traveled on through more sand and brush, passing before T'eng-k'ou (Tungor in Mongol), the only place we have seen on the right bank of the river since passing Tan-kai-mao-to in the Ordos. It consists of a dozen houses and, *mirabile dictu*, there is a vegetable garden outside it where potatoes and cabbages are said to thrive. It used to be, before the Mohammedan rebellion, much larger, and it existed even, so report says, in the Yüan period, when it was a place of great importance and of possibly considerable size.* It is supposed by some writers to have been Prester John's capital, but I am inclined, for reasons given previously, to place that at Ho-k'ou.

The sand dunes on the left bank attain, in front of T'eng-kou, to the size of hills; especially is this the case around a little hamlet called Sabokto. This name has a Mongol look to it, but I am inclined to think it is Chinese and should be read *Sha-po to*, "Many sand hills"; at all events, that would be a good way to transcribe the name in Chinese. Just beyond this place we cut across a big bend of the river, thus shortening our road several miles. When here it suddenly began blowing such clouds of dust that we got lost; the sky at moments was totally obscured. The wind blew in narrow currents; at one moment we were lost in dust and a few minutes later we reached a spot where no wind was blowing, to again be wrapped in dust a few hundred yards farther on.

We stopped for the night at Ho-kuai-tzŭ where my rest was disturbed by part of the family passing the night helping a ewe in a difficult case of parturition, and by my carters and a couple of travelers feasting on dead horse cooked with lots of garlic, a dish fit for a king, they said.

Coal of a poor quality is mined some twenty *li* west of Ho-kuai-tzŭ and made into coke, which sells, so the *chang-kuei-ti* said, but I believe he lied so as to squeeze me a little, for three cash a catty, while coal brings two. The coal used at San-tao ho-tzŭ comes from this mine.

We are now abreast of the Yin shan, which borders here the Yellow River along its right bank. It, like its continuation, the

* Col. Prjevalsky, in 1871, came from Pao-t'u across the Ordos country, and reached the Yellow River at this point, but he makes no mention of any place on its right bank but speaks of the town of Ding-hu on the western (left bank). "This small town had been entirely destroyed by the Dungans. * * * The only inhabitants of Ding-hu are the garrison, numbering at one time a thousand men." See Prjevalsky's *Mongolia*, I, 221. Though the name Ding-hu looks very much like T'eng-kou, it is the present Sabokto.

Chu-tzŭ shan to the north, is formed of stratified reddish brown sandstone dipping eastward. The mountains on the west side of the river are of similar formation with a westerly dip. The gravel covering the country in spots is of gneiss and disintegrated conglomerate, and in the drifted sand much hornblende is to be seen.

January 14.—At Ho-kuai-tzŭ the willow brush and bunch grass cease, the soil becomes stony (sandstone), and the road is over rising ground, the foothills of the Alashan range. Watch towers, which are found on all roads leading to China when one is close on to the Great Wall, are noticeable on either side of the river, and are excellent points for compass bearings, as are also the *obo* or stone heaps.

The valley of the Yellow River is here not over three miles in width, the mountains to the west are called by the Chinese Hsi shan ("Western Hills"), a name they retain as far as Chung-wei Hsien, where we lose sight of them ; they are the Alashan mountains of our maps.

We stopped for lunch at Erh-tzŭ tien on the bank of the river. This is the only hovel between Ho-kuai-tzŭ and Shih-tsui. My men, who are always hungry, no matter how much they eat, thought to improve their porridge by the addition of some of my butter. They took, by mistake, a big piece of Marseille soap and seasoned their food with it. The boy soon discovered their theft and told them of it. They came to me in a body with long and anxious faces asking if their lives were in danger. I said they would probably die, as even an external application of soap to a Chinese frontiersman was very dangerous, an unheard of thing in fact, what then must become of them who had taken such a large quantity internally. Useless to add that their stomachs did not feel the least worse for the unusual condiment.

On leaving Erh-tzŭ tien we went for a short distance along the bank of the river where it rises about fifty feet above the low water mark. The cliff showed some twenty-five feet of coarse gravel of sandstone, gneiss and granite, on top of which was the same thickness of honey-combed loess. The same strata were visible on the right bank. This loess had not been washed down from higher levels but was, I judged, a true sub-aerial deposit.

As we entered Shih-tsui we met two drunken Mongols riding camels. One tried to make a row and swore he would shoot one of the "*sao Man-tzŭ*" as he called us. He took his gun off his back, tried his best to strike a light with his flint and steel to ignite the slow-match, but was so drunk he could not succeed, and we laughed at him so much that he finally lashed his camel in a fury and galloped off.

At Shih-tsui the mountain range on the right bank of the river comes abruptly to an end in a ledge of rocks, and that on the left bank deflects to south south-west. The name Shih-tsui, or "Point of Rocks," is hence a most appropriate one for this locality. Officially it is known as Shih-tsui shan and in Mongol it is called Hotun jéli.* It is nominally the southernmost point in this direction on Alashan soil, but it is governed by Chinese officials and is an integral portion of the Ning-hsia Department, The road to the residence of the prince of Alashan branches off from the road we had just come over between Kang-tzŭ tien and Kuan-ti. This palace of the Alashan Wang is called by Prjevalsky Din-yuan-ing or Wei-ching P'u, but no one whom I questioned about it knew of any other name for it than Alashan Ya-mên or Wang-yeh Fu ("The Prince's Palace").

There are now some fifty or sixty Chinese families, mostly Shen-hsi people, living at Shih-tsui-tzŭ, but before the Mohammedan rebellion there were several hundred, and the ruins of the old town cover the ground for half a mile around. Moored to the bank of the river I noticed a number of large pontoons or mud scows made of willow planks, like those seen at Ho-k'ou. It is a wonder that such miserably build things can carry any cargo, and above all that they can reach Pao-t'u,

January 15.—Coal at Shih-tsui is brought from the Hsi shan, about twenty miles away ; it costs half a cash a catty, or five hundred cash for a cart load.†

* On the map of the River Hoang ho, accompanying Mr. St. George R. Littledale's paper on his recent journey across Asia, *Geographical Journal*, III, 445, et seq., this place is called Sudwisashan! On the same map San-tao ho-tzu is placed on the bank of the Yellow River, whereas it is several miles away from it. It is true that this name applies to all the Christian hamlets located thereabout, and there may be a little one on the river bank, though I did not hear of one.

† Huc appears to have crossed the Yellow River in front of Shih-tsui (his Che Tsui Dze). He says that the coal mines and the potteries of this place are its sources of wealth. The town was much larger in his time than at present. See Huc, *op. cit.*, II, 2, et seq.

The inn people tell me that the road to Ho-k'ou *viâ* Teng-k'ou and the Ho-tung (*i. e.*, the south side of the Yellow River) is very good, and that it only takes ten days to reach Pao-t'u by it. This is the road I wanted to travel over and was obliged to give up the idea of following on reaching Hsiao nor. But it is just as well I did not try it; my carters have proved themselves, times without number, unable to keep on the high road; what would it have been had we taken a cross road!

Shih-tsui is of special interest to foreigners, for here lives one of the pioneers of western civilization in Eastern Asia, the German trader Graessel, an energetic man who is equally known for his wool (camel's) gathering, as for his Shopenhauer-reading, camel-riding proclivities. He, the Belgian Splingaerd, who lives at Hsia-yü kuan, and the late Dalgleish of Kashgar, have done more than any other three men living to introduce foreign ideas and a respect for European methods of trade in these remote regions. But, ye gods! what a life they all have had to lead! Once a year Graessel goes to Peking, sees a few Europeans, gets, for a week or so, in touch with the outside world, and then returns to Shih-tsui or the Alashan Mongols for yet another year of dirt and discomfort.

We left Shih-tsui by nine o'clock and pushed on rapidly to Ping-lo Hsien, traversing a country covered with detached farms and little hamlets. For miles we followed a huge irrigation canal from which ran innumerable ditches leading the water all over the broad valley.* This stupendous work has converted an alkaline, wind-swept, sandy plain into a fertile district, where rice, wheat, millet and fruits of various kinds are raised in great abundance.

About nine miles from Shih-tsui we saw, about a mile on our right, a branch (or rather a remnant of a branch) of the Great Wall terminating at the steep base of the Hsi shan. We passed through Hsia ying-tzŭ—a Christian village, Shang ying-tzŭ, Huang-ch'i chiao, a bustling market town where we took lunch, and finally pulled up at Ping-lo Hsien, a miserable, dilapidated place, lost in the sands which, on the north side of the town, have drifted to the height of the top of the walls. An alkaline plain, in a great measure unsuitable for agriculture, surrounds the town, and the *raison d'être* of such a place is hard to find.

* Cf. Huc, *op. cit.*, II, 4-5.

January 16.—We made an early start as we had to reach Ning-hsia by dusk, before the city gates were closed. The Hsi shan grew higher and more rugged as we advanced, and the right bank of the Yellow River, some three or four miles to our left, rose above the stream a hundred feet or so, the country behind it sloping very gradually upward. On a few peaks of the Hsi shan we could see a little snow.

The country south of Ping-lo is very poor, alkaline deposits cover large areas with a thick white coating. Farms are few, the people congregating in the villages, of which we passed quite a number.

We stopped for half an hour at Li-k'ang P'u to eat a *momo** and drink a cup of tea, and then pushed on as rapidly as we could, but not fast enough, it turned out, for it was night when we reached Ning-hsia, and the city gates were closed when we pulled up before them. There are no suburbs on the north side of the city—a measure of precaution adopted since the Mohammedan rebellion, so we had to pound on the gates and shout wildly till we aroused the warders, and my boy explained to them that I was a foreign envoy *en mission extraordinaire.* Off they rushed to the Ch'en-tai's Ya-men for the keys of the gate, and, having opened it, escorted me with lanterns to a fairly good inn on the high street. The first impression I gained of this famous city was very disappointing; nothing but low, newly built mud houses, with a row of willow trees on either side of the street. We passed many vacant lots scattered about, and not a few ruins; in fact Ning-hsia is just rising for the fifth or sixth time in its history from its ruins.

The inn was clean but of course there were no comforts; if you want luxuries of any kind in northern China you must carry them along with you for none are to be found, even in the best of inns. There is only one Mohammedan inn in the city, and this one is only tolerated, for Mohammedans are not allowed to pass the night inside the city; they may only come in during the day to transact their business and must go back to the suburbs by dark where they have their homes.†

* A roll or small loaf of bread of wheat flour.

† The late Mohammedan rebellion is not apparently the cause of this measure, for we learn that as early as the beginning of the 17th century, when Benedict Goës went to China (1603-1607), the Mohammedans of the Su-chou in northwestern Kan-su (and probably elsewhere) were shut up every night within the walls of their own city, which was distinct from that inhabited by the Chinese. H. Yule, *Cathay and the Way Thither*, 582.

The Mohammedans here and in northern China frequently call themselves *li ch'üan*, "esoterists," other Chinese they call *wai ch'üan*, "exoterists." They also say their faith is the "little religion" (*hsiao chiao*), while that of all other Chinese is the *ta chiao* or "great religion." They are the Chinese with prejudices, abstaining from pork, tobacco, and who do not eat unclean food or use unclean vessels; the Chinese of the other persuasions form the unprejudiced part of the population, to whom all kinds of food and every kind of enjoyment are good; these are practically the only distinguishing features between the two faiths.

January 17.—To-day I examined the carpet factories for which this place has been famous for centuries. The wool is bought from the Mongols and each manufacturer dyes his worsteds for himself. I found it difficult to obtain very accurate information about the origin and nature of the dyes used. Brazil wood supplies a red dye, *huai-tzŭ* (seed of the *Styphonolobium japonicum*, according to Williams), a yellow dye, safflower is also used, as is a red dye said to come from Tibet, and which is possibly the *ts'o* of the Tibetans. Another plant called here *tzŭ hua-tzŭ* (*tzŭ* meaning "purple") supplies a light drab, and indigo furnishes them their blues. Aniline dyes, I was sorry to find, have found their way into the Ning-hsia market, but are not much used in dyeing wools for carpets, except for supplying purple. The green colors used come, I was told, from the East (probably Shanghai), and are therefore, I presume, of foreign origin. The manufacturers only dye their wools in summer. In company with Mr. Horoben, of the China Inland Mission, I visited a number of the factories (there are sixteen in the city), in most of which we found between six to ten looms at which both men and women worked. The looms, of the most primitive description, are vertical and the warp is passed over two rollers. The woof is passed in between two threads of the warp without the aid of any instrument, the wool being simply rolled in a ball, and is cut off roughly with a rather blunt knife. When a whole line has thus been put in, it is trimmed with a pair of shears. There is no pattern before the weaver, but he evolves the most intricate and tasteful designs without their assistance or a moment's hesitation.

I found that many manufacturers were copying very common patterns of European ingrain carpets. These were to fill orders given them by various officials who had brought here bits of carpet bought at some of the treaty ports. The usual size of the rugs is that necessary to cover a *k'ang*, say ten feet by six. Prayer rugs, cushions, saddle blankets, etc., are made in larger numbers than any other styles of rugs, as nearly all of them are sold to Mongols or go to Tibet. Besides rugs, Ning-hsia manufactures a good quality of paper, and here the industries of the place cease.*

The town of Ning-hsia is still to a great extent a pile of ruins. The main street (*ta chieh*)—at least the portion of it on which there are shops of any pretension, is not over five hundred yards long. These have in them very few articles beyond the necessities of life and the usual Chinese "notions." The rest of the town looks very deserted, and the large number of soldiers one sees is evidence of the distrust still felt by the government towards the Kan-su people, and especially the Mohammedans. There is but little of the Kan-su element in the present population, the inhabitants are largely from Shan-hsi, Shan-tung, with a sprinkling from probably all the other provinces of the empire.

The members of the China Inland Mission tell me the climate is delightful, a clear sky nearly all the year, but little wind and no snow. The water is strongly alkaline, and no flowers can be raised here; what few one sees are brought from Lan-chou.

January 18.—The coal used at Ning-hsia is mined in the Hsi shan some three or four days from here, and costs, delivered in the city, three cash a catty. The crops, I hear, are good on irrigated land (*chiu ti*), but absence of any facilities for getting the grain to outside markets and their remoteness, deter farmers from raising more grain than the local consumption calls for.

* Father Gerbillon, when at Ning-hsia in 1697 with the Emperor K'ang-hsi, makes mention of the rugs and paper made with hemp "beaten and mixed with lime water."—(See Du Halde, *op. cit.* IV, 372.) He also says (p. 373) that the best mules in China came from Ning-hsia. He furthermore remarks (p. 370) that it was one of the largest and most densely populated cities along the whole length of the Great Wall, the houses built so closely together that there was no room even for courtyards. Before the late Mohammedan rebellion it had already greatly fallen from its high state, for Huc (*op. cit.*, II, 13 et seq.) speaks of the poverty of the city and of the absence of any commerce. Several quarters of the town were ruined and deserted "save for a few hogs wandering amidst the ruins." Most of the people were dressed in dirty rags and looked lank and pale, etc.

I saw in the inn-yard quite a number of sacks of dry rhubarb root *en route* for Pao-t'u. It comes, I am told, from Hsi-ning and is used by veterinaries, especially in treating camels. Some is found in the Hsi shan (Alashan range), but is of an inferior quality.*

I leave to-morrow for Lan-chou in carts hired here for 14 taels a piece, and we are to reach our destination in twelve or thirteen days. These Ning-hsia carts are roomier than those used farther east, but no more comfortable. I leave Ning-hsia as I have done every other town in China, with no desire to go back to it. Like the plaster bust of which La Fontaine speaks, "De loin c'est quelque chose, de près ce n'est rien."

January 19.—Outside the south gate of Ning-hsia there is a miserable suburb where live the Huei-huei, and beyond this extend alkaline flats and marshes on which grow tall reeds that supply the city with fuel for heating the *k'angs*. We passed a few hovels belonging, presumably, to reed cutters, for no other profession would appear possible hereabout.

The road led us nearly due south through numerous little hamlets and across two enormous irrigation canals, which, by the way, one would certainly take as depicted on all our maps, for branches of the Yellow River. These canals are about twenty feet broad between the banks and are in many places bordered by rows of willows. It is said, but I know not on what authority, that the irrigation of the plain of Ning-hsia was executed in the K'ang-hsi reign by imperial order.† These canals, both large and small, are called *ho ch'ü*.

As we advanced the soil appeared slightly less barren; the Yellow River was soon lost to view, but the long low hills which

* That its medicinal qualities have long been known among the Mongols is evidenced by Rubruk's mention of it. *Land of the Lamas*, 284 and Rubruk's *Itinerarium*, 323 and 342.

† Father Gerbillon speaks of the Ning-hsia irrigation canals as follows: "Tous les ans on employe plus de deux mille hommes pendant un mois entier à racommoder ces canaux, qui sans ce soin seroient bientôt comblez par le sable et la terre que cette rivière entraine avec elle." Du Halde, *op. cit.* IV, 373. Irrigation canals of great extent must have existed as early as the beginning of the 13th century, in this district, for we know that when Ning-hsia was besieged by the Mongols under Jingis Khan, in 1209, the inhabitants flooded the Mongol camp "by opening the dykes of the river" (by which the canals must be meant). See H. H. Howorth, *op. cit.*, I, 66.

are beyond it were certainly not over five miles away, as I could distinguish little houses at their base. The Hsi shan took a decidedly western turn and appeared lower than even at Ping-lo Hsien, though it retained the same rugged appearance.

We passed on the road a cart with Jardine and Matheson's flag, coming probably from Chung-wei Hsien, where camel's wool is sold in considerable quantities to foreigners. This trade has fallen off very much in the last three or four years on account of the Chinese middlemen rolling the wool in the dirt so as to add to its weight, and practicing other tricks on buyers.

Everywhere traces of the rebellion of twenty-five years ago are visible—ruined villages and weed-grown fields. The rebellion was especially destructive to dwellings, but Chinese houses are so cheaply built, and contain so little of any value, that it is hard to conceive that they should not have sprung up at once again, were not other obstacles, created, perhaps, by the authorities to perpetuate the memory of the punishments inflicted on the rebels, put in the way of their reconstruction. It was in a village a few miles off our road and on the river bank near here that the rebellion in these parts originated.*

Wang-hu P'u, where we stopped for the night, must have once been a fine place, for ruins of well-built houses and yamens cover the ground for half a mile around the poor hovels which compose the present village. A very large irrigation canal passes through the village, and there are a number of locks through which the water can be drawn off into lesser ditches so as to supply the whole country. This abundant supply of water in the Ning-hsia plain makes it possible to grow rice, which is one of the staple products of this region. It is, however, of poor quality and reddish color, and not to be compared with that grown at Kan-chou in northwestern Kan-su.

* In Gerbillon's time the Ning-hsia plain must have been one vast garden, "On ne voit point de villages dans cette campagne, mais on la peut appeller un village continuel; car les maisons des Paysans y sont répanduës de tous côtez environ à cent pas l'une de l'autre plus ou moins * * * Enfin ce pays est un des plus beaux et des meilleurs que j'aye jamais vue." Du Halde, *op. cit.*, IV, 374. Even in Huc's time the road to the south of Ning-hsia is described as magnificent, with willow and jujube trees growing along the side nearly the whole way to Wang-hu P'u, Huc, *op. cit.*, II, 15.

January 20.—Very litttle can be said of the country we have traversed to-day, save to express astonishment that any one, even a Chinese, should have chosen it to live in. Nearly all the soil is alkaline and reeds are apparently the only product of the land. The few farms we saw were imposing from a distance; they looked like castles, with high crenelated and loop-holed stone walls (probably they were thus built to enable the owners to resist bands of marauders), but when one looked inside them they proved but filthy, tumbled-down dens.

The irrigation canals grow larger as we advance southward. The smaller ones are led across the big ones by plank sluices, just as is done with us.

Ta-p'a, where we stopped for the night, is a very small place beside the ruins of a walled town (*Ch'eng*). Yeh-sheng P'u, and half a dozen other places we passed through before reaching it, are like it—hamlets built on the ruins of former towns. We have seen no traffic on the road since leaving Ning-hsia, only ox-carts loaded with reeds and straw.

At Ta-p'a coal can be bought; it is brought from the Hsi shan twenty miles away, The inn-keeper said it sold for ten cash a catty, and it undoubtedly does when he or his like have the sale of it. The same high authority said it took three days to reach Chung-wei Hsien and six from there to Lan-chou Fu.

The weather remains wonderfully pleasant, just such weather as one usually has at Peking at this time of the year. The nights very cold but clear, the days warm enough to make walking agreeable, and no wind. The barometric variations are wonderfully small during the twenty-four hours.

Ta-p'a is of some importance as it is the first and principal distributing point of the water brought from the Yellow River south of here to fertilize the Ning-hsia plain. At this point three or four branch canals leave the main one, carrying water to the various levels of the plain. This main canal (*ho ch'ü*) we crossed for the first time at Wang-hu P'u; it passes east of Ning-hsia and terminates a couple of miles east of Shih-tsui.

January 21.—Crossing a low range of limestone hills which, branching out from the Hsi shan, abut on the Yellow River a few miles to our left and there form a gorge through which the river flows, we came on its western side to Kuang-wei, the country up to that point uninhabited and untillable; it is too high to be irrigated and there are no permanent streams in these hills. Beyond Kuang-wei farms and villages were surprisingly numerous. One wonders where the people find arable soil in sufficiency to supply their wants, for much of the plain on this side of the Yellow River is covered with ochre-colored sand, which is forever drifting in long and parallel ridges, gaining rapidly on the tilled land and often overturning the houses against whose walls it accumulates. I had noticed this yellow sand in a few spots in the Ordos, and could see no place there from which it could have come, now it would seem that it must have been blown there from west of Chung-wei, from the great "drifting sand" desert which there abuts on the Yellow River.

I killed two antelope just as we came to Kuang-wei and wounded a third, but did not have time to follow it up. These antelope (*huang yang*) are the only game we see, there have been no sand grouse since leaving San-tao ho-tzŭ, no hares, or pheasants, or ducks, though the river is free from ice in many places.

We still have the Hsi shan a few miles on our right. These mountains are—here at least, of igneous formation, not over eight hundred feet high, and stretch as far west as the eye can reach.

We stopped for the night in a tumble-down place called Ts'ao-yüan P'u which we reached long after dark. In the inn-yard were a number of the big-wheeled carts used throughout the Ordos and in some parts of Kan-su, and of which I have spoken previously. I learnt that they only cost 20 *tiaos* to build, or about fifteen Mexican dollars.

January 22.—The road ran along the bank of the Yellow River. I failed to observe any gravel, nothing but loess, washed down here from higher levels. The river is very shoal, with numerous sand banks rising above its surface; it has a rapid current in places, and is, on an average, about two hundred and fifty yards in breadth.

There is now going on a curious process of agriculture which shows how little the Chinese understand saving of labor. The farmers dig up a large patch of the surface of each field, cart it back to their farm-yards and their let the clods of earth dry, when they take a mallet (or a stone hammer with an eye drilled through it in which to fix a long handle), and reduce it all to powder; with this is then mixed what manure they have been able to collect on the road, and this top dressing is laboriously carted back and spread over the field from which nine-tenths of its component parts were a few days before quite as laboriously taken away.*

At Shih-kung-shih P'u, where we stopped for lunch, I heard that there was a cave temple with a colossal stone figure in it not over a mile or so to the north of the village. There are some *ho-shang* living in the temple, which is known by various names, Ta Fo ssŭ "Big Buddha Temple;" Shih Fo ssŭ, "Stone Buddha Temple," or Shih-kung (P'u) Ta ssŭ "the great temple of Shih-kung (P'u)."

I suppose this is another specimen of the Toba dynasty cave temples, of which there are so many in northwestern China. I had been prompted to ask if there were cave temples near Shih-kung-shih P'u on seeing a long ledge of sandstone disposed in horizontal strata a short distance from our road, and on noticing a number of little niches in it like those I had seen in 1887 at Yung-k'an near Ta-t'ung Fu in north Shan-hsi.† Such cave temples are here called Fo-t'ung, "Buddha Caves," and I heard that they were very numerous.

Just as we passed Sheng-chin-kuan tien, "the inn of the Sheng-chin barrier," I shot a big antelope buck, so we decided to stop over night in this lonely inn and have a good meal of antelope steak. The barrier (*kuan*) is about half a mile west of the inn, and is a good landmark as there is a tower (*t'un*) on a point of rocks just behind it. The steak proved delicious, for I still had plenty of good butter bought at Ho-k'uo to cook it with, and the cook made some wheat cakes and with this, together with plenty of vermicelli (*kua mien*) and good tea, I made quite a feast, while the wolves howled at a great rate outside the gate of the inn, attracted by the odor of the fresh meat.

January 23.—The Hsi shan now bend a little north of west, but we saw little of them, for a strong northwest wind began to blow shortly after we started, and though there was no dust

* A similar method of fertilizing the field is practiced in western Kan-su. See *Land of the Lamas*, 98.

† Gerbillon mentions this latter famous temple. The Emperor K'ang-hsi, with whom he was traveling "mesura avec un de nos demi-cercles la plus grande des idoles qui occupe toute une grotte, et il la trouva haute de 57 *Tche* on pieds Chinois." Du Halde, *op. cit.*, IV, 352.

where we were, the mountains were hidden in dense clouds of it. The mountains on the right bank of the Yellow River still run southwest by west and increase in height as we go west. The plain over which we traveled to-day was so flat that we never got a glimpse of the river, though it was not over a mile or two at the utmost from the road.

We reached Chung-wei Hsien by two o'clock and stopped in the east faubourg in a fairly good inn, The faubourg is not large, but quite busy. I noticed some factories (in rooms twelve feet square !) of water-pipe tobacco—and this, I learnt, is one of the chief industries of the place—flour and grain shops, dry goods, blacksmith shops and the usual variety of trades met with in this part of the world, take up the business quarter of this town.*

The Mohammedan bakers of Chung-wei make delicious rolls (*k'ou-kuei*), and I bought good potatoes and eggs, so I will speak nothing but praise of such a place. Coal is brought here from a distance of four or five days to the south, and it costs (at least I had to pay for it) 12 cash a catty.

I laid in a supply of food sufficient to last me to Lan-chou, for until we reach that city, eight or nine days hence, nothing can be bought on the road, and when a Chinese says there is nothing to be bought in the way of food, one must understand it literally.

January 24.—It was 8.30 before we got off from Chung-wei, rather too late, as the day's march proved a long one, and it was nearly midnight when we reached its end. A couple of miles beyond the city we came to a big irrigation canal on the farther side of which are the ruins of a branch of the Great Wall, which now only imperfectly opposes the inroads of the vast sea of yellow sand on its outer side stretching as far as one can see in endless hillocks perpendicular to the direction of the prevailing northwest wind.†

* Huc gives us to understand that he only took three days to go from Ning-hsia to Chung-wei. This is certainly wrong as the distance between these two cities is nearly one hundred and twenty miles. He says (*op. cit.*, II, 21) of Chung-wei "sa propreté, sa bonne tenue, son air d'aisance, tout contraste singulièrement avec la misère et la laideur de *Ning-Hia ;* à en juger seulement par les innombrables boutiques, toutes très-bien achalandeés, et par la grande population qui incessamment encombre les rues, Tchong-Weï est une ville très-commerçante."

† Huc apparently did not follow the river but took straight across the sand hills to Chang-liu-shui. Huc, *op. cit.*, II, 21-23.

In this sea of sand ridge follows ridge, and of such uniform color is the whole scene that all idea of distance is lost, and one cannot tell if a hillock is a hundred yards or two miles away. The wall appears to have been made of successive layers of well beaten loess, and never to have had a facing of brick or stone. It is about six feet broad at the top and fifteen feet high. Outside the wall, some hundred yards, are stone watch towers against which the sand is heaped up at least thirty feet high.

After about a mile through these "liquid sands," as the Chinese call them, we came to the bank of the Yellow River, here at least one hundred and fifty feet below the surrounding country. No ice was to be seen on it for several miles in either direction, as it sweeps out in a swift eddying current of a gorge in a range of red sandstone mountains to the west. Little log rafts were coming down the stream loaded with coal for the Chung-wei market, or carrying travelers from Chung-wei across to a little village on the right bank at the base of the steep, rugged mountains, which here rise some fifteen hundred to eighteen hundred feet above the plain.

We followed the river bank till we reached Sha-pa (or Sha-po)* at the mouth of a gorge which bears the same name. Here begin the big irrigation canals which supply the Chung-wei plain with water, and here also travelers journeying westward usually get taken up beyond the gorge, they, their carts and animals, in a big, flat boat kept there for the purpose at government expense.

We found only three boatmen at Sha-pa and were told that it would take half a day to get the others here, as travel along this side of the river being unusual in winter, they had gone to Chung-wei. We consequently decided to try and get the carts through the gorge, the boatmen agreeing to carry on their backs my instruments and more valuable belongings, for it was more than probable that the carts would get upset a few times on the way. The sands have flowed over the hills in the gorge and reach to the river banks, where rocks and ice are piled up, so that cart travel seemed next to impossible. It took us over two hours to make the two miles around the loop which the river here describes, lifting the carts over the rocks, unloading and reloading them repeatedly, and doubling up the teams to pull them out of the soft sands in which they sunk to the axles.

*Sha po apparently means "Sand hill." The hamlet is at the foot of high hills of sand.

I noticed in this gorge that the water does not rise in flood more than ten feet above its present low water level. The rocks composing the hills on either side are of red sandstone and gneiss. Near the upper end of the gorge on the south side of the river, are several coal mines, before the mouths of which were piles of coke, burnt at the mouth of the mines and carried down the river on little rafts, similar to those we had seen earlier in the day.

Leaving the river here, we traveled due west up a valley in which we passed but one small village, and then going over some hills, where the soft sand gave us much trouble (it took us four and a half hours to travel the last three miles), we reached Chang-liu-shui, where we found accommodations for the night. It was one o'clock before I ate my bowl of rice and mutton and laid down for the night, thoroughly worn out.

January 25.—We continued in a slightly west-by-north direction, first up a loess gorge, then over red sandstone gravel and finally over a brush-covered plain, till we came to a series of sand dunes running west-northwest. Over these we slowly plodded till we reached a miserable hamlet called I wan ch'üan, or "Myriad Springs," a grim joke of doubtful taste, as water has to be hauled here from four miles away, and the surrounding sand hills produce nothing but a little brush.

The road improved a little for the next twelve miles to the west of this place, leading through deep cuts in the loess, but not a drop of water was there anywhere, and only occasionally a little brush relieved the awful barrenness of the land.

We stopped for the night at another miserable post-station which had the appropriate name of Kan t'ang-tzŭ, "the dry station,"* for water is brought here from a distance of ten miles, probably from the Yellow River.

We did not see a single cart to-day, though old cart tracks were occasionally crossed. The road is not suitable for them, the sands are too heavy and fodder is too scarce; it is, however, an ideal camel road, nothing to eat but brush, nothing to drink and plenty of soft sand for the feet. We passed a few small caravans of camels and mules going to Chung-wei, carrying water-

* Huc's Kao-Tan-Dze "village repoussant et hideux au delà de toute expression * * * Les habitants de Kao-Tan-Dze sont obligés d'aller chercher l'eau à une distance de soixante *lis* (six lieues). Huc, *op. cit.*, II, 24.

pipe tobacco (*shui yen*), beans, hides and wool. In places red sand has been blown over the ochre-colored kind, so that it looked as if there were great streaks of blood on the ground. Fortunately for us we have had no wind of late, for in such a country the gentlest breeze would raise such clouds of dust and sand that it would make travel impossible.

The road from Ning-hsia to Lan-chou on the other side of the river, though much longer than that we are following (it takes eighteen to twenty days, I hear, to go over it), is from all accounts very much better, and is usually taken by travelers; I am not aware that any foreigner has ever traveled over it.

January 26.—To-day has been one of comparative rest, we have only gone seventeen miles to Ying-pan shui (or fei, as the last syllable is locally pronounced).* The route all the way led along the southeast side of a range of hills between five hundred and eight hundred feet high, which cut our route a little beyond Ying-pan shui. A little brackish stream flowing southeast passes by this hamlet. There are here the ruins of quite a fine temple and of other substantial buildings, but only two or three very poor inns are now standing, in one of which we found a very imperfect shelter for the night. The Yellow River is about 70 *li* southeast of here, and the roads to Liang-chou and Ping-fan Hsien branch off from that we are following a few miles beyond here to the southwest.

To-day there was a strong wind for a while, and shortly before it struck us I saw a red mist (or dust) rise along the base of the hills on our right. Throughout these barren regions the winds or the strong currents of air observable in the winter months in the middle of the day, follow very narrow and well-defined tracks; they are especially strong along the base of hills, where the air is most heated and radiation greatest.

January 27.—We trudged up and down over endless little hills of sandstone formation, the offshoots of the main range which runs a few miles to our right in a south-southwest direction. The face of the country to our west was covered with such a maze of hills that I could not determine their general direction, which appeared, however, to be southwest and northeast.

* On the Chinese dialect of Kan-su, see Dr. J. Edkins in *China Review*, XVII, 174, *et seq.* A Ying pan is a small walled camp.

There is a total absence of water hereabout; in summer there is probably a little water to be found in hollows, but the people say the country is a dry one. It is strange to find such an arid belt of land so near a section of Kan-su, which is reported to be one of the wettest on the face of the globe. Liang-chou, Kan-chou and the adjacent districts have, from all accounts, quite as heavy a rainfall as parts of southern Japan, and Liang-chou is only six days travel from Ying-pan shui.

Some twelve or fourteen miles southwest of Ying-pan shui we came to Ch'ing ngai-tzŭ where the ruins of temples, ya-mêns, etc., bore proof of the former existence of a large village.

Now there are only three or four families living there, keeping inns and pasturing little bunches of sheep. The owner of one of the inns told me that all the country was well tilled until during the Mohammedan rebellion, about thirty years ago, the villages were destroyed and the people driven from their homes.

Eleven miles beyond this place we crossed the Great Wall and five miles further on came to the village of I-tiao shan. The Great Wall at this point runs across the valley from the base of the hills on one side to the same point on the other. It is of loess mud, twenty feet high, with detached truncated-cone shaped towers along its inner side every few hundred yards and distant about a hundred yards from the wall. I cannot conceive of what use they can have been, certainly not as signal towers, nor can they have added to the strength of the wall or its powers of resisting attacks.

The head of a criminal in a little cage tied to the end of a pole greeted us as we entered I-tiao shan. This hamlet is quite a fine place for these parts, with a couple of shops and several large inns. It is the largest place we have seen since leaving Chung-wei.

January 28.—At I-tiao shan cultivation of the soil begins again, and with it sand grouse which seem, like our quail, to be never found in large numbers away from cultivated fields, reappear. The fields are irrigated and at Suan-huo P'u, a village of some pretension a few miles south of I-tiao shan,* we crossed a large ditch with a clear stream flowing down it, the first running water we have seen since leaving the Yellow River. Another criminal's head exposed in a cage grinned at us as we passed here.

* This must be the same village as Huc's San-Yen-Tsin, although he says that that village was only a few paces inside the wall. (*Op. cit.*, II, 29.) Huc left the high-road here and went directly to Ping-fan Hsien.

Our road led through a complicated system of low sandstone hills, about one hundred and fifty feet high, with a dip of about twenty degrees southwest, and a little beyond them rises a higher range of the same formation. The range to our left is apparently more thickly covered with loess than that on our right, but it is so low I got but a poor idea of it. None of these hills are over five hundred feet in height.

We stopped for tea at Ta-la P'u. The people were everywhere preparing for the New Year, pasting up new mottoes, baking cakes (*mo-mo*) and bread (*man-t'ou*) in great quantities, killing pigs and rigging up swings. The custom of swinging at New Year is observed over all northern China. In Korea also, this custom obtains during certain feasts, but a little later in the year.*

We stopped for the night at Chung ch'ang-tzŭ; this place is, I am told, 170 *li* from Ping-fan Hsien and seven days from Hsi-ning by the direct road, and Lan chou is distant from it 270 *li*, or three days' journey by the route we are following. Between Ta-la P'u and this place there has been a great deal of prospecting for coal. The water, even here in the hills, is terribly brackish, in fact since leaving Kalgan we have only found sweet water in two or three places.

January 29.—A few miles above Chung ch'ang-tzŭ we crossed a low *col* and entered a valley which has been at one time well cultivated, but where now ruins, fallow fields and half filled irrigation ditches are all that tell of its former prosperity.

Below Sha-ho ching, the first village we passed through, the valley broadens rapidly, and farms and villages were visible on every side; along the road the latter follow each other with hardly any interruption. The particular feature of this section is that the soil is composed of alternate and very thin layers of loess and gravel; and so the farmers cover the light loess with a thin layer of stones; this is especially the custom where the poppy is raised. It keeps the moisture in the soil and prevents the light soil being blown away.† Water here is only found at considerable depths, the wells, from which the whole supply is procured, are from one hundred and fifty to two hundred feet deep, and the water is

* In Nipal swinging, as well as kite flying, is popular during the Dassera feast (*i. e.*, beginning of October). H. A. Oldfield, *Sketches from Nipal*, II, 351.

† See also on this custom under date of *February 3*.

very brackish. Drawing water from these wells is a tedious operation, as small wicker buckets* are used and the rope has to be dragged up by a large number of men.

Bands of horses and mules were seen here feeding in the stubble fields, and I heard that mule raising was an important business hereabout.

At Liu-t'un-tzŭ where we stopped for the night, the inn keeper was so busy with his New Year's preparations that he practically ignored us and let us understand that he was obliging us by admitting us to his hovel. Fortunately for us he was poor and could not indulge in a profusion of pyrotechnics, so the night passed quietly and there was little wine-drinking and riotous living.

January 30.—The hills grew slightly higher as we advanced south, attaining possibly four hundred feet. The whole country was of loess, and as the valley we followed (which attains nowhere more than four hundred yards in width) was not exposed to the full violence of the north and northwest winds, the people do not have to cover their fields with stones. Water is evidently scarce, for I noticed reservoirs dug in the soil in which the water from the hills is stored and drawn from when needed as from a well. At Shui-pei ho water is nearer the surface than at Liu-t'un-tzŭ; the wells were not over twenty to thirty feet deep. Shortly before reaching Shui-pei ho the characteristic vertical rifts in the loess were again seen.

I remarked to-day on detached monticules, the ruins of little forts. They reminded me of those François Garnier saw in Yün-nan similarly situated. Probably they were built at the time of the Mohammedan rebellion. I have seen others like them near Lusar and Hsi-ning.

It is curious that while the Chinese attach great importance to having their houses face the true south, very few really do. The compass is far from being in common use among them, and hardly any can find the polar star, though most of them can point out Ursa Minor (*Pei sheng*). I have been asked hundreds of times if a house were straight (*cheng*) or not, and the owner's disgust has always been great when I have shown him by my compass that it was not.

* Wicker buckets are used all over northern China for this purpose.

January 31.—From Shui-pei ho to the Yellow River in front of Lan-chou, the road led through an uninterrupted succession of loess hills, the highest—those nearest the river, rising about six hundred feet. The greater part of the way was down a deep cut in the loess, which here rests on river gravel.

We crossed the river, which is here about three hundred yards broad, on the ice (the bridge of boats is withdrawn in winter), or as the Chinese call it, on an "ice bridge" (*ping ch'iao*).* Entering the city by one of the "water gates," we passed through a labyrinth of foul, muddy streets, then out by the southern gate and finally drew up in front of the house of my old friend, the Curé of Lan-chou, Monsieur de Meester with whom I had stayed when on my first journey to Tibet.† The reception from the good father was the cordial, whole souled one I have always felt sure of receiving from a Catholic missionary in China, and the rest of the day was passed telling each other what we had done since last we had met two years ago.

February 1.—Part of the day has been passed rearranging my boxes, so that they may be all of about equal weight and of proper size to be packed on mule-back. I find the Japanese baskets I bought in Yokohama most convenient. Made of bamboo and very light, the tops fit over the bottoms so that the contents can be added to or decreased without danger of their being shaken up; they are admirable for rough traveling. I have had them lined with water-proof cloth and covered with leather. As they are pliable they can be tied securely to a pack-saddle and can stand lots of rough handling.

* Father Grueber visited Lan-chou Fu towards 1662. Though the city is not mentioned by name, there can be no doubt that it was of it he spoke when he said that, after crossing the Karamuren by a fine bridge of boats they entered a very large city. "Il y avoit (içi) des filles de joye d'une grande beauté. Quoique les filles du Khataï soient belles communement, neanmoins elles sont là plus belles qu'ailleurs, la ville pour ce sujet s'appelle la ville de beauté." Thevenot, *Relation de divers voyages*, II, IVe Partie, p. 5. The word *Lan* may effectively have the meaning of "beauty." *Lan-hsing* means "a beautiful appearance." And the Persians who visited Lan-chou two hundred years earlier also wrote that it was remarkable for the beauty of its women, inasmuch that it was known as the City of Beauty (Husnabad). *Embassy of Shah Rukh*, in Yule's *Cathay and the Way Thither*" (Hakluyt Soc.); I, CCIV.

† *Land of the Lamas*, p. 33 et seq.

Mons. de Meester says that the misery in Kan-su is on the increase. This is not solely attributable to the drought, but to the use of opium and general absence of enterprise and energy. At Lan-chou this winter the public soup kitchens (*chou chang*) have fed over six thousand people, while last year there were not half that many applicants for relief.

Opium cultivation and opium smoking are increasing at a rapid rate.* At Liang-chou, for example, they count eight lamps (*yen t'eng*) for every ten persons; here at Lan-chou it is nearly as bad. It would be wrong to imagine that the native Kan-suites (*pen-ti jen*) are responsible for the increased consumption of opium, it is a result of the rapid and overwhelming influx of Ssŭ-ch'uanese into the province. I do not think I am exaggerating when I say that they form a fifth of the whole population of Kan-su; in the southern portions they are much more numerous than elsewhere, around Hui Hsien, and the warmer and more fertile districts especially. They take the trade, wholesale and retail, and have energy, the one essential thing the Kan-suites are lacking in.

There are three or four Chan-t'ou (Turkestanis)† here selling raisins, rugs, etc., and also seven or eight Koreans with ginseng. These latter people visit the remotest corners of China. In '89 there was one at Ta-chien-lu, where he kept an inn.

The New Year's festivities are progressing as gayly as if the past year had been a most prosperous one. The noisiest feature is the beating of the *yang ko ku*, "the country song drum," a long cylindrical drum which is slung in front of the player by a band passing over his shoulder, and on which he beats furiously with a short bit of knotted cable (or something resembling it). Drums of like shape, but smaller, are usually carried by the wandering stilt-wearing singers one often sees in northern China. To-day processions are marching about the town, some beating gongs and others banging with might and main on *yang ko ku*.

---

* Du Halde says that the trade of Lan-chou consisted in his time in hides from Tartary which came by way of Hsi-ning and To-pa, and in woolen stuffs (*jung*) of which he names five varieties. Du Halde, *op. cit.*, I, 213.

†Grijimailo, in *Proc. Roy. Geog. Soc.* XIII, 210 and 226 speaking of these Chan-t'ou says "The descendants of those Uighurs (of Pichan, Lukchin and Turfan), a people known by the name of Chen-tu, allied to the Sarts of western Turkestan * * *" I think he is wrong in imagining that Chan-t'ou is the name of a nation or tribe, it applies, as I have shown elsewhere, to all Turkestanis or even Kashmiris.

I am told that the *t'ai-p'ing ku** familiar to residents of Peking, is also known here, but I have seen none.

The Kan-su people are literally wild on the subject of official hats; for the most futile reason they don the *kuan mao*, they and all their male progeny down to children of eight or ten years of age. This and the big-sleeved jacket or *kua-tzŭ* are indispensable here, if one would look respectable when making a call, or performing any duty to the living or to the dead. To-day every one, down to the poorest coolie who has not perhaps much more than a breach clout to cover his nakedness, sports an official hat.

The famous Ho-nan anti-Christian and anti-foreign placards and pamphlets have been scattered broadcast over Kan-su, brought here, it is rumored, by the nephew of the Governor General Yang (who is a Ho-nan man, by the way). Liu's now famous book *Kuei chiao kai sha*, "The devil's doctrine must be destroyed," has been brought here by the cart load. The pictures in which Jesus is represented as a "wild hog" (*Yeh-chu*) or a "heavenly hog" (*t'ien chu*) † were torn down from off the high street by quiet little Mons. de Meester and taken by him to the Tsung-tu who was obliged to take action in the matter, and so an anti-Christian riot in Lan-chou was averted.

February 2.—I called on Graham Browne of the China Inland Mission whom I had met here before in '89. He, his wife, children and two lady assistants are very comfortably installed in the city. He very kindly offered to arrange for me with a Chinese bank to have a telegraphic transfer of some funds made from a Chinese bank in Shanghai to its branch office here. Such an operation has never been done, but that is no reason why it should not be now. He told me that on the Ta-t'ung ho not far from Ping-fan Hsien, at the ferry about 20 *li* from the mouth of the river (which is at Hsiang-t'ang), there was a Lo-lo Ch'eng inhabited by a people of peculiar language and having a chief (*Wang*) of their own. This locality would be well worth a visit; it would be interesting to ascertain whether these Lo-lo are a northern branch of the Ssŭ-ch'uanese race of the same name.

* A species of tambourine, in shape like a large fan. On the handle are a number of iron rings. A light flexible rod is used as a drum-stick and the rings are rattled at the same time that it is beaten.

† Poor puns on the word "Jesus" (*Yeh-su*) and "Lord of heaven" (*T'ien-chu*).

I hear that Polhill-Turner of the China Inland Mission, whom I knew at Lusar in '89, when he was studying Tibetan in hope of being able to preach the Word to the Tibetans, has gone to Sung-pan T'ing with his wife, thinking that he might more readily gain access to Tibet from that point. It is the worst point he could have chosen, as the Golok country is between him and his goal, and unless he makes friends with the Sharba and travels with them, he cannot hope to get very far.* He had tried to strike out previously from Kuei-tê, but that place has the same disadvantage as Sung-pan, Panakasum and Golok bar the road to the west.

I saw to-day on the street a criminal wearing the heavy cangue and tattooed† on his left temple with the crime for which he was suffering punishment. He belonged to the *chun liu chien fan* class of convicts or exiles to 6,000 *li* from their homes.

There is a religious sect (some say Mohammedan) in Kan-su, especially numerous near Liang-chou, and called *Chu shih*. These people are vegetarians, but of their doctrines I can learn nothing, nor have I met with any members of the sect.

I have been making inquiries concerning the population of Lan-chou and the results are rather bewildering. Graham Browne puts it at four hundred thousand *at the lowest*, de Meester at eighty thousand, and some Chinese merchants (bankers and tobacco factory owners) at between fifty and sixty thousand.

February 3.—Coming back from the Hsieh-t'ung-ch'ing Bank where I had gone to get my money, I met the Ying-ch'un or "welcoming spring" procession returning from outside the east gate of the city and on its way to the temple of the local god. A man disguised as a woman led the procession and another in a similar disguise followed riding a donkey. This latter, I was told impersonated the imperial princess who first introduced into China

* Since writing the above a Miss Taylor, a member of the China Inland Mission, has passed through the Golok country, reached Jyäkundo and pushed on towards Lh'asa as far as the Naach'uk'a country, where she was stopped and forced to return to Ta-chien-lu.

† This punishment is a recognized one throughout China, but unless one visits one of the remote provinces of the empire, to which such criminals are exiled, one would never see persons thus marked. Tattooing is not practiced to any extent among the Chinese as a means of decorating the person. I have seen a few men with dots picked on their arms and hands, but they had lived with foreigners or traveled abroad. To tattoo is called *chen hua*, "to draw with a needle, to prick a pattern."

the custom of binding women's feet. Then came a lot of men disguised as foreigners and red bearded ruffians. Men beating the *yang-ko ku* and gongs followed these, and finally came a cow drawn by some fifty men pulling on two long ropes. The cow was of wicker work, covered with clay of a reddish brown color, about six feet high and eight or ten feet long and a red gown covered the body. Altogether it was a poor show, but a very noisy one.*

I have decided to leave for Hsi-ning on the fifth, and have hired six mules for fifteen taels, one a saddle mule for myself. They will go as far as Lusar (Kumbum).

I hear that small hazel nuts grow in the mountains south of Lan-chou. They are called *mo* (*mao?*) *chen-tzŭ*. Wild hops (*ma-ku yen*) grow in the warmer southwestern part of the province near Hui Hsien. The Belgian missionaries at Liang-chou make good beer with them.

The western wind which blows so violently down the Yellow River valley and is called here *Huang feng*, or "Yellow (river) wind," is felt from Su-chou, Kan-chou, Liang-chou to Lan-chou, but not to the south of the latter place. It follows the Nan shan.

I have noted previously the peculiar custom of covering the fields in which the poppy is raised with pebbles. I now learn that these pebbles are changed every year, and that this is necessary because "they lose their moisture."

There is some small trade carried on between this place and India, *viâ* Ilchi, Kashgar and Sa-chou. Hindoo traders have reached this place, and Graham Browne told me one can buy Indian goods in the shops.

* In some of its features this festivity reminds one of the Nipalese Gaijatra or "cow festival." See H. A. Oldfield, *Sketches from Nipal*, II, 299-303. Carter Stent, *Chin. Engl. Vocabulary*, 714, says "At the 'welcoming spring,' all the local magistrates, with their escorts, go in procession carrying a gaudily painted image of a cow—each color is symbolical, if yellow predominates, the crops will be plentiful; red, conflagrations will take place; white, floods; black, sickness; and blue, war. This is followed by the god T'ai-sui; who, if bareheaded, is symbolical of heat; with the cap on, cold; if he wears shoes, much rain; barefooted, dry weather. The procession marches to the eastward to receive the spring and returns to the local god's temple to worship, each official afterwards going to his own office. At the magistrate's office a dinner has been prepared called *Ch'un yen* 'the spring banquet,' this, after the magistrate has dined, is taken by the people. Theatricals and merry-making also take place."

February 4.—To-day is *li ch'un*, "the beginning of spring," and the cow I saw yesterday triumphantly hauled through the streets was knocked to pieces and farmers began sowing seed.

The famous woolen factory built by the former Governor General Tso, is now a school of telegraphy under a Shanghai Chinese called Wang. I hope it will cost the government less to turn out an operator than it did to make a blanket, but I doubt it. The telegraph line was brought into this city from Hsi-an Fu last year and reaches now to Liang-chou, Su-chou, and as far as Chia-yü kuan, I believe. It is only used by the government; merchants do not believe in it, or rather in the honesty and trustworthiness of the government operators; they do not wish them to know too much about their business relations for fear of exactions, and rightly enough, I fancy.

I am told that all the Prefects (*Chih-hsien*) of Lan-chou (which by the way is officially known as Kao-lan Hsien) desire, after filling the office for a short time, to be relieved, for the expenses they have to incur here are very great and the perquisites very small. The Governor General gets all the squeezes for himself I have no doubt.

This afternoon the muleteers tied the loads on the frames which fit over the pack-saddles, so to-morrow morning we will be able to get off without delay.

February 5.—We left at eleven o'clock for Hsi-ning. Just outside the west gate of the city there is over the torrent which comes down from the southern hills a fine log bridge of the cantilever kind. This type of bridge is everywhere met with in Tibet, but this is the first one of the kind one sees in this direction when coming from China.

The Great Wall crosses to the right bank of the Yellow River eight miles west of the city and follows the valley on this side till near Ho Chou. It is known here, as in Chih-li, as the *Pien ch'eng*, or "frontier wall."

I got on the way a good photograph of one of the water-wheels used to raise the water from the river to the irrigation ditches. The one represented in this photograph is about seventy-five feet in diameter, and is not the largest one by any means.

They look clumsy but are very serviceable; hardly any iron is used in making them.*

I reached Hsin-ch'eng at 7.30 P. M., and got a warm reception from Father van Belle and a Friday's meal—cold tea, dry bread and lard, used in place of butter. This is the usual style of living among Catholic missionaries. Among the Protestants, Crossette and James Gilmour tried it and consequently both were looked upon as "cranks" by their brethren, the former especially who lived for years an ideal Christian life, having no cares for the morrow, providing himself with neither raiment nor food and giving all to the poor.

Gold is found in the hills near Hsin-ch'eng; a couple of years ago a nugget was picked up by a peasant which he sold for 70 taels of silver. The consequence was that half the population got the gold fever in a malignant form for a twelve month; now, fortunately, they have recovered.

Hsin-ch'eng is inhabited by between four and five hundred families, over one hundred of which are Christian. When the Belgian mission was established in Kan-su a number of Christian families were discovered living here, and in the neighborhood—refugees from Shen-hsi they were, so a father was sent to live with them and weed all heresies and irregularities from out their midst. This was probably filling a long felt want, for these Christians had been ordaining priests without a bishop and these had in turn been baptising, administering the sacraments, etc., etc., probably in a highly irregular way.

February 6.—Crossing the Yellow River on the ice near the mouth of the Hsi ho (or Hsi-ning Ho), we reached Ho tsui-tzŭ, thirty miles from Hsin-ch'eng at 6 P. M. There seems to be a good deal more ground under cultivation than when first I visited this valley in '89. Most of the soil is given up to poppy culture, and is covered with gravel, as around Lan-chou. This mode of protecting the soil is also used when melons are grown, but not for grain crops.

I noticed to-day a great many small caves dug in the cliffs on the north side of the Hsi ho valley near its mouth. The muleteers said that they were made in the troubled times of the Mohammedan

* St. G. R. Littledale also photographed this water-wheel and reproduced it in his paper in the *Geographical Journal*, III, 467.

rebellion to serve as refuges. They appear inaccessible, but may not have been so twenty-five years ago, or they may have been reached by ropes from above, or they may not have been refuges at all and only have resulted from the crumbling of strata of gravel between the loess and the lower red sandstone.

In the inn at Ho tsui-tzŭ were a number of mules carrying beans from Hsi-ning to Han-chung in Shen-hsi. The trip occupies a month, two months in fact the muleteers say, but then they rest repeatedly and for days at a time on the way.

February 7.—We reached to-day Hsiang-t'ang, twenty-five miles from Ho tsui-tzŭ, at the mouth of the Ta-t'ung river. Quite a crowd of people came into the inn to see me and among them was a Salar. He gave me a number of words in his native language and was very communicative and intelligent, though without education. He said the Salar number many tens of thousands and that the term *Salar pa kun* means "the eight thousand Salar families" or "the eight Thousands of the Salar." His people came in past centuries, he knows not when, from some place in the west.

Hsiang-t'ang is largely inhabited by people of mixed T'u-jen origin who came here from Bayan rong. These people have distinctly Tibetan features, more noticeable in the young people. They have no longer any language of their own but use a Chinese patois in which a few Mongol, Tibetan and possibly Salar words are to be found. Most of them understand Salar and a little Tibetan. There are some seventy Mohammedan families living here and the place took sides with the rebels in the late rebellion.

Potanin says somewhere that Li K'o-yung was buried here.* I can hear nothing concerning him, nor are there any ruins of any great antiquity, certainly none of the eighth century in which he lived. I fancy however, that Potanin must have had some good authority for his statement.

February 8.—To-day we reached Kao miao-tzŭ (28.5 miles) and put up in an inn outside the west gate. I was struck while going through the "great gorges" (*Ta-hsia*) with the correctness of Huc's remarks about the danger of traveling through them.†

* *Proc. Roy. Geo. Soc.*, IX, 234. Li-ko-yung was a famous commander in the latter part of the T'ang dynasty. He died in A. D. 908. See W. F. Mayers, *Chinese Reader's Manual*, 117. (*Sub voce* Li K'eh-yung.)

† Huc, *op. cit.*, II, 53.

His memory served him badly however, for he speaks of the danger of the "little gorges," (*Hsiao hsia*) which are nearer Hsi-ning, whereas he should have said the great gorges. The Ta-hsia are really very dangerous, in many places along some ten miles of road, the bridle path is between two hundred and three hundred feet above the river which roars over rocks at the bottom of the cliffs in the side of which the path is cut. Land and rock slides are of continual occurrence, and the rocky path is so slippery that one has to be very careful in traveling along it.

Kao miao-tzŭ is quite a large walled village with a number of shops and inns, but, as every where in this country, not one of the latter is even passably clean. We put up in a Mohammedan inn outside the west gate. Around the yard a number of men were loafing, among them a red gowned, long haired Bönbo lama, the first I have seen in these parts. One of the servants in the inn is an *Ahon* (Mohammedan priest), and my boy, who is well up in the Koran, had a match with him in reciting verses of the sacred book, each of the contestants giving in turn the first phrase of a certain passage and asking the other to finish it. Their pronunciation of Arabic was not so bad that I could not understand a little here and there. There are about twenty Mohammedans living in this place, and probably one hundred and fifty families belonging to the *ta chiao*.

February 9.—The red, argillaceous sandstone characteristic of the Hsi ho basin as far west as the "little gorges" (*Hsiao hsia*), and which first crops up west of Hsin-ch'eng at the mouth of the Ping-fan ho valley, though possibly not identical in composition with the red sandstone of western Ssŭ-ch'uan, appears to me to belong to the same formation. The gravel and débris in the Hsi ho valley rise one hundred to two hundred feet above the river bed.

The climatic conditions west of Lan-chou are perceptibly different from those farther east, cloudy days are in this season of frequent occurrence, and the weather throughout the year is milder (so said Father van Belle at Hsin-ch'eng). The evenings, ever since passing Hsin-ch'eng have been cloudy. I noticed these same peculiarities three years ago when first I passed along this route.

We stopped for the night at Chang-ch'i-ts'ai (twenty eight miles from Kao miao-tzŭ). Speaking to some muleteers here, I heard that in the San-ch'uan* there live Chinese, T'u-jen and Mongols, the two latter races predominating. I heard from another source that these Mongols speak good Mongol, except when they count, when they have recourse to Chinese numerals.

February 10.—I reached Hsi-ning Fu at 2:30 P. M., after a very disagreeable ride in a strong east wind which kept us wrapped most of the way in dense clouds of dust. A few miles before reaching the Hsiao hsia ("little gorges") we passed by the temple of the White Horse (Pai ma ssŭ) and the village of the same name. Both are inhabited by T'u-jen. I fancy the temple is not long for this world; it is built in a sandstone rock which is nearly completely detached from the main ledge and seems to be toppling over.

At Hsi-ning† I was warmly welcomed by my old acquaintances and took up my lodgings at the same inn where I had passed many days in '89. Every one complained of business being bad. Though the crops hereabout are invariably good, lack of capital cripples the most enterprising, so that tradespeople can barely make both ends meet. The bovine pest, which has carried off in the last two years over two-thirds of the cattle of Chinese, Mongols and Tibetans, is still raging. Wool alone has more than doubled in price since '89 (it is now selling for 6 taels a picul of 200 catties).‡ I cannot see where the profit comes in at this high rate, for it costs about 7 taels a picul to deliver it at Tientsin where it sells for not more than 10 taels. I bought a pretty pony for 18 taels from Ch'i-hsiang, the same man who abandoned me in '89

* The San-ch'uan is a district some twenty miles south of this point and of peculiar interest to ethnologists.

† Ysbrandt Ides (1692), speaking of Hsi-ning says that "great numbers of Merchants come to the vast trading city of *Zunning*, in the Kingdom of Xiensi: and the Door of Commerce being for some time opened here, and liberty granted to them as well as *Muscovites* and *Tartars* to trade here, they have with their Wares and Trade, introduced the *Mahometan* Religion, which, as Weeds grow apace, is spread over all *China*, to that degree that there appears more of that accursed Seed than of the true Doctrine of Jesus Christ." *The Three Years Land Travels of E. Ysbrandt Ides*, p. 126. Further on he says that the people of Cambay (Gujarat), Bengal "and other subordinate countries" are those who chiefly resort to Zunning, bringing there diamonds, jewels, elephants' teeth, wax, etc. Ibid., p. 196.

‡ On this curious Chinese habit of counting two pounds as one, 10 taels as 7½, etc., see also under *December 21, 1891, and April 28, 1892.*

PAI MA SSU, "WHITE HORSE TEMPLE," IN HSI-NING HO VALLEY.

at Tankar to return home and get married.* Now he wants to go with me—to the end of the world if I see fit. Marriage in his case has probably proved a failure.

There must be some Scotch blood in the Hsi-ningites, for I find they are very fond of oatmeal and of cracked wheat. The first is called *yen-mei ch'en* and is eaten boiled with the water in which mutton has been cooked, or with neat's-foot oil (*yang-t'i yu*). The cracked wheat (*mei-tzŭ fan*) is eaten prepared in the same way, and is a very good dish.†

February 11.—I rode to Lusar on my newly-purchased pony, a most agreeable change from the headstrong and iron-mouthed mule I had ridden all the way from Lan-chou Fu. Ch'i-hsiang accompanied me, and we joined outside of the gate a party of Hsi-fan lamas from a lamasery near Serkok, who were on their way to Kumbum for the feast of lanterns to be held the day after to-morrow (15th of first moon). The road was crowded with people all on the same errand, Hsi-fan, Mongols, Chinese and chiefly T'u-jen. I listened to the latter talk. Their language is, as I thought, a mixture of all the languages spoken in these parts. Why this hybrid people should have retained to the present day, though living in China proper, its tribal organization is difficult to explain, and speaks well for Chinese administrative methods which can admit of such a thing with no fear of trouble and perfect obedience to their laws.

At Lusar (which name, by the way, is written Lu-sha-erh in Chinese) I received a very hearty welcome, for nearly every one in the village knew me and hardly one failed to greet me as I passed with a *Ta-jen lai-liao* ("His Excellency has come!"). This time I have taken lodgings in an inn in the lower part of the

---

* See *Land of the Lamas*, 117.

† In winter fish are very cheap on the Hsi-ning and Tankar markets, two large ones sell in the latter place for a parcel of vermicelli (worth 30 cash). They are caught in lake Koko nor by the Mongols who make holes in the ice for that purpose. They are all of one variety, yellow-skinned and scaleless, I believe. They are called *chin yü* "goldfish." These fish are also sold split and dried, in which shape they are worth the same price as fresh and are known as *kan pan-pan*. Prjevalsky says of the fish of the Koko nor lake "The only kind of fish that we saw was the *Schizopygopsis* nov. sp., which we captured ourselves; we heard that though there were many other species, owing to the badness of the nets they were rarely caught." *Mongolia*, II, 141.

village, as my former quarters are occupied by traders come here for the fair. I am, however, much more comfortable than on my first visit. I have a large room of three *chien*,* divided into sleeping, reception and dining compartments. Besides this I have on the other side of the court-yard a kitchen, with stabling for eighteen ponies, and rooms for my people on the second story, for which I am to pay $2 a month.

Presents from old acquaintances pour in, the inn keeper brought me a sheep and one of my former followers, Ssŭ-shih-wu, some butter, cakes, *chuoma*,† etc., etc. He declared his intention of accompanying me on this journey, as did also yesterday at Hsi-ning Miao san, the man whom I had to leave behind me in '89 at Jyäkundo and who was, with Liu san, so roughly treated by the Dergé lamas.‡ The willingness of these men to go with me has relieved me of the anxiety and uncertainty in which I had to live for six weeks on my first journey while trying to engage men to travel with me.

To my delight I found a party of Salar muleteers stopping in the inn, and we were soon on friendly terms, especially after I had read them the few Salar words I had taken down at Hsiang-t'ang. Three of these men had thin oval faces, fine eyes and beautifully regular teeth. They were dressed in Chinese garb, but had nothing else Chinese about them. They all spoke fluently Chinese, Mongol and Tibetan. This knowledge they said is indispensable, as nearly the whole male population is occupied driving mules from Salar pa kun to Lusar or Labrang gomba and the neighboring country, either carrying freight or pilgrims (chiefly Mongols) of whom large numbers visit yearly the numerous lamaist sanctuaries scattered through the mountains. They told me that it took four days from here to reach the Salar settlements on the Yellow River, and two days from there to the great lamasery of Labrang. The word *kun* in *pa-kun* is, so they said, the Chinese *t'sun*, "a village." ‖

* A *chien* is the space between two consecutive pillars and rafters, and is usually about ten feet. The size of a room is counted in *chien*, a room of thirty feet is called a "three chien room."

† The root of the *Potentilla anserina*, used throughout northwestern Mongolia and Tibet as a vegetable.

‡ See *Land of the Lamas*, 223 and 297.

‖ In another place I heard that the word *kun* is the equivalent of the Chinese *chien hu* "thousand families, a Thousand," and had the same meaning. See under date of *February 22d*.

February 12.—To-day I made a few purchases, mostly of the little odds and ends required in camp life. A number of people dropped in to see me and to find out what I had come here for this time. Towards noon I went over to Kumbum to see the fair, and try to pick up some curios. I found there quite a number of Lh'asa Tibetans (they call them Gopa here) selling pulo,* beads of various colors, saffron, medicines, peacock feathers, incense sticks, etc., etc. Among the medicines I saw pods of the *Colocanthes indica* (Blume) called in Tibetan *tsampaka* and in Chinese *hsüeh lien* ("snow lotus"), probably because the seeds look like great snow flakes.

I had a talk with these traders, several of whom I had met here before in '89. They were very friendly and jolly. One of them had a *swastika* (*yung-drung*)† tattooed on his hand, and I learnt from this man that this was not an uncommon mode of ornamentation in his country. He said that one often sees at Lh'asa devotees (*Atsara* from India) with the three mystic syllables *Om, A, Hūm*, tattooed on their persons—the first on the crown of the head, the second on the forehead, the third on the sternum. He was very much surprised, however, when I showed him an image of Sachya t'uba tattooed years ago in Japan on my arm. He would not believe it was tattooed, but insisted it was *rang chyung* ("self produced," "come of itself"); I left him in this pleasant belief. K'amba were also quite numerous to-day, but on the whole the attendance was much smaller than in '89 on the same occasion.

In the afternoon, while writing in my room, who rushed in but my faithful friend Yeh Chi-cheng (Yeh Hsien-sheng) my headman on my first journey. The good fellow had received news at Chen-hai P'u of my arrival, and had not lost a minute in coming to greet me. He said that if I wanted him, he would go with me anywhere I said, and that, at all events, he would only go home after I had finished the trip I proposed making to the Salar country.

* Woven in pieces usually thirty feet long and about nine inches broad. The best kinds of this cloth come from Ulterior Tibet. The most popular colors are red, purple, striped and white with red and blue crosses stamped on it. It is used in China to cover saddles with or trim seats of carts. *Pulo* is the Chinese transcription of the Tibetan name of this cloth, *p'ruk*. See Du Halde, *op. cit.*, I. 53.

† A hooked cross. It is a sacred symbol both among the Buddhists and the Bönbo.

Of course I told him I wanted him, not only for that trip but for the whole of my journey; he is too good a man to let slip.

Ssŭ-shih-wu later in the day brought me a fine Tibetan mastiff which I bought for a peck of tsamba and some tea. He had also a live lynx (*shih-li*) which a Hsi-fan had caught in the mountains. It was so fierce that I refused to take it as a present.

In the evening the managers of the Hsiao-sheng huei* came and invited me to the performance to be held on the square this evening and on the two nights following. We were escorted to our seats by the managers carrying lanterns, and found sweets, water-melon seeds and samshu provided for us. The performance consisted of stilt-walking and masquerading, firing off of crackers, etc., etc., the usual tame and slip-shod performance seen all over northern China, but which here, as elsewhere, seems to afford the audience great pleasure.

At a table near us were the likin office officials, and we vied with each other in liberality to the performers, each time they presented them with a string of cash we gave them two, and so it went on for over an hour, till the play has cost both parties some fifteen to twenty *tiao*, much to the delight of the managers and the disgust of the likin people who had not anticipated any one trying to outdo them in generosity.

February 13.—(15th of 1st moon)—Half of to-day was passed at Kumbum sauntering through the fair. I was surprised to see quite a large number of Bŏnbo lamas, recognizable by their huge mops of hair and their red gowns, and also from their being dirtier than the ordinary run of people. I heard that throughout this Amdo country they have numerous small lamaseries and that their belief is very popular among the T'u-fan.

There appears to hang a certain mystery about the famous *tsandan karpo*, the "white sandal wood tree" † sprung from Tsong-k'apa's hair. I now learn that the great and only original

* The lads in every town and village of China give these theatrical performances at this time of the year. Hsiao sheng huei may be freely translated by "young men's amateur theatrical company."

† In my *Land of the Lamas*, p. 67, following Lieut. Kreitner's suggestion, I remarked that this tree was probably the *Philadelphus coronarius*. I have now learnt from Mr. W. B. Hemsley that the tree is the *Syringa villosa*, Vahl. Sarat Chandra Das, *Narr. Journey to Lhasa in 1881–'82*, p. 91, makes mention of a juniper bush at Tashilhunpo sprung from the hair of Gédundrub the founder of that lamasery.

one, on the leaves of which images of the saint appear, is kept hidden away in the *sanctum sanctorum* of the Chin-wa ssŭ ("golden tiled temple"), remote from the eyes of the vulgar herd. So it would seem that I have never seen it, though I have been shown four or five other "white sandalwoods" in and around the lamasery. I learn, moreover, that the images on the leaves, bark, etc., only appear to those who have firm belief, and that the faithless can distinguish nothing extraordinary on them. This, if true, is rough on Huc, who thought he detected the devil's hand in the miraculously produced images *he* perceived on the leaves of this tree.

Some of the Gopa (Lh'asa traders) have their wives here with them. They were out to-day dressed in all their finery and looked remarkably well. Strapping big women they were, with ruddy cheeks and frank open faces, in green satin gowns, aprons of variegated pulo, shirts of raw silk (*buré*), silver charm boxes (*gawo*) on their breasts, and crowns of coral beads and turquoises on the top of their long loosely hanging black locks.

In the Gold tiled temple in the northeast corner near the door is an impress in a chunk of sandstone of a human foot about eighteen inches long and two inches deep and said to be that of Tsong-k'apa. It is placed in a vertical position. On the top of the stone is a little wax; on this the people place a copper cash and then examine the footprint to ascertain their luck. If it is good, then bright spots will appear on the surface of the stone in the foot-mark.

In the evening I again went to Kumbum, this time to "*lang t'eng*," as it is called here, *anglicè*, to see the lanterns and the butter bas-reliefs. The latter were very good—better perhaps than those I saw in '89. In one of the largest ones the central portion of the design was a temple, and little figures of lamas and laymen about eight to ten inches high were moving in and out of its portals.* Another new feature was musicians concealed behind curtains hanging around the bas-reliefs, who discoursed sweet (?) music on flutes, cymbals and hautboys. Four of the largest designs were in the style of the one just described, the others represented images of various gods inside of highly

* When Huc saw this festival there were similar butter manikins. See Huc, *op. cit.*, II, 102.

ornamented borders; in these the main figures were about four feet high.

February 14.—The fête is over and most of the visitors have gone. I also will soon be ready to leave, for I have already bought at least half of my outfit, including four stout ponies, for 70 taels. Saddles (of the Hsi-fan type) are being got ready for them, leather bags for tsamba, flour, rice, etc., have also been bought and filled, and if the money I am expecting from Lan-chou arrives, I can start for Tibet three or four days after receiving it.

The inn-keeper and a number of other persons got up for my benefit a *Kuan-wu*, a fencing, wrestling, single-stick, double sword, spear performance, which was really very good. The single stick and quarter-staff exercises were capital, and an old fellow of nearly sixty (an ex pao-piao-ti or "insurance-against brigand's-attack-agent") went through some marvelously agile single stick and *savate* exercises, but his son was the hero of the entertainment.

Things have nearly doubled in price since my first visit here. This is attributed to the smallness of the crops, but hats, boots, and cotton piece goods have increased proportionately as much as flour and rice.

We have not had a perfectly cloudless day since leaving Lan-chou; in the mornings and early evenings there are always light clouds covering the sky, which disappear later on. Afternoon winds are also *de rigueur.* In these narrow valleys they appear cyclonic in their movement, but I have no doubt they are westerly to northwesterly, and are deflected to the northeast on striking the mountains a few miles to the south of here.*

The population of Lusar is estimated at five hundred families (say two thousand souls), of which more than half is Mohammedan. There is a slight tendence to increase, but it is only due to the influx of Shen-hsi and Ssŭ-chu'an people, who here, as elsewhere, are ousting the native Kan-su people from most branches of trade.

* Hail storms are very common here in the spring and summer. The Kaffir Chinese (non-Mohammedan ones) make little manikins, put a bow in their hands and place them in the position of shooting an arrow. These figures they put in the sixth moon (July to August) on the summits of the various beacon towers (*tun*) on the hilltops, where they are said to ward off the hail.

All the people here insist that there is no difference in race or language between the T'u-jen and T'u-ssŭ, but the Chinese are not observant about these matters and I doubt the correctness of this statement, though I am fain to admit that physically all these people (T'u-jen and T'u-ssŭ) greatly resemble each other.

February 15.—To-day I had to go through the ordeal of a Chinese dinner given me by some merchants and traders. It lasted three hours but the time was not absolutely lost ; I got an indigestion and a few details concerning the trade of these parts.

The musk trade here is increasing, Cantonese and Ssŭ-ch'uanese traders now come here to buy it, paying for good musk four times its weight in silver (*ssŭ huan*, as they say). The best test of its purity is an examination of the color. The Tibetans adulterate it by mixing tsamba and blood with it. The best time to buy it is from the seventh to the ninth moon (latter part of August to middle of November).*

A trail leads from Hsi-ning to Kan-chou *viâ* the Kokonor steppe (*ts'ao-ti*) in ten days; it is frequently followed by traders. The Lo-lo town, of which I heard at Lan-chou from the China Inland Mission people, is, these traders told me to-day, 70 *li* from Hsiang-t'ang and is very small, there being hardly a hundred families in it. The inhabitants are said to be T'u-jen.

February 16.—I have to-day finished buying ponies, securing six more strong ones of Tibetan stock, for which I paid an average price of twenty dollars. I have now got to purchase pack-mules and to complete my stock of provisions, and all this I will do as soon as I receive letters and the money I am expecting daily from Lan-chou. In the meanwhile I have decided to go on a little trip to the Salar country and to see Kuei-tê and the adjacent Tibetan tribes of Rongwa. This will occupy about a fortnight, and on my return here the money will surely have arrived.

* Mongols call musk *owo;* Tibetans call it *latsê.* The best musk they say is "white musk" *tsahan owo* in Mongol, in Tibetan *latsê karpo.* I do not know whether white refers to the color of the musk itself or to that of the hair on the skin covering the musk pouch.

PART II.

SALAR PA-KUN. KUEI-TÊ. KOKO-NOR. TS'AIDAM.

February 17.—I left this morning with three men and a pack-horse carrying my instruments, which I have packed in a padded box divided into compartments. In this I can put my sextant, artificial horizon, bull's eye lantern, boiling point apparatus and thermometers. The box serves me moreover for a table. Well wrapped in a sheet of felt made double over the corners, it can stand a good deal of very rough handling. My camera, bedding, a pot and a kettle complete the load.

The road on leaving Lusar led nearly east-southeast over the loess-covered foothills of the Nan-shan. The loess even on the higher foothills, seems to have been washed down there, as rolled stones are everywhere found in it. In many places we saw holes dug down through the loess to auriferous gravel beds, and in the valley bottoms the gold bearing gravel is also worked. I noticed a little white quartz in the loess and also in the gravel in the beds of most of the streams.

We passed through a number of little villages of T'u-jen, several of probably a hundred families each. A considerable number of the houses are cave-dwellings, or partly of that order, with a front in the ordinary adobe-brick style built against the mouth of the cave. In western Kan-su these T'u-jen alone use cave-dwellings (*yao t'ung*). Such dwellings are found among all these people, and also, I have heard said, among the Tibetan tribes living west of Sung-pan T'ing. The question suggests itself whether these tribes did not teach the Chinese to make such dwellings, and furthermore whether these people, these T'u-jen, are not of the same stock as the now extinct Man-tzŭ cave makers of western Ssŭ-ch'uan. The only cave makers I know of in northwestern

China in the olden days were the Tobas who were not of Chinese, but probably of Tibetan, (or T'u-jen) stock. The question is an interesting one, but it will require much more investigation before we can pronounce upon it.

The T'u-jen women have adopted the Chinese fashion of binding the feet, but only to the extent of deforming them in width, not in length. This is the more fortunate for them as they lead hard lives, doing all the household and most of the field work. They are an ugly lot, short, thick set and very broad-faced, not to be compared physically with the Fan-tzŭ of this same region.

We reached Sha-erh-wan (a strangely Turkish or Persian name, by the way) at 3 P. M. The village has in it several hundred families, the people tell me, and all are Mohammedans.

At the inn where we stopped we were shortly followed by a party of Baron Sunit Mongols on a trip to Labrang gomba. They were in charge of some Salars who had hired to them mules for the trip (seven days) for 1.8 taels a head.

In the evening I held a reception in my room, and the conversation turned mostly on Islam. I learnt that the late Mohammedan rebellion broke out at Bayon-rong, where we will arrive the day after to-morrow, and that the people were incited to it by their priests or *Ahons*. Fortunately for the government dissensions soon broke out among the Mohammedans who came to blows over the question of smoking tobacco, one Ahon from Ho-chou contending that it was permitted them, the others denying this lax interpretation of the words of the Prophet. At Tankar the dissension became so violent that the Hsieh-t'ai* conceived a plan of ridding the town of the whole lot. He had the males of both factions invited to meet him in the mosque, and as soon as they had assembled they were called out one by one under some futile pretext and their heads cut off, and so thirty-five hundred troublesome Huei-huei were got rid of in a day, and Tankar, with a remaining population of a few hundred, knew peace once more.

Since the suppression of the rebellion the Ahons have not been idle. Some have come from Mecca, some from Medina, some from Turkestan, and they have by their preaching incited the Kansu Mohammedans to rebellion by urging them to follow customs contrary to the recognized usages and habits of China. Thus,

* The Colonel in command of that frontier post.

they tried to induce the young men to let their beards grow, parents not to compress their female children's feet, and even encouraged them not to wear queues. In Hsi-ning when the Chen-t'ai* heard that some Mohammedans under forty were wearing beards, he had them called to his Ya-mên and gave them their choice, prison or shaving off their beards, and off went the half dozen long hairs which probably adorned their manly faces.

As to not compressing girls' feet, the Ahons have been a little more successful; some of the native priests have in the case of their daughters let nature follow its course, but nine-tenths of the Huei-huei are as fond of seeing small feeted women as other Chinese are.

Until about ten years ago no Mohammedan was allowed to enter the city of Hsi-ning (none, of course, could then as now reside there) without having an official seal stamped on his wrist at the city gate, and for the first few years after the rebellion the stamp was put on the face, near the corner of the mouth.

It began snowing about 4 P. M. (the first heavy snow I have seen since December 14th last), and when I went to bed (8.30) the snow was still falling fast.

February 18.—The snow fell during the night to a depth of between two and three inches. When we left this morning the sun was shining brightly and the glare was terrible. Fortunately we had all provided ourselves with horse-hair eyeshades. The snow made the narrow trail running along the very steep mountain side extremely slippery. This trail is usually only followed in winter when free from snow; in summer it is impassable. It led first over loess-covered hills, then over disintegrated red sandstone and finally over the porphyritic masses of the main range (Nan shan) by two passes, the first one called Niu-hsin yahu or "ox-heart pass," from a huge mass of bare rock beside it which may possibly have some likeness to an ox's heart. The main pass is the Ch'ing-t'u yahu or "black clay pass," a most appropriate name as the soil on the eastern slope of the pass is of a coal black color.

From the Niu-hsin yahu we looked back towards Lusar, and all the valleys, ravines and anfractuosities we had crossed coming

* Brigadier General. His correct title is Tsung-ping, Chen-t'ai is his colloquial designation.

here were invisible ; the whole country seemed a gently sloping line of hills running north and south. The valleys and ravines we had painfully climbed up or slid down into, seemed but as wrinkles on the broad expanse of reddish earth. It was a beautiful example of loess formation, the subærial and the marine deposits side by side. The loess is being continually redistributed in China by the action of water and the subærial deposits do not cover, I fancy, a fifth of the loess-covered country of northern China. In eastern China (plain of eastern Chih-li and Shan-tung), I imagine that most of the loess is not a subærial deposit, while in Shan-hsi the greater part of it is.

On the south side of the range we reached, after a short but very steep descent, the village of Ts'a-pa, a place of several hundred families with a walled camp, a mosque, a lieutenant (Ch'ien-tsung) and a small garrison. Half the population is Mohammedan, hence the necessity for the garrison.

February 19.—In the hills around Ts'a-pa are numerous T'u-jen and T'u-fan (Rongwa)* villages, the latter people, of mixed Tibetan descent, have retained some of their ancestral customs, but in their mode of living, they are purely Chinese.

Ts'a-pa is a Salar Wai-kun † administered from Bayan-rong T'ing, and is of some importance as being on the route followed by salt smugglers on their way to and from Han-chung in Shen-hsi. These salt traders buy at Lusar, salt brought there by the Panaka or Mongols, who pay no import duties (*likin* or *shui*) to the Chinese authorities, and who can consequently undersell the government monopolists. The Chinese traders take this salt by this mountain route to Han-chung and thus evade all internal revenue taxes, as there are no likin stations on this road.

On leaving Ts'a-pa our road led east by south up a well cultivated valley and then over a low *col* into the broad (for these parts) Bayan-rong valley, down which flows a small stream fed from springs in the Nan Shan. The southern slope of this range

* The terms T'u-jen and T'u-ssŭ apply to non-Chinese peoples of mixed Mongol, Tibetan, Turki and Chinese descent, while T'u-fan, Fan-tzŭ, Hsi-fan apply only to tribes of Tibetan blood, occasionally with a slight admixture of Chinese.

† Besides the Eight *Kun* into which the Salar district is divided, there are five outer (*Wai*) Kun inhabited by a few Salar and a mixed population of Chinese and T'u-ssŭ. See p. 77.

shows, in the little valleys at its base, loess mixed with disintegrated red sandstone and gravel of gneiss and dolerite (?) ; a little higher up appear beds of red sandstone, above this and falling over it, like beds of drifted sand, is the true loess, and finally rising through the latter the black, jagged peaks of the main range. About six miles before reaching Bayan-rong we passed the ruins of quite a considerable village destroyed three months ago by a loess hill-side falling down on it. Such events are of frequent occurrence in a loess country.

Bayan-rong is a small village with a walled enclosure of the dimensions prescribed for a sub-prefecture or T'ing,* on a bluff above the Bayan-rong ho. The western suburbs contain all the inns and most of the shops, and the space within the walls is half empty. All the shops must be very badly supplied, for we could buy nothing in them that we wanted, neither bread, millet, coal-bricks (*mei chuan*), nor meat.

The name of this place is apparently a hybrid one (such names are innumerable in this country), *Bayan* is Mongol for "rich" and *rong* Tibetan for "arable valley." The crops hereabout must be abundant, if one may judge from the number of small grist mills one sees along the river, and so the name given this valley is justified.

The Hsieh-t'ai (colonel) who governs this sub-prefecture has five Wai-kun or "outside" Kun under him. They are Ts'a-pa, Nang-ssŭ-to, Hei-ch'eng, Kan-tu and Kargan. The word Kun (of questionable origin) designates a commune containing, theoretically, a thousand families, but some of them (as Kă-tzŭ kun) have a much larger number of habitations. The term Wai-wu Kun or "five outside Kun" is used to distinguish them from the "eight Kun" inhabited by the Salars. These Wai-wu Kun are not exclusively inhabited by Salars, but have many T'u-jen, Chinese, T'u-fan, etc., living in them. Each Wai-Kun has, theoretically, fifteen villages in it.

February 20.—The road on leaving Bayan-rong led in a south-east direction for about five miles, till by an easy ascent we reached the top of the La-cha shan (a Chinese transcription of the Tibetan word *Ra-jo* "fork"). From there we looked down on an endless maze of rounded hilltops of loess, and higher and more

*The dimensions of all Chinese cities and towns are fixed by regulations.

anguler ones of red sandstone. Our road led along the crest of the mountains for awhile, then by a precipitous zigzag down the side of sheer precipices hundreds of feet in depth, to the base of the mountain at the hamlet of La-mo shan-ken (another hybrid name, *la-mo* or *mä* and *shan ken* both meaning "foot of the pass," the first being the Tibetan, the latter the Chinese expression). This village has only some twenty houses in it; most of the inhabitants are Kargan Fan-tzŭ and Mohammedans. I found the inn where we had stopped for lunch so clean and quiet, and the cooking so good that, though we had only traveled eighteen miles, I determined to stop here for the night.

The Bayan-rong rivulet flows by here, and empties into the Yellow River some eleven miles to the south, near the Wai-Kun of Kan-tu. We will follow this brook to-morrow.

All the people here as well as at Ts'a-pa and Bayan-rong thought I was here to buy wool. They heard a year or so ago that foreigners at T'ien-tsin Wei and Shanghai were wild to get their wool, and so they think I have come here for the sole purpose of securing this year's clip. To say one is a wool-buyer is now a sure way of securing a friendly reception anywhere in this region. When the *flâneurs* about the inn in the evening saw me taking observations with my sextant ("looking at the stars," *kuan hsing*, they call it), they were persuaded it was to see how the wool market would be by the time I got the supply I was now buying down to Tien-tsin.

It is about 45 *li* (fifteen miles) from here to Hsün-hua T'ing on the Yellow River. The Tibetans (here and elsewhere around the Kokonor) call this place Ya-dza k'uar, and the Yellow River is invariably called by them Ch'u-k'a "The river." When the Tibetans living north of the Yellow River speak of it they say *Ma (c'hu) harka* or *haré* "the Ma ch'u there;" when those living south of the river refer to it, they say *Ma (ch'u) tsurka* or "the Ma ch'u here."

February 21.—After about six miles over a stony road down the narrow valley—which must be converted into a broad torrent in the rainy season, by numerous little villages, nearly each one of which possesses a large mosque, we came out in the Yellow River valley, about a mile or two to the east of Kan-tu.* Turning

* R. B. Shaw, *On the Hill Canton of Salar, in Journ. Roy. As. Soc.*, n. ser. X, p. 308, gives Khantus and Mahtus as the titles of the two native Musulman chiefs who rule Salar under the Hsi-ning Amban.

eastward, we crossed the river on the ice a few miles down (just opposite the large Salar village of Kă-tzŭ kun) and followed it down for about four miles till we came to I-ma-mu chuang or the "village of the Imam,"* belonging to the Chang-chia kun. The village is divided into two portions, the "big" (*ta*) and the "little" (*hsiao*, here pronounced *ka*) I-ma-mu chuang. I stopped in the latter one. Here, after some difficulty, we found accommodations in the house of one of the muleteers we had met at Sha-erh wan, and who had advised us to come to his home where he assured us we would be kindly received by his mother. It was fortunate we were able to get lodgings here, for as there are no inns in these Salar villages, if we had been refused admittance at this first village, it is doubtful if we would have been admitted in the next, as I fear we looked like rather suspicious characters.

On either side of the Yellow River valley and at the base of the mountains which border it, there are hereabout a number of cliffs of horizontally stratified loess, gravel and disintegrated red sandstone, some three hundred to four hundred feet thick; these probably marked the former banks of the river. The river, about two hundred feet wide, now flows at a considerably lower level between rather high steep banks composed of red sand, on top of which is about twelve feet of sandstone and granitic gravel, and finally a bed of loess stretching over to the foothills or the cliffs above mentioned.

The Salar men are of short, light build with regular features and oval faces, frequently with not a trace of the Chinese about them, and were it not for the queues they all wear, one would never dream of associating them with that people. The women, though they have a distinctly foreign look about them, have more of the Chinese in their features, especially the eyes which have drawn lids like the Chinese. Their head-dress is peculiar; it resembles somewhat the tiara so often seen in Assyrian bas-reliefs; the Salar wear it black, and, in that following the Chinese fashion, of white when in mourning; women and girls wear it alike. It is probably first put on when puberty is reached. The Salar women do not compress their feet. The jacket and trousers they wear are of blue

* The Imams among the western Kan-su moslems receive as their perquisite, when any animal is butchered, the saddle, or the brisket. When after Ramazan everyone kills some animal to celebrate the event by a feast, some killing an ox, others a camel or a sheep, the hides belong to the Imam.

cotton and wadded, and are of the ordinary Chinese pattern, but the sleeves of the jackets are red or black. The men's dress is purely Chinese, the hat, perhaps excepted, which is rather of the pointed Kokonor Tibetan pattern but with a wider rim, faced with lamb's skin. The Ahons* wear a white turban and most of them have clean shaven heads, but when abroad they put on a false queue, so as not to get in trouble with the Chinese authorities. All of them go about with a rosary of ninety-nine beads in their hands, and attend the mosque three times a day where they sit on antelope skin rugs or else on woven rugs brought from Ilchi (Ho-tien).

These Salar bury their dead with their heads to the north (as do all Chinese Mohammedans), the body is washed and wrapped in a sheet, but no coffin is used. The graves they cover with black and white pebbles arranged in patterns, and a stone is placed at the foot of the mound which is about two feet high.

Several Ahons passed part of the evening with me and were very communicative. They told me they had no written traditions concerning their people, that it had come down to them that the first Salar who came to China, arrived in this valley in the third year of Hung-wu of the Ming (A. D. 1370). They came from Samarkand, driven thence by internal discords, and were only two in number, leading an ox laden with all their worldly goods. They settled where the large village of Kä-tzŭ kun now stands. They were soon followed by others, and the villages became more and more numerous, so that now there are more than a hundred Salar villages (divided into eight Kun, as previously stated) in which live between eight thousand and nine thousand families.†

* The word Ahon is the Turkish *Akhund*, in common use throughout Turkestan.

† "They (*i. e.*, the Salaris) have a tradition that their ancestors came from Rúm or Turkey. The story is as follows. Their spiritual guide or religious teacher, some seven hundred years ago, sent them forth on a pilgrimage, giving them a sample of earth with instructions to wander until they should reach some country whose soil should weigh the same, measure for measure, as the sample which they bore with them. From land to land they roamed, weighing the earth from place to place, till they came, by way of Tibet, to *Sálár mês* (Lower Sálár). Here the earth was found to come nearer in weight to their sample than it had been anywhere else. Still it differed somewhat. They were preparing to march further when it was discovered that some of their camels, laden with religious books, had strayed. In search of them they penetrated into the hill country which lay at the side of their road. Here their task received its accomplishment. They weighed the soil and found it exactly

SALAR WOMAN OF I-MA-MU CHUANG.

All the men are taught to read and write Arabic (and some say the Turkish forms of these letters are also occasionally used) which they use in writing their own language, which is Turkish with a slight admixture of Chinese, Tibetan and Mongol—and possibly *t'u hua.* I obtained here a considerable vocabulary; I have, of course, transcribed the words phonetically—and where the sounds approximate Chinese, I have followed Sir Thomas Wade's system of transcription.* They have no written books save the Koran, at least so I have been told wherever I have inquired, at Lusar, Sha-erh-wan and elsewhere.

February 22.—The head Ahon of the Salar is at present Han-Pao (it is pronounced Hambo, but I presume it represents Han-Pao) Ahon, he is a Hsi-ning man, and has a residence in the Ta I-ma-mu chuang. All men among the Chinese Mohammedans, Salar as well as others, have a Chinese name of the usual type, and also a Mohammedan one; thus the son of the woman of this house is called Osman but for the world he is Ma Ch'eng-hsi.†

The eight Kun‡ constituting the Salar pa-kun are Kä-tzŭ, Chang-

balanced an equal measure of that which had been given them by their spiritual teacher. Here, therefore, they rested from their travel, and finding the hills inhabited they formed a settlement, to which they gave the name of *Sálár-gés*, or Upper Sálár, though to what language the affix belongs I do not know." R. B. Shaw, *op. cit.*, 305. I have a vague recollection that this tradition is not original with the Salars, and I think that I have heard of it among the Mongols.

* See this Salar vocabulary in the appendix.

† Col. Yule in speaking of the Mohammedans in Burmah says "Every indigenous Mussulman has two names. * * * As a son of Islam, he is probably Abdul Kureem; but as a native of Burma, and for all practical purposes he is Moung-yo or Shwepo." *Narr. of the Mission to the Court of Ava in 1855, p. 152.*

‡ Shaw, *op. cit.*, 309, says that the Salars number "about forty thousand, and they live in villages consisting of scattered farmhouses, each on its own land. Groups of four or five villages each are administered by local chiefs called '*Imák*,' who again are subordinate to the two governors above mentioned." He further adds that "the Sálárs know themselves as *Mumin*, or 'the Faithful,' an Arabic word." Salar is, however, found as the name of one of the great Turkoman tribes now under Russian rule and residing around old Sarakhs, and numbering about five thousand families. The three nations of the Salars are named Yalawach, Githara, and Karawan. They have an evil reputation even among Turkomans, and are said to be generally hated. Lieut. A. C. Yate, *Travels with the Afghan Boundary Commission*, 301. M. P. M. Lessar calls them Salyrs, estimates them at five thousand seven hundred kebitkas (in 1882), and says they are the weakest of the Turkoman tribes. *Proc. Roy. Geog. Soc.*, V, 11. See also W. W. Rockhill, *The Land of the Lamas*, 39 et seq.

chia, Némen, Ch'ing-shui, Munta, Tsuchi, Antasu and Ch'a-chia. Kä-tzŭ kun is the oldest and largest; it is said to have over thirteen hundred families living in it.

We left Ka I-ma-mu chuang by the same road we had come by. While getting up the steep river bank my instruments came very near being ruined by the pack saddle turning and the horse carrying it thrown into a deep rift in the loess; fortunately he fell on his back and as the whole load was, in his struggles, shifted around to his belly, nothing was materially damaged, but we had a hard time getting the load and the pony out of the hole.

It was necessary in passing at Kan-tu to ask the officer commanding the post (a Ch'ien-tsung) to supply a guide to take us over the mountains and find us a resting place in whatever Kargan village we might have to put up in. This he at once did and we pushed on without any loss of time. By an easy ascent we reached the top of a short valley, the Radzu-p'o, near which is a large Kargan hamlet, one of the thirty-eight inhabited by this tribe of Tibetans, and then, following the crest of the hills we finally descended to the village of Rdo lung ("Stony Valley") and got good accommodations in the house of the chief, who has, by the way, the Chinese rank of Po-chang or "Head of Hundred."

The Kargan have for the most part been converted to Islamism by the Salar, though a small portion of the tribe has remained Buddhist.

The Kargan women have adopted, in a measure, the Salar dress with a little more color about it, They wear a long gown of dark blue, broad trousers and their hair is done up in a knot at the back of the head, with a crown of red cloth bound around it and showing the hair through the middle, and a big silver needle is stuck diagonally through the hair on the crown of the head. The men wear the pointed Tibetan cap, short woollen jackets with red collars, and a kind of Tibetan boot with red, blue and white cotton tops.

Their language is a mixture of Tibetan and Chinese. Thus they say *ta lu ré*, "This is the highroad;" *chi-gi ré*, "How many are there?" etc., etc.

The men among the Kargan and other Fan-tzŭ tribes of this region occupy themselves making or repelling attacks on neighboring villages, keeping watch over their homes and property, and so have been obliged—unquestionably to their great regret, to abandon all the work, both at home and in the fields, to the women. In doing so they have also copied the example of their religious teachers, the Salars.

It is difficult to get any idea of the number of these Mohammedan Tibetans, for Chinese Mohammedans include them among the Huei-huei, and only call Fan-tzŭ those among them who have not come into the fold of Islam.

The Kargan have but a very few sheep. They are tillers of the soil (*rongwa*), and raise wheat, barley, peas and a few vegetables. Their houses are of the half Tibetan half Chinese style usual in this country, and they (the Mohammedan part of the tribe) are certainly more advanced in civilization than most of their compatriots of the same race who have adhered to the old faith.

We got some excellent bread from the Po-ch'ang. Bread-making is a blessing the Kargan owe to the Mohammedans, for Tibetans are not bread-eaters, or rather bread-makers, as the miserable cake they eat is not worthy of the name.

The Kargan and all Rongwa eat tsamba, but usually dry instead of making it into dough. It is served heaped up in a bowl with some little brass spoons stuck in it. The proper way to eat it is to take a spoonful and throw it into the mouth without letting the spoon touch the lips, and afterwards to take a draught of tea to wash the dry flour down. It is doubtless a cleaner way of eating tsamba than the one usually followed, but I must say I prefer the dirtier method, it is more palatable.

February 23.—Last night was the coldest we have had since leaving Lusar, the thermometer this morning at seven o'clock marked +6°.2 F. After passing over the hills to the west of the village we re-entered the Yellow River Valley; for a while our way led along the crest of some hills from whence I could see that at some comparatively recent geological period the loess must have filled the valley, raising it some five or six hundred feet above its present level. Diluvian rains (such as still occur in summer) perforated the loess, created subterranean streams into which the superincumbent loess finally dropped and was then carried to lower levels; the adjacent loess at the same time subsiding without losing its characteristic stratification and covering the lower rock formations, moulding itself on them. These new loess beds were in turn perforated in the same manner, and so on till the present level was reached. This process is continually going on; I have remarked it at every stage of its progress. The presence of erratic blocks of gneiss and granite at twelve or fifteen hundred feet above the river bed are puzzling, if loess is a subærial deposit, and such blocks are of frequent occurrence in this part of the Yellow River Valley.

We passed through a number of Hsi-fan (Buddhist Kargan) villages. The men of two of these were posted on the hills around their houses and in every coigne of vantage, armed with long matchlocks, swords and spears. They were at war with each other over a question of pasturage; a man or two of one or the other party had been killed each day for the past week. To-day the party whose score was lowest was expected to attack the other to square the reckoning.

Just before crossing the Yellow River to reach Fei-tzŭ-ch'uan,* where we proposed spending the night, we passed through the ruins of what must have been a prefectural city (*Hsien*). The walls, all that now remains of this place, which is called K'ang Ch'eng, are divided in their greatest length at about a third from the southern side by a transversal wall. This Ch'eng occupies a commanding position of great natural strength, the river bluff in front, a steep gorge to the west. It is said to have been built in the T'ang period, sometime in the seventh or eighth century probably.

We crossed the river in front of Fei-tzŭ ch'uan on the ice. The stream is here about fifty yards wide and has a swift current. This point marks approximately the boundary between the Bayan-rong and the Kuei-tê sub-prefectures (*T'ing*). A direct trail leads from Fei-tzŭ ch'uan over the mountains *viâ* Ts'a-pa to Hsi-ning in two days. In coming this way from Ts'a-pa over this route one must follow the Ts'a-pa stream down to its mouth, instead of going eastward up the valley we followed on leaving that place.

In the house where we have put up lives a most intelligent Ahon, he has been to Mecca by way of Russia and the Suez Canal, he told me, but he did not describe his route clearly enough for me to identify many places along it. He said most pilgrims from these parts go to Mecca by way of Shanghai or

* Fei-tzŭ-ch'uan is the Kan-su pronunciation of Shui-ti ch'uan in Pekinese, meaning "water and earth stream" or "valley."

Canton, and the route through Tibet and India does not appear to be ever taken by them. On returning to their country, these Chinese Hadji wear green, black or white turbans.

He told me that in the forty-sixth year of Ch'ien-lung (A. D. 1781) a Salar Ahon called Ma Ming-ching of the village of Su-a-shih, fomented a rebellion which was quickly quelled by the Chinese troops. Ma is said to have disappeared, but this, if I remember rightly, does not agree with the account of his end as contained in Wei Yuan's *Sheng wu-chi.**

The Chinese pâtois spoken here is nearly unintelligible to us. It contains such expressions as *kinder*, "this one," *kunder*, "that one," *she li ka la*, "come in," etc., etc.

February 24.—About two miles west of Fei-tzŭ ch'uan we passed through Kao-chia chuang, a good sized village, where are stationed a lieutenant and fifty soldiers. This village is the last Chinese one we will see until we reach Kuei-tê, all the numerous hamlets we will pass through are T'u-fan or Rongwa ones, and for six miles beyond Kao-chia chuang the valley is thickly studded with them.† The largest village we saw to-day was that of Li chia. The males of this place were in arms and stationed on every hillock round about. They had killed yesterday two men of a neighboring village, with which they have a long-standing feud, and were expecting to be attacked to-day by the dead men's clansmen.

After passing this village we entered the Li chia gorges (*hsia*), about a mile and a half long, formed by a ridge of schist and coarse red granite, which here cuts the valley from north to south. The trail is at this point very bad and extremely narrow, in some places barely wide enough to admit of a loaded horse pushing along it; with that it is several hundred feet above the river which tumbles along over huge boulders at the base of the rocks; when snow is on the ground it must be a very disagreeable path to travel over.

A little beyond the gorge we turned to the south, up a lateral valley, its mouth marked by coarse red sandstone bluffs and boulders of weird shapes resembling those of the Garden of the

* Cf. *Land of the Lamas*, 40, and *Sheng wu shi*, VII, p. 35 et seq.

† Kao-chia chuang means "the village of the Kao clan," Li chia chuang, "the village of the Li clan." Tibetans, with the exception of these tribes, have no family or clan names.

Gods at Manitou (Colorado). This valley is thickly wooded with shrubs in the lower part, and with pines, spruce and birch trees in the upper portions.* I was surprised to find many of the shrubs and birch trees budding; though it is true that these little valleys, all trending north and south, are admirably protected from the prevailing westerly winds. We followed it up for several miles and then, passing by a low *col* into an adjacent one to the west, reached the little Rongwa village of Ssŭ-ké (or Sé-kê).

We experienced some difficulty in gaining admittance to a house as the inmates feared I was one of the Hsi-ning T'ung-shih,† and that they would consequently be squeezed and have to supply me with *ula*. Finally we got into one, by offering to pay my board bill in advance, and in a few minutes I was on the best of terms with the woman who owned it. The people here are all Bönbo and there are several lamas of that sect living in adjacent houses.‡ In one end of the house (it is of logs and is not divided off into rooms; one end is a stable, the other a dwelling) was a big Tibetan stove that heats, by means of flues, a Chinese sleeping *k'ang* placed behind it. I noticed a little altar in a corner with a wooden bowl on it filled with grain, wool and yak hair, first fruit offerings probably, and beside it lay a *damaru* ‖ and a couple of grimy volumes of Bönbo sacred literature. One of these I examined; it was a funeral service and was in the usual Bönbo jargon, three-fourths Buddhistic in its nomenclature and phraseology.§ The altar and books belonged to a lama who came in later on to have a talk. He asked for some rice to offer on the altar, in exchange for which he gave me some butter and *ma-hua-erh*, wheat cakes made in long strips plaited together, and cooked crisp in hemp oil; a favorite dish all over China, Mongolia and Tibet.

Over the stove hung a small prayer-wheel which turned in the heated air as it ascended toward the big smoke hole in the roof.

* On the flora of this section of country, see Prjevalsky, *Reise am oberen Lauf des Gelben Flusses*, 216 et seq.

† Interpreter attached to the Ya-mên of the Hsi-ning Amban. See *Land of the Lamas*, 52 et passim.

‡ Prjevalsky, *op. sup. cit.*, 198, makes mention of these "Shamans," and of their powers as medicine men.

‖ Small hand drum used by both Buddhist and Bönbo lamas.

§ Its title was *Zab-ch'os dji k'rod gngos-pa rang-grol-las sngon tur gro-vai ch'os spyod bag-ch'ags rang grol.* The colophan read *Rdo-rje kro-po lod-kyis mai sgrib spung-du par-du bsgrubs.*

There were also on the bank of the brook which tumbled down the hill beside the hamlet, wheels (or rather barrels) turning by water; and similar ones are to be seen in or near all these Rongwa villages. They occupy little log hutches, and turn by a horizontal overshot water-wheel, the axis of the wheel and the prayer barrel being the same. In front of each house is an incense burner where spines of juniper (*shuka*) are burnt morning and evening in honor of the tutelary and household gods.

These Rongwa show considerable ingenuity in carrying water to their little fields along the hillsides; they use troughs dug out of long logs or poles supported where necessary on high props, to carry the water on to the fields and also from one side of the valley to the other.*

To finish up the evening we had singing, and I awarded prizes to the best singers, or rather to those who sang the longest. The singing was very poor, the best performer was one of my men; he improvised his songs as he went along, but none of them had anything in the world to commed them, not the smallest poetic idea or even originality, but every one was delighted with the performance.

I should not omit mentioning that a few miles after leaving Fei-tzŭ ch'uan we passed in front of a large lamasery perched on the summit of a very steep hill, some eight hundred feet high, towering above the left bank of the Yellow River. It was the Sachung (or Shachung) gomba of the orthodox Gélupa sect and has some fifteen hundred lamas. It ranks third among the lamaseries of this sect in Amdo, the first being Kumbum and the second Labrang.† It has a small gilt-tiled roof temple (*chin wa ssŭ*), but though its

* R. B. Shaw, *op. cit.*, p. 311, speaks on the authority of some Salars whom he met at Yarkand, of the following tribes living near the Salar, "the Daza, Si-fan or Ch'uan Rung, Khun-mo, Kopa and Turun." The first are the Mongols, Ta-tzŭ or Meng-ku, Ta-tzŭ being the usual name given that people by the Chinese. Of the Si-fan I need say nothing here, having discussed the term in other works. The term Chuan Rung is either an opprobrious one given them by the Chinese and meaning, as Shaw states, "Dog Rongwa," or else it is a hybrid term, *Ch'uan* in Chinese and *Rong* in Tibetan, both meaning a fertile valley fit for agriculture. The Khun-mo are in all likelihood the K'amba, the Kopa are the central Tibetan people called in Amdo Gopa, and the Turun are the aboriginal tribes called by the Chinese T'u-jen.

† Labrang (written in Tibetan *bla-brang*) means "the residence of an ecclesiastical dignitary," the French term "palais épiscopal" corresponds exactly to it. The real name of this famous lamasery is, I believe, Trashi-chyil (Bkra-shis k'yil).

possession is a source of pride to the inmates of the Gomba, it is not to be spoken of in the same breath with the great prototype of such edifices at Kumbum.

Some 30 or 40 *li* west of this lamasery, and on the north side of the river, is a Bönbo lamasery with some two hundred inmates; it has a printing establishment. The most famous Bönbo lamasery in this border-land is, I have been told, a day's ride south of Sung-pan T'ing in northwest Ssŭ-ch'uan. It is called Jarang gomba and has some two hundred *akas** in it.

The Kuei-tê Rongwa carry on a considerable business with Lusar, Kuei-tê and Hsi-ning in birch wood ladles, yokes, wheel tires, pestles, etc. They themselves use birch bark to make little buckets and ladles, sewing it with woollen thread or else with strips of bark. These utensils are very roughly made. The birch tree is called *hua shu* in Chinese, and in the Tibetan of these parts, *to-hua*.† The pine tree they call *sumba* (Chinese *sung*), and the poplar *maha* (in Chinese *liu yang*).

February 26.—I got some good photographs of the villagers this morning. I find the best way to get them to stand for their photographs is to tell them that the Kodak is a toy, a kind of telescope, in which one sees the object in the finder instead of having to hold the apparatus to the eye. I have only to ask one of them to come and see for himself, and telling the person whom I want to photograph to stand still so that his friend may see him, while the first looks in the finder I push the button. This simple method never fails.

One of the inhabitants showed me how he hollowed out mortars from birch logs. He placed a short section (about six inches in diameter) of the trunk between his feet, and with a bit of hoop iron sharpened on one edge and fixed in the end of a handle about two feet long, he, little by little, scooped the wood out of the

* The term *aka* is used in Tibetan as a general term for all lamas. This latter term is only used to designate the ordained monks or gélong. Prjevalsky says that the "Tangutans" salute each other by saying "*Aka dĕmo.*" This is not quite correct; the words used are *aku dĕmo*, *aku* is the Kokonor Tibetan equivalent of the Central Tibetan *Ku-zu* (*sku gzugs*) meaning "body," "is your person well," —just as the Chinese say "*shen shang hao.*"

† In the Bat'ang country birch bark utensils are also in common use. See plate XXIII. At Lit'ang the birch tree is called *drapo*, but Jaeschke gives *ta-pa* (*stag-pa*), in which we probably have the correct form of *to-hua*.

center till he had hollowed out a mortar. The ladles, yokes, etc., are made with adzes and axes of Chinese manufacture.

From Ssŭ-ké the trail (it is in reality the highroad between Hsün-hua T'ing and Kuei-tê) led over a *col* into a deep gorge, and then through birch woods to the top of the Ts'a-ma shan from where we could see Kuei-tê, some fifteen miles away. The descent from this pass to the valley was about four and a half miles long, extremely rugged and precipitous, and I should say that in wet weather or when snow covers the ground it would be impassable.

In the valley around Kuei-tê the river débris is at least a hundred feet deep, and consists of angular stones brought down from the adjacent mountains, and rolled pebbles. The valley is, about the town, between two and three miles wide, and, wherever possible, under cultivation, irrigation being, of course, used. Numerous Fan-tzŭ hamlets of eight or ten houses with a few knarled poplars and fruit trees growing around them, are passed before one reaches the little town itself The fields are now being irrigated, and the road is turned into an irrigation ditch.

Kuei-tê* I found smaller than Bayan-rong; inside the wall is the Ya-mên and the garrison's quarters, in the faubourg to the east and south of the ch'eng are a couple of hundred families of Ta-chiao Chinese and one family of Mohammedans (La chia) of about forty members, which is a *Hsieh-chia* family (or brokers for Tibetans who resort to this place). Mohammedans have not been allowed to live here since the rebellion, when they killed the official commanding here and had to flee.

We found lodgings in a fine inn in the suburbs, but experienced great difficulty in getting any food, there was no bread to be bought, as the people here only eat *man-t'ou* or "steamed bread," no rice, no millet, tsamba or even *mien*. We have fortunately been faring well all along the road wherever we have stopped, for none of my men can cook; but here no one will cook for us and so we

* Prjevalsky, *op. sup. cit.*, 215, reckons the population of Kuei-tê at about seven thousand souls, one half Chinese the other Kara Tangutans of the Dunzsu (*sic*) tribe. The women, he adds, were much more numerous than the men. This was in 1880. The present population is, all the adjacent villages included, certainly less than this. As to his Dunzsu I am unable to explain this term, though it would seem to be a Chinese one. It is, I think, misleading to call Kuei-tê an oasis as Prjevalsky does.

had to go to bed feeling rather grumpy, and after having supped on tea and bits of biscuit found in the bottom of my saddle-bags.

February 27.—The principal trade of Kuei-tê is in lamb skins; a little musk is also brought here, and wool is becoming an important staple of trade, but the Tibetans have suddenly got such wild ideas of the great price foreigners are willing to pay for it, that they are holding it back and refusing to sell any for three or four times the price they would gladly have accepted three years ago.

Pears, peaches, apples, jujubes, watermelons,* are grown here, as is also a little cotton, but of a poor quality. Wheat, millet, hemp, broad beans and peas are the principal crops, and good potatoes sell for six or seven cash a pound. Cabbages, onions and a few other vegetables are also plentiful, at least I hear all this, but I regret to say that with the exception of a few potatoes and a couple of hard pears I have had no corroborative evidence of the truth of my informant's statements. Every thing else is very dear, more than the short distance from here to the place of production and purchase (Hsi-ning) would seem to justify.

A little dried rhubarb root goes from here to Hsi-ning and thence eastward, There are several thousand pounds of it ready for shipment in the inn in which we are stopping. Travel to Lan-chou and all points east of here is usually done by way of Lusar and Hsi-ning, as the trail down the Huang ho valley is too bad.

A hundred steps from my door in a little cage tied to the end of a pole, is the head of a T'u-fan of this place, who three years ago tried to stir up a rebellion. His bleached and grimacing skull tells of the fate which overtook him and his plans of ambition and reform.

Kuei-tê T'ing is officially designated as a *Fan chŭn min fu*, "a military sub-prefecture for keeping the savages in order." There are twenty-four lamaseries in the sub-prefecture, with several thousand lamas and ever so many incarnate saints (*huo Fo*). The Chinese spoken here is of the same description as that I noted at Fei-tzŭ ch'uan, though it differs considerably from it—wonderfully so, considering that the two places are hardly thirty miles apart.

* Cf. Prjevalsky, *op. sup. cit.*, 215 et seq. He says that not only watermelons but melons grow here, also apricots and a small variety of cherry.

Thus, they say here ***kushli***, "that;" ***kuerh***, "this;" ***ku-ak-shli***, "who is this?" ***ma-la***, "early morning," etc., etc.

West of Kuei-tê on the Yellow River, distant a two days' ride, is Gomi Wahon—called on our maps Balekun Gomi and inhabited by tent-living Tibetans (Hsi-fan). There is a trail leading directly from Kuei-tê to Tankar, *viâ* Sharakuto and passing by Ka (or "little") Gomi or Gomi t'ang five miles north of the Yellow River.*

Two Bõnbo lamas came to-day and sat in the inn-yard for a while, and I got a couple of shots at them with my kodak. They are very numerous around here and are very popular with the agricultural Tibetans, but not so much so with the pastoral tribes, who nearly all belong to the Gélupa sect of the orthodox Buddhist Church.

Very little snow or rain falls, I am told, at Kuei-tê, but at present, though the soil is clear of snow (in fact the buds on the trees are beginning to swell), it is thick on the mountain sides all around. It is a fearfully windy place and the people all insisted, when I asked the direction of the prevailing winds, that it prevailed from every quarter.

In the afternoon to-day while on a walk through the town, I met a big Tibetan chief on the street, and asked him to come and take tea with me at the inn. He was a wizzened up old fellow of about fifty-five, with a very bright and cunning eye. His name is Lu-bum ku,† and he is the great chief of the Panaka south of the Yellow River, and a friend of my old acquaintance Nyam-ts'o Pur-dung, of whom he reminded me strongly in his manners. He offered to take me through his country and to make my stay there agreeable, and I was sorry I had to decline his offer, as I have always found these Panaka chiefs reliable ***when*** once they had given their word.

In the evening—to wind up a well employed day, I got together in my lodgings, all the muleteers in the inn, gave them a feed and lots to drink and got two Tibetan women from the hills to sing and dance for us. The singing was of the usual miserable style, and the dancing, or posturing and shuffling about, as poor as

---

* Ka gomi is Prjevalsky's Cha gomi. He says that Kuei-tê is 69 Kilometers from Balekun gomi. See Prjevalsky, *op. sup. cit.*, pp. 214, 215.

† Meaning, probably, "Body of ten thousand Nagas."

the singing. The women got very drunk and I had to turn them out after awhile. In their song, in which first one woman sang a verse (which she improvised), and then the other, they spoke of mountains, living Buddhas, horses, saddles, temples, a hotchpot of everything they hold beautiful, with feeble attempts at descriptions of each. The dancing consisted chiefly in swinging the arms and body slowly about, one dancer walking around the other, a poor attempt at a darkey shuffle. None but the Kuei-tê Tibetans have this dance, which they have borrowed from the Chinese of this town.

February 28.—We left this morning for home (*i. e.* Lusar), after being delayed some time getting an order (*piao*) for the ferry boat to take us across the Yellow River.* This boat is supposed to take every one across free of charge and whenever called upon, but the boatmen squeeze travelers terribly and delay taking them across until well paid for so doing. The *piao* got us taken across at once, and I was pleased to be able to carry a lot of poor pilgrims and travelers at the same time over with me.

We followed down the left bank of the river, through willow brush (*sha-liu*), sand and gravel, until nearly opposite the Ts'a-ma shan, which we had crossed on the twenty-sixth, and then turning up a valley leading to the La-chih yahu or La-jé la in the Nan-shan, ascended as far as the village of Kajang (Szechenyi's Kaschan) where we stopped for the night.

The road all the way from the Yellow River to Kajang was in a loess-covered valley, showing a good deal of clay and red conglomerate. The bottom of the valley was filled in places, and to a depth of several hundred feet, with angular bits of stone, granite, gneiss, etc., brought down probably from the summits of the main range to the north by the summer rains, after being detached by the action of the cold.

We passed quite a number of Fan-tzŭ villages near which I noticed *obos*,† in the tops of which were stuck amidst the brush-

* Prjevalsky, *op. sup. cit.*, 215, makes out the Huang ho at Kuei-tê to be 108 meters (354 feet) broad. He gives in the same passage as the altitude of the town above sea level 7,183 feet. Elsewhere he makes it out to be 7,500 feet. My observations place the town at 7,634 feet above the sea.

† *Obos* or stone piles erected on the top of passes or near temples or sacred structures. They are also known in Tibetan as *lab-ts'e*. Obo is the Mongol name for hem. It is probably the Tibetan word *do*, meaning "a pile of stones."

wood always put there, huge wooden arrows, some of them twenty feet long. On the brushwood were hanging thousands of little tufts of wool, taken probably by shepherds from their sheep as they passed the sacred spot,* and little pieces of cotton on which charms are printed (*lung-ta*) hanging from long strings running from the *obo* to some adjacent tree or rock. I could not learn whether these *obo* with these peculiar arrows were built by Bönbo or Buddhists. Many prayer-wheels turned by water, and receptacles for *tsa-tsa* † (*tsa-tsa k'ang-ba*) made of logs and looking like diminutive cabins were also very numerous all the way up.

Kajang (or Karang) comprises two villages or rather hamlets, Lower Kajang and Kajang Ch'ien-hu, a quarter of a mile higher up the valley. We stopped at the first named place, where live six or eight families of Chinese and where there are two inns. In the other village, which is on the west side of the valley, lives the native chief, who has the rank or title of Ch'ien-hu or "Thousand Families."

On the west side of the valley facing Lower Kajang are extensive ruins of what I took to be an old Chinese fortified camp or Ch'eng, but of which I could learn nothing save the name, Ku Ch'eng (*i. e.*, "Old Town,") in Chinese and Ch'e-rgya t'ang, in Tibetan.

February 29.—Last night two men belonging to the La-chia Hsieh-chia of Kuei-tê, who are accompanying us over to Lusar, told me that the profits they derived from their business at Kuei-tê have been very much reduced on account of all the members of their clan having a share in them. They have to keep open house for Tibetans, supplying them during their sojourn at Kuei-tê not only with lodgings for man and beast, but also with food. Then the Ya-mên has to get its squeezes, and so do various other parties, and the Hsieh-chia have little left. And all this simply because

* On the habit of hanging bits of rag or a little wool on sacred monuments confer the custom as known in Mohammedan countries, and also Emil Schlagintweit, *Buddhism in Tibet*, p. 198. The custom is not unknown in Christian countries. See a note by W. Copeland Borlase on "Rag Offerings and Primitive Pilgrimages in Ireland," *Athenæum*, April 1, 1893, 415–416.

† Little clay cones usually made in moulds and deposited either in these special hutches or else in ch'örtens. See *Land of the Lamas*, 257.

being born in a family occupied at a certain trade, every member had rather attach himself to this same business than strike out for himself; this is Kan-su enterprise!

My man Hai Chi-hsiang is a Hsieh-chia, but his father deemed it advisable to take up some other calling in life, so, he being a Bachelor of Arts (*Hsiu-ts'ai*), joined a profession where brains are requisite, and opened an "office for the protection of families" (*pao-chia chü*) *alias* a blackmailing agency. When he sees two men quarreling on the street, he threatens to hand them over to the authorities unless they pay him a certain amount. If a couple of young men are seen gambling or violating any of the innumerable municipal ordinances, half of which have "fallen long ago into inocuous desuetude," he bobs up and threatens his victims with exposure and gets a few cash out of them. Strange as it may seem such Pao-chia chü are common all over northern China.

About four miles above Kajang the valley forks, and we see the La-jé Pass (in Chinese La-chih yahu) about two miles to the north-east. At this point in the valley there is a fort commanded by a Ch'ien-tsung with some eighty to a hundred soldiers; it is called Ch'ien-hu Ch'eng, "The Camp of the Thousand Families," referring to the designation of this district, or rather to the title of its native chief. Such forts are innumerable all over western Kan-su, but the presence of these soldiers is only so far of use that it prevents the population rebelling against the imperial authority, otherwise acts of violence may occur daily, hourly, in the immediate vicinity of these forts among the Salars, or Tibetans, and the troops will not interfere—it is only "a fight among Fan-tzŭ and unworthy of notice."

The ascent of the La-chih shan was very steep but over a good trail; the descent was precipitous, and, as the gorge down which we had to go was filled with ice, on top of which was a little water, it was very bad going. At the mouth of this gorge we passed through the Nan-mên ("South Gate") in the Great Wall (*Wan-li ch'eng*), which passes at Lusar and goes thence by Ch'en-hai P'u to Ts'ama-lung at the eastern end of the defile leading to Tankar. We were now in the Nan-ch'uan valley, which has its mouth at Hsi-ning. Passing through the village of Djaya, I went up the valley a couple of miles to visit a place of great interest to me, Ch'ü-k'or t'ang, where Huc passed several months waiting for the arrival on the Kokonor of the great caravan on its way to

Lh'asa.* The name Ch'u-k'or tang ("plain of the prayer-wheel") belongs properly to a T'u-fan village near a little lamasery consisting of half a dozen white washed houses perched on some shelves of rock a hundred feet or so above the valley, and which is called Ch'ing fang meaning, probably, "Abode of Purity."

I was told that in 1890 the Grijimailo brothers staid eight or ten days here collecting birds and plants. They were not mentioned by name, but from the description given me I cannot doubt that they were the "Olosu" referred to.

I arrived at Lusar at dusk and was pleased to learn that a Mr. Rijnhardt, of the China Inland Mission, had come from Hsi-ning to bring me the money I had asked for at Lan-chou. Not finding me at Lusar, he returned yesterday to Hsi-ning where I will have to go and see him.

March 1.—I found out this morning that my cook, Kao pa-erh, whom I had brought from Kuei-hua Ch'eng and had left here while I was away to look after my things, has been looking into them besides, had promenaded about bedecked in all my finery, been out shooting the vultures around Kumbum, much to the dismay of the lamas, for they are *quasi* sacred, being the last, though temporary, resting place of most deceased lamas. To one man he had lent one of my ponies, to another he had given some of my clothes, and to all he had said that we were such devoted friends that what was mine was his. I called him up, gave him a good rating and told him that I would abandon him here to get back to Kuei-hua as best he could, with neither money nor clothing. for I would not pay him any wages, and the clothes on his back were all mine, paid for with my money and only lent to him. I have no intention of carrying out this threat, it would be biting my nose to spite my face with a vengeance. I have at best to eat bad food made with poor materials, and he knows how to prepare very tasty messes, such as no one I could get could

* Huc, *op. cit.*, II, 145 et seq. He calls it Tchogortan. His "grande montagne taillée à pic," in the flank of which are the dwellings of the lamas who live in this place, is only a cliff some 200 feet high. This little lamasery was destroyed in part during the late rebellion, but from Huc's description of it I doubt if it was any larger in his day or different from what it now is, though he seems to imply that there was a building in the bottom of the valley at the foot of the cliff, in which the hermits lived. I could find no trace of any such building.

possibly make. I cannot punish myself to the extent of dismissing him, but I will wait for all my men to come and beg me to keep him, which they will surely do, though to-day they all vow that dismissal is too light a punishment for him.

During my recent trip we were four men with five horses, and got all our food at the inns where we stopped and also feed for our horses, yet the expenses for all have only been a tael of silver ($1.15) a day. This was because I managed the whole thing myself, and no squeezing was possible.

March 2.—I went to-day to Hsi-ning to get my money at the China Inland Mission house, where I found Messrs. Hale and Rijnhardt. The latter had kindly ridden all the way from Lanchou here to bring me my money. I asked him to come and pay me a visit at Lusar, and we will ride up there together to-morrow.

I put up at the inn where I have always stopped, and was so fortunate as to secure a copy of the "New description of the Hsi-ning Department" (*Hsi-ning Fu hsin chih*) for 18 taels.* It is very rare, as the blocks and nearly all existing copies were destroyed in the burning of the Ya-mên during the Mohammedan rebellion. It was written by a Tao-t'ai called Yang in the Ch'ien-lung reign, and contains much valuable information on this frontier country, its inhabitants, monuments, ethnology, etc., besides valuable itineraries to Tibet, etc.

The son of my former friend, Fu T'ung-shih, came to see me to-day, and I gave him some presents for transmission to his father who has not come back from K'amdo since we went there together in 1889, and also some for himself. I suppose the father has made a pretty good thing out of his three years of foreign service in a country where he can play the big man.

March 3.—I got back at dusk to Lusar accompanied by Rijnhardt who cut a funny figure riding with very long stirrups a diminutive pony of mine, and looking very foreign, notwithstanding his Chinese rig and surroundings.

Yeh Hsien-sheng, who had accompanied me to Hsi-ning, did not come back with me, as he had difficulty in settling up our

* This book, together with a number of other things, were sent by me to Lan-chou to be taken to Shanghai by Mr. Brown. The boat in which he descended the Yang-tzŭ kiang capsized, and this valuable work and a number of other things, I am sorry to say, were completely ruined.

1. Brass kettle, used in Mongolia and Koko nor. (U. S. N. M. 167221.)
2. Copper pot (Koko nor). (U. S. N. M. 131187.)
3. Red leather and leopard skin tsamba bag. (U. S. N. M. 131201.)
4. Copper kettle (Shigatsé). (U. S. N. M. 131188.)
5. Goatskin bellows. (U. S. N. M. 131043.)

accounts with the inn-keeper Ma Shao-lin, who was short of money, and did not want to pay me back 50 taels I had lent him in February to help him settle his accounts at the New Year.

I have put all my money matters into the hands of the Hsien-sheng who is the best and most reliable fellow I have met with in China, and for whom I have a very soft spot in my heart.

March 4.—Most of my time to-day has been spent in repacking my boxes, weighing them so as to apportion the loads, and fixing everything for the start. All the things I don't require, together with the things I have bought on the way, I am sending down to Shang-hai.

Besides the camp outfit, bought at Kuei-hua Ch'eng, I have got here the following supplies which I have had packed in leather bags such as are in universal use in Tibet and Western Mongolia.

191 Catties * of tsamba (*t'sao mien*).
160 " " flour.
45 " " candles (five to a catty).
42 " " ch'i-tzŭ (kind of little biscuit).
140 " " rice.
50 " " vermicelli (*kua-mien*).
80 " " *fu ch'a*, brick tea (for barter).
20 " " " " " (for use of party).
20 " " brown sugar.
20 " " Hami raisins.
5 " " rock candy (*ping t'ang*).
5 " " candied jujubes (*mi tsao*).
5 " " candied apples, apricots, etc.
25 " " butter.
4 " " tobacco, (*tsa-pa yen*).
4 " " Chinese condiments, ginger, red pepper paste, *kan fen* (a kind of vermicelli), vinegar, onions, etc., etc., and a few other odds and ends.
5 pecks chuoma (*potentilla anserina*).
5 " dry jujubes.

*A catty (*chin* in Chinese) weighs about 1⅓lbs.

Besides these I have six boxes containing goods for barter,* and for presents, my papers, change of foreign clothing, money, horse-shoes, shoeing outfit, etc., etc., weighing altogether three hundred and thirty-six catties or about four hundred and fifty pounds.

The two tents, each with thirteen iron pegs and a hammer, weigh together sixty-six catties, and the kettle, ladles, tongues, grate, teapots and *batterie de cuisine* in general about twenty-five more.

There are six riding saddles of Tibetan pattern, which I have found much less apt to rub horses' backs than the Chinese or Mongol kinds, seven pack saddles, also of Tibetan type, five pair iron chain-hobbles with padlocks, the same number of yak-hair hobbles, and a supply of thick, soft felt for repairing packs, plenty of hair rope and pack thread. I have also provided a suit of summer clothing and two pairs of boots for each man.

Our armament consists of two forty-four calibre Winchester carbines, a ten bore Scott shotgun and a forty-four calibre Colt's revolver; I have also a Remington forty-four calibre rifle with one hundred cartridges to present to the Dzassak of Baron Ts'aidam, to whom I promised it in '89, and a small revolver for his steward Dowé, who guided me in '89 from the Ts'aidam to Jyäkundo.

I have five hundred rounds of Winchester ammunition, twenty-five ten guage cartridges loaded with buck-shot and two hundred loaded with No. 4.

Altogether I have reason to believe that my preparations are complete in every respect, save perhaps money, of which I have only about 700 taels. I have been careful to take two of every essential article, so that I will be able to split up my party and make rapid trips away from the main route without putting the men left behind to any inconvenience.

March 5.—Yeh Hsien-sheng brought in to-day a fine mule which he bought for 25 taels at Hsi-ning. He left a little later in

* A full list of these would take up too much space, but I can recommend to travelers going into Tibet the following articles: Satin ribbon 3 inches wide (red, blue, yellow and green are the colors preferred); flat mother-of-pearl buttons, large needles, thread, small Japanese lacquer rice bowls, gunpowder, razors (Chinese), copper wire, pocket looking-glasses, snuff, Chinese mouthpieces for pipes, thumb-rings, snuff bottles, hatchets, *hsiang-pien* tea, broadcloth (red and purple), jack-knives.

the day for Chen-hai P'u and Toba, where he hopes to be able to buy a few more mules at moderate prices.

I have been shown a copy of Tsong-k'apa's *Sung-bum*,* printed here, it is a cumbrous work in sixteen volumes printed on thin Chinese paper, the leaves of Tibetan size and shape, two feet long by four inches broad. It costs between 60 and 80 taels, so I cannot, to my regret, buy it.

The organization of Kumbum (which may be taken as the prototype of all large Gélupa lamaseries) is as follows:—The elders (*Rgan pa*) of the lamasery appoint, for terms of three years, four officers who manage the temporal affairs of the convent and who are respectively called Ta Lao-yeh, Erh Lao-yeh, San Lao-yeh and Ssŭ Lao-yeh. The first looks after the finances, the second after all such things as come under the cognizance of the Hsi-ning Amban's Ya-mên, the third Lao-yeh attends to the convent's trading with the Mongols and Tibetans, and the fourth Lao-yeh is steward of the University or La-lang and regulates the fare to be supplied the members on the rolls of the different colleges, to one of which all lamas must belong.

Besides these four officials there are magistrates or lama officers (*Seng kuan*), also chosen by the Rgan-pa for three years, and called Gékor, whose duty it is to see that the rules and regulations are observed by the *akas*, and who have, as assistants, the Ch'ü-lin-ba, called by the Chinese Hei ho-shang, or "Black lamas," who are primarily water-carriers,† as their name implies, but are chiefly known as the Gékor's executioners and assistants.

The four colleges composing the university are each presided over by a lama with the title of *Ji-wa*, and the name Lar rgyad, or "Eight-Lar," is applied to the establishment and directors collectively. The great college or Iké La-lang is managed by an Iké Ji-wa who is also Proctor of the University. The second is the medical school or Män-ba La-lang with a Män-ba Ji-wa at the head, the third is the Ch'ü-ba La-lang or theological school and is under the rule of a Ch'ü-ba Ji-wa, and the fourth Ji-wa manages

* This is the most famous work by the great reformer Tsong-k'apa, who lived in the 14th century, and was a native of Kumbum. His Lam rim ch'en-po ranks next in importance to his Sung-bum.

† Carrying water to fill the big tea cauldrons from which the lamas employed in reading the sacred books are daily supplied.

the Teng-kor La-lang or college of contemplation (or asceticism).* These positions, which are of profit as well as honor, are reserved for Chinese *akas* of the Hsi-ning circuit, such people being known as the *Li t'su* ("inner tribes"), while all Panaka and Mongols, called generically *Wai tsu* or "outside tribes," are excluded from them, and even the San-ch'uanese and other T'u-jen are comprised in this latter class.

In the fourth moon of every year each college sends out its agents among the Panaka and Mongols to collect donations for the support of the institution. They assess each tent or home according to its means, and to one they present a piece of cotton cloth (*lao pu*), which obliges the receiver to give as a return present a horse; to another family they present a pair of boots which is acknowledged by handing them an ox, and so on. Returning to Kumbum in the eighth moon, with the horses, cattle, sheep, butter, wool, etc., they have thus obtained, the live stock is sold at a good price to Chinese who, when known to the San Lao-yeh, are given easy terms for payment.

All lamas whose names are on the rolls (*t'o*) of the lamasery receive daily allowances of tea and a yearly allowance of meal, the tea is brought to them daily in the buildings where they prosecute their studies, and they on their side bring there with them their tsamba and butter. There are three thousand seven hundred lamas at Kumbum.

---

* Conf. as to the organization of this famous lamasery, Huc, *op. cit.*, II, 119 et seq. Sarat Chandra Das, speaking of the theological studies pursued by the lamas of Tashil'unpo, says: "For a period of three years from the date of entrance they are regarded as *Rig-ch'ung* or monks of the primary stage, after which they are called *Rig-ding*, *i. e.*, those of middle stage. Monks of five years' standing are called *Rig-ch'en*, *i. e.*, monks of the higher stage. They are permitted to pass an examination in the sacred books to obtain the rank of *P'al-chenpa*. The most intelligent among the *P'al-chenpa* go up for the degree of *Kah-chan* (called *Rab-champa* at Lh'asa), which is something like the degree of D. D. Those who fail in this examination go to the Buddhist college of Gyantsé, where there are eighteen *Ta-tshangs* or classes, to graduate themselves as *Tung-rampa* or Bachelor of Divinity." *Indian Pundits in the Land of Snow*, 8. Speaking of the degrees conferred at Lh'asa, the same writer says: "The *Ge-tshul* (novice monk) goes up for the degrees of *Tung-rampa*, *Kah-chan* or *Rab-champa*, which may be likened to the B. D. and D. D. degrees of the European universities. * * * The successful candidate applies for the highest initiation into the Lamaic order of *Ngag-pa* (esoteric initiation) when he becomes eligible for the posts of *Khan-po* (professor) and Head Lama of a monastery." *Ibid.* 5.

The various high dignitaries of the Gélupa sect, most of whom recognize Kumbum as their *alma mater*, keep up (at their own expense or at that of the tribe among whom they have taken up their abodes) an establishment here known as a K'arwa (*mk'ar-wa*),* where they reside perhaps a portion of the year, and where the people of their district find free board and lodgings. These K'arwa are recognizable by their red painted outside walls and by the front doors opening in the middle, all other buildings having white walls and small doors. There are eighty-three K'arwa at Kumbum, the oldest and first one in importance is the Tsong-k'a k'arwa, dating from the foundation of the lamasery.† The highest dignitary residing in any one of these Kumbum K'arwa is the A-chia Gégen (or Hutuketu),‡ then comes the Pé-chia Fo-yeh and some forty other "Living Buddhas," of high degree.

The lamas who own houses may not receive rent of any kind from those who stop with them, the latter present them with a few presents (*li wu*), and the host makes up for his liberality by the squeezes he is able to make on all the purchases of his guests.

Among the customs peculiar to this great lamasery is the following:—when a lama has committed a crime entailing his expulsion from the lamasery, an arrow is run through his ear,|| the paper wrapper of a brick of tea is put on his head, and he is driven across the bridge on the road to Hsi-ning, which marks the limit of the convent's property in that direction. Cases of murder are disposed of by the Amban at Hsi-ning.

Kao-pa-erh, my cook, condemned recently to dismissal, is trying to ingratiate himself with me by giving me the best dishes he can prepare. By the same irresistible means he has won the men over to his cause, and they have hinted to me that I will find it most uncomfortable in camp without him. I will await a formal

---

* The foot-note on p. 88 of my *Land of the Lamas* should be corrected so as to conform with the explanation of the term *K'arwa* given above.

† Tsong-k'apa derived this name from Tsong-k'a, a village which possibly occupied the spot on which Kumbum now stands. At the Tsong-k'a K'arwa are kept the two big "black snake" whips used by the Hei ho shang. This K'arwa is the only one in the gomba allowed by law to have them.

‡ The village of A-chia or A-chia chuang is only a few miles south of Kumbum.

|| A similar punishment is in vogue in China. The *Shen Pao* of Shanghai, of April 4, 1886, mentions certain criminals at Port Arthur who had arrows run through their ears.

appeal for mercy from the culprit and the other men, so that they may not fully realize my weakness.

March 6.—Yeh Hsien-sheng brought back three more good mules bought at an average price of 27 taels. This is more than I had wanted to give for them, but it is money well invested, if I only get them as far as the Ts'aidam, for even there they are worth twice this amount. I have told him to buy two more, and then my preparations will be complete.

I am waiting for a party of Chamri Fan-tzŭ to arrive here to hire yaks from them to carry my goods and guide me as far as the Muri-Wahon country towards the southwest corner of the Koko-nor. I heard yesterday that they would probably reach Lusar in a day or so. This tribe is the largest one among the Panakasum, and they make themselves everywhere respected—or feared, so to travel in their company will be an additional safeguard in traversing the Koko-nor steppes.

March 7.—Last night as I was going to sleep all my men came in a body and, having kotowed,* besought me not to leave the cook behind, but to pardon him "just this once," and take him along. I said I would give the matter careful consideration, that my word was engaged to dismiss him, and that I could not lightly break it.

This morning the cook came in, made his kotow, admitted that he had behaved very badly, but begged to be forgiven. I gave him a second edition of the sermon I had delivered to him when first found sporting in my clothes, and told him I would take him on probation, adding that should he behave badly again, no matter where we might be, in the wildest part of the wilderness of north Tibet or among the savage Tibetans, I would abandon him to his fate, without money, food or pony, to shift for himself.

* Among themselves Chinese Mohammedans do not kotow, but bow and say, "*Salam aleikum*," to which the reply is, "*Aleikum salam.*" I may note here that among the Hsi-ning Mohammedans the husband and wife do not use in speaking to each other, their *ming-tzŭ* or name, but simply the expletive *hai!* If they have a son, the mother will speak of her husband as the father of so-and-so, and the father will speak of his wife as so-and-so's mother. For example, if the boy is named Erh-li, the father speaking of his wife will call her *Erh-li-ti ma-ma*, and she will speak of him as *Erh-li-li t'a-t'a* or *lei-tei*. Old people who have grandchildren speak of each other as *ani*, "the old woman," and *aje* "the old man." These latter expressions are Tibetan.

Shortly after this my dinner was served, and it was the best I have had since leaving Peking.

To-day I gave each of the men 20 taels on account of wages (they get 5 taels a month), and leave of absence to go say good-bye to their families and settle their affairs. Rijnhardt left for Hsi-ning, so I have seen the last of foreigners for many a long month to come, but I am so accustomed now to being all the time with Asiatics that it is more of a strain to converse with Europeans than with them, more irksome to comply with the foreign customs of the missionaries than with those of Chinese and Tibetans.

March 8.—I went out walking to-day and got some fairly good photographs of Kumbum. The gold-tiled temple had its roof regilded last year and looks very gorgeous. While photographing I was surprised to see a large wolf trotting along not five hundred yards from the lamasery. The lamas do not allow any animals (sheep excepted) to be killed on their property, and so pheasants and wild pigeons wander about its precincts like barn-yard fowls.

To-day was a market-day at the temple and I bought a few odds and ends for my ethnological collection, among other things some large agate beads such as the T'u-fan and Fan-tzŭ women wear on the cloth bands hanging down their backs and fastened to their hair. They come from the Tung-lu (Liao-tung, probably), and are called in the trade *Han ma-nao* (Chinese cornelian ?). Amber in rough pieces is also procurable here. The Fan-tzŭ call it *su-ru*, and when I objected that this was the Tibetan name for "coral," they said that the latter was *hsu-ru*. This may be true here, but su-ru *is* the usual name of coral in Tibet.*

The weather at night has been so cloudy since I have been here that I have had to give up taking observations by stars east and west and confine myself to the sun, which is much more certain, as the days are nearly invariably clear, though often windy.

March 9.—I have invested in another fine mule which, in Tibet, will be worth four times the price I gave for it—if it lives to get there. All caravans going this way to Tibet take as many mules as they can with them, also horses; they consider it the best way to invest their money.

* I know of no name for "amber" in Tibetan. Jaeschke and several other writers give *spos shel*, which means, literally, "perfumed crystal."

I heard this morning that some thirty or forty Na-chia Panaka (living near Muri-Wahon) have arrived here, and are now camped in the ravine above the village, with some two hundred yaks loaded with salt, hides, etc. I intend trying to hire some of their yaks to carry my luggage to their country, as the Chamri I was expecting have not turned up.

I managed to get 105 rupees from a Tankar trader; I wanted some six or seven hundred, as sycee is of little use in Tibet, but they are very scarce this year, much more so than in '89.

March 10.—Ssŭ-shih-wu, who had gone to Shang wu-chuang* to say good-bye to his wife and family got back to-day bringing the pack saddles and crupper-sticks (*ch'iu-kun*) I required. Shang-wu chuang makes a specialty of manufacturing these saddles, which are made of birch wood, also sheath knives and swords for the Tibetans and Mongols. The crupper-stick is universally used for mules throughout China and Tibet, and is also sometimes used on pack horses and yaks; it is a great deal better than the ordinary crupper. Broad breast-bands of wool are always used, no matter what the pack animal may be. Between the two the saddle is kept immovable, and if the pads under the saddle are well aired and scraped, there is little danger of the animal's back ever being galled. Should this, however, occur, the universal practice in these parts is to put warm urine or else tea on the chaffed parts. The former will rapidly reduce any swelling. Throughout China and the adjacent countries mules receive much more care at the hands of their owners than horses, in fact the horse is looked upon as an inferior animal to the mule, and I think deservedly so.

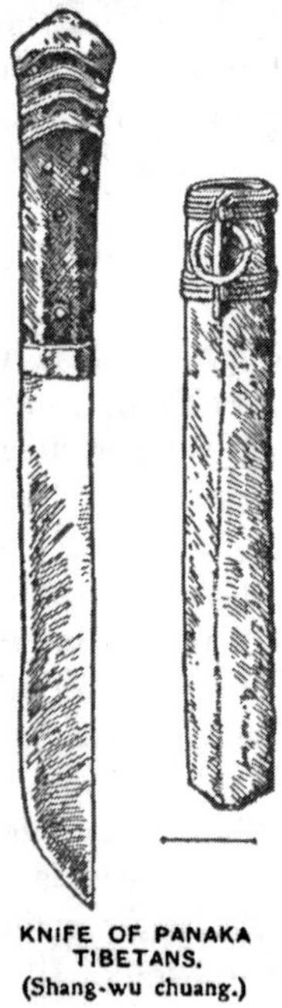

KNIFE OF PANAKA TIBETANS. (Shang-wu chuang.)

March 11.—The headman of the party of Na-chia Panaka I had been expecting, came to see me early this morning, but he could give me no assurance as to when he would be ready to go home,

* A group of five hamlets about fifteen miles north of Chen-hai P'u.

"perhaps we will be ready in ten days, perhaps in a month, the blue sky above only knows;" so we could come to no agreement.

Shortly after he left a Chamri Panaka from somewhere near Kuei-tê came and offered to hire me yaks for two pieces of cotton (*lao pu*) a head, this would be equivalent to 1.2 taels in silver, to go to Muri-Wahon, and I gave him two pieces to clinch the bargain. In the afternoon he came again and returned me the cotton, he could not go, news had just been brought him that his village had got into a fight with a neighboring one, and he had to hurry home to take his part in the scrimmage.

Time being of value, and as I have set my heart on leaving here on the 14th, I sent two of my men to a village not far away called Chung-t'ai, to try and hire yaks from a party of Su-chia Panaka reported to be camped there. They came back towards dark and said that these Panaka being quite as uncertain as to their future movements as those camped here, they had hired donkeys from some of the villagers, for which I am to pay 1 tael a head as far as Muri-Wahon, which district they agree to reach within ten days. This pleases me well, donkeys carry the same loads as yaks (one hundred and sixty pounds) and travel faster and behave on the road in a much more dignified way. Yaks, even the tamest ones, are savage beasts, like their owners.

March 12.—I took all the horses and mules to-day to Toba (Hsin-tseng P'u) to have them shod by a smith of local fame. I was entertained while there by the relatives of Yeh Hsien-sheng, who gave me a good dinner and took me to visit the famous mosque which occupies the center of the little town. It was built, I was told, by order of the Emperor K'ang-hsi in the sixth year of his reign (A. D. 1666), and he also had built the large mosque in the village of Chen-hai P'u* near by. It is faced all over with fine large tiles, with flowers and arabesque designs in various colors on them, and the roof is covered with turquoise blue tiles. All the tile work was made at Ning-hsia. Like all Chinese mosques, it has no minaret, but a little detached pavilion in its stead, with one story reached by a flight of a few steps. The interior of the mosque was, of course, empty, but a tablet with the Emperor's (K'ang-hsi) name or style on it occupied the center. The build-

* Tchin-hai Pou of d'Anville's map. (Carte Genl[e] du Thibet, IV[e] Feuille.)

ing has, in the last twenty odd years, become rather dilapidated, and only recently permission has been granted the Ahons to repair it. A handsome subscription book was shown me, and I contributed my mite towards the much needed work.

The village of Ta-nei-k'ai, about two-thirds of a mile south of Toba on the road to Lusar, is built in the half cave, half house style peculiar to the T'u-jen of this region, but is inhabited by Chinese, or at least by people claiming to belong to that race, in which case it is the only village of this kind inhabited by them in this region. Toba, if my memory serves me right, was a place of some importance in the seventeenth century when the Jesuits make mention of Armenians residing there.*

March 13.—A San-ch'uan T'u-jen came to see me and from him I got a short vocabulary of his language, which is, as I thought, about eight-tenths Mongol, the residue being Tibetan, Chinese and, to the best of my knowledge, a heretofore unknown lingo, probably the original language of the T'u-jen of this part of the Empire.† My informant said the T'u-jen were called in his language *nutan-ni kun*, I fancy that this half Mongol word is but a translation of the Chinese *t'u-jen* or "people of the soil." Curiously enough the word he used for "Tibetan" *Tébé*, is nearer our name

* "Les Armeniens qui étoient à *Topa* paroissoient fort contents du Lama qui en est le maître." Du Halde, *op. cit.*, I, 41. He apparently quotes Père Regis. On the map prepared by the Roy. Geog. Soc. to illustrate Mr. St. G. R. Littledale's journey, previously referred to, this place is erroneously called Dabachen.

† Potanin says that on the left bank of the Yellow River, and also in the valley of the Ta-t'ung ho, live a people called Chiringols, who speak Mongol strongly mixed with Chinese and another element which must be their ancient language. These people say that the Ordos country is their original home. Potanin thinks they belong to the same race as the Daldy of Prjevalsky, and Mr. Deniker, from whom I quote the above, says that this conclusion appears highly probable, as the northwest section of the Ordos is at the present day called Daldi. He (Mr. Deniker) inclines to believe that the Chiringols and the Daldy are of Turkish stock. Deniker, *Les populations turques en Chine*, in *Bull. Soc. d'Anthropologie de Paris, 3e Série, X, 206 et seq.* Potanin's Chiringols are unquestionably the San-ch'uan T'u-jen. As to Prjevalsky's Daldy, I am unable to form an opinion; see, however, my *Land of the Lamas*, 44, *note*. Chiringol is certainly not a tribal name, but that of some stream (*gol*) flowing through the country inhabited by this people, possibly the Mongol equivalent of the Chinese San-ch'uan or "Three streams." The people inhabiting this district are undoubtedly of mixed descent, certainly not pure Turks like their neighbors the Salar. The Daldi of the Ordos are the Talat Ordos Mongols. See p. 29.

for this people than any I have heard elsewhere. The Mongols, it will be remembered, say *Tangut*, so the *t'u-hua* word is not directly derived from that language. Of the unexplicable words in the vocabulary, I will only note here *miengo*, "silver;" *nara*, "sun;" *sára*, "moon;" *bulé*, "boy;" *akur*, "girl;" *rjigé*, "ass;" and *Mioré*, "cat."

The San-ch'uan people are said to number several thousand families, their language is also spoken in the Cho-mu ch'uan, which lies to the east of Bayan-rong and is probably contiguous to San-ch'uan. The San-ch'uanese are divided into a number of *gens* taking their names from the families of their chieftains, thus there is the Li T'u-ssŭ, Ch'i T'u-ssŭ, Cho T'u-ssŭ, etc. They are quite as devout Buddhists as the rest of the Mongol race, and count a living Buddha among them, the Pé-chia Fo-yeh, who resides, however, at Kumbum, though he has a K'arwa in the San-ch'uan.

This evening all the loads were made up, bills were settled and everything got ready for the start to-morrow. The donkeys will only come over here to-morrow from Chung-t'ai and it is probable that we will only get a few miles on our way; but starting is always a most difficult thing in these parts, and the nearly universal practice is to camp a few miles out of town and there collect the caravan.

March 14.—We actually left Lusar this morning, though we straggled out by twos and threes, and the donkeys only reached camp at A-chia chuang, some four and a half miles southwest of Lusar, at midnight.

This T'u-fan village near which we have camped is famous as the birth place of one of the most saintly of the Kumbum Buddhas, the A-chia Fo-yeh. It is one of the ten villages which give this broad valley the name of Shih ta t'an, and it is recognizable by two high poplars which grow near it.

It began snowing heavily towards 4 P. M., and by 11 P. M., when it cleared, about four inches of snow had fallen. I put up my tent, but the men preferred the open, as all these frontiersmen do when the weather is not too execrable.

The dogs went and lay down far from the camp and kept up a fierce barking all night, as is their custom. We hobbled the horses and mules two by two with padlocked chain hobbles; this is the best precaution I know of in these countries of horse thieves as it is impossible to drive away animals so locked together, then we sat around the fire until near dawn, talking over our adventures of three years ago and all agreed that there was no life so agreeable, so free from care as that we were now entering on. How long will these sentiments last?

March 15.—Before we left this morning a Hsün-i, sent by the Ch'ien-tsung of Ch'ing-shih pao, the warden of the Sharakuto road and of the Hung-mao pan-tao pass which we have to cross to-day, came and asked to see my passport. As a sign that he was detailed by the Ch'ien-tsung (lieutenant) he bore that officer's official hat, but notwithstanding these credentials I refused to show my papers to him, but sent the Ch'ien-tsung my card and told him to go to Hsi-ning, if he chose, and there find out who I was. The idea was to get a squeeze out of me, as it was believed I was a foreign trader going to the Panaka country to buy wool. This Ch'ien-tsung is, I learnt, in the habit of exacting squeezes from all Tibetans coming this way with salt or other produce to sell at Lusar, though they are by right exempted from the payment of any duty to the Chinese.

The ascent of the Hung-mao pan-tao pass, called in Tibetan Ta-mo ri, and which leads into a valley at the mouth of which is the little frontier post of Sharakuto, proved most trying, for neither we nor our horses or mules were yet broken into climbing, and the mountain side of shaley rocks, with here and there porphyry up which the trail led, was exceedingly steep.

From the summit we could see to the east the La-chih shan, over which we had passed when coming from Kuei-tê, and before us to the south, some two miles away, was the dark *massif* of the Yeh-niu shan, or "wild ox mountain," stretching westward to Sharakuto, and which is also visible from Kuei-tê, from which place it bears about north-northwest.

We camped on the south side of the pass, at the first spot where we found water and grass, at a place called Feng fei (shui) ling, about fourteen miles east of Sharakuto.

March 16.—The trail led down to Sharakuto through a stony, uninhabited valley in which flows a little stream. We passed on

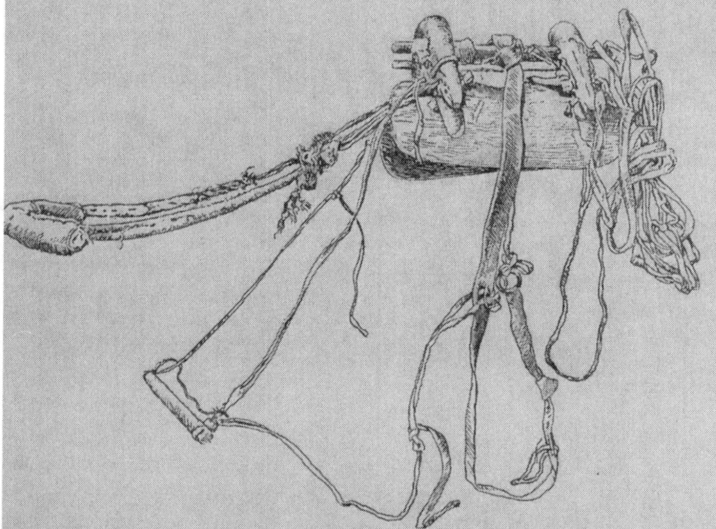

1

2

1. PACK SADDLE for YAKS (Lh'asa). (U. S. N. M. 167234.)

2. PACK SADDLE (Koko nor). (U. S. N. M. 167235.)

the way a large drove of salt-laden yaks coming from the Dabesu gobi, and belonging to a party of Chamri Panaka, who passed us by without a word of greeting or recognition.

A mile or two before coming in sight of Sharakuto we saw at the foot of the mountains, on the right side of the valley, a few tents, some of Mongol type, others of Tibetan, but all inhabited by Kung Dzassak and Tolmok Mongols. Some thirty or forty (others say seventy or eighty) families out of the two hundred composing this latter tribe are Mohammedans and live at Fei hsia, 40 *li* from Shang-wu chuang, which is north of Toba about eighteen miles. The chief of the tribe has the rank of Kung ("Duke"), given him by the Emperor of China, who bestows on him annually 12 *yuan pao* of silver (600 taels) and six pieces of satin, the usual allowance made a Mongol Kung. He lives at Morjia, near Gomba soba, in the Hsi-ning ho valley.* These Mohammedans had, eight or nine years ago, a protracted controversy with the Mongol Wangs of the Koko-nor, who wanted to forbid them professing Islam, lest they might rebel. The Mohammedans finally made a compromise by which they were allowed to follow their own faith, but agreed to keep some lamas among them to read Buddhist prayers.

I camped about one-and-one-half miles south of Sharakuto† where good grass and fuel were abundant, and sent my head man to inform the Shou-pei or Captain of my arrival. Shortly after, an interpreter from his ya-mên, a Pa-tsung (Sergeant), and an escort of five soldiers, all armed with spears and matchlocks, and carrying a tent, made their appearance, and said that they were detailed to escort me to the Wayen nor and inform the chief of the Chamri tribe of Panaka living near there that due courtesy must be shown me. The interpreter, who is a Hsieh-chia, said that the Shou-pei had received advice of my coming from the authorities at Hsi-ning some time ago. He had also been advised that six or seven foreign women had been authorized to visit the Koko-nor to "preach religion" (*ch'uan chiao*) which, by the way, my informant thought a most unwomanly thing to do, as it certainly is in the eyes of all Asiatics. He asked me if I had seen

* I camped at Gomba soba (or sarba) in 1889. See *Land of the Lamas*, 118.

† This place is called Shéné hoto by the Panaka. The Chinese name of it is Hala hu-to ying. The name is Mongol and means "Yellow town" (Shara hotun).

these women, knew anything about them, and if such an extraordinary thing would be allowed in my country, and I was fain to admit that such proceedings were not of rare occurrence, but that these *ani* were harmless if treated kindly, but if harshly, then the troubles of that country were about to begin, to last until it had been "civilized" and the original owners had become unrecognizable for ever more or had been wiped off the face of the earth.

From where we had camped we could see on a hillside about three miles north of the town the Tungor gomba, a lamasery of some celebrity, where live about five hundred akas.

From Sharakuto a trail runs south to Gomi-t'ang, a day northwest of Kuei-tê and about five miles north of the Yellow River. Another trail leads hence southwest to Gomi-wargan (or Wahon, on some maps called Balekun gomi) which is two days west of Kuei-tê. A road leads from Sharakuto to Tankar which is distant twenty odd miles; and finally a trail (though it is really the *highroad* to Tibet) leads along the south shore of the lake* to Dulan-kuo and thence to Baron Ts'aidam.

March 17.—We were unable to start to-day on account of the sudden illness of old Miao san. He is fifty-six years of age and has been leading a rough-and-tumble life, so the climbing over the Hung-mao pan-tao has worn him out. I fancy also that he is not over anxious to go on this journey and wants an excuse to slip back home and pocket the twenty taels I gave him the other day and get all the good clothing, etc., I have supplied him with. He groaned and tossed about all day in great pain but when finally I said I would send him back to Hsi-ning as I could not wait his recovery and had no medicine to give him, and told the Hsien-sheng to ride over to Sharakuto and take him behind him on his pony and make arrangements for his getting home, he braced up very fast and was soon off. It will be one man less to feed, always an important consideration in the country we are about to visit.

The T'ung-shih says that some years ago a foreign Hsieh-t'ai (Colonel) with twelve or thirteen soldiers and provided with Mongol tents came here by the Hung-mao pan-tao route. While

* Prjevalsky has explored this route along the lake, and I believe that Potanin has also followed it.

camping at Feng-shui ling he was trying to put a cartridge in his shot gun when the shell exploded and the load lodged in one of his men. When they had got beyond Sharakuto the man died and was buried beside the road. He added that he would point out the grave to me to-morrow. I repeat this story for what it is worth, but Asiatics are such wasteful liars (the exceptions only confirm the rule) that there may not be a word of truth in what he said.* The only Colonel I know of who has been here is Prjevalsky.

March 18.—We got off in good time this morning, and about one and one-half miles from camp crossed the Jih Yueh shan ("Sun and moon mountain") which marks the boundary between China and the Koko-nor. This hill, called by the Tibetans Do-rnirta, is but a spur of the Yeh-niu shan, and of inconsiderable height and very easy ascent. It connects to the north with the range running along the south side of lake Koko-nor, and on its western flank is the basin of the little Tao-t'ang ho (Rhirmo yong or djong in Tibetan) the only river I know of which flows into the Koko-nor from the southeast.†

Beyond the Jih yueh shan‡ stretches a rolling plateau well covered with grass but very badly watered, we saw on it but very few tents, though many may have been hidden in protected nooks where the fierce winds cannot reach them.

---

* What Sir John Bowring says should be borne in mind by all travelers in Asia. "My experience in China, and many other parts of the East, predisposes me to receive with doubt and distrust any statement of a native, when even the smallest interest would be possibly secured by falsehood. Nay, I have often observed there is a fear of truth, *as* truth, lest its discovery should lead to consequences of which the inquirer never dreams, but which are present to the mind of the person under interrogation. Little moral disgrace attaches to insincerity and untruthfulness, their detection leads to a loss of reputation for sagacity and cunning, but goes no further." Sir John Bowring, *The Kingdom and People of Siam*, I, 105–106. My own experience is that Asiatics often lie for fear of displeasing, or so as not to commit themselves, or from suspicion of the motives of the interrogator, but rarely from maliciousness.

† According to Prjevalsky it is the Ara gol which empties into some ponds along the shore of the lake at its southeast corner.

‡ Timkowski, *op. sup. cit.*, II, 275, calls this the Je choui chan, signifying "hot spring mountain." "La source chaude, coule vers le lac Koukou noor; une autre d'eau froide, au nord, donne naissance à la rivière de Si-ning." Most Chinese authors write the name as I have done, meaning "mountain of the sun and moon." See *Jour. Roy. Asiat. Soc.*, n. s. XXIII, 97, where it is also (p. 105), however, called Jih-ya la shan.

Some eight miles from Sharakuto we passed an abandoned fort or Ying-pan, called by the Chinese Tsahan Ch'eng and by Tibetans Kar t'ang, both terms meaning "White fort;" then crossing the Tao-t'ang ho and a range of hills some four hundred feet high which divides the basin of this little stream from that of the Wayen nor, we entered the latter plain and camped in another abandoned Ying-pan which stands one-quarter of a mile north of the little lakelet of Wayen nor.

At no very remote period (geologically speaking) this lake may have been of considerable size (four miles from east to west and possibly two to three from north to south), but now it is not over one-quarter of a mile in its greatest width and exceedingly shallow.

In the eighteenth century this, and in fact all the country around the Koko-nor, belonged to the Mongols,* while the present Koko-nor Tibetans occupied the country to the southwest, extending through most of the mountainous region south of the Ts'aidam, including the valley of the Alang and Tosu-nor, which latter region was then occupied by the Arik or Arki Tibetans now living north of the Koko-nor. The name of this latter tribe was, by the way, in all likelihood the same as that of the lake now called Alang by the Mongols, who probably made the alteration so as to make a poor pun on the name of their much feared neighbors.†

All the clans of Koko-nor Tibetans belonged to eight tribes with the cognomen *Na* (or *Nag*), so they became known by the hybrid term of Pa-na ka, or Pa-na-ka sum "the eight Na families" or "the three (divisions) of the eight Na families." The latter designation appears to be of more recent date than the former and refers, I am told, to the three sections of country over which they are now spread, *i. e.*, the tribes north of the Koko-

* Khoshotes or Eleut Mongols, according to Timkowski's Chinese authorities of the Eighteenth century "Le pays qui entoure le Koukou noor (ou Khoukhou noor), est habité par des Oeloet, des Torgaut, des Khalkha et des Kho ït * * * En 1509 cette contreé fut conquise par les Mongols. Au commencement de la dynastie mandchoue, actuellement régnante, Gouchi Khan des Oeloet, venant du nord-ouest, fit la conquete de ce pays, il envoya un ambassadeur à la cour de Peking, et fut confirmé dans sa dignité." Timkowski, *op. sup. cit.*, II, 270-280. See also H. H. Howorth, *op. sup. cit.*, I, 497, et seq.

† When the *Hsi-ning Fu hsin chih* was written (A. D. 1759), the Arik Fan-tzŭ lived along the Tieh-li nor (*i.e.*, Tongri ts'o-nak, the Tibetan name of the Tosu nor). See *Journ. Roy. Asiat. Soc.*, n. s. XXIII, 98. For the various meanings of the words Alang or Alak, Areki or Arik, see *Land of the Lamas*, 158.

SU-CHIA PANAKA AT MURI-WAHON.

nor, those south of it, and those living south of the Yellow River or Ma* h'aré Panaka. This name of Panaka or Panaka-sum they have now adopted as their ethnic appellation, and they speak of themselves, as "we Panakasum" (*Na-ts'ang Panakasum*).

The country these Tibetans first occupied was mountainous, of difficult access, and the Golok were too near neighbors for comfort. So they began moving northward taking possession of first one slip of Eleut Mongol land, then of another, till now they have driven the Ch'ing-hai Wang's Mongols to Dulan-kuo and the Muring Wang's to around Tankar and the immediate neighborhood of the Chinese. Thus they obtained not only finer pasture lands than they originally had, but an easy access to the Chinese markets and consequent higher prices for their goods, and whenever they have seen lands which have seemed to them desirable, they have taken possession of them, and held them against all comers. To these sources of profit they have added others derived from *razzias* on their Mongol neighbors, and even on Chinese travelers.

The Chinese saw with unconcealed displeasure this migration, and probably they at first prevented it taking too great proportions and lent their aid to the Mongols in their efforts to keep the Tibetans to their mountains. But with the outbreak of the Mohammedan rebellion in Kan-su, in fact even earlier, probably as soon as the T'ai-ping rebellion broke out, all China's forces were employed elsewhere, and the Panaka were left to do and move about as they liked, and thus they have come to occupy the country they now control. The movement of these tribes northward is still going on, small bands or single families are constantly coming from south of the Yellow River to live in the pasture lands south of the Ts'o non-bo (Koko-nor).

The Panakasum have never paid tribute to the Emperor, but within the last few years the Hsi-ning Amban, as a means of conciliating them has given yearly to each of the principal chiefs among them three piculs of barley. He has also conferred on all of the chiefs official buttons, but they care, very rightly, more for the barley.

As far as I can learn the Panaka are divided into the following bands:—

* The Yellow River is called Ma ch'u in Tibetan. *Hsi-yü tung wen chih*, XXII, says this word (written *rma*) means "yellow," but dictionaries do not thus explain this word.

1° Bands living north of the Koko-nor.

Arik	10,000	families
Dabjé	4,000	"
Konsa	2,000	"
Bumtok *	2,000	"
Honsang	300	"
Yasho santo	300	"
Rémung-shérab	200	"
Rusér	100	"
Tatsa	200	"
Topa	200	"
Nardza †	200	"

2° Bands living south of the Koko-nor, but north of the Huang ho.

Chamri	5,000	families
Tub-chia	1,000	"
Wutushin	500	"
Narta	100	"
Rjyäkor	100	"
Rärin ‡	250	"
Chu-chia	75	"
Na-chia	70	"
Ku-chia	50	"
Su-chia	50	"
Shurtsang	50	"
Gonwa	50	"
Atchok	100	"
Mirka	75	"
Wangsht'ah'a	100	"
Kuri	?	"
Gona	?	"
Kuar-sotsang	?	"
Shang-chia ‖	?	"
Yangyu	?	"
Tawo	?	"

* They live near Dulan-kuo, in the hills to the east of that place, I believe.

† The Topa and Nardza bands live in Korluk Ts'aidam.

‡ Divided into Rärin shuoma or "lower Rärin," and Rärin gongma or "Upper Rärin."

‖ Not to be confounded with Shang chia in southeast Ts'aidam.

There are probably a few more bands, but I have been unable to learn their names, nor have I been able to obtain more than rough guesses as to the number of families in each.*

The Chamri, who form by far the largest band of the South Koko-nor Panaka, do not certainly exceed five thousand families, and most of the other bands, such as the Na-chia, Su-chia, are under a hundred. So it will appear that the Panaka living south of the lake are numerically inferior to those living north of it, even if, as in fact appears proper, we discount heavily the figures I have given above.

I have left out of count the Ma h'are Panaka, those living south of the Yellow River, who, I have been told, are more numerous than those to the north of it. Old Lu-bum-gé, whom I met at Kuei-tê was one of the most influential chiefs of these southern tribes.

Supposing the above estimates correct, we have:

N. Koko-nor Panaka	19,500	families
S. Koko-nor Panaka	8,500	"
Mahari Panaka	9,000	"

or, estimating four persons to a family, about 158,000 souls.

The estimate given above of the numerical strength of each band does not appear excessive, except for the four first bands of the North Koko-nor Panaka, in which case it would perhaps be wise to strike off ten per cent., and then I would be inclined to accept the result as roughly correct.

The Wayen-nor Ying-pan, where we are stopping, was built three years ago (in 1888) when there was a great rush to the newly discovered gold fields of Gork, which lie about south of here four days travel. One has to cross the "Three days' desert," (Kurban tara in Mongol, Do t'ang, "Stony Plain" in Tibetan), then Ta hoba of the Chinese (Ch'u-rnang of the Panaka) is reached, and near here, in the mountains inhabited by the Su-chia Panaka, the gold diggings are found. First discovered in 1888, the Hsi-ning Amban leased them to a Chinese for one hundred and eighty ounces of gold (three thousand two hundred and forty

* The names of the principal chiefs now ruling these tribes are Chamri Solo, Ch'ü-gyal Da-lä-rgya, Na-chia Ta-kō, Konsa Lama Arabtan, Konsa Pei-hō, Rémung Shérab, Ta-tsa Guru, Bumtru Séku, Mogalo, and others with like harmonious names. It must be noted that these names are frequently the same as that of the tribe to which the chief belongs.

ounces of silver) a year, which sum he had to collect as best he could from the people who came to work in the diggings.

Villages of log houses soon sprang up, and in less than two years about three thousand ounces of gold had been taken out of the diggings. Then the rude appliances in use were no longer serviceable and the placers were abandoned.

The T'ung-shih tells me that the Hsieh-t'ai of Tankar will proceed in two months time to Dérgé to there meet the Hsieh-t'ai (Colonel) from Ta-chien-lu, with whom he is to confer on the important question of whose "sphere of influence" Dérgé is to be placed in, will the Viceroy of Ssŭ-Ch'uan or the Hsi-ning Amban's delegates squeeze it. Ssŭ-Ch'uan, I fancy, will be given authority over it, but from what I know of Dérgé, it will not make very much out of it.

March 19.—The T'ung-shih and the escort left us at Wayen nor, but the headman of the Panaka living near by was informed by the former officer that I was not to be molested in any way, but to be allowed to proceed peacefully whichever way I chose. So much *kung shuo* ("empty talk"), for no one cares a cash if I am molested or not, on the contrary, every one would like to see me forced to give up the journey.

About three miles west of the Ying-pan we came to a short but steep descent of about one hundred feet through gravel and loess lying in horizontal strata, each stratum from eight to twenty feet thick.* Then we crossed a succession of low hills, and ravines, and passed by the little walled Rongwa village of Tumba, where the agricultural Tibetans come yearly to sow and reap their crops of barley, going during the winter farther south to the Yellow River. A mile farther on at Ch'abché (one of the numerous little valleys we had to cross) we saw a number of black tents and many sheep and yaks. Leaving this behind us we entered another lacustrine plain, similar to that of the Wayen nor but stretching north and south and with a small stream flowing through it and emptying, I was told, into the Huang ho, or possibly into the Huy-huyung, a large river which has its source to the west of here.†

* This whole country shows how active an agent erosion can be in altering the topography of an extensive region. Lakes and rivers which we know existed a century or less ago have been completely obliterated, chains of mountains have crumbled away and are now little more than hillocks.

† In or near the bank of the Dabesu nor (Ts'aka nor).

On this stream, a little to the north of our route and where it issues from the mountains, is the village of Kaba (or Gaba) talen where live some twenty to thirty families of Chinese Mohammedans, Hsi-fan and also, if report be true, a number of Chinese fugitives from justice, who have committed crimes in the Nei-ti (China proper) and have found refuge in this secluded spot. The place bears a bad reputation among Tibetans and Mongols. A little farming is done around the village and a small crop of barley is raised.

We camped near the river nearly two miles from the village, with which we thought prudent not to hold any intercourse. The country so far belongs to the Chamri Panaka tribe, but to-morrow we will enter the country of the Shaner Panaka.

March 20.—The trail led over the foot hills of the range which hides the Koko-nor from us and whose southern base we have been following since leaving Sharakuto. This range has no name that I can hear of, at one place it is called by my Chinese Erhte-shan at another Lao-hu shan, and so on. To the south the country stretches out for miles an undulating plateau, the little ridges traversing it having a general southwesterly direction. Some forty miles to the south I can distinguish a chain of mountains trending apparently southwest by west, but of no great height. They are probably on the farther side of the Yellow River.

Black tents were quite numerous all along the route, and we passed a few whose denizens told us they had but recently come from near Labrang gomba, to the south of the Yellow River. This country is the Tibetan's land of promise, plenty of grass, water, wind, and pusillanimous Mongol neighbors, whom they can bully and rob.

We camped in a stony valley called Erhté, down which flows a good sized stream, the Erhté ch'uk'a, and where there are a number of tents of Shaner Panaka, at one of which we bought a sheep for a brick of tea and some red handkerchiefs. Some Sharba* from Sung-pan were camped near us, but, as is their custom, they would have nothing to do with us fearing lest I were a T'ung-shih anxious to squeeze them. These enterprising traders are found in every nook and corner of the Koko-nor and have got all the trade with

* The Sharba are Chinese traders from Sung-pan T'ing in Ssŭ-ch'uan. See *Land of the Lamas*, 54 and 112.

the people, which should by rights have belonged to the Kan-su traders if they had only a little more push and energy.

We made camp at about noon, just as the west wind began its daily violent performance, and to-day, as usual, it kept it up to sunset. I noticed very few yaks hereabout, all the cattle are half-breed yaks (*pien niu* in Chinese) and domestic cattle (*huang niu*). I am told everywhere that the cattle plague, which has been raging now for over a year, has destroyed most of the cattle, and has been especially fatal to yaks. What would become of the Tibetans without yaks is difficult to imagine, dwellings, food and fuel, they owe all this and much more, to these useful, ugly beasts.

March 21.—Some six or eight miles to the west of Erhté the trail took us higher up the foot hills, and we passed into another little basin, that of the Hato, which empties, I was assured, into the Kaba talen stream (but of this I have my doubts, and it would appear to me much more probable that it flows into the Gunga nor). The country is covered everywhere with grass, but it is of little use as pasture land, as water is miles away, except during a brief period of the year when the rain water collects in the hollows. The small herds we saw have all to be driven daily four or five miles to water.

When about eight miles from Erhté ch'uk'a, I caught a glimpse of the Gunga nor or "Egg lake." It bore about south-southwest from us and was probably four miles away. It appeared to be a very small sheet of water, hardly deserving the name of lake. It receives a number of streams, the principal being the Huyuyung, which, as I have said, comes from the west. It may have an outlet into the Yellow River, or one of its affluents, but my men assured me it had none.

To the south of this lake is a chain of mountains, trending in its eastern portion in a southeasterly direction, but becoming parallel to the chain to our right at its western extremity. This range appeared to be slightly higher than that to the north of our route—useless to say that my men assured me that it had no name, though each peak in it is provided with a high sounding one. The whole country hereabout shows signs of rapid erosion, every depression I see has been cut out of the loess and gravel by the action of water. All the elevations are of the *mésa* type, of uniform height, with steep sides and flat tops.

About five miles before making camp we passed a few tents of Tashio Tibetans, near which small herds of camels were grazing, an unusual sight, for Tibetans do not often own these useful but patience-trying animals.

At Hato, where we camped, we found an abundance of pebbles and sandstone boulders (hence the Mongol name of *hato*, "stony"), but very little grass. The stream which flows by this place is of quite a respectable size, and in the rainy season must be a formidable torrent. Some fifty tents of Narta Hsi-fan are scattered about here, and we availed ourselves of their proximity to buy a sheep, for which I paid a small brick of tea (*fu ch'a*) and a piece of red cotton cloth (*hsiao mo-hun*), the whole of the value of six mace of silver. A sheep lasts the party eight days; when we have only rice to eat it takes two cups full a day, or if we only have vermicelli (*kua mien*), one and a half catties. A brick of tea (five catties) lasts us from five to six weeks. Rice is decidedly the most economical food we can use and the best for travelers.

The west wind blew to-day with its accustomed violence, it has been blowing nearly incessantly since we have left Sharakuto.

March 22.—Shortly after starting this morning we passed a caravan of several hundred yaks laden with salt. The owners were Chu-chia Tibetans and the salt was brought from the great salt lake, the Ts'ak'a or Dabesu nor ("Salt lake"), about three days west of here. The Tibetans buy the salt from the Mongols (of the Wanka tribe), who obtain it by evaporation. The price paid for it by the Tibetans is about a *sheng* (a little over a quart) of tsamba for a bushel (*t'ou*).

Three miles from camp we entered a sandy waste in which the only vegetation was a few thorny bushes projecting out of the tops of sand hillocks; the sand had drifted around them till but a little portion of them showed above ground. The trail led over a succession of undulations trending southward. Some ravines or *nullahs* we crossed, showed in their sides (thirty to fifty feet in depth) alternate layers of gravel and loess.

When about eight miles from Hato, we came in sight of the Huyuyung, a good sized stream (for these parts) some twenty-five yards wide and about four feet deep. This stream, I am told, has its source on the very edge of the Ts'ak'a nor. We followed up its left bank to Ts'o kadri where we camped, the river bottom, everywhere thickly covered with alkaline efflorescence, and hardly a blade of grass to be seen anywhere.

Shortly before reaching the river we passed through a sand bank where I saw quantities of the little univalve fossil shells which characterize the loess. A covey of partridges rose at our approach, and a few antelopes (*huang yang*) scampered away on sighting us—except these we saw no living creature.

We are now within five or six miles of the southern range, which, I am told, bears here the name of Ch'ermar (or Ch'émar). The hills to the north of the road are considerably higher here than farther east, and a few peaks have snow on them, but not so much as on the mountains to the south.

Again to-day the west wind has blown with great violence. I have noted that the temperature is higher when it blows than when it is calm.

March 23.—We crossed the Huyuyung River on the ice, and I was assured that this was the only time of the year when this stream could be traversed, as the quicksands, with which its bed is full, render it impassable, except when frozen over. Travelers going to Muri-Wahon have, except at this season, to follow the Huyuyung up to its source, a day's journey to the west. On account of the impossibility of fording this stream, all Tibetans living in winter along the base of the mountains to the south of the Huyuyung, and who are desirous of using the fine pasturage to the north of it, cross to the north side before the ice breaks up.

Leaving the river we took a southwesterly course across the Ch'émar t'ang, which has, within a very recent period, formed one of the largest of the lakelets or sinks with which this region is covered. In fact it must even now, in very rainy years, be converted into a swamp, and a little stream, whose dry bed we crossed, connects it with the Huyuyung.

Near the southwestern extremity of the Ch'émar mountains, as viewed from this point, I had pointed out to me some ruins which are said to be those of a Chinese fort (*Ying*). They are called Mar-k'uar or "Red fort."

While traversing the depression just mentioned I saw large numbers of antelopes (*huang yang*) and wild asses, also some sheldrakes and a small, light brown colored bird, with a black patch on its breast. This little fellow is an agreeable twitterer, a rare gift among birds of these regions.

Some seven miles from our camp of yesterday we came to a stream flowing north, and called the Tsatsa ch'uk'a (or gol), and finding the banks of the rivulet covered with fine green grass, we decided upon passing a day here to let the animals feed, as they have had hardly anything to eat, except a quart or two of barley daily, since leaving Sharakuto.

The spot on which we camped was one any Mongol or Tibetan would have held to be an ideal one; it was sheltered from the west winds by a low range of hills, which here intersect the Tsatsa ch'uk'a; there was good water, grass, dry dung for fuel, and stones to build a hearth with; no one could ask for more.

In the hills behind our camp I found a number of the little shells characteristic of the loess, though I noticed no loess. The wind blew furiously from noon well into the night, but the temperature in the middle of the day was quite warm; the thermometer rises daily now in the sun to about 60° F.

In looking over my notes on Tibet from Chinese sources,* I find (p. 98) that in the eighteenth century a road leading from Hsi-ning to Lh'asa passed by the Wayen nor, and after following up the left bank of the Huyuyung for some distance, struck south across the mountains to the Tosu nor. It passed along the north bank of this lake and then, by the road I followed in 1889, led to Karmat'ang and the source of the Yellow River. This itinerary shows, furthermore, that at that time (say 1750) there was another small lake (Sini nor) between the Wayen (Bayan) nor and the Gunga nor, about thirty miles west or west-southwest of the former. We also learn from this work that at the time it was written the whole country between Sharakuto and the Ts'aidam was inhabited by Mongols, and that Tibetans (Arik Fan-tzŭ) were then occupying the fertile pasture lands around the Tosu nor and Alang nor.

March 24.—To-day has been a most enjoyable one, no wind in the morning and the thermometer in the sun at noon going up to 78° F. A Sharba trader rode by but, though he spoke a few words to one of my men, who was a little way from camp, he

**Journ. Roy Asiat. Soc.*, new series, XXIII, 97, et seq. This road is also laid down on d' Anville's map (Carte Genl[e] du Thibet). See also Dutreuil de Rhins, *L'Asie Centrale*, 355 et seq.

could not be induced to approach us; he feared there was some T'ung-shih in the party who might attempt to squeeze him.

I went to try and shoot an antelope, but only saw a band of fifty to seventy-five wild asses on the Ch'émar t'ang, and it was impossible to stalk them, as there was neither cover nor a gully on it. A number of little streams flow across the plain from south to north; they come from the mountains along its southern edge and disappear in the ground near the northern border of the plain.

Ssŭ-shih-wu, who has passed much of his life among the Tibetan tribes of this neighborhood, tells me the chiefs or *Pönbo* receive in the eighth month of the year from their clansmen presents of cattle, horses, sheep, pulo, butter, etc., which constitute the only salary they get. Their duties are, however, not onerous; they command their people in case of war, and with them watch over the pasture lands of the band, trying always to gain more acres and to resist the encroachments of stronger tribes.

March 25.—We left early, as it was a long way to the Muri ch'u, where we had to camp, and where the donkeys hired at Lusar were to leave us. We passed around a spur projecting from the mountains to the south, but apparently not belonging geologically to the same formation, for it is of igneous, while the range itself appears to be of metamorphic rocks (fine grained bluish limestone and granite). A considerable portion of this spur has been covered up by loess, leaving here and there a peak a hundred feet or so high sticking up out of the surrounding grassy plain. From the main range a huge amount of *débris* (limestone and granite pebbles) has been carried down, forming enormous cones of dejection, stretching into the plain a mile or more beyond the base of the mountains at the mouth of every gorge.

The Muri-ch'u (or ch'uk'a) we found to be a good-sized but very shallow stream, flowing north-northeast over a bed of rolled stones, its banks rising vertically about twenty feet and showing that the plain is but a very thin layer of loess and sand over a thick bed of gravel. Erosion has changed the whole face of this country in very recent times, and this change is still going on rapidly.

The Na-chia and Chu-chia Panaka live here, some hundred tents of them in all. It is a fine pasture land, but water is scarce.

We camped on the Muri ch'u about a mile from where it leaves the mountains and near the ruins of an old Tibetan camp marked by numerous cooking stoves and altars of stone plastered with dung. These stoves differ slightly from those used to the north of the Koko-nor. The annexed cut and elevation of one will enable me to dispense with further description of this ingenious contriv-

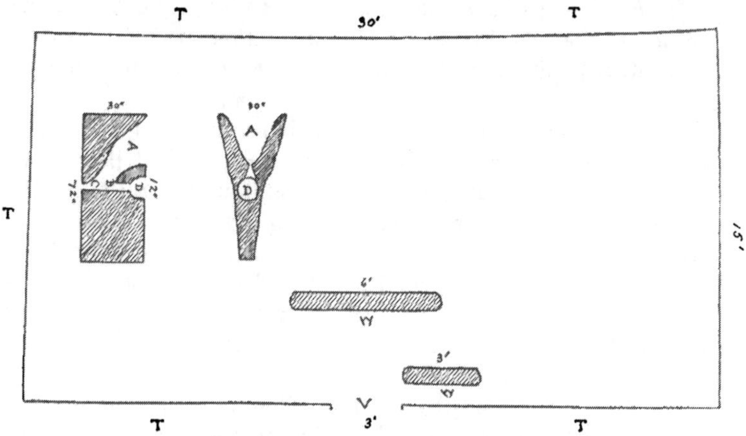

ELEVATION AND PLAN OF TIBETAN TENT.

T, T, T, Tent.
W, W, Low interior walls.
A, Place for fuel.
B, Fireplace.
C, Ash hole.
D, Opening to receive kettle.
V, Door.

ance. This cut also enables one to understand the interior arrangement of Tibetan tents. On the altar, which is built some little distance from the tent, juniper spines (*shuka*) are burnt morning and evening. The low wall inside the tent keeps out the wind.

I can see from here stretching to the northwest, some twelve miles away, the Huyuyung, and I am told that still about eight or ten miles farther on is the Ts'ak'a nor, from which point Dulan-kuo is reached in a day. The mountains, at the base of which we have camped, rise rapidly to the west of us, and we can see in that direction a number of snow-covered peaks. I can hear of no general name for this range, though the people speak of the Muri la, the Wahon la, the Sayi la, etc., each peak having its own name; but though, after all, it is well provided with names, a foreigner will come along some day and give it another; I, however, waive my right to do so.

Between the Tsatsa ch'uk'a and this place we saw some three hundred wild asses, also quite a number of wild pigeons and sheldrakes. These latter neither Mongols nor Tibetans will kill, because their plumage is partly yellow, and they look upon them as "lama birds"; in fact, they call them by that name.

March 26.—Yeh Hsien-sheng and Ssŭ-shih-wu went early this morning to the sub-chief of the Na-chia, whose tent is on the slope of the Muri la, about a mile and a half from ours, to hire yaks to carry our luggage to Shang in the Ts'aidam.

In a few hours they returned, Ssŭ-shih-wu bearing the chief's sword, by which I at once knew that a bargain had been made and that his sword was the guaranty that bound him to it. The bargain was not a very good one; for eight yaks and two men I have to pay ten small bricks of tea worth 4.0 taels, two bricks of fine tea, of the same value as the first, and eighteen pieces of red calico (*hsiao mo-hun*)* worth 46 tael cents a piece; total, 13.08 taels, but these goods are valued here at 25 taels.

I endeavored to induce the sub-chief, Wang-ma-bum by name, to take me to Shang *viâ* the Tosu nor (the trail I have previously referred to as known to the Chinese in the last century), but he said it was impassable at this season of the year on account of the ice and the enormous quantities of snow on the mountains. This trail, he explained to me, led over the Amnyé Malchin (the most sacred mountain of the Panaka and K'amba), and is only practicable in the seventh and eighth months, when some of the Na-chia, Chu-chia and Su-chia Panaka take it to hunt yaks and dig rhubarb near the Tosu nor. It takes about fifteen days to reach Shang by this road.

I had been led to believe that the Golok confined their raids to the Mongol country, but I now hear that a party of them made a razzia in this valley last year.

The grass has all been eaten up around here by the flocks and herds of the Tibetans, and so my ponies and mules are not profiting much by the rest, especially as from our proximity to the black tents and the irresistible inclination of this people for horse stealing, we have to tie the mules and horses close to the tents from dark to dawn. We will leave here to-morrow and probably find

* Called *Räs rlung* in Panaka Tibetan.

good grazing up the Wahon valley where Tibetans have not been since last summer.

The donkey men go back to-morrow to Lusar, and I have given them my home letters and telegrams, which they will deliver to the Inland Mission people at Hsi-ning, by whom they will be forwarded to Lan-chou where there is a post and telegraph office.

March 27.—Passing over the foothills of the Muri la, in the depressions of which were some thirty to forty tents of the Su-chia and Na-chia tribes, we saw from the highest of them a corner of the Ts'ak'a nor glistening in the distance. Turning southward, we entered the mountains and followed up the course of the Wahon ch'u (or ch'uk'a), a clear mountain torrent of considerable volume which is probably the principal feeder of the Huyuyung. The mountains rose precipitately on either side with hardly any vegetation or even soil on their flanks of granite, and the bottom of the valley was so thickly strewn with *débris* that one might well have thought that dynamite had been used to blow the rocks to pieces, so finely were they shattered.

A few miles up the valley we found, at the base of a nearly vertical wall of red and rose-colored granite, fine, long, green grass, and here we camped, and the animals had soon filled themselves with the succulent food and were able to enjoy a long and well-earned rest. This place is called Wahon omsa ("lower Wahon").

Old Wang-ma-bum, our guide, is a queer specimen of the Panaka Tibetan; a little, wizzened-up fellow of about fifty, with shaven head and no beard,* a piercing eye and spare but well-muscled body, only imperfectly wrapped in a big sheepskin *ch'uba*. His pet exclamation is *Om mani*, or *yim dén-ba*, "it is true," either one or the other of which he appends to every ten words he speaks. The Tibetans of Central Tibet he calls Gopa, which word I take to be a corrupt pronunciation of Bo-pa (Bod-pa).† He has traveled not only to Lh'asa, but also into the Golok country. Of these latter people he says that they have at the most five chiefs, and that their country is so poor that they cannot buy

* The Panaka pluck out their beards with tweezers (*chyam ts'er*), one of which every man carries suspended around his neck or hanging from his belt. The Lh'asa people frequently wear moustaches.

† Pronounced Beu (or Peu) ba in Central Tibet.

tsamba or flour, twelve bowls full of which are counted as the price of a sheep. Sheep are rare among them, but they have large numbers of cattle. They live in black tents like the Panaka, and he has never heard, as I had, that any inhabited caves. They eat chura and butter like other Tibetans, and, of course, drink quantities of tea (from Chiung-chou).

March 28.—The *débris* in the bottom of the valley increased in quantity as we advanced, and to-day it is in many places over a hundred feet deep on either side of the stream. Numerous skulls of mountain sheep (*Ovis poli, pan yang* in Chinese, *Rnyen* in Tibetan) lay scattered about, and the guide told me that this splendid animal is very common all through these mountains; we saw none, however, only a few wild asses and half a dozen yaks.

The Wahon ch'u, less than a mile above where we camped last night, disappears under the mass of *débris* which fills the valley, so we had to ascend to the snow line and there let our animals slack their thirst with snow; they had, however, to go without food, not a blade of grass was to be seen, only a little moss growing here and there on the stones around the place where we camped. We gave our ponies and mules a little barley and they huddled together under a ledge of rock near our camp to get away from the piercing wind.

The place where we camped is known as Wahon jamkar, from it the pass we have to cross is visible, and it looks appalling, a wall of snow from the base to the very summit. It will prove a difficult task to scale it.

In the afternoon about an inch of snow fell, and during the night the thermometer fell to +14° Fahrenheit.

I tried in the evening after dinner, when all were placidly and contentedly seated around the fire, to get some information from Wang-ma-bum concerning the number of persons in the different bands of Panaka. He was very communicative until I said that I wished he would repeat what he had just said, that I would like to write down the figures he had given me. He refused and said, rather excitedly, that if I wanted to talk he was willing, but if I proposed writing down what he said he would not say another word. He imagined, probably, that I wanted to use the information gained in estimating the resources of each band, so as to be able to raid their country some day with a party of my own people.

I ascertained, however, from the old fellow, that the Chamri were the most numerous (five thousand families) of the Panaka between the Yellow River and the lake (Koko nor), the other bands ranging from fifty or sixty tents to one hundred and fifty and two hundred, also that the Panaka south of the Yellow River were much more numerous than those north of it. During the Mohammedan rebellion some of the Panaka bands, among others the Su-Na-chia, that of my informant, moved from their present location to Shang-chia in the Ts'aidam, and only came back to their present location when troubles were over.

March 29.—This has proved a terribly hard day. The rocks which covered the bottom of the gorge were entirely hidden by snow, over these we plunged and slid for nearly two miles, when we found ourselves at the foot of the principal ascent. By this time it was past noon, but we stopped to reconnoitre the pass and readjust the loads of the mules and yaks. The guide and Yeh Hsien-sheng returning reported the pass nearly closed, and Wang-ma-bum suggested that we should turn back and take the Ts'ak'a nor and Dulan-kuo route to Shang. I refused, and insisted that we could cross the pass if no time was lost in talking and we went about it in the usual *ka-lé, ka-lé,* "slow, slow," way.

After trying the pass itself and finding it absolutely impracticable from the great depth of soft snow, we attacked it by the mountain on its eastern side, and up its steep sides we struggled, where the sharp stones cut the feet of horses and men, and after innumerable falls we finally made our way to the summit. It took us four hours to reach it, though the distance was not over a mile and a half by the zigzag trail we followed.

From the top we saw a maze of mountains to the south and east, and to the west the broad reddish plain of the Ts'aidam was dimly discernible. The prevailing color of the mountains was brick red, and very little snow was visible anywhere on them, even on the great range to the south of the Ts'aidam—the Kun-lun of our maps.

The south side of the pass was steeper than the one we had just ascended, but snow covered it so deeply that we made the descent without danger by simply sliding down through it. Reaching the valley bottom, we found the snow over four feet deep, and the yaks could not get through it till we had opened a trail with the mules, who were of infinitely more service to us in this trying place than the yaks of whom we had, however, expected wonders.

To add to our trouble it began snowing heavily before we got below the snow line, and darkness overtook us, so we scraped away the snow from a large flat rock and put up our tents, but were too worn out to either eat or sleep. When I had lit a candle we all burst out laughing as we looked at each other; we were as black as negroes, and our eyes were so swollen and blood-shot that the tears ran down our ebony cheeks even in this dim light. Had the sun shown during the day our sufferings would have been terrible, notwithstanding the horse-hair eye-shades we all wore.

The pass we had crossed bears no name, though it should properly be called Wahon la, being at the source of the Wahon ch'u. It is approximately 16,500 feet above sea level, and from its western flank issues the Tsatsa gol, which flows through the northeastern corner of the Ts'aidam, while on its southern side the Tsahan ossu or "White River" has its source. The road we propose following will take us down the course of this latter river—whose very existence has not heretofore been suspected, until near where it enters the Ts'aidam plain.

The place where we camped is called Kukusé, a Tibetan mispronunciation, I fancy, of Koko ossu, "Blue River," the name of a rivulet which empties into the main branch of the Tsahan ossu, a mile or so lower down than this camp.

March 30.—We left by daylight, as we wanted to reach some place where we could procure fuel and cook a little food. After a few miles through deep snow we reached the main valley of the Tsahan ossu and left the snow behind. The snow line on this side of the Wahon la, as I shall call this mountain, is at least a thousand feet lower than on the northern slope. The predominant formation is still granite.

We noticed in the distance several large herds of wild yaks, hares, very large crows, a variety of bird that I took for a flicker, and a small greyish brown bird were also quite numerous. I saw quite a number of skulls of big-horns (*Ovis Poli*).

The general direction of the range before us is west-northwest and south-southeast, and its summits rise 2,000 to 3,000 feet above the valley, which in places is, perhaps—counting its width from the summits to the north to the crest of the southern range, two to three miles wide. Many patches of loess are visible on the mountain sides, and along the river bank there is a great deal of gravel and broken, angular pieces of stone. Reddish clay is abundant, I should have noted, on the southern slopes of the range we have just crossed.

We sighted two or three hundred yaks drinking in the river, and I wounded three. It was a glorious sight to see the whole herd dashing across ravines and through snow drifts up a lateral valley. I followed them for several miles, and though two of the wounded animals were losing quantities of blood, I failed to get again within range, for the melting snow and the slippery clayey soil were too much for my pony. I did not want to take any Ts'aidam ponies with me into Tibet, experience had proven them to be worthless for the kind of work I had before me, and so I had to give up the chase, as I could not afford to overwork the good little Konsa pony I was riding.

We camped on the bank of the river in a miserably bleak spot where the wind and the driving snow made it most uncomfortable for us all night, and where our cattle got very little grass or rest. A couple of bears came wandering about among the rocks near us, but we were all too tired to think of shooting. From what old Wang-ma-bum tells me the Tsahan ossu is the same stream which I crossed in '89, in the Ts'aidam, when on my way to Baron kuré, and which is there called Shara gol. It is like all the rivers of this region, much shallower and of smaller volume in its lower course than at its head, much of the water being lost in the sands and swampy grounds when it leaves the hills.

March 31.—We moved down the Tsahan ossu about ten miles and came to a spot where grass and fuel were abundant, and where we decided to rest for a day, as much for the sake of the yaks and mules as for our own. We are all suffering terribly from snow blindness, even the Panaka have not been spared. We passed a hot spring (*hotun ossu*), but the weather was so bad, the snow driving in our eyes made us so anxious to reach camp as fast as possible, that I omitted taking the temperature of the water. I doubt if it was much over 70° Fahrenheit.

On the mountain side near where we camped we saw some wild yaks, and I shot a fine young heifer; the meat is, though I don't care for yak meat, most acceptable, as we have exhausted our supply of mutton, and we have still three days traveling before we reach Shang.

Every evening, when the two Tibetans who accompany me and who camp away from us under the shelter of our luggage piled up in a semi-circle around them, have got their frugal meal of meat and tea ready, one of them arranges in two rows twenty-six bits of burning dung, and on these he puts a little *shuka* in which tsamba, butter and salt have been mixed (the two latter ingredients to make it burn the better); then they both stand facing the south and, bare headed with joined palms, shout in a wild and apparently angry tone, a long prayer to the gods, among which the Amnyé ("forefathers")* are especially mentioned, asking their protection for themselves, their flocks and herds. Then they make three prostrations, and finally circumambulate the fire keeping it on their right side and never ceasing their furious praying.

My sextant work, surveying and drawing, in the terribly inflamed condition of my eyes, has become most painful. I find some relief in holding my face over the boiling kettle, the steam soothes the pain considerably. This is the usual remedy used by the natives.†

Wang-ma-bum, though passed fifty, vaults on to his horse's back by resting his left hand on the pummel of his saddle and grasping in his right his long lance, its butt end resting on the ground. This is the usual way for an armed Tibetan to get into the saddle, and is a very graceful one.

---

* For a list of the Amnyé see *Land of the Lamas*, 94. Each Amnyé is supposed to reside on a certain high peak, usually some great snow-covered mountain. Gesar (the Chinese Kuan-ti) is one of the most powerful Amnyé. There are many mountains besides those mentioned in the list referred to above to which this word is prefixed.

† Father Acosta, in his *History of the Indies*, (Hakluyt Soc. edit), I, 288, tells us that when once crossing the Andes he was greatly troubled with snow blindness, and, "being troubled with this paine, and out of patience, there came an Indian woman which said to me, 'Father, lay this to thine eies, and thou shalt be cured.' It was a piece of the flesh of vicuñas, newly killed and all bloody. I used this medicine and presently the pain ceased, and soon after went quite away."

April 1.—The whole day was taken up by work in my tent, writing up my notes, working out my route sketches, and, last but not least, doctoring my eyes.

Last night the thermometer fell to −10 Fahrenheit, but as there was no wind, the cold was quite bearable. To-day at 2 P. M., it stood (in the sun) at +54° and at 7 P. M. it had fallen again to +8°. The two or three inches of snow which fell yesterday, have already disappeared in exposed places; throughout all this region it melts with wonderful rapidity.

April 2.—The trail continued down the Tsahan ossu valley, the *dêbris* (loess and gravel) at the mouths of the lateral valleys was in many places over one hundred feet thick. Some miles below camp a good-sized stream, coming from the southeast, empties into the river. From this point onward for over six miles the valley is considerably broader than higher up, and must have been quite a "park" before the *dêbris* from the mountains on either side had filled it with rows of low hillocks, cut through here and there by torrents. We see no signs of anyone ever inhabiting this splendid pasture land, only a few old hearth stones and some manure show that man ever passes this way. In summer, I am told, the Rérin gongma—"Upper Rérin" (to distinguish them from the "Lower" or *chuong-ma* branch of the tribe living near the Muri ch'u), travel this road when on their way from Shang to Lusar. To-day has been the second since we left Lusar in which there has been absolutely no wind. Last night again was very cold, the thermometer falling to +0° before 8 P. M. The ice on the river is in places two feet thick. We saw a few wild yaks, some hares and magpies.

A few miles beyond where we have camped to-day, the river takes a west-northwest bend, and though it has in this part of its course several considerable affluents, the volume of its water is less than higher up its course.

April 3.—Three miles below our camp of last night we left the Tsahan ossu, and passing over some gravelly hills and across some alkaline flats entered the basin of a little affluent coming from the Koko k'utul ("Blue pass"). The ascent was very easy, although we had to flounder for half a mile before reaching the summit through very deep snow which filled every hollow. The hillsides were covered with fine grass, and we saw many Hsi-fan fire-places; the Rérin camp here in summer.

From the summit of the pass we could distinguish, apparently only a few miles away the Bayan gol (lower course of the Yogoré) and the reddish yellow plain of the Ts'aidam, behind which rose the South Ts'aidam mountains (our Kun-lun).

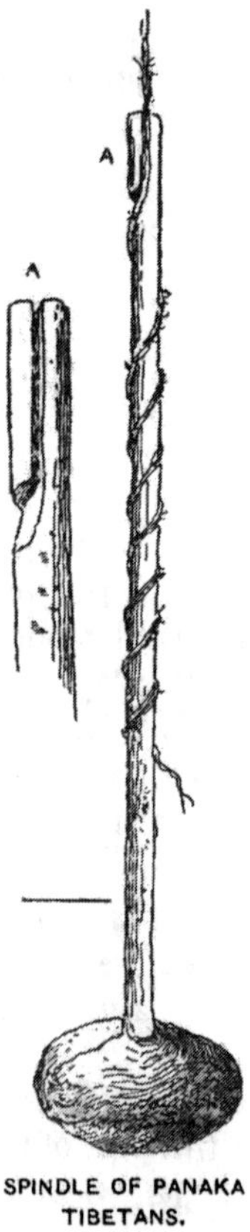

SPINDLE OF PANAKA TIBETANS.

The descent was very steep for the first thousand feet, as is the case with nearly all southern slopes of passes throughout this region, over a mass of *débris* (mostly limestone), then we came to a gently sloping valley, covered with fine grass and juniper trees scattered about on the hillsides, and in sheltered nooks were numerous black tents belonging to the Rérin. This valley leads down to the Mongol town of Shang, and is inhabited in the upper portion, called Kéter gun ("come twice") by Rérin Panaka, and in the lower, known as Dérben chin (or Jya-ma bji, "Four catties"), by Shang Mongols.*

The temperature this evening is much warmer than that we have heretofore experienced since leaving Lusar at the same hour. At 7 P. M. the thermometer stood at +23° Fahrenheit, while yesterday at the same hour it was +4°.8.

My Panaka guides were much worried because they could not make their burnt offerings this evening, they had no argols on which to burn the incense, and insisted that cedar wood, with which we had built a roaring fire, was not suitable, though I called their attention to its fragrance.

April 4.—Some Rérin Tibetans stopped us about a mile below camp, but seeing that we were well armed let us proceed. No Mongol or Chinese traders ever venture to come this way as these Panaka would levy such blackmail from them that they would be ruined. As we advanced, the hills on our right—the last southwestern slopes of the range through which we have been traveling

* I could obtain no satisfactory explanation of these names.

Bonbo lamas in Inn-Yard at Kuei-te.

Camp of Rerin gongma Panaka near Shang.

since leaving Muri-Wahon, dwindled away to insignificant hillocks, their southwestern extremity a rocky spur some four hundred to five hundred feet high, abutting on the Yógoré gol. The hills on our left (the southeastern side of the valley) were higher, with two distinct peaks, that farther down the valley called Noyen hung, probably fifteen hundred feet high.

We stopped at some Rérin tents to buy a sheep, and I availed myself of the opportunity to photograph the camp. While so doing a small boy came running towards me but a woman seized him and shouted out "don't go near him, he can make a hundred soldiers come out of that box!"* The Chinese are often quite as foolish. While traveling to Kuei-tê two soldiers passed me while I was using my prismatic compass. One said to the other "He is looking for gold deposits in the river, he can see them by looking through that little box he has in his hand."

About ten miles down the valley we came to some fifteen Mongol tents, the farthest camp the Shang Mongols have in this direction. They live in dread of their thieving neighbors, the Rérin, but the latter appear to be in nearly as great dread of them, for while we were trying to buy the sheep, I asked one of the Tibetans to guide me to Shang as I wanted to ride ahead of my party and feared to lose myself, but he refused for fear of the Mongols in the lower part of the valley.

The distance to Shang proved greater than we had anticipated, over twenty-four miles over sandy soil. When near the Yógoré we passed some land under cultivation, irrigation ditches being cut from here to the river. We had some difficulty in fording the river in front of Shang, as it was nearly three-fourths of a mile wide and quite swift, though fortunately shallow. There was still a good deal of ice on it, in places eight or nine inches thick.

The new Tibetan governor of Shang (he had arrived a week or two after my first visit to this place in 1889)† took me for a trader and tried to squeeze me before allowing me to enter the town. He sent a number of envoys to confer with me, the first a poor devil of a Jack of all trades, called Shára-wánza, who had been my

* Moorcroft when in Kunduz says, "Baba Beg apprised me that some persons had been telling strange stories of us to the Mir; amongst other things, that we had a fortress concealed in our packages, with artillery which went off of its own accord, and had the power of discriminating friends from foes." W. Moorcroft, *Travels in the Himalayan Provinces of India*, II, 419.

† See *Land of the Lamas*, 144 et seq.

factotum during my first visit here, then a Chinese trader, then a dirty Tibetan from Tsang, and finally his steward. Each one told me that the K'anpo insisted on my leaving Shang, as it was Tibetan governed territory, and the Tashil'unpo lamas would be much vexed if they learned that he had allowed me to visit it. I finally sent the Hsien-sheng to him with my passport, visiting card and a *k'atag*, and told him that I was astonished at his incivility, that his predecessor had treated me with great politeness, given me a fine tent, entertained me, and that we had parted the best of friends. He apologized, said he was not conversant with official customs, and begged me to make myself at home, regretting that he had no tent to lend me. Later in the day I learned that ever since my first visit the crops had failed, and that most of the cattle had died from the murrain which has swept over all the Koko-nor and adjacent country, and that I had been considered the cause of all the trouble.*

April 5.—Although I staid at Shang nearly a fortnight in 1889, and knew nearly every living soul in the town, only a very few have vouchsafed to recognize me this time. The Chinese here assure me that this is a Mongol custom, a strange one to say the least, and confined to this place, as far as my experience goes.

Everything is fearfully dear here this year, two pounds of butter are exchanged for a sheep, barley sells for a tael of silver a bushel (*t'ou*). I sent the K'anpo a small present to-day and he promised to send return presents to-morrow.

My Panaka guides left this morning with their yaks, as there is no grass around this place. Before leaving they begged for first one thing and then another, until I got mad with them and turned them out of my tent. These people are insatiable, and one should be very careful when dealing with them, never to give them anything until they have completely fulfilled the bargain made, whether it be to guide or do something else for you. If

* Shang pays a yearly tribute to the Panch'en rinpoch'e of Tashil'unpo of 3 *yuan-pao* (150 taels). The lama who governs the district for him receives annually from each *ta chia* (*i. e.*, all the tents occupied by members of a same family, married ones included,) twelve sheep, one each month. He on his side gives yearly to each family a little *k'atag*, and in return he receives from each a certain number of lamb-skins, nominally "to line his clothes." The second lama (colloquially called the K'anpo) gets whatever he can squeeze from the people. All the property which a person had in actual personal use at the time of his death, such as clothes, boots, saddles, horses, gun, etc., goes to the lama on his demise.

one begins from the start to make them small presents to keep them in good humor, they will pester one's life out. This remark applies to Mongols also, though in a less degree.

To-day has been very hot, the thermometer in my tent at 1.30 P. M. stood at 78° Fahrenheit, and in the sun at 87° Fahrenheit. It is positively oppressive, the change has been so sudden.

I heard that the Djassak of Baron, my former acquaintance of '89, is now living at Oim, a little valley opening on to the Iké gol and a day's ride from here. The Hsien-sheng will go there to-morrow to see Dowé, my former guide to Jyäkundo, and learn if he will assist me this time.

April 6.—Most of my time to-day has been taken up buying barley, hair hobbles, ropes, and various other necessary odds and ends, and also ethnological specimens. Flat pearl buttons, small jack-knives and needles were in great demand, five buttons or needles buying a pair of hobbles. For a fine matchlock I gave an Alashan saddle-rug, a brick of tea and a jack-knife.

I was very sorry to hear to-day from a Chinese trader just arrived from Oim that Dowé had lost the sight of one eye, and that the other was in a very inflamed condition and of little use to him, I fear he will not be able to accompany me.

There are here four Mongol lamas from Manchuria, one a Solon. The latter is waiting to join the yearly caravan from Tankar to Lh'asa, which is due in the Ts'aidam in May. He is a fine looking fellow as white as I am, and has quite a European cast of features. Eastern Mongol lamas like living here, as the usage of the country admits of their having wives, whereas in Tibet or their own country such a thing would not be tolerated.

The meteorological record to-day in the shade, from 6 A. M., to 7 P. M., is as follows:

HOUR.	TEMP.	ATMOSPHERE.	
6 A. M.	+35° F.	Calm.	Cirro-stratus $\frac{10}{10}$
7 "	39°.1	"	" " "
10 "	44°.3	"	" " "
12 "	68°	Light N. W. breeze	" "
2 P. M.	67°.5	"	" "
4 "	61°.2	"	" "
6 "	53°.2	Very light S. breeze	Ciro-cumul. Strato. cirrus "
7 "	51°	"	" " "

These figures are all much higher than on the same date in 1889.

April 7.—I heard that the present K'anpo on arriving here was horrified at the morals of his subjects, he imposed heavy fines on all offenders, but from what I learn he has not yet been able to produce from among the people a candidate for the *Prix Montyon* or any other prize for virtue. There will never be a *rosière* in this country.

Last night the Solon lama told me a curious yarn which I learnt was widespread among the Mongols. He said that some five hundred years ago the Emperor of Russia (or a foreign Emperor, for *Olosu* has either meaning), desirous of knowing what was in the sun, had taken fifty Mongol men and as many women and, shutting them up in a crystal casket which had the power of flying, had started them off on a voyage of discovery to the sun. Since then nothing has been heard of the explorers, and the Mongols bear a grudge against this Emperor, whoever he may be, who practiced such cruelty on their people.

We are now in the month of Ramazan, and all the Chinese here fast very strictly, only drinking tea between sunrise and sunset, but my men, being travelers, are free to eat when they will or, rather, can.

A very fine quality of rhubarb grows in the mountains south of Shang. The Chinese dig the root in the fifth and sixth moons, when the shrub is as high as a man. Rhubarb is called *shara butuk* by the Mongols, they use a good deal of it as a dye, but its medicinal properties are unknown to most of them.

In Taichinär a great deal of excellent licorice (*sha-nyar* in Koko-nor Tibetan) is found, but it has no marketable value. Around Kuei-tê and on the Huyuyung it is also abundant, and I have seen a little of it for sale at Kumbum.

In the evening the Hsien-sheng and Dowé arrived from Oim, and the latter showed great pleasure at seeing me again. He brought a message from his chief asking me to come and camp near him, where grass and water were abundant. Should I wish to visit the Tosu nor, he added, as he had learned from my Hsien-sheng that I wanted to do, Dowé was to guide me and bring me back to Oim by an easy road through the mountains.

Dowé told me that in 1889, after he had left me at Jyäkundo, he returned to Nyamts'o Purdung's camp and stayed there several days. The old chief told him to tell me that should I return to the Ts'aidam in two years, as I had said I would, I was not to come back to Nyam-ts'o, as his people had been greatly displeased at the friendliness of the reception given me, they contending that I had only come to take treasures out of their mountains and streams. Should I show myself again there, the old chief went on to say, he feared his people might revolt and kill both him and me.

The old Tibetan who had guided me from Jyäkundo to Kanzé, Dowé also told me, had been seized by the people there shortly after my departure and some said that they had killed him, while other reports had it that the Ch'ien-tsung, Lu Ming-yang, had been able to deliver him from the mob and get him safely, though after much trouble, out of town.*

Dowé has only recently returned from Lh'asa where he went with his Dzassak, leaving here in the fourth moon and getting

* The following letter from Fu T'ung-shih and two other petty officers accompanying him, and of whom I have spoken in ***Land of the Lamas***, 133, ***et passim***, was forwarded to me at Shanghai and tells of what befell my two servants left by me at Jyäkundo in 1889, when I had to make a rush through Dérgé and the Horba country to reach Ta-chien-lu. From other sources of information opened to me on my second visit to Ta-chien-lu, the story in this letter is corroborated. It runs as follows, after the usual flowery preamble:

"After Your Excellency had left this district the local lama and the tribesmen heard of you, so they armed themselves and went several *li* in pursuit 'to kill the foreigner,' but they could not overtake you and returned. They then seized your servant Liu, and Miao Ting-hsin, near the T'ung-tien River (Yang-tzu kiang), bound and beat them and commanded them to tell where the foreigner was and deliver him up, or be decapitated as traitors for intriguing with a foreigner to make trouble in Tibet.

"Twelve days later we heard of this, and hurrying to the place we settled the matter by paying official fees, 10 and 11 rupees, and giving a bond that no foreigner should ever come to disturb Tibet.

"At the Erh Tao Ho (probably at the ferry over the Dré ch'u) the two men were again arrested, and we went there, arranged the matter, and paid 1 rupee for fees. Liu Ch'un-shan and his comrade Miao, when they reach you will themselves relate all their fears and sufferings.

"The above-mentioned bond which we and the local headmen gave is of the greatest importance. If you, Sir, should not exercise magnanimous forbearance, but should in your anger send troops against Tibet, we who have pledged ourselves would be entirely ruined and charged with treason and bribery.

"Hence we now write to beg of you to bounteously forgive what was done and thus receive public gratitude as well as our heartfelt thanks for the personal favors which you will have shown to us.

"Thanking you for all your kindnesses to us and with best wishes for your welfare.

"Your stupid brothers,

"HSIEH WÊN-CH'ANG,
("Civil officer.)

"CHANG CH'ÊNG-CHIH,
("Military officer.)

"FU PING-CHING,
("Interpreter.)

"Knock their heads and submit this letter, 5th moon, 14th day (1889)."

back in the ninth. He says that when they passed Nagch'uk'a they were warned that if ever they led foreigners into Tibet they would be put to death. I do not believe the whole of his story, though I think it probable that, in view of Bonvalot's recent journey, they may have been warned against guiding foreigners.

April 8.—The K'anpo has forbidden anyone serving me as guide on my proposed trip to the Tosu nor. Neither Mongols nor Chinese may go, nor must anyone hire me pack animals. If I want to go I can go by myself. Dowé reported this to me, and I at once went to see the K'anpo and have it out with him. He received me very courteously in a little room arranged in true Tibetan style, and I conversed with him through a Chinese interpreter who translated what I said into Mongol and this was again translated into Tibetan by a Shigatsé man of the K'anpo's suite. I preferred this roundabout way as I could then hear all the side talk of the K'anpo with his people without his suspecting that I understood him.

He denied emphatically that he had issued orders forbidding Chinese to accompany me to the Tosu nor, the prohibition only extended to his Shang-chia Mongols, for he feared if the news came to the ears of the Tashil'unpo authorities they would be displeased at his allowing a foreigner to travel about in Shang under their guidance. I, of course, he went on to say, might "go to the sky" if I saw fit (he meant the devil, I suppose), he had nothing to do with my movements. I told him that the people were saying that the drought of the last two years had been caused by my first visit here (he himself had started the report), and I begged him to state now in the presence of the crowd which surrounded us, that this was nonsensical. This he did, with poor grace I must admit, saying that the Mongols were very ignorant and superstitious, and that he himself was new to official life, and if he had appeared discourteous to me he had not intended to, and begged I would accept his excuses.

I presented him a few odds and ends as a present, together with the obligatory *k'atag*, and after swallowing a few cups of tea took my leave.

A Chinese trader from Shang-wu chuang arrived to-day and reported that when at Dulan-kuo he had heard from some Korluk Mongols that twenty-two foreign women were on their way to the Taichinär and Tibet.* The air is full of reports about foreigners, and everyone fears their advent, though no one can say why.

April 9.—Three camels I hired yesterday to carry my luggage to the camp of the Dzassak of Baron Ts'aidam, in the Oim valley, got here at about 10 A. M. to-day, and it was 11 before the loads were on them and we were all ready to start, I with Dowé, Ssŭ-shih-wu and Chi-hsiang for the Tosu nor, and the Hsien-sheng and Kao pa-erh, with the camels and mules, for Oim.

Just as I was about to mount my pony, it was taken dangerously sick, and though Dowé doctored it, blowing a decoction of saffron water and salt up its nostrils, it was too ill to be of any use, so I had to take another and leave my own behind. It had probably eaten poison-weed, which is quite common hereabout. Everyone held that the sudden illness of the pony was a very bad omen for the success of the journey, and many, Dowé among others, shook their heads ominously.

We followed up the course of the Yógoré, taking a rough trail over the steep foothills along the left bank, the ground composed in great part of disintegrated granite and a mixture of clay and sand. There was a great deal of water in the river which, in places, was one hundred and fifty feet wide, though nowhere over four or five feet deep. Mosquitoes swarmed along the river banks in the willow brush, fine big ones they were, worthy of New Jersey. We camped in the brush near the river about fifteen miles from Shang, and sat around a blazing fire of dead wood, the heat from which was very pleasant, for in these mountains the sun has hardly set, no matter how hot the day has been, before it grows bitterly cold.

When we had finished drinking a big kettle of tea, my men, in true Mongol fashion, put the leaves on the hearth stones on which the kettle rested; this practice is held to be equivalent to burning incense or making an oblation to the gods, and is usually observed by Chinese frontiersmen, even though they profess Islam. In case a hearth stone cracks they are always careful to smear it with a little butter—"for good luck" they say. These are the only two customs observed by Mongols in connection with the fire-place, and they are, I believe, of Tibetan origin.

* This may refer to a number of Swedish women who arrived in Eastern Mongolia (or Kuei-hua ch'eng) sometime during the winter of 1891–'92, or in the spring of '92, "to proselytize the heathen."

Dowé says it takes six days to travel around the Tosu nor, which would make its circumference about eighty miles, and this agrees fairly well with what old Wang-ma-bum, my Tibetan guide from Muri-Wahon told me, when he said it was about one-quarter the size of the Koko-nor. Dowé also said that the Amnyé malchin is so far from the Tosu nor that it is barely visible from the west end of the lake on a clear day.

April 10.—It began to snow about midnight, and by 5 o'clock this morning there was four inches of snow on the ground, so we had to wait in camp until 8.30, by which time the sun had melted most of the snow on the level ground and we could travel comfortably.

We stopped at a small camp where Dowé's brother-in-law lives and bought a sheep from him, as I found that we had started out with only a shoulder and neck of mutton. The sheep we bought had four horns, and we saw in the little flock from which it was taken a large number with the same deformity. Six horns are not uncommon, I was told, but the Mongols try to kill off such animals.

We crossed the Yógoré near the mouth of the Kado gol. When I first visited this valley in '89 I wrote down the name of this little stream Kâtu gol, but Dowé, a good authority on all such subjects, says its name is Kádo, a Tibetan expression, meaning "mouth of two (valleys)."*

We camped near the mouth of the valley leading to the Dúring (or Dúrun) ula, a trail I had followed in 1889. Before we reached camp all the snow fallen during the night had disappeared and the ground was as dry as before. The soil in the bottom of the valley is a mixture of loess and granitic gravel, the loess has evidently been washed down and rests on top of the gravel, which is of angular bits of stone detached from the adjacent range by the disintegrating action of the frost.

Dowé says that while at Lh'asa last year he heard that in the recent Sikkim trouble between the British and the Lh'asa people, the P'yling ("foreigners") had killed three thousand (!) Tibetans, while the latter had only killed one British officer, who had been

* See *Land of the Lamas*, 153. In the same work instead of Yógoré, I wrote the name of that river Yohuré; the Dzassak of Baron assured me, however, that Yógoré was the correct pronunciation.

stabbed by a wounded man whom he had got off his horse to assist.*

April 11.—It blew very hard in the night and I feared the wind would be followed by snow, but in the morning the sun shone brightly and we got off by 7.15. We followed the whole day the bank of the Yógoré, over a mass of *débris* of sandstone and basaltic rocks of gravel, loess and rolled pebbles. We found fine grass growing around the springs, which are very numerous hereabout in the valley bottom. We also saw two small coveys of partridges, some hares, magpies, eagles, crows and hawks.

The only gorges of any length we saw opening on to the valley of the Yógoré are the one leading to the Dúring ula and one on the west side of the valley and a few miles farther south, and called Kókosé. As far as we could see up this latter gorge it was one deep mass of broken rocks, over which tumbled a brook. The *débris*, which in places filled the gorges of the Yógoré, is in many places from a hundred to a hundred and fifty feet thick. The river is very swift and about three and one-half feet deep.

We stopped about half a mile north of the mouth of the Kókosé to drink tea, and at this point, or a little beyond it, we came in sight of the two principal peaks in this portion of the range and the only ones on which there appeared to be much snow, the Turgen ula and the Tsáhan hórga, one on either side of the valley.

A few miles farther up, on reaching the edge of a little lateral gorge, I saw a large herd of wild asses, and I killed three, but lost two in the river and the third dropped dead after swimming the river, and we had not time to dress it. I also wounded one of a large herd of wild goats, but the smallness of the bullet of my carbine made me lose my game, as it usually does unless I hit it in a vital spot.

The Yógoré valley narrowed considerably above the Kokosé gorge and the path was very bad, most of the way a mere goat trail and in places very dangerous and slippery.

We made about twenty-six miles and camped at the junction of the Alang gol with the Yógoré, a place marked by three fine springs and also by a large obo. It is known as Kawa obo.†

*I believe this officer was a major, of whose death I remember reading at the time in the Indian papers.

† Meaning, probably, "the white obo."

The Caroline mountains were visible from here stretching east and west to the Alang and Tosu lakes. The valley along the northern flank of this range, which I have called after my wife, is known as the Ts'o-do lung, "the valley of the two lakes," and is a broad one for this country, averaging a half mile in width.

At Kawa obo, where the two rivers meet, the Yögoré is perfectly clear, while the water coming from the Alang nor is of a reddish brown color, derived, as I found out in '89, from the stream flowing through beds of clay brought down from the mountains along the south side of the valley.

April 12.—We reached the western extremity of the Tosu nor by 5 P. M., after riding along the foothills on the south side of the valley. On the way up I killed a large female wild ass. It is the last one I shall ever shoot, it is butchery, too much like killing a domestic animal, and I see no sport in it.

We camped on the edge of the lake which forms at its western extremity a little bay separated from the body of the lake by a strip of land projecting from the south side. This part of the lake is called "Head of the lake" (Ts'o-go). The bank of the "head" is covered with a mass of water grass which looks like short brown fur in its present dried state. There was only a very little water free from ice on the Ts'o-go, and this was covered with wild fowl, geese, sheldrakes and several varieties of ducks and teal. The banks of the To'o-go were literally covered with bones of yaks which Dowé said had met their death by getting mired. The lake rises in the rainy season ten to fifteen feet higher than its present level.

The lake, on which the ice was piled up, is apparently no where over two miles wide and runs nearly due east and west a distance of about forty miles. On either side rise low mountains of reddish sandstone (?), and beyond its eastern extremity can be seen two pyramidal-shaped snow peaks, probably the Amnyé malchin ula. The lake's Tibetan name of Tong-ri ts'o-nag, or "lake of a thousand hills," is a highly appropriate one, surrounded, as it is, by mountains on every side.

When the moon rose over the lake and shed its rays on the waters of the Ts'o-go, the ice of the lake and the snow peaks around it, leaving the neighboring gorges in deep darkness and magnifying the height of the hills, the sight was a most beautiful one. This lake is the largest I have seen in this region, second only to the Koko-nor. I fancy it is of very inconsiderable depth, the overflow from it is very small, most of the water in the Yógoré is supplied from springs along its course and from four or five affluents, the Seldum gol, Alang gol, Kokusé gol, Kado gol, etc., nor does this lake, in all probability, drain a very large extent of country to the east, receiving in all likelihood only the drainage from off the mountains along its shores.

The Tosu nor is considerably lower than the Alang nor, which I made out in 1889 to be a little under 14,000 feet above sea level. A series of boiling point observations made on the bank of the Tosu nor gives it a mean altitude of 13,180 feet above the sea.

The valley of the Ts'o-do lung from the Alang to east of the Tosu nor was less than a century ago inhabited by the Arik tribe of Tibetans, now living north of the Koko-nor. It is possible that the name of Alang, now given to the lake, is a Mongol perversion of the name of this tribe. The Mongol word Alang has an offensive meaning and was, I imagine, given the lake in later days by the Ts'aidam Mongols who must have had a very hard time of it with these truculent Panaka for neighbors.

April 13.—I passed the day in camp taking sextant observations and surveying the surrounding country. I secured a lot of little univalve shells* from the lake and noticed two or three varieties of small fishes, one about five inches long and of a light brown color, the others with catfish-like mustachios and a flat, sheep-like head, but we had no means of catching any.

I tried to shoot some wild fowl, but could not bag one. Dowé begged me not to fire off my gun, as it would surely cause snow to fall. I promised him 10 taels if it did, and then he was most anxious for me to blaze away at anything and everything for the rest of the day.

Dowé told me that near Sa-chou there are wild men. They make their beds on reeds and feed on wild grapes, which they also know how to dry. They are of the size of ordinary men and speak a language of their own. Two were captured by some Mohammedan Hsi-fan, but one soon died and the other escaped. He, Dowé, places the home of these *Gérésun kun*

* *Planorbis albus* (Müller) and *Limæa peregra* (Müller), both European species.

between Sa-chou and the Lob nor. The persistency of these stories of wild men in this region is strange and highly interesting.*

---

* In my previous work on Tibet (*Land of the Lamas*, 116, 150 and 256), I had occasion to refer to wild men and to some cases where bears appeared to have been taken for human beings by terrified travelers. A—— K—— heard of these wild men in the same region. "Wild people exist in some of the valleys of the northern range (of the Saithang). They have thick and dark skins, are well built and apparently well fed. They wear no clothes except skins; nor do they dwell in either tents or huts, but live in caves and glens and under the shelter of overhanging rocks. They are ignorant even of the use of arms in the chase, and lie in wait for their prey near springs of water or where salt incrustates. They are said to feed even upon rats, lizards, aud other small animals. They are remarkable for their swiftness of foot, and when pursued even a horseman cannot easily catch them. Whenever they see a civilized man they run away in great terror. They are said to know how to kindle a fire with the aid of flint. They flay the animals they kill with sharp edged stones. Sometimes, but very seldom, they steal goats and sheep grazing in the valleys." *Report of Explorations * * * made in 1879-'82, by A—— K——*, 50. In the same report he mentions meeting with a wild man, when I think he saw a bear. An old Mongol woman living north of Saithang "advised us to return to our tent before evening, because a *demo* (brown bear) had lately committed great ravages in the neighborhood. We met no bear, but the old woman's son, who accompanied us for some distance, pointed out to us a wild man, on an opposite spur about two miles off, coming towards us, but who on perceiving us turned back." Ibid., p. 52.

Douglas Forsyth, *Journal Roy. Geo. Soc.*, XLVII, p. 6, says: "There are numbers of encampments and settlements on the banks of the marshy lakes and their connecting channels; perhaps there are as many as a thousand houses or camps. These are inhabited by families who emigrated there about one hundred and sixty years ago. They are looked upon with contempt by true believers as only half Musselmans. The aborigines are described as very wild people—black men with long, matted hair, who shun the society of mankind and wear clothes made of the bark of a tree. The stuff is called "luff," and is the fiber of a plant called "toka chigha," which grows plentifully all over the sandy wastes bordering on the marshes of Lop." Wild men are said to live on the lower Tsangpo, in Tibet. The Mongol Lama Sherab jyats'o says that in Pemakoichhen (north of Mira Pedam) the Lh'opa "kill the mother of the bride in performing their marriage ceremony when they do not find any wild men, and eat her flesh." See *Report on the Explorations in Sikkim, Bhutan and Tibet, from 1856 to 1886*, p. 7.

Du Plan Carpin, *Historia Mongalorum*, 648 (Edit. Soc. Geog., Paris) refers to wild men living to the south of Omyl (or Cummyl, *i. e.*, Urumtsi) in a great desert. "Sylvestres homines qui nullo modo loquuntur, nec in cruribus habent juncturas; et si quandò cadunt, per se surgere sinè aliorum adjutorio minimè possunt; sed tantam discretionem habent quòd faciunt filtra de lanã camelorum, quibus vestiuntur, et ponunt etiãm contra ventum; et si aliqui Tartari vadunt ad eos et vulnerant eos sagittis, ponunt gramina in vulneribus et fortiter fugiunt antè eos."

Dowé told me also of a mission (?) of Yingili Menggu (*sic*) now on its way to Peking with presents from the Yingili Emperor, but I can make nothing of this story.

April 14.—We started for Shang and made good time down the valley. On the way I saw a big bunch of wild goats, but as I was riding alone a couple of miles ahead of my men and had only a revolver, I failed to get one, though I got several good shots at them.

Game is very scarce in the Ts'o-do lung. When first I visited this valley in 1889 it was teeming with yaks, antelopes, asses and bears. A disease has destroyed nearly every antelope in the country, and the yaks have also disappeared, probably driven farther south by the Mongols of Shang and Baron who hunt them a great deal, their flesh being the only meat a great part of these people use during the winter.

We crossed the Yógoré about two miles east of Kawa obo. The men in single file rode their ponies across the ice without accident, though it cracked ominously. As I started to cross Dowé shouted out, "*Séms chung, séms chung, Pönbo-la!*" ("Look out, look out, Sir!") but too late; the ice gave way under my horse and we both disappeared in the water, which was very deep and swift and about a foot or so below the lower surface of the ice. My baggy ch'uba and trousers held me up and I caught on to the ice, where I was able to cling, though the current threw my legs against the ice with such violence that I could not draw myself out, but the pony was swept under. I shouted to the men to throw themselves flat on the ice and creep out to me, which they did, and after much trouble got me out, none the worse for the ducking. For several hours we tried to break away the ice to get the pony and especially my saddle, also my note books and instruments, which were in my saddle-bag, but to no use; we finally decided to try it the next day, for the stream was now swollen by the water coming down from the snow hills.

We again camped at Kawa obo, and I passed the rest of the day trying in vain to dry my sheepskin gown and leather breeches in the sun and over the fire, after wrapping myself in my blankets, as I had no other clothes with me. I am glad it was not the mule with my sextant and camera which was lost; on the whole I think I am in luck, though my men look very gloomy over my misfortune.

April 15.—We were able to find the pony which had been swept some distance down the river. The saddle and bridle were still on him and nothing was much damaged. I regret the loss of the pony, which was one of the best ones I had, though very undersized; I will not be able to get such another in this country.

We left Kawa obo by 9 A. M. and camped a little below the entrance to the valley leading to the Durun ula, where we found very good grass and dry brushwood. Though this point is only twenty miles from our camp of last night we halted here, as the horses have had little or nothing to eat for the last five days. Partridges are quite plentiful hereabout, and we saw a large herd of wild goats and some geese a little higher up the valley. It snowed and hailed slightly towards 2 P. M., but it was clear again in a short while, though violent gusts of wind blew all through the day and night.

While writing in my tent after supper my two Chinese, who had been holding a secret consultation for some time a little away from the camp fire, came to me and said that, as I had Yeh Hsien-sheng to look after my affairs and a cook to prepare my food, I did not require their services, and that they proposed leaving me as soon as we got back to Shang. I replied that I was delighted to have them go, that I was tired of them and of the continual wrangling and bickering they had kept up ever since leaving Lusar. The fact is these two men are disgusted at not being able to squeeze me more, and are jealous of the confidence I show the Hsien-sheng.

I only fear that Dowé will take this desertion as another proof of my bad luck, and will either refuse to accompany me or use it as an argument to prevent others from doing so, all his professions of friendship notwithstanding.

April 16.—We got back to Shang this evening after a hard ride of thirty-three miles, only stopping at Dowé's brother-in-law's to drink tea. We came down the right side of the river, a far better road than that we had followed in going, and one which should be followed when the river is not too high, though even by taking it one has to ford the river twice between the Kado gol and Shang, and four times between the former place and the Tosu nor, and any of these fords may be very dangerous when the current is as swift as it is now.

The people at Shang, from whom I had borrowed a tent when I first arrived here, kindly gave up their tent to me and prepared me some food, as I had told my Chinese that I would not allow them to approach me or do anything more for me.

The Mongols all begged me to reconsider my determination to have nothing more to do with my two Chinese, but I refused most emphatically. Dowé then declared that he could not accompany me as my luck was too bad and he might have some mishap befall him. Since his first journey with me he had lost the sight of one eye, and the other is now very weak. It might well be that I was the cause of his misfortune. All this and a great deal more occurred to him now, and he decided to cut loose from me.

I ordered my Chinese to return to me all the things I had bought for them before leaving Lusar, clothing, blankets, etc., and turned them out of the compound. Before going to sleep I sent for old Ma Shuang-hsi, an old Chinese trader from Shang wu chuang, near Hsi-ning, whom I first met here in 1889 and who is anxious to join his fortunes to mine as he has lost all the money he came here with, or rather he can collect no money or goods from his Mongol debtors. He agreed promptly to accompany me to Oim, where my other men are camped and where I will make final arrangements about his permanent employment.

April 17.—My final departure from Shang was not a triumphal one, nearly every one shunned me, only two or three Mongols (among whom Dowé was conspicuous by his absence) escorted me out of the village, which I left by eight o'clock, accompanied only by Ma Shuang-hsi.

We traveled very slowly for the ponies and the pack mule were very tired and hungry, as I had not been able to buy forage or grain at Shang, and they had had no grass to eat since the day before yesterday. We followed a general westerly direction up a narrow valley called Hultu, in the mountains skirting the Ts'aidam plain, then crossing a couple of low but steep hills, we entered the valley of the Ara ossu which marks the boundary between Shang and Baron Ts'aidam. The lower course of the Ara belongs to the latter district, the upper to Shang. We followed up the stream, which flows between tolerably high, bare and rugged hills to a point called Tsahan hada, or "White Stones," where the valley branches and where we found good grass and water. Here we camped for the night and, to my surprise, while we were eating our supper, Dowé joined us, looking rather shamefaced and in a very pleasant humor. He explained his absence by saying that he had been too tired and foot-sore to follow me, that he had had to walk most of the way as his pony was played out, etc., etc.

I turned the conversation to other subjects and we talked of foreign religions, monks, nuns, propagation of religion and the comparative merits of the different faiths. Dowé, like most Buddhists, is very liberal. A Mongol or a Tibetan will always meet you on the common ground of *läs* or "good work," just as a Chinaman will on that of *li* or *tao*.

The night was so pleasant that we did not put up the tent, but piling up the luggage and saddles to windward, lay down on our saddle blankets and felt comfortably warm with nothing but our sheepskin ch'ubas over us.

April 18.—A few miles above our camp of last night we climbed a steep but not very high hill on which a few junipers were growing, and reached the summit of the Koko k'utul or "Blue pass," thus called from the bluish color of the mica-schist on the hillsides.

From here we descended into a narrow valley leading north-west and called Arachedo, down which flows a good-sized brook, emptying probably into an affluent of the Iké gol a few miles to the north. Cutting across the valley we crossed another low pass (Oim k'utul), and on its western slope I saw my blue tent and a quarter of a mile below it six or eight Mongol tents, forming the camp of the Dzassak of Baron and his immediate retainers.

I felt as if I had reached home again and looked forward with great pleasure to a few days of rest, for I was weary of wrangling with Mongols and Chinese and wanted a little solitude. On the whole I was pleased with the success of my trip to the Tosu nor, where, by the way, the Mongols said I had gone this time, as well as in 1889, to angle for the fish of gold which lives in its water. The K'anpo of Shang asked Dowé (whose name is written, I now learn, Rdo-pi) when we got back there from the Tosu nor, whether I had caught the fish of gold in the lake, because he sup-

Mongol Women of Shang.

Mongols of Shang.

posed I had only gone there this time for that purpose, having failed to catch it in 1889.

Dowé told him that I had caught nothing, that I had not taken so much as a stone away from the lake. "But what did he do at night?" insisted the K'anpo. "He went to sleep in his tent at an early hour," replied the other. "Aya!" said the lama, "what in the world did he go there for, if that is all he did! But where is he going to now?" "He is going to the Lob nor," said Dowé. "That's it, I thought as much," petulantly exclaimed the K'anpo, "he has caught the fish and horse of gold of the Tosu nor, and now he thinks he can catch the golden frog which lives in Lake Lob; but he cannot, no one can catch it but my master, the Pan-ch'en rinpoch'e of Tashil'unpo."

My men were surprised to see me without the two men who had started out with me from Shang, but when I had told them of their desertion, they evidenced no astonishment and declared themselves ready to follow me anywhere. I now first learnt from that that Ssŭ-shih-wu and Chi-hsiang had tried to debauch the Hsien-sheng and Kao-pa-erh when we were camped at Muri-Wahon. It was their intention to run away from me there, when they could have got back to their homes in a few days, and I would have been unable then as now to get back from them the 20 taels I had advanced to each of them before leaving Lusar.

I sent the Hsien-sheng to the Dzassak's with a few presents, the Remington carbine and a hundred cartridges, a jack-knife, some sugar, dried fruit and a k'atag, to make inquiries concerning his health. He sent me an invitation to dine with him to-morrow, when I will ascertain if Dowé will come with me as guide; I fear, however, that he will not. The Hsien-sheng heard him telling the Dzassak of my recent bad luck, one pony knocked up, another drowned, my men abandoning me, etc., and then he had said that he would not go with me farther than the Taichinär. The private chaplain of the chief is a lama from Tashil'unpo, and he is opposing tooth and nail my project of visiting Lh'asa territory. Time and lots of patience will possibly enable me to make some kind of a compromise with the chief and his counsellors, but I am terribly wearied with these vascillating, unreliable Mongols, one never knows exactly how one stands with them, one minute they appear to be your devoted friends, the next they will not even recognize you. Then their cowardice is so great that they will hardly ever stand by you in a tight place, unless it is so hopelessly tight that they can only get out of it by trusting to you, when they become a dead weight upon your hands.

April 19.—The Dzassak sent a white pony for me to ride on to his tent where I was to dine with him, and I was told that this was quite the correct thing, to send a pony of any other color would not have been so exquisitely polite.

I found him much fatter than three years ago, especially about the head, but he still wore the identical little black satin Chinese cap (*mao-t'ou-erh*) he then had, but which now rests very unsteadily on his crown. Two lamas were seated in the tent, the one reading from the Kandjur, the other mumbling prayers, but both of them listened, notwithstanding, to all we said. The one reading the Kandjur was the Tibetan from Tashil'unpo; he has a bad face, and did not disguise his displeasure at seeing me here.

The Dzassak has brought back from his recent journey to Lh'asa a lot of brass lamps, prayer-wheels and various religious implements which now give a certain furnished look to his tent, but it is still a pretty poor looking place, though he may possibly have lots of pretty things locked up in the big boxes ranged along the side of the tent.

His wife, this year no longer fearing me, came in shortly after my arrival with her daughter, a pretty little girl of eleven or twelve, and made a bad kind of doughnut—*ma-hua-erh*, the Chinese call these twisted, greasy cakes—on the top of a box, rolling out the dough with a not too clean crupper-stick. We drank a great deal of tea and ate ma-hua-erh, *chuoma*, chura, tarak and mutton, finishing off with a cup of Chinese samshu. The conversation was for the most part very foolish and bored me intensely, still I had to reply to all the stupid questions put to me, as for example, which is the best country I had ever visited? Had I ever visited the country of people with a hole through their bodies and that of the Cyclops? (The *Shan hai ching's* legends are apparently current in Mongolia.) Were there many treasures in the Ts'aidam? Will next year be dry or wet? Who is the *Pusa* of my country? etc., etc.

Finally after two hours of this, I told the chief that I had come to the Ts'aidam for two purposes, to see him and to ask him to let me have a guide to the Tengri nor.

He replied that there was no such lake, that no one in his country had ever heard of it, but the Tibetan lama whispered to him "*yō*" ("there is"), and then the Dzassak said: "We will talk about this at our leisure some other time," and dismissed the matter, when I took my leave.

In the afternoon the Dzassak came to my tent, poked his nose in everything, had me explain the sextant, the kodak, the guns, the artificial horizon, the thermometers to him, ate a huge quantity of Chinese chow I had got ready for him, smoked my water-pipe, and finally told me he would certainly do all he could for me, escorting me through the Taichinär himself. He would even go with me to Lh'asa, he added, had not a letter recently reached him saying the Tibetan authorities had closed the *chang lam* this year to all comers, for fear some foreigner might worm his way into the country. He was perfectly well aware that I knew he was lying, but I thanked him effusively, begged he would not take so much trouble on my account, and finally got him to leave, and I went to bed utterly played out.

April 20.—The Hsien-sheng and Ma Hsuang-hsi (or Lao-han, as we call him,) started for Shang to-day to get the black pony, which had been taken ill when I was starting for the Tosu nor, and secure the services of a Taichinär Mongol who had offered to guide me into Tibet, or wherever I chose to go.

The morning was lost for either rest or work, first one Mongol came in, then another, and finally the Dzassak, who wanted to look through the telescope of my sextant. He was accompanied by Dowé, who told me that everyone at Shang thought I was angling for the sun when they saw me looking at its image in the artificial horizon, and that they feared they would be plunged in darkness if I caught it.

The Dzassak prolonged his visit till near evening, and as my Mongol speaking Chinese had left, I had no one to help me and had to talk Tibetan to Dowé, who acted as interpreter for me. Some men with the Dzassak told me that kuldza (*Ovis Poli*) were very numerous in the mountains around this place, and they promised to bring me one or more.*

The Dzassak brought the Remington carbine I had given him and took some lessons in firing it, he will soon have exhausted the supply of cartridges I gave him and the gun will be useless.

* I also heard that leopards were very numerous in the adjacent mountains. The Dzassak had killed three a few months previously.

I told him this, but he said that the moral effect produced by his possession of such a weapon was incalculable. The Goloks, he told me, would never attack him when they heard that he had it, and he intended to let them know of it at once.

April 21.—This has been a day of rest, no one bothered me with foolish questions—at least for any length of time. A young Halha lama, awaiting here an opportunity to go to Lh'asa, came into my tent for awhile, but he left me to myself and amused himself cutting out paper figures with a pair of scissors, showing wonderful expertness, making the most intricate designs, some of them very pretty, and all with Buddhist symbols (*vajras* especially) in them.

The day was oppressively hot towards noon (the thermometer in the shade at 11.30 A. M. stood at 87° Fahrenheit), but by nightfall it was nearly freezing.

Kao pa-erh, who has lived with the Eastern Mongols near Kuei-hua Ch'eng, has told me he had frequently witnessed their burials. The body is put on a frame and dragged away by a horse; if it falls off, it is left to be devoured by wolves and vultures, or else it is burnt and the ashes are moulded into a little human figure, which is stored away in the house of the family in a small white cotton bag.

In this part of Mongolia all corpses are exposed on the hillsides to be devoured, but strangely enough I have never seen any skeletons. The Chinese and Mongols say that vultures are able to eat the bones, which they first break by carrying them to a great height and then letting them fall.

I passed part of the day in taking an inventory of my belongings and repacking my boxes, in each of which I hid some of my money, so that all should not be stolen if one box were broken open. I find that the two men who left me at Shang have stolen a number of things from me, brick tea, sugar, snuff, buttons, knives, etc. Hai Chi-hsiang I had suspected of crookedness for some time, he is a worthy son of his father, the blackmailer.

Dowé came to camp in the evening while I was making some star observations. He told me his people call Ursa Major *Dolón Burhán* "The seven Buddhas," and Ursa Minor *Altán kátasún*, or "the golden nail," the latter a better name, I think, than the one we use. He asked me for a few sheets of paper on which to have written the Dorjé chö-pä do (*Vajrachêdika sûtra*), which he wanted to put in one of the charm boxes (*gawo*) he wears around his neck. He says this work is one of the favorite ones among Mongols for this purpose, for it is a most potent charm.

Dowé told me also that the Tibetans test the quality of tea by burning some leaves on a coal and smelling the smoke.

This camp is most inconvenient, there is absolutely no water in this gorge, only a few little patches of snow. All the water we use has to be brought from near the Iké gol nearly two miles away; the grass, however, is good, and it is well sheltered.

The people here are all very anxious to get money not goods for everything they sell, they say they want to buy yaks (*djomo*) in the K'amba country to replace those which have died during the last year or so from disease—the Dzassak has lost two hundred head, but none died in K'amdo to the south of here.

April 22.—About two inches of snow fell this morning between five and ten o'clock, but by noon, when the thermometer stood at 52° Fahrenheit, it had nearly all melted. At 2 P. M. it began to snow again and continued until five, when the sky cleared.

The Shang Mongols, and to a less extent all the Ts'aidam people, write charms on the jaw bones and shoulder blades of sheep and suspend them in long strings over their houses and tents in lieu of the more commonly seen *lung-ta* ("wind horses") used throughout Tibet and other parts of Mongolia.

The living Buddha I met in this country in 1889 has "made his pile" here and left the country for Sérkok gomba.* He came here in 1887 or 1888 from near Jyäkundo, a very poor man, but left here with several thousand sheep and other valuables, the gifts of the faithful—it is astounding how these Mongols will let themselves be fleeced by a pack of ignorant rapscallions such as most of these lamas are.

---

* I visited this famous lamasery in 1889. See *Land of the Lamas*, 98. Tibetan authors give the name of this lamasery as Ser-k'ang gomba, "the lamasery with the golden house." Its official name is Gadän dam ch'ös ling, and it was anciently known as Amdo Gomang gomba. This latter name probably means "the Imperial lamasery of Amdo,"—implying that it had been built with funds supplied by the Emperor of China.

April 23.—Yeh Hsien-sheng and the Lao-han got back to-day from Shang. They had much difficulty in getting my black pony back, as the man in whose charge I had left it first swore it was dead, then that he would only deliver it to me, finally that I had promised him 8 or 9 taels if it got well. My men had to appeal to the K'anpo, give him an ounce of silver (in lieu of a *k'atag*, the rascally lama had the impudence to say), pay 3 taels for medicine, and even then they had to threaten that if the pony were not forthcoming I would write to the Amban at Hsi-ning about it. The pony is to be here the day after to-morrow in charge of the Taichinär Mongol Panti who has agreed to accompany me to Tibet. He is to be given a horse, saddle, etc., and 6 taels a month as wages.

I heard that my two deserters are in hard straits at Shang; they have had to sell all their belongings, down to their knives, to get food and see no prospect of getting back to Hsi-ning. They sent me word that they would come back to me with great pleasure, but I would not have them again on any account.

The Dzassak left on a *tournée* to-day to allot to his people land to till this year, as no one holds land in severalty, it is all the property of the chief, nor may the same soil be cultivated two years in succession; it is usually left fallow three or four years. Those of the people who till the soil pay to the Dzassak annually one bushel (*t'ou*) of barley per family, while those who are only herdsmen pay him about the equivalent in butter or sheep. All the fields are irrigated, and are in the mountains where alone the soil is not alkaline and the water is pure. They yield from forty to fifty times the seed sown.

The crop last year was a complete failure, so it happens that the women are abstaining from washing themselves the whole year, a time honored method of averting the wrath of Heaven.*

April 24.—Tsul-k'rims Panti the Taichinär guide, arrived to-day, and I like his face, it is energetic, and to his other virtues he adds that of not being loquacious, but answering all questions in a straightforward way and then remaining silent till again spoken

* Mongols and Tibetans hardly ever wash their clothes. Speaking of the former Rubruk, says: "Vestes nunquam lavant, quiâ dicunt quod Deus tunc irascitur, et quod fiant tonitrua si suspendantur ad siccanduum. Immo lavantes verberant, et eis auferunt." *Itinerarium*, 234.

to. He has been several times to Lh'asa; when going there the last time he passed at Muktsi Soloma a couple of foreigners with Chan-t'ou servants and donkeys (evidently Carey and Dalgleish).

After a little persuasion, having had a good feed and a long smoke, Panti told us his story.

Until a few years ago he had lived on the Naichi gol, where his brother is a headman (*Jalang*), but one day his wife deserted him for another man of the tribe. There are no marriage ceremonies among this people,* and the woman is at perfect liberty, if she does not like her husband, to leave him and take another. Panti, however, felt aggrieved, he gave out that he was going to Lh'asa, sold his few belongings and started off, but only went as far as the mountains. From there he stole back in the night to the Naichi gol, drove off his happy rival's ponies and set out with them for the Alang nor, whence he proposed traveling to the Golok country. It was his intention to try and get a band of these robbers to come back with him to his native country and lay the whole land waste. When he had got to the Alang nor he met a party of yak hunters from Shang, and to them he told his tale of woe. They persuaded him to give up his project of revenge and to go with them to Shang. There he gave in his allegiance to the K'anpo by presenting him as tribute one of his ponies, then taking a half interest in a wife (such practices are common in these parts) and in a hovel, he settled down to the exercise of the various trades in which he was proficient, blacksmith, tailor and carpenter, and here my men found him, anxious to return once more to his native Taichinär and once more try his luck at marriage.

The Dzassak has promised me a letter of introduction to the Dzassak of Taichinär, and Dowé is to give me the names of all the stages where water and grass can be found between the Ts'aidam and the Tengri nor;† I don't know that either of these documents will prove of any use, but I can get nothing else from them. Dowé, however, is excusable, his eyesight is so bad that he could be of no possible use to me, he is in constant pain and sits most of the time with his face in his hands.

---

* See note under date of *April 25*.

† The list of names he gave me was a mixture of names of places along the high-road to Nagch'uk'a, with one or two of places he had heard of near the Tengri nor. It was of no value whatever, so I do not reproduce it here.

I hear that there are a number of boys among the Ts'aidam Mongols with such strongly marked European features that some of them were recently refused permission to pass Nagch'uk'a when on a pilgrimage to Lh'asa, the authorities there insisting that they were Russians in disguise. The youngest of these half-breeds (?) is between six and seven years old.

The Ts'aidam Mongols only live in the mountains during the winter and early spring, going down to the foot of the hills in the month of June or thereabouts and remaining there, mosquitoes notwithstanding, drinking, singing and making merry (so said my informant) till late in the autumn.

April 25.—As regards marriage among these people, when a man and woman, after cohabiting for awhile, have decided to be man and wife, the parents of the girl, if pleased with the marriage, give her a dowry of cattle, sheep, a tent or whatever they can afford. As far as I can learn endogamy and exogamy are both allowable.* The Dzassak of Baron, whose name I should have said is Targyä, is a poor man, he married the daughter of a wealthy man of Shang called Lama Wangbo, who gave his daughter as a dowry several hundred yaks, sheep, horses, jewelry, clothes, etc., and she never loses an opportunity of reminding her husband that the wealth of the family is all hers. She makes all the purchases or sales herself, and is rapidly adding to her belongings, an easy thing by the way as a chief has prior rights to anyone else in the country as regards trading, and most of his tribesmen are not only in debt to him but he alone can always sell them such things as they stand in need of or have a wild and irresistible longing for and of which he usually has a stock on hand.

Most of the men I see here who have been to Lh'asa have brass army buttons on their gowns, and Panti tells me that they are

* That marriage by purchase still exists to a certain extent among the Mongols, I have no doubt. Rubruk says of Mongol marriages: "De nuptiis eorum noveritis, quod nemo habet ibi uxorem nisi emat eam, unde aliquando sunt puelle multum adulte antequam nubant * * * Servant gradus consanguinitatis primum et secundum, nullum servant affinitatis. Habent enim simul vel successive duas sorores. Nulla vidua nubit inter eos, hac ratione, quia credunt quod omnes qui serviunt eis in hac vita servient in futura, unde de vidua credunt quod semper revertetur post mortem ad primum maritum. Unde accidit turpis consuetudo inter eos, quod filius scilicet ducit aliquando omnes uxores patris sui, excepta matre. Curia enim patris et matris semper accidit minori filio." *Itinerarium*, 235.

sold there seven for a tanka (about twelve cents). The future traveler in these regions will be surprised to find among the women's ornaments a number of Hong-kong ten cent pieces, and some small Japanese silver coins; I, however, am responsible for their appearance here, I brought over a hundred with me and bought various curios and barley with them, they were in great demand.

It is customary among the Ts'aidam Mongols for the males from the age of thirteen to thirty-three to wear their hair in a number of short plaits about six inches long hanging from the crown all around the head. At the age of thirty-three they may wear one long queue in Chinese fashion. This custom is not universal, at all events many of them wear the viril queue long before their thirty-third year. The women until they reach a marriageable age, or until married, usually wear their hair in Tibetan style *i. e.*, innumerable small plaits falling around them like a cloak and held together at the bottom by a ribbon covered with shells and pieces of turquoise or coral beads. When married they wear their hair in two big plaits falling on either side of the face and covered with a broad black satin ribbon passed under the belt.

I learn from Dowé that the Dam Sok Mongols living along the Lh'asa highroad north of Nag-ch'uk'a are of the same stock as the Ts'aidam Mongols (*i. e.*, Eleuts). They were located in their present haunts by the Mongol Emperors to keep the Tibetans back. At that time the Ts'aidam was inhabited by Tibetan tribes and the present Alashan Eleuts lived in the upper Hsi-ning ho valley where they built a fort the ruins of which I saw in '89, a stage to the west of Gomba soba. The ruins at Nomorun hutun in Dsun Ts'aidam were also built at this time, and likewise to keep back the Tibetans.*

*I think that my informant has got things pretty badly mixed up. Prjevalsky's remarks on the Dam Sok given below and Mongol history enable us to straighten out his story and assign an approximately correct date to not only the emigration of these Mongols to Tibet but also to the building of the Nomorun hutun and occupation of the Ts'aidam by the Eleuts. The second story given in the text may be *partly* true, as is also Prjevalsky's, which runs as follows: "After the subjection of the Yegurs, some of the Oluith troops returned to the north, but others settled in Koko-nor; their descendants are the Mongol inhabitants of the present day. Some hundreds of them emigrated to Tibet, where their posterity has multiplied and now numbers eight hundred Yurtas divided into eight koshungs (banners). They live six days' journey to the southwest (*sic*) of the village of Napchu, where they cultivate

Another Mongol told me a more credible story. He said that when in 1779 the Panch'en rinpoch'é Paldan Yéshé passed through the country south of the Koko-nor on his way to Peking, a number of Mongols asked him to protect them from the Panaka Tibetans then pushing northward. He told them to go to the country just south of the Dang la, which forms the northern border of Tibet. Here they went and took up their abodes in the country they still occupy and in which they are under the jurisdiction of Tashil'unpo, not of Lh'asa as might be supposed from their living in a region ruled over by that country, but the sovereignty over the Dam Sok was ceded by the Lh'asa government to that of the Panch'en rinpoch'é. The Dam Sok have eight Débas or chiefs, and the Mongol language is still spoken by the old men of the tribe; in dress and manners they are now thoroughly Tibetan.

It snowed to-day from 7.30 A. M. to 2 P. M. and between four and five inches of snow fell. There was a light east breeze blowing, which usually accompanies snow, though on one or two occasions a snowfall has been preceded by a rather strong westerly wind.

April 26.—The Dzassak paid me another terribly long visit to-day. He said he could not write to the chief of the Taishinär, but he commissioned Dowé, who is to accompany me as far as the latter chief's home, to tell him that I was a very good man, a friend of his and that he would be doing him a personal favor if he gave me guides, supplies, and such pack animals as I required. Of course all this means nothing at all, the message will never be delivered, and Dowé at the last moment will back out of accompanying me.

The Dzassak, who was in an amiable frame of mind, brought about by the gifts I had presented him in fulfillment of a promise

the soil and bear the name of Damsuk Mongols, after the little river on whose banks they are settled." Prjevalsky, *Mongolia*, I, 152.

Two explanations may account for the presence of the Dam Sok Mongols in the locality they now occupy, either they are a remnant of Latsan han's forces with which he invaded Tibet in 1705, or else they belonged to Dalai Kungtaichi's Koko-nor Eleuts, and drifted to Nagch'u to escape the attacks of the Sungars. As to Nomorun hutun, I fancy it was built in 1723, when the Chinese defeated the Koko-nor Mongols who had revolted under Lobzang tandjin. See H. H. Howorth, *History of the Mongols*, I, 522, et seq. On the Yagara, see also the present journal, under date of *June 2nd, 1892*.

made him in '89, said all the Mongols liked me for I dressed and lived as they did, whereas the Russians who had been here had frightened the people with their foreign dress and arms and scorned their food and drink.

The Dzassak gave me the following information concerning the Mongol chiefs in the jurisdiction of the Hsi-ning Amban (Hsi-hai Meng-ku, the Chinese call them).* There are three Wang and two Beilé:

Ching hai Wang,
Muring Wang,
Ch'ing Wang (Mahari Wang in Tibetan),
Koko Beilé,
Erké Beilé.

Each of these five chiefs receives a yearly imperial gift, handed him by the Amban, of 24 *yuan-pao* (1,200 taels) and eight pieces of satin.

Then there are two Beisé:

Korluk Beisé,
Hargé Beisé,

who receive an annual present of 16 *yuan-pao* and eight pieces of satin.

The Tolmok Kung-wang,
Boha Kung,
Dundura Kung,
Bitcheren Kung,†

receive 12 *yuan-pao* and six pieces of satin. Lastly there are thirty-two Dzassak, each of whom receives yearly 2 *yuan-pao* and four pieces of satin.

Some of these chiefs only rule very small bands, the Bitcheren Kung for example, who lives on the Ta-t'ung River north of Hsi-ning Fu, has only four or five families under him. Under each chief holding his position under a commission from the Emperor,

* The Koko-nor Tibetans call the eastern Mongols Harchimba or Mar Sok, "Low country Mongols;" the western Mongols they call Yar Sok or "Upper country Mongols." According to my informant there are forty-three chiefs among the Koko-nor Mongols. Timkowski, *op. cit.*, III, 272, says there are twenty-nine, three Wangs, (iun vang), two Beilé, two Beisé, four Kung and *eighteen* Taichi.

† Bitcheren means "little."

is a *Tosalakji* who receives his from the Hsi-ning Amban. Under this latter officer are *Hosho-dzangé*, *Mérin*, *Jálang* and *Sumen-dzangé* appointed by the head of the tribe (*hosho*), who also gives them official buttons of rank.*

April 27.—There is quite a difference in the Mongol spoken here in Baron and that of Shang, not only in the pronunciation, but also in the vocabulary. Then there are tabooed words. Thus in Baron Ts'aidam, salt is called *hsiu*, not *dábesu*, because the latter word entered into the name of the grandfather of the present chief. A number of similar cases have been mentioned to me.†

I paid my last visit to the Dzassak to-day; he has proved himself a great bore and a terrible beggar, and, considering that I have got absolutely nothing out of him, he has made a pretty good thing out of my visit. The lama who is reading for his benefit the one hundred and eight big volumes of the Kandjur, which it takes him about a year to drone through, told me that he got for the job, besides board and lodging, ten ounces of silver and a piece of pulo of about 5 taels value.

The Dzassak told me that he had heard that some robbers had some time ago stolen a horse from my K'amba friend Nyam-ts'o Purdung. The old chief took the revolver I had given him in '89 and, accompanied by two of his sons, followed them up, wounded two of them and got his pony back. Since then his thieving neighbors, the Golok, had been so filled with dread of him that they had left him in perfect peace, for, they said, the foreign gun he had got from the *p'yling* can kill a hundred men at a shot.

---

* The sons of chiefs (*i. e.*, Wang, Kung, Beilé, Dzassak, etc.) bear the courtesy title of *Taichi* in the Ts'aidam.

† Tibetan words are of frequent occurrence in Ts'aidam Mongol, for example: *ma lung*, "ear ring;" *shugu*, "paper;" *rgya-ma*, "scales;" *natsa*, "ink;" *suru*, "coral;" *chyutso-k'orlo*, "watch;" *kaiyü*, "porcelain cup;" *largya*, "sealing wax;" *karma*, "star;" *litsé*, "seal." Tabooed words are common in Chinese. Besides the tabooing of characters occurring in the names of emperors, the people refrain from using many words because certain others with the same sound have unlucky meanings. Thus in western Ssŭ-ch'uan soldiers and boatmen do not use the word *kai*, "to boil," but say instead *chang*. Boatmen will not use the word *tao*, "to arrive," but *lung*, for another word pronounced *tao*, means "to upset." Instead of saying *tao ch'a*, "pour out tea," they say *yao ch'a* or *chun ch'a*, etc.

The Panaka Tibetans call Shang, Gongma Ts'aidam or "Upper Ts'aidam;" Baron and Dsun they call "Middle (Barma) Ts'aidam," and Taichinär is Shuoma (or Lower) Ts'aidam. Formerly the country to the west of the Taichinär, and called Karsa,* was inhabited, but now it is a desert only visited occasionally by gold diggers from the Chan-t'ou country (Ilchi probably).

In conversation to-day with the Hsien-sheng he told me that the Hsieh-chia used formerly to give the Mongol or Tibetan chiefs presents to secure the privilege of transacting their business at Tankar, Hsi-ning or elsewhere. At the present time they have to get a license from the Amban and of course are still obliged to buy the good will of the people with whom they wish to trade. Their profits are, as I was told at Kuei-tê, greatly curtailed and they barely make a living.†

April 28.—The Dzassak has promised to have camels here early to-morrow to take my things as far as Tengelik. He says he will not accept any pay for the use of them, that he puts them at my disposal. I am heartily tired of Oim and the Dzassak, and delighted to get away, even if it is to go down to the swamp of the Ts'aidam.

I have noted somewhere ‡ that Chinese traders make use of certain terms only known to themselves to express numerals. These terms (called *yen-tzŭ* in western China and *t'iao ka-erh* at Peking) vary in each locality and even in each branch of trade, horse traders, inn keepers, flour dealers, each trade has its own. Curiously enough Hsi-ning Fu and Ta-chien-lu (Ssŭ-ch'uan) have the same *yen-tzŭ* in general use; they are as follows:—

1. Ch'ien-tzŭ-erh.
2. Ch'ou tzŭ-erh.
3. Ts'ang tzŭ-erh.
4. Su tzŭ-erh.
5. Nien tzŭ-erh.
6. Nao tzŭ-erh.
7. Tiao tzŭ-erh.
8. K'ou tzŭ-erh.

* Prjevalsky, Carey, and apparently Bonvalot, visited this section of the Taichinär, which the first named traveler calls Gast or Gass.

† Conf. p. 93.

‡ See p. 15 and 64.

9. Sao tzŭ-erh.
10. Ch'ien tzŭ-erh.
11. Ch'ien tzŭ ch'ien.
12. Ch'ien ch'ou.
15. Ch'ien pao.
20. Ch'ou ch'ien.
25. Ch'ou pao.
55. Nien tzŭ nien, etc., etc.

April 29.—We broke up camp early, though the Dzassak only sent two miserable she-camels instead of the four he had promised me. I gave Dowé, who brought them, a good scolding and told him what I thought of his chief whom I had treated like a gentleman and who acknowledged my kindness by this shabby trick. I left all my traps on the ground for him to get to the village of Baron as best and when he could.

About three miles below our camp we entered the valley of the Iké (or Eké "Big") gol, which is a little broader in this part than the Oim valley and susceptible in spots of being cultivated. The mountains on either side of the stream (which is eight or ten yards wide and about three feet deep), are of coarse, bluish granite, those on the west side from eight hundred to a thousand feet high and rising precipitously; those on the east side sloping more gently and not so high. The valley led north-northwest for about eight miles, and we passed some twenty-five tents in this distance. Then we came to its mouth and the broad Ts'aidam ("salt marsh") lay before us. The plain was covered for miles beyond the foot of the mountains with a thick bed of *débris*, sand and gravel, the low ranges of hills bordering it to the north vaguely discernible through the mist which nearly always hangs over this forlorn country.

Leaving the Iké gol, which must find its way into the Bayan gol or one of its affluents (possibly the Tsahan gol) somewhere to the east of the village of Baron, we took a northwest direction across the plain, cut here and there by low sand hillocks, and for the last five or six miles before reaching the village, covered with brush, willow (*sha-liu*) and white briar (*pai-tz'u*).*

* Suhai in Mongol. Prjevalsky says that this "white briar" is the *Kalidium gracile*. He also calls the coarse bunch grass growing here and in the Gobi the *Lasiagrostis splendens*. See also under date of *May 4th*.

I found the village a little larger than in '89, but quite as miserable looking, many of the hovels had caved in on the soft, spongy soil, and huge pools of reddish iridescent water now marked the spots where they had stood. The houses, however, are of little use to the Mongols, who only use them as store-houses, living themselves in tents in the courtyards. Some twenty families are living here now, many of them were comparatively well off when I first visited this country and then lived in the mountains, since then they have lost all their cattle and sheep and have had to come to this miserable place.

The grass is long and fine around here this year, had I known it sooner I would have come here directly from Shang and saved myself a lot of trouble and all the things I have given away to the chief. Dowé promised to be here to-morrow with my luggage, but I doubt if he is. On Prjevalsky's map, this village is called Khyrma Baron Dzassak. I take the word *Khyrma* to be a poor transcription of the word *kérim* "village." It is more usually called Baron* kuré (*kuré* also meaning village), or Baron Baishing, the latter word meaning "house." The Tibetans call such villages *k'angsar*, Baron k'angsar, Dsun k'angsar, etc.

April 30.—There is a good silversmith here and I availed myself of his presence to have him do a little work for me, solely that I might see how he proceeded. He told me that when he was a boy a Tibetan silversmith had come to the Ts'aidam for awhile and that he blew his bellows and watched him work, this was all the teaching he had ever had. The style of his work is purely Tibetan, and very good considering the clumsiness of his tools. He uses a goat skin bellows, the top with two flat sticks sewed to it with rings in which to pass the thumb and fore-finger. With the right hand he opens and shuts the bag, and by pressing it down expels the air through an iron nozzle, covered with clay, its mouth in a little fireplace about four inches broad. This fireplace is also surrounded, except on the side nearest the smith, by a little clay wall about three inches high. The fuel is charcoal made from the dead willow stumps found near the village. The smith uses a small anvil made in the shape of a cube and resting on a piece of wood, and he has a very small crucible in which to melt the sil-

* Baron in eastern Mongol is pronounced *baragon*; it means "south," literally, "right side."

ver. The silver having been melted into a button (whatever object he is making the process is the same), is beaten out into a thin plate, cut into pieces of the desired shape which are then soldered together, borax and a blowpipe being used in this last operation. The ornamentation consists in pearlwork and in twisted or pearled wire;* to make the latter the silver is cut into thin strips, then passed through a bit of iron pierced with holes of various sizes till it has the desired dimension, after which a little iron instrument is used to cut it slightly and to shape it like a string of very small silver beads. These wires are afterwards soldered on the plain silver work. I saw this man make a ring and I bought from him several other articles, and was shown a number of handsomely finished charm boxes, all made in this primitive fashion.

I heard that in Baron Ts'aidam, there are about one hundred Akas (gélong, gétsul and gényen,† but mostly of the last category, which does not here preclude marriage). This shows the very large proportion of those who embrace a religious life, for the whole population of Baron is only estimated at three hundred families.

As I expected, the camels did not arrive to-day from Oim. I fancy it snowed heavily in the mountains yesterday, for very dense masses of clouds have hung over them the whole day; down here in the plain, for the first time in several months the sky has been perfectly clear the whole day, and I have been able to get time sights both in the forenoon and afternoon.

May 1.—The Dzassak, his wife, the Tibetan lama his chaplain, Dowé, and the luggage arrived this afternoon and I will get off to-morrow. I bought some butter, tsamba, flour, etc., from the Dzassak who, with his wife, tried their best to cheat me in the quality of the goods and by using short weights and measures. I told him some pretty disagreeable truths, which he did not, however, mind in the least, he only cared "to take the cash and let the credit go." He asked me what could be done to prevent the village tumbling down and stop water oozing up from the soil;

* Occasionally the Tibetan "barley grain" (*nas dro*) pattern is used by Mongol silversmiths. Borax, called *ts'a-bla* in Tibetan and *peng-sha* in Chinese, is found in Korluk Ts'aidam and exported thence to China.

†*Aka* is the generic name for all lamas. *Gélong* is an ordained monk, *Gets'ul* and *Gényen*, brothers, or monks who have only taken the minor vows.

Mongols from Baron Ts'aidam.

I told him, nothing, the only thing he could do was to have a new village built on higher and drier ground at the foot of the mountains. This he declared was impossible, it would be in too close proximity to the Panaka and the Golok who could get within reach of his people before they would be aware of it, futhermore there was no water to be had at the foot of the mountains. I suggested digging wells, but he would not believe that water could be had by that means. Here the village has been since it was first built, forty-six years ago, and here it will remain.

To-day again the atmosphere has been perfectly clear and I could see due north of here, some fifteen miles away, the end of a low range (possibly six hundred feet high) which runs along the right bank of the Bayan gol; this is the Sarlik ula or "Yak mountains" and near to its extremity the Shara gol (or lower Tsahan ossu) is said to empty into the Bayan gol. To the north-west we can see, probably thirty miles away, some low peaks, forming the eastern extremity of the Emnik ula which range forms the southern boundary of Korluk and separates it from Taichinär in that direction.

The great southern range stands out grandly to-day, covered with snow down to 13,000 or 13,500 feet above sea level. The Burhan bota, over which runs the highroad to Lh'asa, is plainly discernible. I hear another explanation here of the name of this famous pass. The Mongols say *bota* is a corruption of *bodé*, "wheat." "The Buddha's wheat" is therefore the meaning of the name; but I fancy that "Buddha's cauldron" is, as I have elsewhere noted,* the correct interpretation. There are, by the way in the mountains of Baron, a number of peculiarly shaped rocks to which the natives have given names. One is "Gésar's hat," another "Gésar's saddle," yet another his boot, and so on. A small ruin in heavy cut stone on the road to Dulan kuo a little above Dorung charu, and about which no one knows anything, is said to be *Kuan gyur* (*bsgyur*) "built by Kuan-ti" (Gésar). Everything odd or of unknown origin is attributed to him in these parts.

I also learnt that the present poverty of Baron is not alone attributable to the drought and cattle plague, but also to the rapacity of the Dzassak himself. Thus when he went last year to Lh'asa he exacted from his people one hundred head of sheep, to

*See *Land of the Lamas*, 139, note 2.

eat on the way! Sixty pack horses and six men had to accompany him at their own expense, so that the trip only cost the chief between three and four hundred taels of his own money.

May 2.—The Dzassak gave orders that the four camels which he had at first said were to carry my luggage to Téngelik should only go as far as the frontier of Dsun, one day's march from this place, and he forbade the driver supplying ropes to tie the loads on their backs. A rather violent scene ensued. I abused him and Dowé roundly, and told them that they ought to be ashamed of themselves, I had shown the greatest generosity in all my dealings with them and they repaid me by acting in a contemptibly mean way. The result was that the driver was ordered to go with me to Téngelik and ropes were supplied to tie the loads on, but I left the chief and Dowé in high dudgeon and told them that I would tell everyone I saw of their stinginess and bad faith.

The trail led west-northwest by west through brush, sand and swamp across the Ulásutai gol ("Pine tree river"), a miserable little rivulet, and thence over firmer and drier ground to the Burúsutai gol ("Tent frame (?) river"), Prjevalsky's Burgasutai gol, which marks the boundary between Baron and Dsun. Here we found grass and pools of water in the bed of the river, which, like most streams in these parts, flows underground at the base of the mountains, and we camped near the tent of a headman (*Mérin*) of Dsun. This Mérin was an intelligent man of about fifty, with a good knowledge of local affairs and quite communicative. He took me for a Turkestani from Ilchi, and said that some of my people visited the Ts'aidam every year in the eighth moon to trade and that there are some Mongols inhabiting my supposed country. He talked a good deal of a Mohammedan town (Huei-huei hutun) to the west of the Lob nor, but he himself had not been there; I fancy he referred to Ho-tien.

He told me that the population of the Ts'aidam (exclusive of Shang, where there are five hundred families) was a little over three thousand families, divided as follows:—

Baron,	300 families.
Korluk,	1,000 families.
Dsun,	200 families.
Erké Beilé,	100 families.
Koko,	150 families.

Wangk'a (Dulan kuo),	150 families.
Taichinär,	1,000 families.
Other divisions	200 families.
Total,	3,100 families.

This agrees fairly well with the information given me by Dowé in 1889.*

He told me furthermore that his master, the Dzassak of Dsun, was now reduced to poverty. About a year ago he had been taken ill (from what he said I fancy the disease of the Dzassak is dropsy), and that he had had to fee so many lamas to pray for his recovery that all his cattle, horses and sheep had been sold to satisfy their demands. The worst of it was that he was no better, and he could no longer get prayers said for his recovery—no money, no lama.

May 3.—The trail led through bog and sands northwest by west for a couple of miles, when we found ourselves due south of, and about a mile away from, the village of Dsun kuré, where live about as many families as in Baron kuré. We did not visit the village but pushed on, turning a little south of west. After crossing the dry bed of the Sangen gol we rode about seventeen miles, and then stopped at a spot called Shudengé, where there is a little brackish water and some coarse grass. Southeast of this spot a ridge of reddish rocks project from the main chain and marks the entrance to the Burhan bota k'utul. This very conspicuous landmark is known as Sang Amnyé.

Were it not for the strong winds of this region, which pile the sand up around the willow trees growing over a large belt of country at the base of the mountains along the southern edge of the Ts'aidam, these trees would appear of quite respectable size; as it is only their smaller upper branches project above ground. The natives dig the trunks out to use as fire wood and for lumber.

The Dzassak of Baron has sent as camel driver a man called Damba, the same who guided me from Baron kuré to Shang in 1889. He is quite a wag and has a somewhat remarkable history. The son of a Tibetan from Ulterior Tibet (Tsang) who had come to Shang with a Tashil'unpo lama sent to govern that country, and of a Mongol mother, he was left here with the latter when his father returned with the lama to Tibet. By the time he was

* See *Land of the Lamas*, 136–137.

twenty-five he had a few head of cattle, some sheep and ponies. Once while camped in one of the valleys in the south of Baron two Goloks came and carried off all his worldly belongings. A few hours after their departure he came back to his tent and found himself a ruined man; without the loss of a minute he followed on the Goloks' trail, overtook them in the night while they were asleep, crept up to them, cut their throats and regained possession of his lost property.

For this act of courage he was much praised by his people, but apparently his head was turned by his own audacity, for shortly after he himself turned brigand and, in company with another Baron man, pillaged all the adjacent Mongol and Panaka country. Unfortunately his tribe (*hosho*) was, as is the custom, responsible to the other Mongol tribes for his rapines, and so it had to pay so many fines for his evil doings that finally his chief (*Nôyen*) decided to have him shot.

Two men held his arms apart while another, a few feet away, levelled his gun at him and slowly applied the match, but the powder only flashed in the pan. Again the matchlock was primed and again it hung fire. Three times this occurred and then the chief saw that Damba was not to die; he pardoned him and having admonished him to lead an honest life sent him home. This happened ten years ago, and since then, for various acts of bravery, among which he mentioned with pride the killing of a large bear in a hand to hand fight, he has been rewarded first with a white button then with a blue one, and finally with the title of *Baturha* or "The Brave." He has never, since his reformation, been able to do more than earn enough to keep body and soul together, but his poverty weighs lightly on him, he looks on it as a just punishment for his having killed the two Golok. The Buddhist theory of rewards and punishments has its good side.

Last night Damba amused us by singing songs in Chinese, Lh'asan, Panaka and Mongol styles. He took off the Chinese admirably and I laughed until the tears ran down my cheeks—a rare treat (not the tears but the laugh); I have not had such a one for the last six months. The Mongol song told of a journey to Lh'asa, of the difficulties of the road and the beauties of the sacred city. The Panaka one had endless couplets, something in the style of the songs in Milarāpa's *Lubum* and his *Namt'ar*. "If you see a young man coming, riding a fine grey horse, if his dark blue gown is trimmed with leopard skin and on his fur hat is a blue button of rank, you may know him to be a young chief. If you see a young man coming, riding a milk white horse, if his gown is of yellow and he looks like a Buddha, he is a young lama," and so forth *usque ad nauseam*. The last and most popular couplet was too bad for translation, a common thing with Tibetan and Chinese songs, but very unusual in Mongol ones which are usually quite sentimental.

May 4.—After a detour of a few miles through sand dunes, to take us clear of the bog and lakelets just beyond Shúdengé, we again took a west-northwest by west direction over a bare, gravelly stretch, covered to our right with willows (*suhai*) and white thorns, till we reached, after about twenty-three miles, a spot called Shara tolha or "Yellow head." Here we found a little water and grass and pitched our tents. The name given this place is derived from a small, bare, yellow hillock near by.

Yesterday and to-day we have had in view to the north a low range of mountains, running east and west and apparently about forty miles off. It is the Ėmnik ula, previously referred to, which bounds Dsun and Taichinär to the north and Kórluk to the south.

The climate of this Ts'aidam must have undergone wonderful changes within a very recent period, such huge masses of *débris* from the mountains to the south as we have traveled over to-day and on several other occasions suggest torrential rains such as, I am told, have never occurred within the memory of man.

The Mongols of the Ts'aidam have a saying to the effect that a Chinese eats with his food three pecks of dirt a year, a Mongol three pounds of wool, a Hsi-fan three pounds of gravel. Never was a saying truer. The wool from our clothing, the dust blown by the winds, the hairs in the milk and butter, the grit in the meal, the filth in the kettles, the ashes from the fire, the dry dung our only fuel, all contribute to make the vile messes we have to swallow daily nasty beyond description, and still the day may come when we will long even for them, a pleasant thought in truth!

The only edible products of the Ts'aidam are two kinds of berries which grow on species of thorns and called *harmak* (Chinese *halamaku*), and *mori harmak*, "horse harmak" (Chinese *k'ou* *chieh*);* also a root called *Sodzum* in Mongol, in shape like a turnip, and which, when roasted in the ashes, has a whitish pulp with yellowish fibres running through it. Its taste is insipidly sweet, something like a frozen potato.

May 5.—Continuing over a gravelly soil, here and there mixed with loess, we came after a few miles to an old walled Chinese camp (*ying-pan*), called by the Mongols Nomorun hutun, and about a mile east of the Nomorun gol; this point marks the boundary between Dsun and Taichinär. This camp was probably built by the Chinese in the seventeenth or eighteenth centuries, during one of their great expeditions into Tibet.† It is square, three hundred and thirteen yards to the side, the crenelated walls about sixteen feet high and made of sun-dried bricks, and it has gates on the east and west sides, and small bastions at the angles and two on each face. Willows and brush grow now inside the walls and a Tibetan recluse is the only inhabitant. The brush extends for many miles round about it, but the Dsun Mongols have cleared patches of it and till the soil, irrigation ditches bringing the water from the river a mile away. There were a number of Mongols ploughing when we passed, the plough closely resembled in shape the Chinese, and was drawn by a camel.

Some eight miles west of these ruins we came to a tomb of some Mohammedan saint now long forgotten. Chinese Mohammedans call such buildings *ma-tsa* (*i. e.*, mizar), but this one is known to Mongols as the *ungerhé báishing* or "domed house." It is made of sun-dried bricks and in the usual style of such buildings throughout the Mohammedan world. The western side of the dome has fallen in, but the rest of the building is in a good state of preservation. I found no inscription which could help to throw light on its history. The Mongols told me it was built by Turkestani people—a safe guess at all events.

Eight miles west of the *ma-tsa*, nearly all the way through willow brush, we came to the Téngelik swamps, scattered around

* There are three varieties of thorns: the "white briar" (*pai tz'u* in Chinese), on which the harmak grows; the "black briar" (*hei-tz'u* in Chinese, *chibeké* in Mongol), and the "yellow briar" (*huang-tz'u* in Chinese), on which the mori harmak grows, I believe. Prjevalsky (*Mongolia*, II, 167,) gives the name of the "white thorn" as *Nitraria schoberi;* the yellow briar is probably his *Rosa pimpinellifolia*. See also p. 33, where its Eastern Mongol name is given.

† See p. 158, *note*.

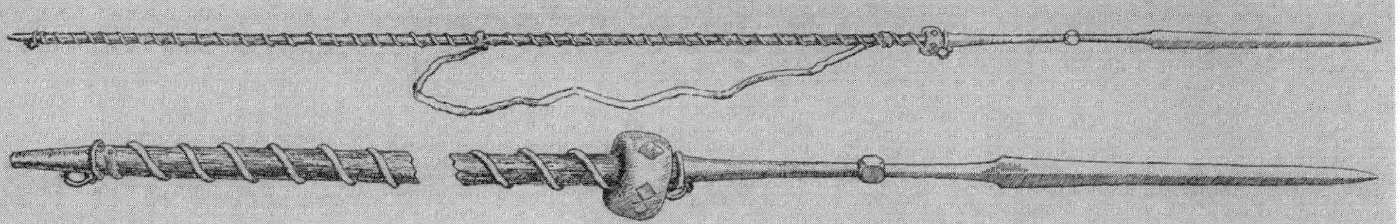

1

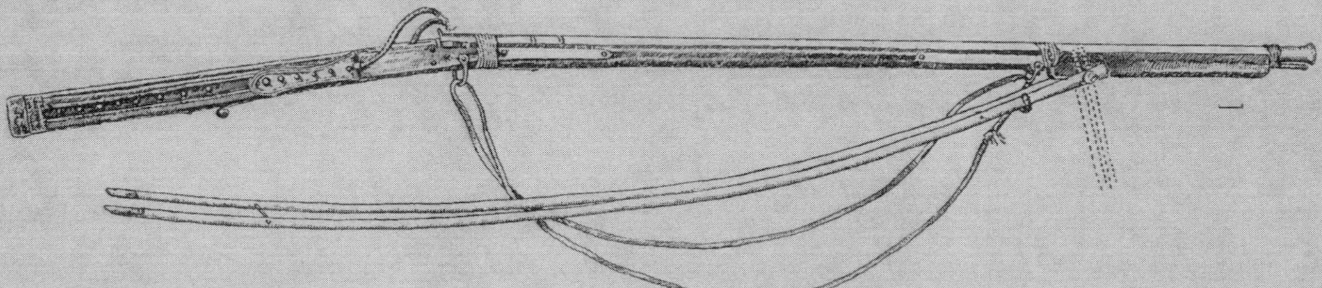

2

1. SPEAR, shaft of cocoanut wood wrapped with iron (Po-yul). (Property of the author.)

2. MATCHLOCK AND FORK. Stock covered with wild ass skin, barrel made in the Ts'aidam (Koko nor). (U. S. N. M. 131042.)

which are ten or fifteen tents. We found very little grass, except in the most swampy parts, where our ponies could not go, but swarms of fine big mosquitoes were everywhere. The day was very hot, the thermometer at 2 P. M. stood at 72.4° Fahrenheit in the shade; after dark, however, my sheepskin gown was not too warm.

The camels from Baron leave me here, but Damba went before dark to one of the tents and brought two men back with him, who agreed to carry my luggage to Golmot or the Naichi gol for eight mace of silver for each pack animal. We will rest here to-morrow and then travel westward as fast as we can, reaching the Naichi gol in five days.

May 6.—I learnt from Panti, who, as I have previously said, is a Taichinär Mongol, that west of the Taichinär proper are the two districts of Kangsa and Kas (Prjevalsky's Gast or Gass) belonging to it, but now uninhabited.* Until about fifteen years ago it was occupied by Mongols, but Huei-huei from the north raided them and so it was abandoned. The Kas nor (probably Prjevalsky's Chong Kum kul) is as large as the Tosu nor, but when saying this Panti naturally included in his estimate of its superficies all the swamps near the Kas nor; in like manner he divided all the central morass of the Ts'aidam into two large lakes, the Golmot nor or western lake and the Téngelik nor or eastern lake.

My men have been trading to-day with the Téngelik people, and I saw Panti sell one man a string of dried rhubarb root. The Mongols use this root as a dye to color yellow the hats, boots, coats, etc., of lamas. They do not know of its medicinal properties, though the Chinese do.

The Taichinär Mongols have quite a reputation in these parts as witches. When they want to bewitch a person, they first ascertain very exactly his name, age, etc., and having procured a hair from his head or a nail paring, or such like thing, they make a little image of a man or woman, as the case may be, and in it they put the hair. Then when certain magic formulas and other hocus pocus have been recited, it suffices to prick the image in a certain part to occasion violent pains in the same part of the body of the chosen victim, or even to make it die.

*See Prjevalsky, *Mongolia*, II, 168). He calls the Taichinär Taiji. Baron he calls Burun.

Crimes among the Ts'aidam Mongols are punished with fines paid to the Noyen or Chief, the injured person or his family. This is also the custom of Tibet. Murder is punished by the imposition of a fine which the whole hosho of the criminal has to pay to the Chief of the victim and his family. To kill a lama is a much greater crime than to kill a layman. In the case of the victim being a lama, as much as one horse for each family is frequently demanded of the hosho of the murderer for the gomba of the murdered lama.

May 7.— We left at seven o'clock with four pack horses, three oxen and a camel carrying our luggage, so that my own mules travel with empty pack saddles. It is very hard on them any way wading through this awful bog, with hardly any grass to eat and only a few handfuls of barley daily.

We traveled a little over thirteen miles in a west-northwest by west direction till we came to Bólang on the edge of the great central morass, where we found a little brackish water and grass. Mongols do not camp usually at this spot for fear of wolves, which are very numerous and fierce hereabout. I bought at Téngelik some ox-hide water jars, each holds about ten gallons. The Taichinär Mongols make them as follows: Cutting two pieces of hide into the desired shape, they sew them together so that the jar has a short neck and small mouth. Then they fill the soft hide with wet clay and let it dry thoroughly, after which the clay is broken up and taken out and the jar retains the shape given it, so long as the outside of the skin is kept dry.

I bought also six pecks of ***harmak*** berries, they taste like poor wortleberries, but are not so very bad when cooked with rice, and they help eke out our little supply of food. Things are very expensive in this part of the Ts'aidam, a brick of tea (*ta ch'a*), costing 40 tael cents at Lusar, is exchangeable here for 4 ewes; a pair of boots, worth 300 to 400 cash, is the price of a fat wether.

One of the two men driving the pack animals is called Rna (a Tibetan name, by the way), he is a great talker and singer. He told me this evening that last year the Chamri Panaka of Chamri Solo raided Korluk Beisé, but were defeated by the Beisé, who killed four of them and took two prisoners. The Beisé took the heads of the slain and his prisoners to Hsi-ning and requested the Amban to punish the latter. One was put to death and the other was ransomed by the Chamri, and so the affair was apparently settled. The poor Mongols, however, were not to enjoy their victory, the Chamri closed the road to Hsi-ning on them, and, so as not to have to travel there by the roundabout way of Sa-chou, Kan-chou and Liang-chou, they had to pay them 2 *yuan-pao* of silver, one hundred head of horses and one hundred pieces of pulo.

Rna told me also that he met Carey when he came to Téngelik in 1886 to buy barley. He said he had ten Turki men, thirteen Ili horses and sixty donkeys. He (Carey) gave him a *yuan-pao* to purchase barley for him, and, though he could only make himself understood by signs (one of his Turki men spoke Mongol, however), he was very kind and considerate and much liked by everyone, but the other foreigner (Dalgleish ?) was very cross.

May 8.—The trail to-day led most of the way through scrub willows embedded in loess and sand, and occasionally over gravelly soil absolutely devoid of vegetation. At Tagur (sixteen miles from Bolang) we crossed some fields in process of irrigation, and filled our jars with water, fearing we might not find any farther on. Panti said the water at Tagur comes from the Uneren gol which flows from the Kuo-shili range to the south, but I did not notice a river bed broader than a gutter, and it is probable that this river flows under ground except when tapped.

At Toli éken (*éken* means "upper"), where we camped, there was a little coarse dry grass and the usual scrub willows, but hardly any water. As far as my experience goes Shang is *the* garden spot of this region and Baron next to it in fertility.

May 9.—We traveled about twelve miles to-day, most of the way along the north side of a line of sand dunes and amidst willow brush. When about half way we passed some three miles to the south of a pool, or lakelet, called Íké talé námehá, "Big sea springs (?)." We camped at Tsáhan kol or "White leg," where we found fairly good water and grass. There were a few tents near Tsáhan kol, and the inhabitants warned us to look out for wolves which are very numerous.

May 10.—The trail led through mud and over shaking bog where willows and thorn bushes grow and where mosquitoes are enormous and ferocious. The muddy ground was covered with a white crust of salt, a quarter of an inch thick, under it was liquid mud in which the horses sank to their bellies. We saw in this swamp a few orange legged snipe and pheasants, and stranger still, a few tents, the latter at a place called Tugetä, a couple of miles beyond Tsáhan kol. What can ever have induced human beings to have chosen such a place to even stop in for a day, is beyond conception; it makes one believe that they actually like such surroundings. A few eastern Mongols bound for Lh'asa were also camped here, waiting for the passage through the Ts'aidam of the big caravan from Tankar to Tibet.

The Túgetä gol, which we crossed some eight miles from Tsáhan kol, is a good sized stream, about six inches deep and ten feet broad; beyond it we replunged into the swamp till we reached a little bit of raised ground, comparatively dry, and where we found a spring of pure water. This spot is called Tolä, and here we camped.

The guide's plan is to go to a point on the Naichi gol about a day's ride south of the village of Golmot, which I have no desire to see, especially as it is said to be only about a fourth of the size of Báron kuré; this would give it about five houses. From Tolä the village of Golmot (this name means something like "many rivers") bears northwest.

We saw a few sheldrakes, but, though I would like to have shot one as a specimen, my Mongols begged me not to.

May 11.—Through the same swamps and then over a sandy plain, with thorns and a few bunches of coarse grass growing here and there on it, we traveled for over nineteen miles, till we came to the banks of the Naichi gol.* On the way we crossed two little streams, the Tumta Tolä gol and the Huito Tolä gol, the former quite a stream with a good current, the latter a mere ditch. The Naichi (Naichiyin or Kurban Naichi) gol is a large stream flowing between banks about twenty feet high and divided into numerous channels, good-sized willows and dense brush growing on the islets. The river bottom is about three hundred yards wide. I learnt that there is another and more important branch

*A—— K——, coming from the absolutely bare region which extends from near Lh'asa to the Ts'aidam, was so struck by the brush growing around Golmo that he spoke of it as "a densely wooded forest, six miles broad and about one hundred miles long. The forest trees, named by the Mongolians *humbu*, *harmo* and *chhak*, are about six or seven feet high." *Report on Explorations of A—— K——, made in 1879-'82*, 44.

of the river about six miles west of here, so at least Panti says, but it may well be that it is quite another river, Mongols are not very particular about such matters.

There are a few tents near the place at which we have camped, but they look very miserable, and I hear that the people hereabout are very poor. Last year in the eighth moon eighteen Goloks suddenly made their appearance here, having come from the upper Naichi valley, and in a few hours they rounded up between fifty and sixty horses, one hundred head of cattle and some five thousand or six thousand sheep, which they drove back to the mountains. The Mongols followed them for a few miles in a half-hearted way and then came back, very glad that they had not seen anything of them. These Taichinär Mongols are greater cowards than even those of Eastern Ts'aidam, these latter are held to be very "big livered men" by the former.

The plain of the Naichi gol is bare, and sheep and cattle nearly starve on it, while to the south in the mountains are rich and abundant pasturages, good water and plenty of fuel, but the fear of a Golok raid keeps the Mongols from venturing there, though they could stay there in perfect security for eight months of the year, for the Golok never raid the Ts'aidam but from June to October.

The people hereabout tell me seriously that the Naichi gol flows to Sa chou and probably empties into the Lob nor. The Yellow river, Chinese geographers say, issues out of the Lob nor to reappear at Karma t'ang, passing apparently under the whole Ts'aidam.*

To-morrow I will send Panti and Yeh Hsien-sheng to see Samtan Jalang, Panti's elder brother, who, besides being one of the headmen (*Jalang*) of this district, is a professional guide for parties going to Tibet. Panti thinks that if I can secure his services I will be able to go wherever I want in Tibet. He lives on the west branch of the Naichi gol, where there are a great many more tents than here.

May 12.—Yeh Hsien-sheng went to Samtan Jalang's but found he had gone to sow his barley patch in the mountains. A man was sent after him, and it was said that the Jalang would be at my camp in two days. The Hsien-sheng got back to camp a little after noon, but Panti, who had gone with him, stayed behind to see his people.

* Conf. remark about Yellow River at Pao-t'u, p. 26.

It was very warm to-day, at 11 A. M. the thermometer in my tent stood at 101° Fahrenheit. In the afternoon I was able to get a bath in the river, and two of my Chinese were so imprudent as to do the same thing. I won't say when I got my last one, but it was considerably more than two months ago. Shortly after one of the Chinese was taken with chills and cramps, this, of course, will confirm the fellow in the belief that a man is a fool who washes himself, and he, for one, will never do such a thing again.

The people living round about here have been offering to sell me barley, butter (of sheep's milk), chura* and such odds and ends as they think may please me. I found barley cheaper here than at Baron and Shang, fourteen pecks selling for an ounce of silver.

I hear that at present Taichinär is badly governed; the Dzassak died a while ago and left a son, a minor, to rule in his stead. There is no Tosalakji and the Hosho-dzangé is at Hsi-ning where he is attached to the Amban's Ya-mên, consequently the various headmen have it pretty much their own way.

Physically the Taichinär Mongols differ considerably from those of the eastern Ts'aidam; one might suspect a certain admixture of foreign blood in them, Turki in all probability. They are more heavily built, and taller than the other Eleuts of the Ts'aidam, and many of them have quite heavy beards. Their features, however, are purely Mongol, though perhaps their noses are more prominent and more inclined to be aquiline than is usually seen among this people. The women are fatter than those farther east, but of about the same height. It is commonly stated that there are in Shang two men over six feet, two in Dsun and three in Baron. These are the recognized giants of this country.

A man between thirty and forty, came to my tent to-day whose appearance made me for a minute hold my breath; I thought I had found a European in disguise, a fellow "crank," so foreign were his features. He had blue eyes, reddish black hair and a very freckled face, he was however, a native of the Taichinär.

---

* Chura was already used by the Mongols when we first hear of them. "Residuum lac quod remanet post butirum, permittunt acescere quantum acrius fieri potest, et bulliunt illud, et coagulatur bulliendo, et coagulum illud siccant ad solem, et efficitur durum sicut scoria ferri, quod recondunt in saccis contra hyemen. Tempore hyemali, quando deficit eis (Moal) lac, ponunt illud acre coagulum, quod ipsi vocant grice (griut aut griut), in utre, et super infundunt aquam calidam, et concutiunt fortiter donec illud resolvatur in aqua, que exillo efficitur tota acetosa, et illam aquam bibunt loco lactis." Rubruk, *Itinerarium*, 229.

The Mongols call Lh'asa *Tsu*, but I am not quite clear in my mind whether this refers to the Kingdom of Lh'asa or to the city of that name, though the latter is usually called Baron tola in Mongol.

May 13.—Panti came back this morning and all his braggadocio about guiding me anywhere and fearing nothing has vanished, after a day's yarning with his relatives, who have told him a lot of nonsense about the danger to which he will expose himself by going to Tibet with me. To-day he is undecided whether to go or not, his brother, the Jalang, will be here to-morrow and then we can all talk the matter over together and he (Panti) will see whether he shall go with me. He told me that he had met at his brother's tent a man who had been to the Tengri nor, and who said that the only road from that lake led to Lh'asa and Shigatsé, so he (Panti) believes, though I have persistently told every one who has questioned me that I did not want to go to Lh'asa, that I want to reach that city by this roundabout road.

Panti told me that while in Shang, Baron and Dsun, it was common, if not usual, for two men, not relatives, to have one wife in common, all three living in the same dwelling, this practice did not obtain in Taichinär and Korluk.*

May 14.—The stories I have heard of late concerning the ferocity and number of the wolves in the Ts'aidam are certainly true. Last night they killed and nearly devoured a horse tied to a tent about half a mile from here, and a few days ago they ate three cows belonging to an old man who has a tent less than a quarter of a mile from my camp. The Mongols do nothing to destroy these pests, in fact they appear very much afraid of them.

Although deer and other game abound in the mountains south of here, it has been forbidden to kill them for the last thirty years. The then Dzassak heard in a dream the deer begging him to protect them as these mountains were their last refuge, so he issued an order forbidding his people killing them.

The atmosphere to-day was very clear and I could distinguish to the north (Panti says five days ride from here but he is probably wrong) a short range of mountains with one snow covered peak bearing 185° (magnetic) from my camp. Panti says it is covered

* Conf. what is said under date of *May 29th*.

with snow all the year, and is known as the Halang ossu mengku or "Hotwater snow peak." If it is as far as Panti says, it is in Prjevalsky's Ritter range.

The mountains to the west of the mouth of the valley of the Naichi gol are called Toré ("Birch tree") Kuo-shili, those to the east of it Talen-tak ula. A trail leading to the Alang nor crosses the latter range by the Hashken k'utul and passes by the Dinsin obo (Prjevalsky's Dynsy-obo). West of the Toré Kuo-shili the mountains prolonging the range bordering the Ts'aidam to the south are called Sosanang, and a direct trail from Hajir to the upper Naichi gol valley crosses this range by the Sosanang daban.

While on the subject of local names in Taichinär, I may note that the river called by Prjevalsky Batygantu, and by Carey Pataganto gol, and which empties into the great central morass near Hajir, is the Baternoto gol or "Mosquito nest river," a most excellent name for a river in this country. The Horghway gol of the maps, in the same section of country, is the Horgon gol, and the Khorgoin ula, the Horgon ula. *Horgon* means "a point of rocks." In the Korluk country the Kurlyk nor of the maps is the Korluk nor; the Toso nor, the Tosu nor; the Chakang-namaga, the Tsahan námeha or "White Springs;" the Khatsapchi springs the Hatsápji námeha, and Chonju is Tsonju.

Panti's brother did not turn up to-day, as I had hoped and expected he would. I am most anxious to see him, for not only is it important for me to secure him, but on his favorable reply to my request depends the decision of Panti, who is a most valuable man. And then the suspense in which I have now been living for a month is most trying. If I can once get into the uninhabited region south of here, I will make it impossible for anyone to desert me, until I get to the inhabited parts of Tibet at all events, but all these people are like children when it comes to taking a decision about anything, money will not always decide them.

May 15.—Samtan Jalang made his appearance this morning. He is a very serious looking man of fifty-one, with an intelligent face, perfectly self-possessed and of good address. He is as poor as his brother and as anxious to make money. He speaks Tibetan fairly well, but preferred talking Mongol, which the Hsien-sheng translated for me into Chinese. He said that he was aware of what I desired of him, but he could only agree to go with me into Tibet if I first went to Hajir, showed my passport to his Noyen and got his consent to his accompanying me. This I, of course, knew was all twaddle, but I replied quite seriously, saying that this long journey to Hajir was quite unnecessary, that the Noyen would not be able to read my Chinese passport, and that the Hsi-ning Amban had informed him and all the other chiefs of the Ts'aidam that I was to visit this country, and so he could have absolutely nothing to say about my movements. My object, I went on, was to reach India by the shortest possible route; that is to say, through Tibet. I had official business to transact in India and must reach that country promptly. After a good deal of "empty talking" the Jalang said that there was a road to India *viâ* the Tengri nor and Shigatsé, that not only was it short (six weeks) and easy, but was well known to him. He said that the only danger for a foreigner traveling in Tibet was the more than likely refusal on the part of the Lh'asan authorities to let him travel in their country, but by taking the route he suggested this would be avoided, as it lay entirely without the territory under the rule of Lh'asa. Since the Lh'asa Amban had arranged matters with the Yingili of India, trade was open between Shigatsé and Darjeeling, and foreigners (he did not say of what nationality) were freely visiting and trading at the former place. He thought he could take me by this route.

I agreed to give him 50 taels of silver if he took me to the Tengri nor and twenty-five more if we should reach Shigatsé, also a like amount to his brother. I would furthermore provide them with ponies and supplies to come home with and a gun for their defense. Should they not be able to come back by the road by which we were about to follow, I further agreed to take them with me to India or China and send them back to the Ts'aidam by Kuei-hua Ch'eng and Hsi-ning Fu.

Everything having been settled satisfactorily, I gave the Jalang a few presents and twenty-five taels of the promised amount, and he started home to settle his affairs and rejoin me on the upper Naichi gol, where we will stop for a few days to get the ponies and mules in good condition, as I hear the grazing is excellent there.

May 16.—The day has been oppressively hot, the thermometer in my tent reaching 94° Fahrenheit. Though it has been calm, little whirlwinds have at frequent intervals swept across the plain, all coming from the west.

We will have to leave our baggage behind us to be brought to the Naichi valley by the Jalang, as the camels on which we had counted are in too poor condition to do the work, and ponies will have to be got. The Jalang will come by the Sosanang daban, a shorter but rougher road than the one I will follow.

I am more and more struck by the marked difference in the features of the eastern Mongols (Halhas) and these Taichinär people. One would hardly imagine they belonged to the same race. While the Halhas are comparatively of small stature, light complexioned, and frequently with fine, regular features and no beard, the Taichinär people are tall, coarse in build, dark skinned, deep voiced, with heavy features and bearded, and frequently with hair on the body and limbs, a nearly unknown peculiarity farther east.

There is a young Halha lama now stopping with the Jalang waiting for an opportunity to go to Lh'asa. He came here to-day with him and asked me if I could not assist him. I told him that if he chose, he could come with me and that I would give him food on the way and hire a pony for him to ride, the Mongols hereabout being in the habit of hiring ponies for the journey to Lh'asa for 5 taels a head. He accepted with great glee. He will join me on the upper Naichi gol at the same time as the Jalang. His name is Zangpo, "The good one," pronounced here Sambo.

PART III.

FROM THE NAICHI GOL TO NAMRU DÉ NEAR THE TENGRI NOR.

May 17.—We broke up camp on the Naichi gol this morning, leaving behind three loads of barley, flour and tsamba, to be brought on in a few days by the Jalang. After following up the river over soft sand we came, after a few miles, to the foot of the Talen-tak (or tagh) mountains, which have their western extremity on the eastern side of the Naichi gol. The sand blown from the Ts'aidam by the prevailing winds is piled up on the foot-hills to a depth of several hundred feet. The mouth of the Naichi valley is about six miles wide and covered with granitic gravel and sand. The river flows at the mouth of the valley along the base of the Toré ula, so we were unable to make out correctly its course, only catching occasional glimpses of it from the top of some sand dune. The mountains to the west of the river are, as I have already noted, the Toré kuo-shili or Toré ula.

Turning around the end of the Talen-tak mountains we crossed a little stream coming from the southeast and called the Kara-sai, and then rode up a side valley leading to the Kano pass.* *Kano*, I am told, means about the same thing as *k'utul*, *i. e.*, "pass." When half way up the valley we found a little grass and some terribly brackish water, and, as it was nearly dark, we camped here.

The mountains visible from this camp are mostly composed of some shining black stone (basalt, probably), covered here and there with loess, with numerous patches of alkaline efflorescence. *A propos* of alkali, it is perhaps worth noting that on all mountains south of the Koko-nor lake alkaline efflorescences are particularly abundant in the highest parts of the ranges, not, as I would have supposed, in the bottom of the gorges or valleys.

---

* Prjevalsky crossed this pass in his journey of 1879–'80. He calls it Gono.

To the east of where we have camped I can see a high but short series of bare, jagged needles (probably of basalt) trending south-southeast.

May 18.—Crossing the Kano pass about two miles above where we camped, we rode in a southwesterly direction for some three or four miles, when we reached the Naichi gol, the country everywhere absolutely devoid of vegetation, only a mass of *débris* and sand. The river (some sixty to seventy-five feet wide and about three feet deep in the middle) flowed between high vertical banks, disclosing alternate horizontal layers (each about a foot thick) of loess and gravel.

The black, jagged peaks, noticed yesterday from our camp, appear from the Naichi valley to be about six miles away; from all the little gorges which seam their flanks, enormous masses of *débris* have been swept down into the main valley.

After about eleven miles along the right bank of the Naichi gol we crossed the Shugu gol, a stream nearly as large and deep as the Naichi itself and coming from the east-southeast where it rises in the Shugan mountains, and three and one-half miles farther up we found a convenient point for crossing the Naichi gol, and a good camping ground on the river bottom along the right bank with plenty of green grass and willow brush. This spot is called Tsahan tohé (or tohä), and Panti said that from this point on grass was abundant throughout the Naichi valley.

There is a trail leading up the Shugu gol and to the Alang nor, and about two and one-half miles lower down the Naichi gol is another lateral valley also on the east side of the river, up which runs another trail leading into the basin of the Alang nor. It is by this latter trail that the Golok invariably come when they raid Taichinär.

Prjevalsky calls the mountains to the south of the Shugu (his Shuga) gol and the bend of the Naichi gol by the unpronounceable name of Gurbu-gunznga mountains. The first part of this name may be Mongol, *Kurban*, "Three," the second has a Tibetan look about it, but no one I have questioned on the subject, and I have asked dozens, knew of any name, let alone this horrible one, for this range.

The subject of the exaction of the Chinese T'ung-shih is one on which Mongols and Tibetans are always willing to talk. Panti

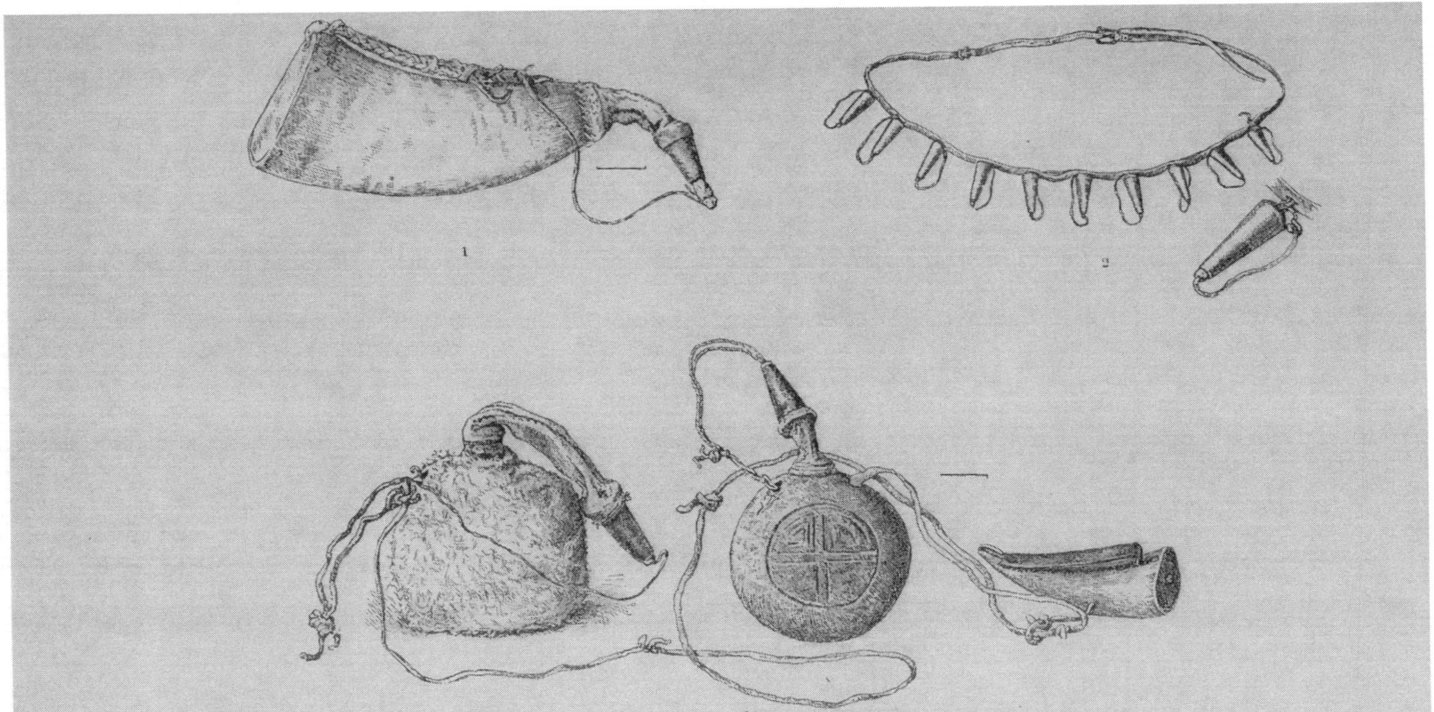

1. POWDER HORN. Ovis Poli horn (Ts'aidam). (U. S. N. M. 131183.) 2 BRASS CHARGERS (Ts'aidam). (U. S. N. M. 131057.)
3. POWDER FLASKS, and horn primer with horn made spring. (U. S. N. M. 131032.)

told me that whenever a T'ung-shih visited Taichinär he exacted a sheep a day for his food and a present from each hosho of six ponies and six pieces of pulo. Of course any delay in complying with this requisition, the first part of which is made on the authority of an ula order, enabled the T'ung-shih to exact double the quantity.

May 19.—About two and one-half miles west of our camp of yesterday we crossed a low col, called the Koko-tom k'utul, from the summit of which we could see the Naichi gol stretching westward some forty miles. To the south were visible some snow peaks rising behind the chain bordering the river in that direction. Panti said they are known as the Naichi mengku or "Naichi snow peaks," and that they are "the elder brother" of the Halang ossu mengku in Korluk. They correspond in position with the western portion of Prjevalsky's Gurbu-gunznga Mountains, though they may possibly be his Mt. Subeh.

The rock on the Koko-tom pass is sandstone, through which run numerous thin veins of white quartz, with nearly a vertical dip, so that traveling over them was extremely disagreeable, the quartz projecting six or eight inches above the adjacent layers of softer stone.

The Naichi above the Koko-tom flows between broad, low banks, most of the way covered with grass, with numerous patches of "black thorn" (in Mongol called *ch'ibeké*) and scrub willows.

Having crossed again to the right bank, we camped in a clump of ch'ibeké, and would have enjoyed the spot thoroughly had it not been for the heat and the mosquitoes.

We had finished taking our tea when we saw three thin, ragged and bare footed men limping down the road towards us. They were young lamas from eastern Mongolia on their way home from a pilgrimage to Lh'asa and Trashil'unpo. They had left that city over two months ago, each one with a little tsamba, tea and butter, a bellows and one small earthen pot, together with a few prayer books purchased at Lh'asa with the money they had begged, carried on the *k'ur-shing* strapped across their shoulders. They had expected falling in with some well provided party on the way, from whom they would certainly have got additional supplies to help them on, but they had met no one. Then the snow was deep and they had lost their way and so, long before they reached the Ts'aidam country, they had exhausted their provisions. Then they had picked up the old bones they found along the route and breaking them, had boiled them and drank the greasy water. They had chewed up the leather soles of their boots, had eaten grass, and by so doing they had been able to cross the Angirtakshia pass and enter the Naichi valley. Farther up the valley they had found a dead colt and had feasted on that as long as it lasted, and then slowly, and by very short stages, they had come down this far. Yesterday they met an old Mongol herding horses a few miles above this place, they had asked him for food and he had said he had only a few handfuls of tsamba to live on till more was sent him from Taichinär Ts'aidam, and "the blue sky above only knew" (*kôko téngri môtiché béné*) when that would be. But they had threatened to kill him if he did not give them something, and so he had handed over to them his little bag of tsamba, and they had got another meal.

They squatted around my fire, and in no time had swallowed two kettles of tea, four or five pounds of mutton, a couple of pounds of butter and a bag of tsamba, enough to have killed any three men with ordinary capacities, but a Mongol's is not of that description. We gave them some old boots and enough food to take them to Golmot ; their expressions of gratitude were quite touching. They told us that when at Trashil'unpo it was reported that two foreigners were on their way there from India to settle details of trade with Sikkim. The people of Shigatsé had not expressed any displeasure at the news, on the contrary they were glad that trade was to be developed. They further said that it was impossible for anyone to pass Nagchúk'a on the Hsi-ning-Lh'asa road without the K'anpo examining him and questioning him as to his antecedents, starting place, destination, occupation, etc., etc.

When they had traveled to Lh'asa last year they had gone by way of Labrang and the Horba country. It took them three months to walk to Lh'asa from Labrang.

May 20.—To-day we traveled up the valley about seventeen miles, going all the way over the river bottom, which is about a quarter of a mile broad and covered with willows, ch'ibeké and good grass. Saline efflorescences are abundant in the river bottom and on the mountain sides; at a distance, when high up on the mountains the salt makes them look as if covered with deep snow, so thick are these deposits. Again crossing the river near the mouth of the Kara k'utul gol or "Black pass creek," where the disintegrated rock swept down from the range to the north rises over one hundred and fifty feet above the bed of the stream, we camped on a pretty little meadow at the foot of the Buhutu ula, a prominent peak close to the left side of the river and along whose eastern base flows the Kara k'utul gol. The peak on the eastern side of the mouth of the Kara k'utul gol gorge is called Tákelgen ula.

The Naichi gol from Tsahan toh'a to Buhutu is very swift, with a drop of about thirty feet to the mile. Along the bank on either side are many large springs. It may be, however, that the river water (which is of a grayish color) percolates through the loose gravelly soil to reappear beautifully clear in these spring-like pools, thence flowing back into the river.

On the way up we saw the old horse-herder from whom the starving Mongols had taken all his food; I filled his tsamba bag and gave him a few bundles of kua-mien.

The only game I have so far seen in the valley has been a few partridges, met with this evening, and a small bunch of wild asses seen lower down the valley.

I passed an hour this evening trying to wash the dirt out of the butter made of sheep's milk, and bought at our camp on the lower Naichi—Camembert cheese is fragrant compared to it. I washed and salted it, but it is still horrible, bad luck to it, for it is all I have and all I will get for months to come, and so I must get accustomed to it. Perhaps some day I will like it!!

May 21.—We moved up the valley about twelve miles to Tator, to the west of Amtun ula and at the mouth of a lateral valley in the mountains on the south side of the river. This lateral valley is called Atak Naichi or "the lower Naichi." The next lateral valley above this is called Tumta (or "Middle") Naichi, and another yet above it, also in the southern range, is called Eken (or "Upper") Naichi. The road to the Naichi daban ("pass") leads up the last named. It is on account of these three valleys that the upper Naichi valley has been called Kurban Naichi, or "the three Naichis."

Tator, where we camped, is the same place marked on Carey's map as Amthun. The valley above Buhutu is broad, in some places not less than a mile in width, and the grass is positively luxuriant. We saw on the way a bunch of at least a hundred wild asses, with a great many colts, all six or eight months old.

The trail leading to the Sosanang daban starts a little to the west of Tator. Panti says Hajir can be reached in five days by taking it.*

To the east of the mouth of the Atak Naichi valley is a high têton called Nyul-chan t'onbo, or "Silver peak,"—to the west is a similar one called Ser-chan t'onbo, or the "Golden peak." These têtons mark the Atak Naichi very plainly.

The river bottom at Tator is covered with a little creeping plant, now in bloom. The flower looks like a diminutive apple blossom, and it is the first flower I have seen on the whole journey; Mongols call it *aura kashim*.†

A little snow fell on the surrounding hillsides, but only a few flakes came into the valley. The mountains to the west of the Amtun ula are not so bare as those lower down the valley; a little grass grows on their flanks, and the rocks are less exposed to view; but, taking them all together, they make up about as barren and inhospitable a picture as one can find. Even the loftiest peak in these mountains has nothing grand or imposing about it; it is simply bleak and barren, and looks much the worse for wear and tear after long centuries in this vile climate.

May 22.—We moved up the valley to near the mouth of the Eken Naichi, where we found splendid grazing and plenty of ch'ibeké, which, when dry, makes excellent fuel. We will remain here until we make the final start for Tibet. This spot is called Kuré bori, or "Village site," from the ruins of a former camp. The Mongols used to keep their flocks here and till patches of ground, but for the last seven or eight years there has only been a very few of them who have ventured to come here for fear of Golok raids.

* Cf. *Journey of Carey and Dalgleish, Roy. Geo. Soc., Supplemental Papers*, III, 42. It is there said that it is eighty miles to Golmo *viâ* the Sosanang (Sosani) daban.

† *Myricaria prostrata*, Hook., f. et Thoms.

I saw, on the way up the valley, two bunches of kuldza, one of eight head, the other of five. I was able to get within good range of them, but was so excited that I missed them twice, and they ran off, crossing a high, precipitous hill, over which I could not follow them. We saw, also, the largest single herd of wild asses I have ever come across; there were between three hundred and four hundred head in it. On the other side of the river, just opposite our camp, I noticed a large bunch of orongo antelope, the first I have seen on this journey.

The valley around Kuré bori is over two miles broad; to our west we have the Umeké ula (Prjevalsky's Ymykeh), and farther west the Dzuha ula (Prjevalsky's Dzukha Mountains). A trail leads along the west side of the Dzuha to the Tsahan daban, and thence to Hajir; this route is followed by the Hajir people when going to Lh'asa by the Angirtakshia road. Due south of our camp we can distinguish, beyond the mountains at the head of the Tumta Naichi, the peaks to the east of the Angirtakshia daban; they are covered with snow which fell on the 20th. The Atak, Tumta and Eken Naichi valleys are not over seven miles long. Beyond the range at the head of these valleys comes the Angirtakshia range (Prjevalsky's Marco Polo range), distant about fifteen miles south of it.

The other peaks visible from our camp, such as the Umeké, Dzuha (which the Mongols divide into "Big" (*Iké*) and "Little" (*Baga*) Dzuha), hardly merit the name of "snowpeak" (*mengku*), at least this year, for there is hardly any snow visible upon them. The mountains to the west of the Sosanang daban are called Kubché ula, as far as Kansa-Kas country. The Kubché ula therefore, includes Prjevalsky's Columbus range and the western portion of his Marco Polo range.

There stands out on the north side of the valley, about three and one-half miles away, and bearing nearly due west from our camp, a detached rocky hillock, called Soyu lung. On this side of the valley, due south of it, is the mouth of the Eken Naichi, up which runs the road to the Naichi daban, the pass over which Carey and Dalgleish came in July, 1886. The Soyu lung is a valuable landmark.

May 23.—I heard that in the mountains to the northeast of this camp copper is found, and the natives insist that gold and silver are also abundant there. Samtan Jalang camped at Kuré bori during the greater part of last year with his little flock of sheep and his few ponies; he was then the only living being in this gorgeous pasture land, everyone feared the Goloks too much to venture here.

To-day I went down the valley as far as the Atak Naichi to see if I could not get a shot at the big horns (*kuldza*) we had seen when coming up the valley. We sighted eleven of them, but they got sight of us also when we were a mile off, and though we followed them for hours over the hills, we failed to come up with them or even see them again. While high up on the hill-sides, I saw the mountains in the Angirtakshia * range beyond the Atak Naichi, they appeared much higher and more covered with snow than those seen in the same range beyond the head of the Tumta Naichi.

While the thermometer in the valley rises during the day to above 70° Fahrenheit, it falls in the night to +14° or 15°.

May 24.—The morning was cloudy and towards noon we heard the rumbling of thunder, and shortly afterwards snow began to fall, but only heavily high up on the mountain sides.

At about four o'clock, Samtan Jalang, Zangpo, and a man leading two camels loaded with the things I had left on the lower Naichi gol, made their appearance. They had been five days on the road (crossing the Sosanang daban), but had found no grass before reaching the Naichi valley.

When we had finished tea the Jalang put on a portentously solemn expression and said that it was reported that a dispatch had reached Taichinār Dzassak *viâ* Korluk from the Hsi-ning Amban, by which all the chiefs of the Ts'aidam were forbidden to supply guides, ponies, provisions or camels to a certain foreigner with a Pekinese cook and several Hsi-ning followers, who was desirous of going to Tibet. The Jalang had not seen the dispatch, neither had anyone he knew of, but he entertained little doubt as to its existence, and he thought it referred to me. I

* A—— K—— says this range is so called "on account of a grass which grows in abundance here, which is used in medicine and is also burnt as an incense before idols." *Report on the Explorations of A—— K——, made in 1879-'82*, 42. This explorer, coming from Lh'asa, entered the Naichi valley by the Naichi k'utul. He makes the average breadth of the valley to be three miles and its length fifty. The valley must have been well peopled at the time he visited it (November, 1879). *Op. sup. cit.*, 43.

replied that it could not refer to me, for the Amban at Hsi-ning knew my name and rank and all about me, and so he could only refer to me by name and not as "a foreigner." I pulled out my passport and explained that it authorized me to travel in the Koko-nor and Ssŭ-ch'uan; how could I get from the first to the second country except by way of Tibet, India and the sea? This seemed to satisfy the Jalang and the camel driver who had vague notions of geography, and after a good deal more talking and explanations the subject was dropped.

I have an idea that the whole thing was got up by the Jalang to impress the camel man with his desire to comply with the well-known rule of the Mongols of this country, of refusing to assist any foreign travelers wishing to enter Tibet, and that he (the Jalang) was going with one duly authorized to visit that country by the Chinese authorities. Furthermore, he was careful to have me say in the hearing of the camel driver—who will repeat every word he has heard to everyone he sees in the Ts'aidam—that I was to give him (the Jalang) only 25 taels for the whole journey. He told me that his neighbors were very jealous of his good luck, that they said I had given him 600 or 700 taels to guide me to the Tengri nor, and that this would dispel their suspicions.

May 25.—Again the Jalang started the subject of the Amban's orders to the chiefs of the Ts'aidam, and again I had to talk over the whole subject with him and his brother, and once more everything was settled to the satisfaction of all concerned, myself only excepted, for my patience is worn threadbare. I wish we were south of the Koko-shili mountains, I would not mind these Mongols grumbling then so much, for they could not get away from me.

The Jalang says that between the Naichi daban and the Angirtakshia daban there is no grass, and that both these passes are, moreover, steep and difficult. He suggests going a little farther up the valley and crossing the Sharakuiyi daban, the one over which the Hajir pilgrims usually travel. From the top of this pass, which is of very easy ascent, it is all down hill to the top of the Angirtakshia pass, if one follows the highroad, but if one takes the trail to the west of the highroad, and this is the one he suggests following, one enters the valley of the Ch'umar (Namchutu ulan muren) directly after crossing it.

We have fixed on the 27th for our departure, it is a peculiarly lucky day, being the first of the fifth moon.

One of the Mongols went up the Eken Naichi valley to-day to try and kill a kuldza, but only brought back a wild ass. He reported that there were thousands of yaks visible on the mountain sides, a little above where he shot the *hulan.* We will have to try and shoot one soon as we have been without meat for the last two days.

May 26.—We had quite an excitement to-day. Towards noon we saw three horsemen driving a good-sized flock of sheep and some ponies before them down the valley. We took them for Goloks, and, quickly arming, we left two of our number to watch the camp, and sallied forth to meet the foe, my Mongols very much excited. The foe turned out to be two Mongol men and a woman, Taichinär people, a little braver than their fellows, and who have been in the valley for the last three months. They said they would stay here for another month and then go down to the Ts'aidam.

It hailed a little in the afternoon and some snow fell on the mountain sides. We all talked over the question of the route to follow on leaving here. Samtan Jalang, who is henceforth to be our guide, has suggested a route nearly parallel to the highroad *viâ* the Angirtakshia to Nagch'uk'a, but considerably to the west of it. It will take us west of the Amdo ts'o-nak and the Tengri nor (Drolmä nam-ts'o) to Sachya djong, from which place Shigatsé or K'amba djong can easily be reached. It will keep us entirely off Lh'asa-governed territory, where opposition to foreigners is to be feared. The only serious difficulty the guide fears is getting across the Tsang-gi tsangpo (Yaru tsangpo), where we will have to take the ferry or traverse a bridge, in both of which cases we may have to submit to embarrassing interrogatories from the people in charge.

The Jalang says that it is unquestionably the fear the lamas entertain of foreigners propagating their religion in Tibet and thus taking their power and wealth away from them, the ruling and wealthy class, which has caused such strenuous measures to be adopted to exclude foreigners from the country. .

May 27.—To-day was the first day of the fifth moon, a very lucky day on which to start on a journey. We broke up camp and moved up the valley about eight miles to a spot called Tabu obo, or "The five stone heaps," near the base of the Umeké. The valley here reaches its maximum width, nearly four miles, one mile of which is river bed. A little above this spot the river flows in great part underground. The grass is not as good here as lower down, and it is considerably colder, there still being a good deal of rotten ice on the river. Above this point there is no more willow or ch'ibeké.

The Jalang says I have too much luggage for such a journey, but I do not think I can cut it down; every pound I have is either food, some indispensable camping article or an object collected. The food will go only too quickly, and, moreover, I suspect the Jalang of wanting to add to his own worldly goods all the things I might leave behind.

The Jalang said that two days' ride due west of here, say about fifty miles, there is a lake called Hara nor ("Black Lake"), some three miles broad and about as long as from Tabu obo to the Atak Naichi. It is surrounded by mountains, around it grows no grass and its water is slightly brackish. No foreigner has visited it, and he suggested that we should go there. I had very reluctantly to refuse, as I feared tiring the horses and mules.

Towards six o'clock snow began to fall on the hillsides, accompanied by an east to southeast breeze, which here, as in Kan-su, usually precedes or comes with rain or snow. I am told that in the eighth and ninth moons (September–October) it blows so hard in the Naichi valley that it is uninhabitable, but by the tenth moon the winds are at an end (or have shifted). On the whole, very little snow falls in the valley, and it is one of the best I have seen in this region, much better certainly than the transversal valleys running north and south, which are colder and more denuded.

The mountains along both sides of the Naichi gol are of sandstone and granitic rock.

May 28.—About eight miles above Tabu obo we left the Naichi valley and rapidly ascended over the hills along the Sharakui (or kuiyi) gol for about three and one-half miles, when we camped, it not being possible to cross the range and reach water the same day.

The Naichi valley, to the west of where we left it, retains the same westerly direction as far as the eye can reach; for the first three miles above the mouth of the Sharakuiyi gol it is between two and two and one-half miles wide, after which it seems to contract considerably. From our camp the Dzuha ula bears northwest and the Umeké east-northeast, while the Sharakuiyi daban bears due south. Prjevalsky, on his map, has misplaced these mountains, putting the Umeké to the west of the Sharakui ula (his Sharagui), whereas the latter is in reality contiguous to the former on the west.

The Sharakuiyi gol ("River of the yellow thigh bone") is a clear mountain rivulet tumbling down over granite boulders from the snow covered pass. The road up to the latter looks very easy. The grass around our camp is just beginning to turn green and the ground is covered with yellow and violet tulips (called *ma-lien hua* by the Chinese and *ji-ji ser-bo* and *ji-ji nonbo* by the Mongols),* and a very little edelweis, called in Mongol *kechígena*.† The grass is of the same kind as that growing in the higher parts of Colorado and New Mexico, a short, very fine bunch grass.

It began to snow at 2 P. M. and by seven, when it stopped, over four inches had fallen, just enough to make it difficult for the horses to graze.

The Jalang states that people from Hsin-chiang (Chinese I suppose) built last year three walled camps (*mk'ar*) in the Lob nor country, nominally to protect the farmers (?) who had gone there. This year they are building another camp in the Kansa-Kas country. The Jalang believes Chinese troops will be stationed in these camps and that they will soon be in the Taichinär country, squeezing the Mongols and behaving generally like real Goloks.

May 29.—It snowed all last night and this morning there were six inches of snow on the ground. We decided to wait here for a day to let the snow melt a little.

The Jalang says that fourteen years ago he went to Lh'asa over the road by which he is now taking me. He guided a party of Halha Mongols in which were a number of women and children. They were afraid to follow the highroad lest they should fall in with the Goloks. This trail is only known to a very few people and is used by very small parties, when they are afraid to follow the main road.

* *Tulipa* (§. *Orithyia*) sp. aff. *T. eduli*, Baker. The Mongols call these plants by their Tibetan names. *Ser-bo* means "yellow," *non-bo* "blue."

† *Iris Thoroldi*, Baker.

1. SADDLE (Dérgé): saddle pads of red leather, with gold leather ornamentation (Po-yul). (U. S. N. M. 131049.)
2. CHAIN HOBBLES, wrapped with worsted. (U. S. N. M. 167237.)
3. TIBETAN WHIP (Namru dé). (U. S. N. M. 131029.)

I am assured that in the Taichinär a woman may not have several husbands, but it is permissible for a man to have two wives.* In Tibet, the Jalang says, children are usually spoken of as belonging to such and such a family, not as the offspring of such and such a father.

My Mongols say that precious metals and also iron and copper have been found in the Naichi valley but they fear to even speak of their presence lest there be an invasion of Chinese and Chan-t'ou. The latter come occasionally to this valley to hunt; last year a party of over a hundred of them came here for that purpose. In hunting yaks one must never shoot at a solitary animal for, if it be wounded, it will surely charge the hunter. If a yak is wounded when he is in a little bunch of five or six head, he will run with the rest from the hunter. A yak bull, whose horns have a sweep backwards, is always dangerous. A curious custom observed alike by Mongols and Tibetans is to smear on the fork of their gun a little of the blood of any animal they may kill.

May 30.—We got off by 7 A. M., and by a very easy ascent of about eight miles reached the top of the pass. The last four miles before reaching the summit were over blocks of granite and loose slate hidden in nearly a foot of soft snow ; it was very tiresome to pick our way over these sharp stones and we and our animals had many a bad fall. The hills on either side of the pass are entirely covered with broken up granite and slate, like all high peaks in this region, and are bare of any vegetation. To the south we saw from the pass a broad undulating plain, running east and west with a pond here and there and bordered to the south by a low range of dark hills, the Koko-shili. We only descended about five hundred or six hundred feet over low hills of gravel and clay on which not a blade of grass grew but with here and there little moss-covered hummocks. After getting clear of the foothills surrounding the pass, we took a more westerly course over absolutely nude ground, cut occasionally by the dry bed of some torrent, till we reached a grassy slope on the first line of foothills leading up to a splendid snow-covered peak called by the Jalang Kuan-shong k'utur and which appears to me to be Prjevalsky's

* Ts'aidam Mongols, when questioned on this subject, have usually denied that polyandry existed in their own district, but have admitted that it was common in all the other districts of the country.

Mt. Kharza. This spot is known as Ch'u-wu doksai and is the only place so far where there was any grass; unfortunately there was no water, but we found enough snow in a hollow to supply us with a couple of jars of water, enough for our own wants. On this, the south side of the range, no snow, or very little at all events, can have fallen these last few days, as none is now visible; at this altitude, however, it thaws very rapidly.

Fortunately we brought with us several bags full of argols, for there were none to be found anywhere about camp. In this country it is always well to carry a small supply of dry dung, it weighs but little and may often prove invaluable and save one's boxes or pack saddles from being used as fuel.

On the way to-day we saw a few solitary hulan stallions, some orongo antelope and pronged horned antelope (*huang-yang*), but not more than twenty head in all. The whole broad valley of the Ch'umar is dreadfully desolate looking, it might quite appropriately be called Mar lung or "Red valley," for the whole face of the country is of a light brick red color.

May 31.—We traveled to-day about eleven miles in a southwest direction over soft, gravelly soil, crossing six little streams of brackish water, the overflow of four pools a little to the right of our line of march. These streamlets flow into the Ch'u-mar.

Although the country over which we traveled to-day seemed level, we descended about six hundred feet. We camped by a streamlet, near which we found a little grass. We could not possibly get to the south side of the valley in one day without tiring the animals overmuch. From this camp, which my Mongols call Ch'u-marin dsun kuba, or "North branch of the Ch'u-mar," we can see due south of us about three miles the Ch'umar River, where it forms a good-sized lakelet.

Now and then during the day it hailed and thundered, then the clouds swept swiftly by and we saw all the mountains around us. The Kuan-shong k'utur peak I now see marks the junction of the range bordering the Naichi gol on the south, and the Angirtakshia range, although the two ranges are already in reality united at the Sharakuiyi daban, as is shown by our now being south of the Angirtakshia, after having only crossed one range between it and the Naichi gol. Nearly due east of our camp and apparently at the eastern extremity of the Angirtakshia range rises a high pyramidal snow peak (probably Prjevalsky's Subeh Mountain and the "Snowy Peak" of Carey's itinerary); my Mongols call it Amnyé malchin mengku, a most unsatisfactory appellation, as there are several others bearing this name in the Panaka country. Our view to the west (or rather northwest by west) terminates at a huge snow-covered "*massif,*" connected with the Kuan-shong k'utur by comparatively low hills. This great snow peak, for which I can learn no name, must be Prjevalsky's Shapka Monamakh or his Mt. Jingri; this latter name I take to be his mode of transcribing *Gangri* or "snow peak." From where we have camped this snow peak appears to be distant some forty miles. To the south the Koko-shili daban, over which the high road to Lh'asa passes, trends east-southeast, and the western extremity of this range is, as well as I can make out, a little north of west, where it seems to sink to the level of the surrounding country.

I have suffered yesterday and to-day very much with inflamed eyes, and have been glad to pass part of the day in my darkened tent. At night I took a few observations for time and latitude, but the strain on my eyes was very painful, and I could not read the vernier very well. The wind, the alkaline dust, the glare of the sun on the snow, have not only got our eyes into a fearful state, but the skin on our faces is cracked and bleeding. Fortunately I have a good supply of vaseline; it is much better than butter or mutton fat, though it softens the skin a little too much.

This camp is on very nearly the same ground as Carey and Dalgleish's of the 16th July, 1886.*

June 1.—June was ushered in with the thermometer at 13° above zero and half an inch of snow on the ground. About three miles southwest of our camp of last night we came to the north branch of the Ch'u-mar, a miserable little streamlet, about six inches deep and ten feet wide, of dark red water. It flows here in a general east-southeast direction along the edge of a salt lake about a mile wide and two miles long. The salt on this lake forms a crust about half an inch thick and through it we had to break our way with considerable difficulty, as the mules sank repeatedly up to their bellies in the mud under it. There is here an inexhaustible and as yet unworked supply of fine white

* See *Journey of Carey and Dalgleish*, 41.

salt when the salt lakes farther south and now being used are exhausted, but that is in the far future; salt is the one thing the Ts'aidam and Northern Tibet are immensely rich in. A stream coming from a short range of hills southwest of the salt lake flows into it. It is larger than the Ch'u-mar itself (at this time of the year at all events). The Ch'u-mar comes from the west-northwest and has its source "a great way off," the Jalang says, probably thirty or forty miles.

When we finally got out of the salt lake we continued over soft water-soaked gravel, nearly as bad as mud. and quite as devoid of vegetation, in a general southerly direction, till we reached the dry bed of a stream (there was a little water flowing a foot or so under the surface) where we camped, the mules being terribly tired from the hard day's work. We saw on the way a few orongo and some gray geese, and at the spot where we camped there was quite a pile of orongo horns, left by Mongol hunters, for had they been Tibetans they would have carried the horns off, as they are much prized among them as tips to matchlock forks.

It hailed frequently and very heavily during the day, with thunder and a strong west breeze. I learnt that all the country south of the Kuon-shong k'utur range and west of the Angirtakshia belongs nominally to the Karsa Tibetans now occupying the district called Yagara, south of the Dang la range and along the highroad to Nagch'uk'a. When they occupied this country the Golok did not venture to pass through it when raiding the Ts'aidam, and it is said that at the present day they pay the Karsa an annual sum to have the right of way through it. The present head chief of the Yagara Karsa is Karsa Ado, the second is Karsa Pésung-gunlo, the third is Karsa Tsédur.

June 2.—About five miles in a southwest direction, over gravelly soil, brought us to the southern and most important branch of the Ch'u-mar (Ch'umarin baron sala, or Namchutu ulan muren, "the red river of the meadow," my Mongols call it),* a rather rapid stream about thirty feet broad, and a foot and a half deep, flowing in several channels over a bed of soft sand at least a quarter of a mile wide. We experienced a great deal of difficulty getting across as the bed of the stream was full of quicksands, and we

* Prjevalsky's Naptschitai-ulan-muren.

had to unload the mules and carry the loads across on our backs. The river has a general east-northeast direction, its water is of the same dark red color as that of the north branch. Beyond the river the ground rises slightly but remains of the same gravelly nature as to the north of it. After about six miles we came to the top of a sharp but short descent at the foot of which were two lakelets and a few patches of grass. This is the Elesu nor or "Sand lake," which has an outlet into another stream emptying into the Ch'u-mar, probably some ten or twelve miles to the northeast. The water of these lakelets is quite sweet and the sand hillocks which surround them to the south are covered with what in this region is considered excellent grass. A few geese and some sheldrakes were swimming on the water, on which there was, to my surprise, no ice, and over two hundred orongo were grazing near by, and better than all, we found wild onions growing in great abundance in the sand. So pleased were we at having something green to put in our miserable food (we had had nothing of the kind for over two months), that we decided to camp here for a day, and our joy was complete when in the evening I killed three orongo and all hands were able to gorge themselves with meat.

Panti and his brother had a row in the evening, the former saying that his brother was making a fool of himself by trying to take me by a road of which he knew nothing, instead of traveling by the highroad. The Jalang replied that he knew what he was about, and would reach Shigatsé by this "upper road," as he calls it, or "bust" (or words to that effect). I had to interpose and tell Panti that it was my desire to travel by this route, that the highroad, which had been explored by the Russians, had no charms for me and that I would not take it even if the Jalang wanted to go that way.

June 3.—The sky this morning was covered with ominously black clouds and a snow storm was impending. Panti went from one little sand hill to another reciting *mantras* and waving his rosary towards the four cardinal points, blowing lustily the while to drive the storm away. This ceremony the Chinese call *t'ang yü*. At 2 P. M. it began to snow, with accompanying thunder and light west-southwest breeze. It ceased at 4.30 P. M., something over three inches of snow having fallen. Just as the storm was about to break, the little lama, Zangbo, burnt some *shuka* and recited *mantras*, so that the horses and mules should not stray. He was delighted when the storm was over to find our stock all huddled together in a nook in the hills. Panti, on the contrary, looked very downcast, he said that if the Jalang had done the proper thing by me he would have dispelled the storm, for he was an expert at *t'ang-yüing*. Zangbo modestly remarked that while he could charm horses (*t'ang ma* in Chinese), he knew nothing about charming storms; it was a separate branch of the science, and little known in his country; the Ts'aidam Mongols have learnt how to *t'ang yü* from the K'amba.

I overhauled all my loads to-day to see if I could cut them down, as the mules show unmistakable signs of fatigue, and I fear they may not reach the journey's end, especially as we fed them the last grain of barley we had to-day. Henceforth they will have to hustle for a living. I hope they will do it as successfully as the dogs, who have thrived on nothing ever since we left Lusar. The result of my examination of the loads has been to throw away about one hundred and fifty pounds of stuff, all of which, under less trying circumstances, would have been of great value to me. All the discarded objects were carefully packed by Panti and his brother, and *cached* in a hole dug in the sand. They said they would take them on their way back to the Ts'aidam.

When looking over one of the boxes I found four sheep's shoulder blades; the Jalang at once appropriated them and had a good time telling our fortune by the lines on them after they had been charred. This mode of divination is called *dala túleje* in Mongol, *sokwa ar* in Tibetan and *shao-chien* in Chinese.* Besides this method of divining the Mongols have also, divination by sheep's droppings, by twelve copper cash, by drawing (the Chinese *shen chien* system), by counting the threads in the fringe of the girdle (odd and even), and by palmistry.

June 4.—Last night was one of the coldest I have experienced on this journey, the thermometer falling to +3° Fahrenheit. The wolves gave us a concert and the dogs responded lustily the

* See *Land of the Lamas*, 34, et seq. The ancient Peruvians had wizards called *Achicoc*, who told fortunes by maize and the dung of sheep, giving replies to those who consulted them according as the things came out in odd or even numbers. See *Rites and Laws of the Yncas*, by Clem. R. Markham (*Hakluyt Soc.*), 14. Also on Tibetan modes of divination. *Journ. Roy. Asiat. Soc.*, n. s., XXIII, 234, et seq.

whole night long, so we got but little sleep. We waited in camp until the sun had thawed our tents and they could be folded up, and got off by nine o'clock. At seven o'clock the thermometer, in the shade, stood at +18°, and at 7.30 it marked, in the sun, +66°.

A very gentle ascent of seven miles, the latter half over grass-covered hummocks, brought us to the foot of the Koko-shili éken k'utul, or "Upper Koko-shili pass." A good-sized brook flows down from the pass, the hills rising not over eight hundred or nine hundred feet above the level of the Elesu nor. This stream empties into the latter lake, but when near it, it flows under the sand. The Koko-shili, or "Blue hills," (or, rather, "alps," for *shili* means a "grass-covered hill") is, as the name implies, a low range of dark-colored hills, without a single prominent peak.* The point at which we are crossing them appears to be very near the western extremity of the range, and hence this part of it, so says the Jalang, is known also as the *tolha*, or "head" of the range. To our west these hills seem to be lost in a maze of low hillocks, forming the southwestern limit of the Ch'u-mar basin.

We camped about two miles up the pass, as the guide feared there would not be good grass near the summit on the other side, and we cannot make forced marches. We saw a great many antelopes (*ling yang* and *huang yang*) near the foot of the pass, and on the way up I noticed six yaks feeding on the side-hills. The ground was everywhere covered with their dung, so I fancy they are quite numerous in these hills.†

June 5.—Two miles above our camp of last night we reached the summit of the pass, the ascent all the way being absolutely without difficulty. The descent was even easier than the ascent; the hills to their summits were covered with grass, and from the great quantity of yak droppings on this, as on the north side of the range, I fancy that this must be a fine place for a sportsman; the innumerable little depressions between the hillocks composing the range give exceptional facilities for stalking. The whole range, from north to south, is not over ten miles wide, and the

* Conf. Prjevalsky, *Reisen am oberen Lauf des Gelben Flusses*, p. 123.

† Prjevalsky, *Op. sup. cit.*, 129, refers to herds of one thousand head of yak seen by him in this region in 1872–'73. On the flora and fauna of this country, see Prjevalsky, *Op. sup. cit.*, 108–113, 123–124.

south side, along our line of march, is chiefly composed of slate and siliceous limestone.

After crossing the range we took a due westerly course along the foothills over a yielding reddish gravel, with an occasional snow-covered hummock and a few grassy hollows. We had now the great Dungburé range in view, about thirty miles to the southward, trending, as well as I could see, east-southeast and north-northwest. This range is an imposing one, with numerous high peaks, not a few covered with snow far down their dark, steep flanks. One of these peaks, from its supposed resemblance to a conch shell, has given the hybrid name of Dungburé to the range.* In Tibetan *dung* is a "conch shell," and in Mongol *buré* has the same meaning. This, at least, is the explanation of the term given me by a number of Mongols, but I don't think that they, any more than the Tibetans, are very trustworthy etymologists, especially as none of my informants could write, and had to trust implicitly to apparent similarity of sound, a dangerous guide in the languages of this part of the world, and, in fact, in any.

Between the Koko-shili and the Dungburé are several short spurs of no great height, of red sandstone apparently, and all parallel to the main ranges; a number of little streams flow on either side of these, all emptying beyond our range of vision into the Nam-ch'utola muren.

We passed near a solitary yak bull, and when the dogs ran at him, he turned and charged not only them, but the whole party of us, his long shaggy coat bristling all over, and his huge bushy tail standing straight out behind him; it was a magnificent sight. He looked very vicious, and I did not dare to try and kill him with a ball from my light carbine, and I feared that if only wounded he might damage the mules with his long horns. So when he had snorted and pawed around us for awhile, we let him peaceably turn around and leisurely trot off. We saw a couple of wild

* This range is possibly the Tung-p'u-lo-t'u of the Chinese. In the Wei-tsang t'u chih we find mention of a Tung-p'u-lo-t'u ta-pa-na (daban). See *Journ. Roy. Asiat. Soc.*, n. s. XXIII, 92. Explorer A—— K—— says of its name, "*Dung* means a shell and *bura* blowing. This place is so called as it is said that when one of the Grand Lamas went to see the Emperor of China the gods came down to welcome him here and blew the shell." *Report on the Explorations of A—— K——, made in 1879–'82*, 40.

asses, two or three antelope, a great many hares, and a few small birds, but my surveying keeps me too busy to give much time to shooting while on the march.

We camped well up on the foothills at a spot where we found good water and plenty of grass, and which we called Hára daban, "Black pass," from a low col just north of the camp. The Koko-shili are not here over three hundred feet high, but a few miles to our west they rise to perhaps six hundred feet.

June 6.—It snowed so heavily in the night (six inches on the level) that we were unable to move from camp. We all turned out at 5 A. M. and scraped the snow off the grass so that the stock could get something to eat. Towards eight o'clock the Jalang came to my tent and after telling me that he thought it prudent for us to henceforth ration ourselves very closely, and that we must keep an eye on everyone to see that no food was purloined, he remarked that the continual bad weather (which was exceptionally bad for even this region) was keeping us back very much and that some means must be taken, and without any delay, to put a stop to it, for otherwise we should have exhausted our supplies long before we could get to the inhabited parts of Tibet. He had learned from the K'amba the way to charm storms and he wished to put his knowledge at my disposal. I told him that I trusted he would do everything in his power to assist us and that I begged him to set to work at once.

He asked for some tsamba, butter, sugar, and raisins, and then kneaded the tsamba into a number of miniature sea monsters (*mêlêkê*), snakes and bears, and manufactured a good supply of little tsamba pellets in which he mixed the sugar and raisins. He then burnt on a bit of dung some shuka, butter and tsamba to attract the attention of the gods by the perfumed fumes, and assisted by Zangbo, chanted certain prayers. Still chanting, the Jalang poured tea over some of the tsamba pellets and then went outside of the tent and first facing the west, then the east, then the north and finally the south, scattered a little of the oblation in each direction, calling on the gods to accept it. Then he once more turned to the south and then to the west and recited some *mantras*.

After this he came back to the tent, and for the rest of the day and far into the night kept up mumbling charms, going occasionally outside to wave his prayer beads, blow lustily to dispel the storm clouds and burn a little shuka on an improvised altar of a big piece of dry dung. When any black cloud came too near us or a little hail fell, the Jalang's face grew sterner than usual, and he burnt a few of the little *mélèké*, snakes and bears.

While resting during the day the Jalang told me that in this ceremony all the gods of the thirty-three regions of space were invoked, and after offerings had been made to them, they were told that we were on a long journey, that the snow was keeping us back, its whiteness blinding our eyes, and that if we were detained beyond measure our food supplies would give out before we could reach men's dwelling places. "You are all powerful, oh gods, be pleased to accept these offerings, the best we have to give, and stop the snow falling, save us from the tempest and from starvation! If you do so we will always give you of our best, but if you are deaf to our prayer, I will burn these images of *mélèké* and *bamburshé* (bears), the like of which you show yourselves to be, vile, loathsome, cruel beasts!" In the evening there was some heavy thunder and lightning, and a little rain also fell, but the storm passed to the east of us, and the Jalang was happy.

June 7.—The Jalang had to burn up all his little snakes and bears and talk pretty roughly to the gods, but he finally got them under control, for no snow and very little hail fell during the night. The medicine man was consequently very proud, and insisted that, had it not been for him, we would have been snow-bound for at least a week. He blew very vigorously at the clouds this morning, and after a while said we could start, that it was all right.

We continued over very soft gravel, in which our horses sank to their knees; it was as bad as quicksand; the incessant snowing and raining has turned these hillsides into shaking bogs. We crossed three little rivulets, meeting at the foot of the hills and flowing southeast around one of the short red sandstone ridges in the main valley and parallel to its axis. We then came, after about nine miles, to a rather dry spot, covered with fine grass and abundant water, where we camped. The Jalang, who, I fear, is cursed with a lively imagination, said this spot was called Olon horgo, but whether this is true or not, it does just as well as any other name, and is better than such names as "Camp Washington," "Camp Despair," or the like, in which some travelers seem to revel.

We are here very near the head of what I suppose is the valley of the Namchutola, whose southern feeders must be vastly more important than any we have yet seen. Though we have apparently traveled over level ground, I find that we have ascended since the day before yesterday (camp at Hara daban) over four hundred feet, and our present camp is at the respectable altitude of 15,700 feet above sea level. We knew there must be a difference before I had taken any boiling point observation, for at these great altitudes one's breathing accurately indicates the slightest changes of elevation; as soon as we got settled here my men remarked that there was a great deal of *yen chang*, their mode of expressing the difficulty of breathing experienced at high altitudes.

I found hares wonderfully plentiful around camp and killed a dozen in less than an hour. The Jalang and Zangbo, who are *lama kun*, would not eat them, but we, who are *hara kun* ("black men"), feasted on them, and I filled a bag with cooked pieces for my future delectation while on the march.

June 8.—An inch of snow fell during the night and this morning the ground was softer and more trying on the animals than ever. After a few miles in a westerly direction, we turned southwest, and after crossing some steep red sandstone hills and wading through heavy red sand for several miles we came to the north branch of the Namchutola muren (or ulan muren), here about fifteen feet broad and a foot deep. A heavy hailstorm with a good deal of sharp thunder here overtook us, but was rapidly swept eastward, and again the sun shown brightly, but in less than an hour it was hailing again, and sunshine and hail alternated during the whole day with accompanying variations of the thermometer, now at 70° and a few minutes later at 45°.

From the summit of the red sandstone range we crossed in the early part of the day, I distinguished to the north the Koko-shili hills stretching westward eight or ten miles, but so low that they hardly deserved the name of hillock; this marks apparently the end of that range.

A pony went dead lame and two mules gave out and fell under their loads, so we had to camp near where they lay down, only ten miles from our camp of yesterday. I reduced the weight of the luggage a little by throwing away all my shot cartridges; every extra pound tells on the poor mules, and we are still weeks, possibly months away from our journey's end.

I saw no living creature to-day save two yak bulls; even sheldrakes have abandoned this region of mud and storms.

June 9.—We continued in a southwest direction along the foot of a sandstone *mêsa*, which here bounds the basin of the Namchutola, and camped in a hollow at its foot at a point where the valley takes a westerly bend. Before us to the east, in the valley bottom, were five little red sandstone *pitons*, which we called Tabu tolh'a or "the five heads"; these mark accurately the position of our camp. This little valley trends southwest, its lower end a few miles south of here near the left bank of the middle branch of the Namchutola.

Hail, wind and mud have greatly impeded our progress; for the last two or three days we have been obliged to lead our ponies, as it is impossible to ride through the deep, soft mud. To-day two broken-down mules and a lame pony have added materially to our troubles. At the great elevation at which we have now been for ten days, the animals shrivel up and lose their strength with wonderful rapidity. No feed, no shelter, muddy, alkaline water and hard work is rather trying on the best of horseflesh, and on such as we have, and with four months of hard work to their credit, it is no wonder they are utterly done up.

The rivulets that trickle down from the hills behind our camp are strongly saline and dyed of a dark red color, the prevailing hue of this region.

The men are in a grumpy frame of mind; their daily ration is a cup of tsamba and a spoonful of butter. A brick of tea (about eight pounds) is calculated to last the party four weeks. We have had no meat since eating the hares at Olon horgo. Once a day we eat a mess of *mien* and wild onions, or a little rice with *harmak* berries, dry jujubes or *chuoma*. We drink, however, oceans of tea and smoke incessantly. I have still a little *chura* (dried cheese) left, it is, when well soaked, a great addition to plain tsamba. Kao pa-erh, the cook, does wonders in the way of preparing our food, he makes it quite appetizing and is making our supplies last very well, though he is a great eater himself, as is also the Lao-han; the other men say the former steals from their rations.

1

2

3

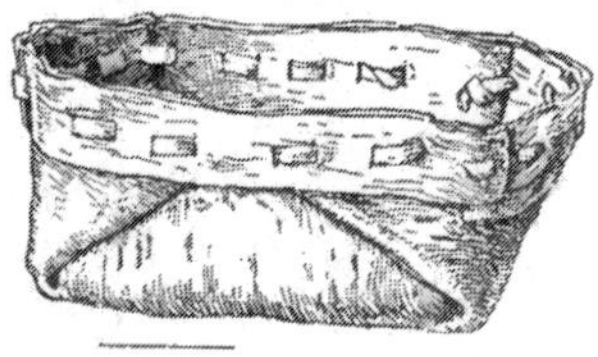

4

5

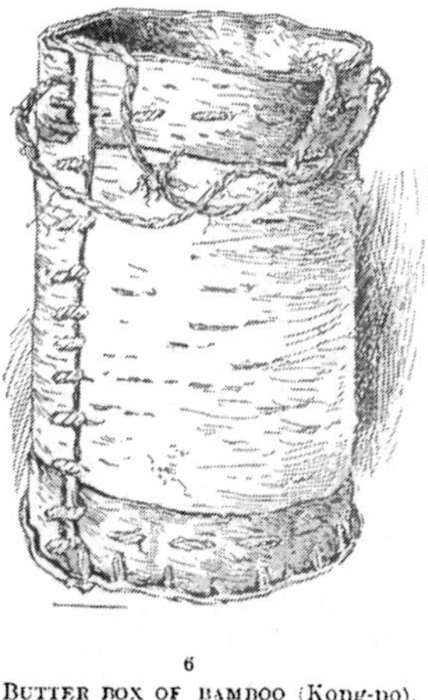

6

1. Butter box (Koko nor). (U. S. N. M. 167214.)
2. Butter box of bamboo (Kong-po). (U. S. N. M. 167213.)
3. Butter box (Lh'asa). (U. S. N. M. 131061.)
4. Birch bark cup (Bat'ang). (U. S. N. M. 167228.)
5. Milk pail (Namru dé). (U. S. N. M. 167226.)
6. Birch bark pail Rong-wa of Kuei-tê). (U. S. N. M. 167226.)

June 10.—We took a southwest by west direction and made for a high snow-covered peak, apparently the culminating point of the mountains to our right and left, and therefore christened by us Namchutola tolh'a or "The Head of the Namchutola." We followed the left bank of the middle branch of the Namchutola, crossing two good-sized affluents which, though now nearly dry, flow in rock-strewn beds over a quarter of a mile in width. These feeders come from the adjacent hills and cannot be over six or eight miles long, hence one may conclude that at certain seasons of the year the rainfall here must be extraordinarily heavy. To the south appear low ranges of red sandstone running east and west, and beyond these again rise the peaks of the Dungburé, in this part apparently of no great height.

As we neared the base of the Namchutola tolh'a, the ground became hummocky and the grass fairly good, though short. We passed by several lakelets and finally made camp beside four small pools of sweet water fed by the melting snow on the summit of the mountain. Bunches of yaks were on every hill, and that readily accounted for the shortness of the grass in the neighborhood. It is wonderful what huge quantities of grass these animals eat, a herd of a hundred would, I believe, find barely enough on a good, rich meadow three miles square. Fortunately their droppings supplied us with an abundance of much needed fuel, and we were able to keep a big fire burning continually, a thing we had not done for many a day.

In the afternoon, seeing a bunch of yaks less than a mile from camp, I started out after them, and by taking a circuitous route was able to get within a hundred yards of them. I broke a fore leg of one with my first shot, and wounded three others badly before they realized that they were being shot at. Then they broke for the higher hills and, though the wounded ones lagged behind and were never out of sight, I was unable to come up with them, so distressing was the effort to walk even slowly and with very frequent halts at such a high altitude. My face was blue and congested and my heart beat so violently that my gun shook when at my shoulder as if I were palsied, and so I had to give up the chase with chagrin, for we were all very hungry.

We called the little pool near which we camped Shiré nor or "the green sod lake," and the animals enjoyed the grass so much that we decided to rest here a few days.

June 11.—The Jalang says we ought to reach the Tengri nor in twenty days, eight days from here to the Murus, and twelve from that river to the lake. From the Tengri nor to Shigatsé he counts eight to ten days march. Twelve days march from here, he says, will surely bring us to Tibetan tents, a most devoutly to be hoped for event as our provisions are decreasing so rapidly that if we are much longer on the way and I have no better luck shooting, we will surely have to kill one of our mules or horses for food.

There are a great many larks* (*pai-ling* in Chinese) here; their singing is a most agreeable relief from the deep silence of the desert, which is only broken by the rumble of thunder or by the moaning of the wind. These birds are only now laying their eggs, I have found a number of their nests in the grass, each with three or four little mud brown eggs in them.

This place used to be inhabited (temporarily I presume) by the Golok. I found to-day near our camp a lot of mani-stones and several hearth stones. We all turned out to try and shoot something but saw nothing, not even a hare. Kao pa-erh fortunately found a quantity of onions and brought back a small bag full.

June 12.—Again we went out to try and shoot something and I killed a fine fat ass, and everyone is in better spirits (the Jalang and Zangbo, of course excepted, who won't eat it) than for the last four or five days.

I got a sight of the Amnyé malchin mengku, the high pyramidal snow peak noted May 31st upon crossing the Ch'u-mar valley. It bears from here 81° east (mag. 261°).

June 13.—About two inches of snow fell early this morning, the storm, as usual, coming from the west-southwest and preceded by an easterly breeze. I fancy there is a regular warm and moisture-laden current from the east, which, on meeting the cold, dry westerly currents prevailing in these regions, results in a hail storm or a sharp fall of snow, as in the present case.

On going out to look at the animals we found one of the mules dying, and I had to put a bullet in its head, for big crows had already plucked its eyes out. It was a fine mule, but had been accustomed to work in towns and to being stabled, and the life I have led it has been too much for it.

* Prjevalsky, *Mongolia*, ii., 145 and 212, calls this species of lark *Melanocorypha maxima*.

I have again overhauled the luggage and reduced the weight a few pounds; now we have not six hundred pounds all told, and I greatly fear the provisions will not last us till we reach some inhabited place. I again talked over the probable length of the journey with the men, and the Jalang insisted that we would reach the Tengri nor in twenty days. Measured on the map we are not over two hundred and fifty miles from the lake, so if the mules hold out, we ought to be there by the 10th of July, and at Shigatsé or some other point on the Yaru tsangpo by the 20th of the same month; but one has to count to so great an extent on the unforeseen on a journey like this that I dare not think I will be so lucky, though I have been wonderfully fortunate so far.

June 14.—Over an inch of snow fell last night. The nights have been so cold on the Shiré nor, and the country so bleak, that the animals have not picked up much, and so we decided to move on. To-day we traveled some six miles in a southwest direction to the foot of a short red clay and sandstone range, trending east and west, and camped in a little gorge just as a violent hailstorm (stones half an inch in diameter), accompanied by very sharp thunder, swept down upon us. This new camp is about 15,900 feet above sea level and we find it oppressive to stand still, let alone to move about; several of the men are sick and we all have headaches and have completely lost our appetites (not a bad thing by the way when one's supplies are as low as ours).

The Jalang thinks we will probably find tents on the Murus where we can buy sheep, but I do not care much whether we do or not, the men have plenty of ass flesh and so I am not worried about them. Last night they ate such quantities of meat—I was awakened several times in the night by the noise they made eating—that to-day they are in a stupefied and gorged condition. The amount of filth they (the good Hsien-sheng alone excepted, who is very gentlemanly in his ways) can eat is simply surprising, hair, dung, blood, all goes, the scum on the boiling pot they hold to be a delicacy; I am not particular, far from it, but I cannot eat the vile messes they revel in.

The night set in with rain and snow, a sure sign of a superior quality of mud and slush for to-morrow. The Ts'aidam is a paradise compared with this vile country.

June 15.—An inch and a half of wet snow covered the ground this morning, enough to prevent the mules and ponies from getting anything to eat. A little after daylight a violent squall of hail struck us, but by 9 A. M. the sun had nearly melted it all and we got off. We trudged up the bed of the stream—which flows from west to east along the base of the Ulan ula, "Red Hills," as we called them, emptying somewhere into the Namchutola or one of its feeders—plunging all the way knee deep in mud and water, till we reached its source and the west end of the Ulan ula. From here we enjoyed a gorgeous view of a perfect maze of mountains, short ranges and little *massifs*, all trending in a general east and west direction. Some eight or ten miles to the west was a beautiful snow peak, seemingly the point where the mountains to our north and the Ulan ula culminate. At its southern base was a lake, its greatest length being apparently from northwest to southeast. The lake we christened Trashi ts'o-nak, "Lake Good Luck," the snow peak I left for some other fellow to name.

A rapid descent of about three miles brought us into a broad valley with a little stream flowing in an easterly direction in a very broad bed to meet beyond the east end of the Ulan ula the Namchutola. South of this broad (and dry, for a wonder,) valley rises the main range of the Dungburé, or rather the western extremity of the range, or Dungburé eken, as the Jalang calls it, a mountain of dark color and easily recognizable by that peculiarity, as all the other hills hereabout are of reddish hue.

The valley in which we have camped, though sandy, is tolerably well covered with grass and, to add to its natural attractions the day has been very pleasant, clear and calm. We walked all the way here, so as to spare our horses, and managed to get them over the ten miles of bad road without any additional signs of fatigue.

I was surprised to-day to see on the top of the Ulan ula (approx. 16,500 feet above sea level) great numbers of light yellow butterflies with small spots of black on their wings. I saw none any where else; unfortunately I was unable to capture any.

June 16.—A very heavy dew fell last night, but the sky was beautifully clear and calm; we enjoyed the peaceful night greatly and all rose this morning feeling much refreshed.

We continued our journey in a southwest direction by a very easy road up the course of a torrent (now nearly dry), which has its source on the west flank of the Dungburé eken, and then crossed a low col, from which we had a fine view of the Trashi ts'o-nak. Lake Trashi ts'o-nak, as seen from the pass, appeared some six or eight miles from east to west and perhaps two miles broad. To the west of it some thirty miles or more away, I saw a fine snow peak. We then descended by a short and narrow gorge leading into another broad valley down which flows a small stream, a feeder of the Toktomai. We had entered the basin of the Murus, the Dré ch'u, the Yang-tzŭ kiang of the Chinese.*

I may here remark that on none of the passes which we have crossed, and many of which were over 16,500 feet above sea level, did we find old snow, so the snow line in this region cannot be lower than 17,000 feet above the sea.

The red sandstone formation disappears on the north side of Dungburé eken and a bluish sandstone takes its place. Just as we were making camp a heavy squall of rain and snow with a southwest wind struck us and drenched us to the skin. Southerly winds are a novelty, we have only had them two or three times, and that within the last few days.

From a little above our camp I had pointed out to me, due south of us, Mt. Buha mangnä. Between this dark, truncated, pyramid-shaped peak and ourselves is a perfect sea of hills, all trending more or less east and west. Nowhere can I see a snow peak; they are extremely rare in this region; we have not seen a dozen so far on the journey.

---

* Cf. Prjevalsky, *Mongolia*, ii, 128. In the light of more recent investigations we are able to correct a number of errors in which this traveler fell. The river in question is known as Murus to the Mongols and as Dré ch'u to Tibetans. From Bat'ang to where it enters China it is called by the Chinese Chin chiang ho or "Gold River;" from the latter point to Sui Fu in Ssŭ-ch'uan, as Chin sha chiang or "Golden sand river," and from Sui Fu eastward, as Ta chiang or "the Great river." Prjevalsky says that Tibetans call it Link-arab at its confluence with the Namchutu ulan muren. The point where the Dré ch'u is forded, on the high road between Hsi-ning and Lh'asa, is called Dré ch'u rabs, "the ford of the Dré ch'u." Probably he refers to this place. He further says (p. 132) that on the Dang la the snow line on the north side is approximately at 5,100 meters (15,728 feet) and on the south side at 5,250 meters (17,220 feet above sea level). I am inclined to believe that it is really even considerably higher than I estimated it.

Yeh Hsien-sheng and Kao pa-erh had a grand row this evening, the former accusing the latter of stealing; they wanted to kill each other and I had a good deal of trouble in quieting them, but the Hsien-sheng will always listen to reason and I hushed up the matter as it won't do for the time being; I told him that when we get to the journey's end I will give him a chance to have it out with the cook. The hard work and poor fare has made everyone cross and snappish; I know that I am terribly disagreeable myself, daily I vent my spleen on the cook and the Lao-han.

We saw one yak and a jackass, but signs of yak are very abundant and the grass has all been eaten very short by them. The grass is just beginning to turn green, a few yellow and white tulips (*ma-lien hua*) and some iris are the only flowers I can see.

June 17.—Several of the horses and mules, though hobbled and side-lined, followed some wild asses in the night, and it took us three or four hours this morning to find them and bring them back. A wild jackass will round up and drive off a bunch of tame ponies in a wonderfully quick and clever way. These animals are most troublesome; more than once I have had to shoot at them to drive them away from around camp.

We descended to the foot of the hills to a little stream which flowed in a south-southwest direction, between low hills of fine bluish sandstone, and followed it for some twelve miles to where it took an easterly bend, to empty into some other feeder of the Toktomai. To the south of where we have camped to-day is another plain running east and west, in which the red sandstone again crops out, forming a short range of hills, and from the top of a hill behind our camp I saw that this sandstone formation extends as far to the west as the eye could reach.* Small ponds and lakelets dot the plain to the south of us, and others appear here and there to the westward. The country seems badly drained, here the waters empty into small sinks, there they flow off to feed the Toktomai.

We saw a great many orongo antelope and hares, but though I failed to kill one of the former I bagged seven of the latter, and we had "a good square meal"—for a change.

* Capt. Bower found this red sandstone nearly 400 miles west of this point in the same latitude. See H. Bower, *Diary of a Journey Across Tibet*, 17.

A few miles above our camping ground we passed an old Tibetan camp, marked by rude stone altars and fire-places such as the Panaka build. Probably the people from south of the Murus come here occasionally to kill yaks, or else it is a rendez-vous for the Golok, from whence they can easily reach caravans traveling on the highroad to Lh'asa, some fifty miles east of here.

A southerly wind has been blowing again to-day and we have had several little showers; the temperature is milder and the air has more life in it. It is lower (15,200 feet) here than any place we have traversed for the last nine days, and every foot tells, as far as the facility of breathing is concerned.

June 18.—We crossed a plain about three miles broad, in which were several lakelets and also a small stream flowing in a southwest direction through a broad opening in a line of low, red sandstone hills. Passing this, we continued in a south-southwest direction over an open plateau, bordered to the south by a range of hills running nearly east and west, but so confused and cut up that it was difficult either to lay them down on the map or indicate their trend with any accuracy. At their northern base, some eight miles away, several rivulets which drain this broad plain meet to form the northernmost fork of the Toktomai ulan muren, "The gently flowing red river."*

Some thirty to forty miles to the west of our route and in the line of the axis of the little plain in which were the two lakelets noticed previously, I saw a fine snow peak. We made about fourteen miles and camped by the river bank, where fine grass covered all the country round. The soil along the Toktomai is a

* Father Grueber, when traveling to Lh'asa, crossed this river, where the Hsi-ning-Nagchuk'a road cuts it. "Le Père s'éloignant ensuite peu à peu de son rivage (*i. e.*, du Koko-nor), il entra dans le Toktokai, païs presque desert et d'ailleurs si sterile, qu'il n'a point à craindre l'ambition de ses voisins.. La rivière de Toktokai arose ce païs, et lui donne son nom: c'est une fort belle rivière, aussi large que le Danube; mais elle a si peu de fond, qu'un homme à cheval la peut passer à guay partout. De là ayant traversé le païs de Tangut il arriva à Retink, province fort peuplée, dependante du royaume de Barantola; il vint en suite au royaume mesme de Barantola. La ville capitale de ce royaume s'appelle Lassa; * * *" Thevenot, *Relations*, II, IVe Partie, p. 1. The district of Reting (his Retink) and Reting gomba are nearly due east of the Tengri nor and on the road to Lh'asa. Reting gomba is about twenty-eight miles from Lh'asa, and has some two hundred lamas residing in it at present. *Report of Explorations made by A—— K—— in 1879–'82*, p. 36.

rather soft red sandstone gravel. We saw several small herds of orongo and an occasional solitary jackass wandering listlessly over the hills.

To-day has been the first since we left the Naichi valley, twenty-three days ago, in which we have had neither rain, snow, hail nor wind; but it hailed not a mile away from camp this evening, and we have heard the low sound of thunder, and, as I write (9 P. M.), it is blowing hard from the east.

The Toktomai is at this spot about twenty feet broad and two feet deep in the middle, with a strong current. I greatly enjoyed a bath in the river; it has put new life in me, but the Chinese and Mongols think I am crazy to jump into such icy water. I noticed numbers of little brown lizards, in shape something like a chameleon, though flatter. I wish I could have taken a few along with me, but my flask of brandy is too precious to waste it on such things, and I have no alcohol, it has all leaked out of the copper can in which I had it.

The weather since we crossed the Dungburé has greatly improved, and is warmer and clearer than farther north. The prevailing winds have become southerly, a quarter from which they never seem to blow in or near the Ts'aidam.

June 19.—For the first time since we left the Ts'aidam, we left off our sheepskin ch'ubas. The day was most delightful until about an hour before sunset when a violent west wind sprang up which died down, however, at 10 P. M.

We followed the river to-day for fifteen miles, crossing it twice on the way, the valley broadening out a little below camp to nearly five miles in width, the bottom land of fine reddish gravel, boggy in many places, the higher ground covered with good grass. The river has a swift current with a fall of about twenty feet to the mile. The mountains on the west side of the valley are considerably higher than those on the east, which are not over two hundred feet high. Nearly due south of us is the Buha mangnä, along whose western flank our route lies, while the highroad to Nagch'uk'a runs some little distance from its eastern base. We saw a few yaks, some wild asses and antelopes; numerous old hearths along the river bank testified to the occasional presence of man (probably Goloks) in this quarter.

The sandstone formation is still visible at our camp this evening, but red sandstone is not so abundant as it was yesterday.

We have all noticed that on rainy or foggy days we feel the effect of the high altitude more than on clear, dry ones.

June 20.—Eight miles below camp the north branch of the Toktomai is deflected due east, around a small hill with a rocky crest, and at its eastern extremity it empties into the southern or main branch of the Toktomai, which flows down a broad valley running due east and west, and some forty miles in length.

Leaving the north branch at the bend, we continued due south for six miles, till we came to the south branch, a good-sized river flowing in a number of channels over a soft sandstone gravel bed a half mile in width. We had not a little difficulty in getting across, as the channels were deep and the sand very soft. There is certainly five times as much water in this branch as in the northern.

We camped near the right bank of the river, and I saw far to the west, probably forty or fifty miles, a large, snow-covered mountain, in or near which, I take it, the south branch of the Toktomai has its source, but the mountains which border the valley on either side take a sharp bend about twelve miles west of our camp, and hide from me the trend of the valley beyond that point. Nothing but a small plain now separates us from the Buha mangnä,* which rises dark and imposing some ten miles to the southeast of us. To the south, in which direction our route leads, I can only see a slight rise in the ground, and the Jalang says this is all that separates in that direction the valley of the Toktomai from that of the Murus.

The grazing is excellent on every side of us, and the weather continues fair. Three days of fine weather! This looks as if the worst of the journey was over, I mean as far as climate is concerned. It blew again in the evening, a result I suppose of the rapid cooling off of the soil at this high altitude.

From what I have been able to learn so far, there are three roads leading into Tibet from the north, and all probably parallel to the

* Called by Explorer A—— K—— Bukhmangne. See *Report on Explorations by A—— K—— in 1879–'82*, 40.

trail we are following.* 1st. By the highroad *viâ* the Angirtakshia; 2nd. West of the one we are following, and followed by the Taichinär Mongols of Hajir, leading over country similar to that we have traversed, crossing no high passes, but along it water and grazing are poor; 3rd. Considerably farther west than No. 2 and leading directly from the Lob nor. This last is followed by the Torgot Mongols and is, I imagine, the one taken by Bonvalot. It is said to be very bad.

I caught a glimpse of the famous Dang la chain this evening; it is the first really imposing range I have seen. Its name is written Grangs la (pronounced in the Lh'asan dialect Dang la) meaning "cold, icy." A good name for it, as along most of its length it rises far above the snowline.

June 21.—A few miles south of our camp of yesterday, we crossed some very low hills which prolong the foothills of the Buha mangnä to the west, and entered the basin of the Murus. From this point we got our first view, in a southeast direction, of an immense snowpeak, probably Prjevalsky's Mt. Dorsi, but called by my guide, Atak Habseré mengku or "Lower Habseré snow-peak."† To the east of it we saw another great snow-covered mountain which I took for Prjevalsky's Mt. Djoma. The Jalang, who ought to know, says its name is Satokto san-koban, meaning something like "enfant terrible." Crossing a rivulet, which probably empties into the Murus about twelve miles east of our route, we ascended another range of low hills and the Murus ("*The* River"), or the north branch of it, if the Jalang is to be trusted (though I have never heard tell of two branches of this river), was before us.‡ Crossing the col we camped about a mile below it; the river about a mile farther south.

* Chinese works, referring to roads to Lh'asa from the north, make mention of (1) a road from Yarkand around the Ts'ung-ling and through Ngari to Lh'asa; (2) a road from Yashar in Ku-che, "It is through marshes and mire and is difficult;" (3) a road by the Murus (this is the Hsi-ning high road); (4) a road from Koliya near Ilchi (Khoten). "It goes due east through the Gobi to Kartsang-guja, thence by way of Pang-t'ang across a lakelet to the Tengri nor, then to the Sang-to lake, which is 200 *li* from Lh'asa. *Hsi-yü kao ku lu*, vi., 8.

† None of the Mongols with me could suggest any interpretation of the word *Habseré*, though it would appear to be Mongol.

‡ As will be seen further on the Jalang was wrong, as there does not appear to be more than one branch to the head waters of this great river in this direction.

Climbing a steep hill directly east of our camp I had a splendid view of the great Dang la range, certainly the most imposing chain of mountains I have seen in Asia. While its eastern extension was far beyond our line of vision, its western end did not appear to be over forty miles away, and from this point it bore 250° west (Mag. 70°). The Atak Habseré bore nearly southeast (E. 155°), the Tumta (or "Middle") Habseré bore southwest by south (W. 210°), and the Èken (or "Upper") Habseré was to the southwest (W. 222°). The Atak Habseré is the most important of the "Three Habseré" (Kurban Habseré).*

The Jalang says that the main branch of the Murus flows some six or eight miles south of the one before us, behind a low range of hills on the south side of the river and near the base of the Dang la.

The hills around our camp are of limestone, a rock we have not seen since passing the Kuan-shong k'utur.

A violent hailstorm swept over us just as we were making camp, and in the evening a strong east breeze blew and there was a good deal of lightning to the south. Grass is getting green hereabout and I picked a number of flowers (*Carex*, *Kobresia*, *Festuces*, *Lagotis*, etc.).

While on the march we saw a number of yaks, wild asses, orongo and huang-yang, but they were all so wild that it was impossible to get a shot at them. Since crossing the Dungburé, huang-yang (*Antilope gutturosa*) have become much more numerous than to the north of those mountains.

We have had no meat for a number of days now, and are reduced to eating onion duff, as I suppose I should call flour and chopped onions cooked in grease; and a pretty poor mess it is!

June 22.—We followed up the course of the Murus for about nine miles over sandy soil tolerably well covered with grass. The river bottom where we came on to it is about six miles wide. To the south it is bordered by a range of very low hills beyond which is another low range running parallel to the main or Dang la chain. In this latter valley is said to flow the southern branch of the upper Murus, or rather the principal feeder of the headwaters of this river.

*A—— K—— calls the Atak Habseré, Atag-hapchiga, and the Eken Habseré, Yakénhapchiga.

I noticed in the river bed (I also saw one yesterday just before making camp), what I took for mud springs, an upheaval of mud and soft stone, all of a reddish color, from which trickled little streamlets.

Having found a spot where the river appeared fordable, it being there divided into a number of channels, we rearranged the loads and sent the Hsien-sheng ahead to try the ford. The water reached to his horse's back and the current proved very strong, but the river bottom was hard, so we took the mules over one by one, and after an hour's hard work everything was landed on the right bank without accident. The water was very muddy and the river much swollen from the melting snows and by the daily rains, but there was no evidence that it ever overflows its bed to any considerable extent.

We camped not far from the river near some pools of water around which there was fine grazing. A violent thunderstorm swept down both sides of the valley from 2 to 5 P. M., with very heavy hail, but we escaped its violence.

The Jalang is turning out to be a vile tempered old savage. He had to-day a quarrel with all the men about his food allowance and his tea. He threatens continually to leave us if I do not comply with all his demands. So far I have been able to restrain myself, but some day I will have to have it out with him. His brother Panti says the Jalang knows nothing of the country through which he is now taking us, that he has never been here before, and that we will never get to the Tengri nor by this route. To all this the Jalang does not deign to reply. He passes much of his time while we are camped seated on some commanding hilltop surveying the country, and when he comes back he invariably says that he has found the landmarks he was looking for and that we are in the right way. I trust more to the compass and maps, poor as they are, than to him, but I say nothing.

June 23.—It rained heavily during the night and this morning it was very cloudy. We followed up the river in a southwest direction for about ten miles, then crossing it where it flows due south and north, we continued in a westerly direction about two miles and camped near some pools of water at the foot of a line of low hills.

1

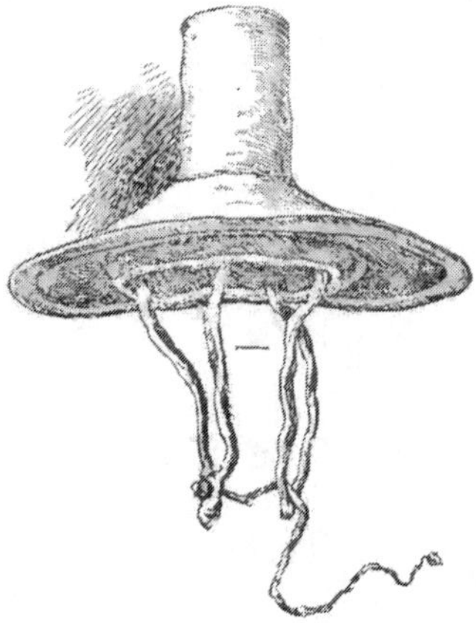

2

3

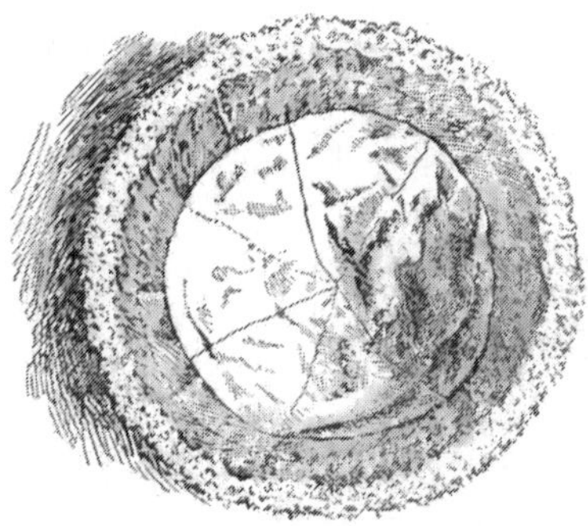

4

1. FELT SUMMER HAT (Ts'aidam). U. S. N. M. 167191.)
3. FUR CAP, lined with felt (Namru dé). (U. S. N. M. 167193.)

2. SUMMER HAT (Namru dé). (U. S. N. M. 167192.)
4. CAP OF TIBETANS and Mongols of Koko nor. (U. S. N. M. 131186.)

The Murus, where we left it, could be traced up as far as the Éken Habseré *massif* in which it certainly has its source. Where we crossed it to-day it was about two feet deep and probably seventy-five feet wide. This does not necessarily imply that we are far from the sources of this great river, as in this region a stream grows with wonderful rapidity. I traced up with my eye the course of the river for about ten miles, and could see numerous brooks emptying into it, quite enough to account for its volume where we crossed it. The Murus' ultimate source is certainly in the snows and ice on the Éken Habseré, which is very nearly southwest by south from our camp of this evening.

A curious feature of the valleys of the Murus and of the Toktomai is the presence there of innumerable little pools or sinks in which is collected all the water that falls in the valley bottoms and over a large area of the contiguous hills. These pools have no visible outlets into the rivers. To-day, for example, we certainly passed twenty-five such lakelets, some of them on the very bank of the stream.

Another heavy thunderstorm at 2 P. M., at which time they always occur, but as usual it kept to the mountains. The Jalang's plan is to go around the Dang la, as we have done in the case of the Koko-shili, Dungburé, etc.; it is a good one and will prove interesting, for I am thus able to define the limits of the basins of all these important rivers, the Ch'u-mar, Namchutola and Toktomai. He thinks that by the day after to-morrow we should reach the head of the Murus valley or, as he calls it, the Dang la tolh'a, the beginning (or "head") of the Dang la. On the south side of this big range he thinks we shall find tents and be able to buy sheep. The south side of such a range must, however, be a long way off, the Jalang's assurances notwithstanding, and we are all getting very hungry. We cannot, I think, be much more than two hundred and fifty miles from Shigatsé. a month's journey, but will we make it in a month with mules and ponies weakening, a guide who is not to be trusted, and the possibility of being stopped by the first chief we fall in with, in case we have not steered clear of Lh'asan territory? The road we are following has been so far a good and direct one, but one big river, or worse still, the impossibility of renewing our supplies, and the consequent necessity of seeking some chief and getting assistance from him, will cause the best laid plans to come to naught.

June 24.—We made fourteen miles in a west-southwest by west direction up the valley of the little feeder of the Murus we entered yesterday after crossing that river. There was a steady though hardly perceptible rise in the ground. Though we have been traveling on what seems level ground since coming to the Murus, we are this evening six hundred and fifty feet higher than when we struck the river three days ago.

Limestone is the principal rock in the hills to the south, and, if I may judge by the gravel and *débris* washed down from the northern hills, sandstone, mostly reddish, predominates there.

I no longer believe in the Jalang's statement that we have been along the north branch of the Murus. There is no south branch, we have had ocular proof of this. Now to explain away the lie, for it was nothing else (and I believe that he has never been this far west before, but probably came along the trail we have heretofore followed as far as the Toktomai, and then cut east and joined the highroad), he says that the Mongols believe that the Murus divides into two branches southwest of here to reunite again to the east of the Buha-mangnä.

The usual 2 P. M. thunderstorm visited us again to-day, and as usual also it came from the west. Since leaving the Ts'aidam we have never had a storm from another quarter. From this camp Èken Habseré bears southeast by south (E. 175°).

June 25.—We are camping to-night at the head of the Murus valley in this direction, and at an altitude of 16,850 feet above sea level. We have also reached the west end of the Dang la range. The country all the way here was of gravel, and for a few miles before making camp the ground was covered with grass-grown hummocks. The hills on either side of us are three hundred or four hundred feet high, but the main range to the north, which bends now in a slightly northerly direction, and is some five or six miles away, rises over two thousand feet above the surrounding country.

We reached camp by 2.30 P. M., and by 3.30 it was snowing hard, with a great deal of thunder, which in these high altitudes, by the way, always sounds like the rattle of musketry. By 5 o'clock the snow stopped falling (three inches on a level), but shortly after a heavy fog enveloped us, and at 7 P. M. the thermometer stood at 25° Fahrenheit. From here the western end of the Dang la seems to be a line of low black hills, over which our route must lay. Along our road to-day limestone and sandstone appeared in about equal proportions, but, I fancy, judging from its rugged outlines, the Dang la is of eruptive formation.

Again to-day we saw quite a large herd of yaks, but they fled when we were a mile away, and we were only able to kill one hare, just enough to give our mess of *mien* a little flavor.

June 26.—We crossed the foothills of the Dang la, taking a west-southwest by west direction. In the first place, we passed six or eight miles south of a small lake, possibly three miles long, and which we called Dzurken ula nor, from its proximity to a black, commanding peak which we thought looked like a heart (*dzurken* in Mongol), and was consequently named by us Dzurken ula. To our west, some twenty miles away, rose a short range of mountains with its central portion covered with snow. This, the Jalang thinks, and I agree with him, must be the snow peak seen from our camp on the south branch of the Toktomai and which I then thought must be at the source of that river.* We have left the valley of the Murus behind; the water from all the surrounding hills south and west of us empties into the Dzurken ula nor. We are at last on the central plateau of North Tibet.† From its flanks flow the Murus, the Salwen and half a dozen other great rivers, and here is also the eastern extremity of the great Central Asian Plateau.

Away to the southwest there is a low ridge running westward and connecting the Dang la with another range of hills, but we have, as we hoped, turned the great mountains. The snow peaks at whose base we are now camped are truly the "Head of the Dang la" (Dang la tolh'a). They rise apparently 2,000 feet above the snow line and, as at least for 1,000 above where we are camped (17,000 feet above sea level) they are without snow, we must

* See *20th June.*

† Politically speaking Tibet begins at the Dang la. All the country between the Ts'aidam and that range is in reality a no-man's land, called usually Chang t'ang or "Northern plain." Capt. Bower uses the word Chang alone, but that only means "the North."

conclude that the line of perpetual snow in this region is at very nearly 18,000 feet above the level of the sea.*

We had our usual hailstorm at 3 P. M., with accompanying thunder and westerly wind. The Jalang thinks that we will see the Dang la behind us in two days, that three days later we shall make the Amdo ts'o-nak and that within eight or ten days, going *tabar, tabar* ("Slowly, slowly"), we shall have reached the Tengri nor. If my charts are anywhere near correct, I do not see how this can be, but the Jalang is a pretty good guesser; even if he has not been in these parts before, he has the true instinct of a guide, he divines where the trail should be, and so far he has done his work very well.

June 27.—We continued to-day in the same west-southwest direction as yesterday, along the foothills of the Dang la, crossing a number of torrents, one about two feet deep and thirty to forty feet wide, but flowing in a bed at least one-third of a mile in width. The soil is everywhere fine gravel and very little grass grows anywhere on it. Our view of the Dang la and its snow fields is absolutely unobstructed. I cannot decide whether there are any glaciers; I am inclined to think there are none. The rocks I see are all limestone and granite. We have camped on the north slope of some low hills, and I fancy that to-morrow we will enter the basin of some river flowing southward. The whole country, as far as I can see, is covered with hills, between which are pools and lakelets receiving all the drainage.

It snowed heavily for about an hour this morning and again in the afternoon, when there blew a strong north wind, but the day would not be complete now without a storm.

June 28.—A couple of miles from camp we crossed a low col, and then took a southwest course over a perfectly bare plain of

* "On the southern declivity of the Himalaya, the limit of perpetual snow is 12,978 feet above the level of the sea; on the northern declivity, or rather on the peaks which rise above the Tibet or Tartarian plateau, the limit is 16,625 feet, from 30½° to 32° of latitude, while at the equator, in the Andes of Quito, it is 15,590. * * * The greater elevation to which the limit of perpetual snow recedes on the Tartarian declivity is owing to the radiation of heat from the neighboring elevated plains, to the purity of the atmosphere, and the infrequent formation of snow in an air which is both cold and very dry." Alex. von Humboldt, *Asie Centrale*, III., 281–326, and *Cosmos* (Harper's edit., 1850), I., 30–32, 331–332. The camp of June 26th was in latitude north 33° 42′. See also note *p. 209*.

gravel, cut here and there by torrents, some with beds over half a mile wide, which empty into a stream flowing westward and which we called, on account of the great quantity of ice on its surface, Kétén gol or "Cold River."

We are now well to the west of the Dang la, which stretches out in a southeast by south direction, as far as we can see. Some twenty miles south of us we can distinguish a short range of black hills, and nearer to us in the same quarter another short range, running southeast and northwest, from which issue several streams emptying a mile below our camp into the Kétén gol. No mountain range of any importance beside the Dang la can be seen, but innumerable little blocks of hills intersect the country in every direction. The soil is very barren; where we have camped there is a little grass, but elsewhere there is only sand and gravel.

The soft wet gravel, through which we have of late traveled so much, has been very trying on the feet of our ponies and mules; every one of them is lame. We will rest here for a day and then push on as rapidly as possible to the Tengri nor.

To-day has been the third fine day we have had since leaving the Naichi gol. It is very enjoyable.

Towards dark we saw a bull yak feeding on the hills west of our camp and we all turned out to get a shot at him. He started off at a great pace when we were half a mile off, and though we followed him till dark up and down the hills we never got near enough to shoot. When one has been very hungry for over a month, stalking is exciting work. There is not even a sheldrake to be seen, not a lark nor a marmot; the silence of this vast wilderness is positively oppressive.

June 29.—Another beautiful, warm day, though quite a thick coating of ice formed on the river last night and the minimum thermometer registered $+13^{\circ}3$, but during the day it went up to 97°. The Jalang passed the morning seated on the top of the highest hill he could find near camp, and when he came back he reported that he had seen Bumza shili (north of Nagchuk'a), also a large lake to the west of us into which the Kétén gol empties. He thinks that by keeping a southwest course we shall pass well to the west of the Amdo ts'o-nak and the Tengri nor, and thus not have to travel on Lh'asan territory but on that of Ulterior Tibet (or Tsang) and that we shall thus not meet any town, gomba or thickly peopled district until we are close to Shigatsé. I agree as to the advisability of keeping a southwest course, but don't believe he saw Mt. Bumza, that is quite impossible, it is a long, long way off.

The men, in expectation of our finding Drupa the day after to-morrow, and in view of the consequent feast of mutton in store for them, have laid in a large stock of onions with which they propose to stuff the delicious sausages (*ch'ang-tzŭ*) they will then make with the intestines, lights, heart, etc.

We have absolutely nothing left to eat but a little flour and tea. To-day I ate my last dish of rice and currants. Henceforth we shall take one meal a day and for the rest of the time content ourselves with tea. Kao has greatly horrified the other two Chinese by smoking tobacco, and they have talked to him so seriously about the matter that he has finally given it up. They will not eat the wild ass meat; they say their religion (Islam) forbids eating the flesh of any animal with an uncloven hoof.

It is curious that Panti, who is asthmatic and suffered greatly from shortness of breath in the Ts'aidam, does not experience any additional inconvenience at the high altitudes at which we have since then lived. In fact, none of the men, save Yeh Hsien-sheng and myself, are in the least inconvenienced by the rarified atmosphere. Kao pa-erh, who is at his first experience of high altitudes, can sleep without even so much as a stone under his head, and that on a full stomach (or as near one as he can get), and not feel oppressed in the least.

It is astonishing how very regular is the pace of our animals; two or three times every day I measure their step, and I invariably find that to keep beside a given one in the line I must take from ninety-eight to one hundred paces of thirty inches in a minute on level ground, and from eighty-four to eighty-eight when on a steep path, either ascending or descending.

June 30.—We got off by 8.15 A. M. The hills to the west-southwest of our camp and over the southern extremity of which we had to pass, are composed largely of flints.* From their summit we caught our first glimpse of a large expanse of dark blue water about twelve miles to the southwest, and on whose western shore rises a steep and bare red sandstone hill. We crossed the

* We called these hills Huo-shih shan, "Fire stone hills."

Kétén gol at its mouth on the shore of the lake, and camped on a green hillslope one hundred feet above the water. The lake is about fifteen miles in its greatest length (northeast to southwest) and in places seven or eight miles wide. The mountains on its western side looked very beautiful as we came down to the lake, with their many shades of red and yellow limestone, with here and there a broad vein of white, the colors brightening or becoming obscure as the sunlight shone upon them or a cloud swept between them and the sun. An end of the lake was at one moment wrapped in darkness, hail poured down and the thunder rattled, but soon all its blue surface glittered in the sunlight, and there was no sound but that of the wavelets breaking on the sandy beach in a gentle murmur.

Around where we have camped I can see many old well-blackened hearth stones; I suppose Tibetans come here to get salt. The water of the lake is nearly undrinkable, and possibly there are deposits of pure salt near here. The grazing is splendid, and the mosquitoes enormous and ferocious.*

July 1.—Our route lay parallel to the shore of the lake over a slightly undulating country. About three miles south of our camp we crossed a good sized though shallow river, which comes from out the hills to the southeast, some ten to fifteen miles away. Farther on we crossed the dry beds of several torrents; they were nearly a mile in width in many places. We camped about nineteen miles southwest of our camp of yesterday, on the bank of another small stream flowing into the lake from the hills which surround it on the south. The water of this stream, like that of all those emptying into this lake, is very brackish, nearly unfit for use. I was unable to detect any outlet for the waters of the lake, though it seems hardly credible that evaporation can dispose of the enormous quantity which must flow into it, and I have seen no signs of its level ever being much higher than at present. My Mongols are persuaded that this lake is the Tengri nor, and I cannot disabuse them of this conceit.

While on the top of a small hill about six miles from where we are now camped, I got sight of some snow peaks to the west, and at no great distance from the lake; and from this point I took

* Later on I learnt that this lake is called Chib-chang ts'o (or T'eb-chang ts'o). I called it temporarily Lake Glenelg.

also what I fancy will be my last view of the western extremity of the Dang la.

To judge from the vast amount of yak's and sheep's droppings and hearth stones which cover the ground where we have camped to-day, numerous caravans must travel over this road. We also found a number of worn out saddle bags, such as are used by Tibetans to carry salt in on the backs of sheep. The two bags hold a load of about twenty pounds. The Jalang says the Amdo Tibetans (from the Amdo ts'o-nak country) travel this way when going to the salt mines in the Dang la. This lake must be one of the numerous *Ts'aka* with which, according to Chinese authorities, this region abounds. It corresponds very roughly in position with the Liarchagan lake of previous maps, and is approximately 15,800 feet above sea level.* The Jalang has never been here, he has finally admitted it to me. All we can do now is to follow our noses, and trust to luck.

The grazing is now good everywhere and our animals are doing well. If only we could do like King Nebuchadnezzar and eat grass! I have nothing but a couple of biscuits (*momo*), some tea and tobacco, and of even the latter only enough for a couple of days, but we all hope to see black tents to-morrow. We had a thunderstorm with rain to-day, the second time it has rained since we left the Naichi gol.

July 2.—We took a south-southwest course parallel to a short range of mountains of no great height on our right. The sandy plain over which we traveled is traversed by a number of small streams flowing, some westward, into a lake which the Jalang saw yesterday some distance to the west, the others emptying into little pools at the foot of the hills, these possibly communicating by underground channels with the former sheet of water.

From the low red sandstone hill on which we have camped this evening, I can see that the hills to the south of the Ts'aka (Chib chang ts'o) run west as far as the eye can reach.

I have to-day distributed to the men the last cupful of tsamba we have; if they could be persuaded to only eat a mouthful a day it might last for ten days, but it won't, I know these people too well. They will, with the exception of the Hsien-sheng, who

* Its name, Chib chang ts'o, is evidently represented by the Chang chong chaka (ts'aka) of our maps.

will do exactly what I tell him, make one or two "square meals," and then live on tea until such time as something better turns up. I distributed among them my own supply of tsamba and chura and have now absolutely nothing but a small flask of brandy which I have treasured up so far in case of an emergency, satisfying my desire for it with an occasional smell of the liquor. We saw no sign of people having been in this region for months past, probably not since last year; we may meet some any time, but then they may have nothing to sell us, or refuse positively to sell what they have, and so it may go on for days. I shot a wild ass to-day just before making camp; it fell at the first shot; we all ran up excitedly but the famished dogs were there before us, and up jumped the ass and made off. Do what I would I could not put my pony into even a trot; he was like his master, too played out for sport. The men took our misfortune with true Mohammedan stoicism; *T'ien ming*, "it is Heaven's decree," was all they said, and mounting their ponies rode on.

July 3.—We traveled to-day about twenty miles, for the greater part of the time in a nearly due southerly direction; crossing two ranges of hills projecting from those to our east, and running due east and west; the stream between them flowed westward. These hills appeared to be composed mostly of shale of a yellowish color. The ground under our feet was of fine gravel, and very little grass was anywhere to be seen. Two miles before making camp we crossed a col, the ascent to which was quite long; I made it out to be 16,500 feet above sea level. From where we have stopped, a couple of hundred feet below the summit on the south side of the pass, we command an extensive view, but I can see nothing before us but mountains and jagged walls of rocks projecting from their summits.

The Jalang says that he followed this circuitous trail, of which he had once heard tell, so that we might not fall in with too many black tents, the people of which might have impeded our progress. This plan has turned out wonderfully successful; it has been entirely too much of a success. Again to-day we have sought in vain for signs of human life; though we are on a well beaten highroad now, no one has passed this way for months past, and no one is such a fool as to live here, I feel convinced.

There is a little bird, I have heard its sweet little twitter ever since we have crossed the Dang la but have never seen it, for it sings at or even before the break of day and just after dark when the rest of creation is still. Its note is plaintive but very sweet; I would like to see the little fellow, he helps so to make life bearable.

July 4.—During the night it rained hard from ten to eleven o'clock, and then for three hours it sleeted. The storm, which was accompanied by thunder and lightning, came as usual from the west. After crossing a little stream flowing westward, we entered to-day a broad valley. At its southern end the stream flowing through it bends abruptly westward and enters a narrow gorge. The upper part of this valley is marked by a curious ridge of rocks, probably limestone, running east and west, and which, from a distance, might be taken for a line of old gnarled and dead trees, so sharp are their outlines. In this valley we came again on the highroad followed by those going to the northern salt mines, and we had to make up our minds to follow it, for no other route led out of the valley. I felt, however, reluctant to do so for where it left the stream at the southern end of the valley, it bent southeastward, a direction I was very loath to take for even a short distance, so apprehensive did I feel lest it should bring me too near to or perhaps on Lh'asan territory, of which I must try at all hazards to steer clear.*

We had to camp near a lakelet on the top of the pass at the south end of the valley we had followed all day, for two of the horses having given out, they could not be made to go a step farther. The ground was soaked, the argols too wet to burn, the only water we could get was muddy and brackish. It was a poor place for a camp, bleak beyond description, the only thing which commended it was the grass. We broke up one of our packing boxes to start a fire and dry some argols for fuel, and with the thermometer at 40°, at an altitude of 16,000 feet and with a cold wind blowing the smoke into our inflamed eyes, we tried to celebrate "the glorious fourth" with a wee bit of dry bread and tea, but it was a failure—no one felt any enthusiasm.

* I think Capt. Bower crossed my route on his way east at the foot of this hill. As well as I can make out, he entered this valley by the gorge down which the stream flows. If he did not cross my route here, he must have done so some twenty miles farther north, but strangely enough his sketch map does not show in this part any stream of any length flowing west, although all those I crossed flowed in that direction.

July 5.—The summit of the pass turned out to be about three miles beyond our camp of last night, but only a few hundred feet higher than it. We rode to-day in a south-southeasterly direction over hills and across dales all trending nearly due east and west, all the water flowing westward and emptying into a large lake some six or eight miles to the west of our route. We also saw from one of the cols we crossed, and some fifteen miles east of it, a large sheet of water which the Jalang thought might be the Amdo ts'o-nak, but, as for four days the weather has been so cloudy that I have not been able to take an observation, I cannot form an opinion. As laid down (conjecturally) on existing maps, the Amdo ts'o-nak is somewhat farther south than the point we have reached.*

After about twenty-two miles over a fairly easy trail we came to the mouth of a little valley whence we could see some twenty-five miles to the south a range of dark hills running east and west, but nowhere any signs of human habitations. All the hills traversed to-day appeared to be of limestone formation, and grazing was fairly good, the grass just beginning to sprout.

It turned out on inquiry to-day that the cook has not only been stealing from my little supply of food but that he has repeatedly robbed the others during the night of some of their provisions. All our supplies are now exhausted, we ate the last mouthful to-night, now we will have to get along as best we can on tea, and then, if we do not meet Drupa, we shall kill a horse; fortunately we have two which are no longer able to carry loads. With the meat we shall be able to get along for quite a while, fifteen or twenty days anyhow, long enough to reach Shigatsé. The Jalang is more and more disagreeable; he will do nothing to assist us in camp, but sits warming himself over the fire, drinking tea and mumbling his prayers.

July 6.—We had a hard day's work of it to get over twenty miles, the distance we try to cover daily. It began to rain shortly

* I am still in doubt whether this was the Amdo ts'o-nak or not. From what I was told later on this lake would appear to be to the south of the Tsacha tsang-bo ch'u. It may well be that my informants (Namru Tibetans who escorted me) intentionally misled me, as they were always very much afraid to give me any information about the country, and I had to get my information in the most roundabout way. According to Captain Bower (*op. cit.*, 49) the Amdo ts'o-nak is considerably to the east-southeast of the one here referred to. See p. 229 and also under date of *July 20*.

after leaving camp, and the rain kept pouring down till 3 P. M. Our route lay south-southeast over a gently undulating plain, the streams which crossed it running southwest by west to empty into the big lake we saw yesterday.*

At 2 P. M. we came to a river flowing westward in a broad flat bed of mud and sand.† We had great trouble in getting across. The water flowed rapidly in a number of channels, and it took us two hours to lead the horses across, a man walking on either side of each pack-animal holding up the load. Several fell in the stream, or sunk in the quicksands and had to be unloaded in the river; fortunately my papers and instruments were got over dry.

* This lake is called, I learnt later on, the Yirna ts'o, and is a soda lake (*bul-tog ts'o*). Its shape is surprisingly like that of the Garing Chho Lake of Capt. Bower, though the Yirna ts'o did not appear to me to be so large. It is impossible that Capt. Bower's Naksung Satu Lake and Garing Chho Lake, which in reality form but one, can be fed by the one small stream which he shows flowing into it from the west. It must receive a large supply of water from the east. The position Capt. Bower gives the Garing Chho is exactly that which the Namru assigned to the Tengri nor (Dolmä Nam-ts'o), and a Tibetan told him (see his *Diary of a Journey Across Tibet*, p. 30) that that was its name, but he suspected that "the villain lied."

† The name of this river is Tsacha tsang-bo ch'u. On some European maps it is figured (but too far north) as the Zacha Sangpo or Yargui tsumbu. The latter name looks as if it might be intended as a transcription of Yirna tsang-po, "the river of the Yirna (ts'o)." There is no doubt in my mind that this river is the Hota Sangpo of Nain Singh, although he makes this river to issue from the Chargut Cho and flow eastward. Speaking of this region (which the Pundit did not traverse), Captain Trotter, in his Account of the Pundit's Journey from Leh to Lh'asa (*Journ. Roy. Geo. Soc.*, XLVII., 110), says: "It appears that the drainage from nearly all these lakes finds its way either into the Chargut Cho, a large lake said to be twice the size of any with which we are as yet acquainted in these parts, or into the Nák-chu-khá, or Hotá Sangpo, a large river which issues from the Chargut Cho and flows eastward. The southern banks of this river are said to be inhabited at certain times of the year by shepherds from the Dé Namru district (north of Dé Cherik). The country to the north of the Nák-chu-khá is believed to be uninhabited.

"The largest river crossed by the Pundit in this section of his travels was the Dumphu or Hotá Sangpo, which receives the drainage of the southern slopes of the Tárgot-Gyákharma range of mountains, and flows into the Kyáring Cho, forming one of the numerous sources of the Nák-chu-khá." The Pundit imagined that the Kyáring Cho was connected with the Chargut Cho, but we now know by Capt. Bower's report that such is not the case. Col. Prjevalsky, *Reisen am oberen Lauf des Gelben Flusses*, 131, mentions a large river, of which he had heard tell, called the Satscha-Zampo, flowing into a lake called Mityk-dschan-su, which, he thinks, is identical with Nain Singh's Chargut ts'o. The other information given Prjevalsky, and referred to by him in the same paragraph, is certainly erroneous.

Just as we made camp, about a mile south of the last channel of the river, a violent storm of hail and rain swept down and drenched every article of clothing which we had so far kept dry, but shortly after the sun shown brightly, and we were able to dry our clothes and bedding before it set.

About half a mile from where we have stopped, I found a deserted camp marked by low dung walls such as are built throughout northern Tibet inside of tents to keep off the wind; it cannot have been abandoned more than a few months ago. Drupa are certainly not far off, I should not be surprised if we fell in with some to-morrow.

July 7.—We got off late; it had rained again in the night and we had to dry the tents before loading them on the mules. We rode in a southerly direction towards a col we could see in the range of hills before us, but we had not gone many miles before we saw a small flock of sheep and some yaks on the hillsides, and a little farther on we sighted some black tents half hidden in a sheltered nook. We kept on towards the hills and camped near some pools of water at the mouth of a valley* and about a mile away from some small black tents around which flocks of sheep were grazing.

While we unloaded the mules, the Jalang and the Hsien-sheng rode over to one of the tents to ascertain where we were and see if they could not buy some food. After a while they returned and reported that they had met a man and two women, who in dress resembled the K'amba Tibetans, but whose language differed considerably from that which they were able to speak. They had had great difficulty in eliciting any information about the country or the road, but finally one of the women, to whom they gave a little mirror, some buttons and a thumb ring, had told them that we were three days' ride (on yak back) from the Tengri nor (*i. e.*, about thirty miles), and only two days' ride west of the Amdo ts'o-nak. They were very much frightened at our advent from the north, and only half believed the Jalang's story that we were Mar Sok (Eastern Mongol) pilgrims on our way to Tashil'unpo, who had lost our way, after the death of our guide some eighteen days north of here, while on the highroad to Nagch'uk'a, and that we had wandered this way in search of pasture for our animals and food

* This valley is called by the Namru, Édjong.

for ourselves. These people sold the men a sheep for the exorbitant price of five rupees, and agreed to give them later on a rupee's worth of chura and butter, but would not part with any tsamba, as they had barely enough for themselves. They gave the men tea and delicious sour milk (*sho*) to drink.

The Jalang also learned that the big lake we had reached on the 30th of June, was called the Téb-ts'ang ts'o,* and that the river we had crossed yesterday was the Tsacha tsangbo ch'u. At first he had been unable to elicit this information, the man had said that we could have no good motive for wanting to know the names of the rivers and mountains of the country. These people begged my men not to mention to anyone they might hereafter meet, that they had sold them anything or had even spoken to them, as there were very strict orders forbidding their having anything to do with strangers. They repeatedly asked the men if there were any foreigners in their party, and seemed much relieved when told that there were none. They said that Lh'asa and Tashil'unpo were both twenty days' ride from here, traveling on yak back, and that they did all their trading at the former city. They belonged to the Namru tribe, and the Amdo tribe lived to the east of them. The most disagreeable bit of information my men brought back was that these people were under the rule of Lh'asa.†

The sheep was soon butchered, and in less than an hour the men were all feasting on the *boudins* (*chang-tzŭ*) they love so to make with the liver, heart, lights, intestines, etc., well seasoned with

---

* Or Chib chang ts'o, as the name was pronounced later on by the Namru Déba and the Nagch'u Pönbo.

† The earliest mention I have found of this tribe of Namru is in Capt. Trotter's Report of Nain Singh's journey, referred to above. The Pundit says that the country inhabited by the Chang pa ("Northerners") is subdivided into the following districts, "designated successively from west to east: Nákcháng Gomnak, Nákcháng Dóbâ, Yákpá Ngocho, Yákpá Jagro, Dé Cherik, Dé Tabârába and Dé Taklung, which latter lies immediately to the north of the Namcho Lake." (*Op. cit.*, p. 108.) All the local chiefs, he goes on to say, "are subordinate to the two Jongpons of Senja Jong, a place of considerable importance lying to the east of the Nákcháng Dóbá district, and containing from eighty to a hundred houses." (*Ibid.*, p. 109.) The Pundit also makes mention of a Nákcháng Ombo or Pembo, to the west of the Nâkcháng Gomnak, where the religion is different from that professed by other tribes of this region. (*Ibid.*, p. 107.) The word Pembo is Bonbo, and the religion referred to is that called Bon or Bonboism. See *Land of the Lamas*, 217–218. I had supposed that all the Bonbo tribes of Northern Tibet lived in the Jya dé, which province I traversed later on.

onions. I had no appetite for food, the starving I had gone through for the last month had taken all desire for it out of me, but I expect I will be able to coax it back in a day or so.

July 8.—The Hsien-sheng and the Jalang went again this morning, and a little ahead of the rest of us, to get the chura and butter the Namru had promised to sell them, and which they would not give them yesterday as it was the 15th of the moon, a day on which they neither buy nor sell. They also wanted to trade one of our worn out ponies for a fresh one. I followed slowly after with the pack mules, and, stopping near the tent, got off my pony to talk with the people and see if my men had finished their trading. They had found the Namru's suspicions fully aroused, he had refused to let them have anything, either chura, butter or even civil words, saying he thought we were foreigners, and, if we were, he and his tribe would kill us all, for that was what the Lh'asa government* had ordered them to do. When I spoke to him he only answered "Go away, I will have nothing to do with you," and turning around he entered his tent and called the women in.

We pushed on up the valley and soon reached the top of the range. On its southern side was another broad valley ten or twelve miles in length and three from north to south, and beyond was yet another range of hills. To our left, some six miles away, appeared a lake probably two or three miles from north to south and eight miles from east to west; this I was told later in the day was the Namru ts'o.

In the valley before us were six or eight tents, each with a little flock of sheep and some yaks grazing round it. We stopped near one about two miles below the summit to ask the road, and found that there were Lh'asa traders in it who had tsamba, butter, flour, etc., for sale; so I camped about a mile away in the hope of buying at once a good supply of food and striking out again in a southwesterly direction before any measure could be taken to stop me.

All my men, with the exception of the Hsien-sheng are very much excited and frightened, the Jalang and I had a big row, and I ordered him out of the camp. For the last fortnight his insolence

* The Tibetan term is Déba djong. Capt. Bower is wrong in calling it "The Deva Zhung's territory," as this word is not the title of a man, but means the government of Lh'asa, the territory under Lh'asa rule.

and laziness have steadily increased. I have had to rely solely on the Hsien-sheng, who fortunately never wavers in his loyalty and devotion to me. When the Hsien-sheng went later in the afternoon to get the flour, tsamba, etc., the traders had agreed to sell, they put off giving it to him until to-morrow, and only let him have about a bushel of tsamba, enough for perhaps a week.

The only person who has come to my camp has been a poor man who lives in a miserable little ragged tent about a quarter of a mile from us. He volunteered to guide me to Shigatsé for twenty rupees and a pony. He said that on leaving this place we would travel for four days through an uninhabited country, after which we should find Drupa, more and more numerous as we advanced, all the way to Shigatsé.* He said that in ten days we ought to make the trip. He denied the story that there were foreigners at Shigatsé, but relieved my men's anxiety about their personal safety by telling them that there was a Chinese garrison and Chinese officials there.

It now looks as if we might reach Shigatsé, or at all events get so near it that the Tibetans will have to send us on to India. Two things are sure, I will not go back the way I have come, and whichever way I go I shall be able to do some useful work.

* Capt. Bower heard, when to the west of Namru dé, that "From Namru a road runs to Lh'asa, by which it would be possible to go straight into the sacred city without meeting a soul." *Op. cit.*, 32.

Sub-Chief of Drupa Tibetans.

Drupa Tibetan of Namru de.

PART IV.

From Namru to Ch'amdo.

July 9.—The fate of everyone who has tried to get into Tibet has overtaken me. This morning by daylight a number of well-armed Tibetans came to camp and said that they feared some of my party were *p'yling* (foreigners), and that they begged us to remain camped where we were until their Déba could come, examine us and see whether we could proceed on our journey or not. So stringent were the orders from Déba-djong (Lh'asa) that if they were to let a foreigner pass through their country, they would all be beheaded. The speaker of the party, who was the headman of the district, asked to see me, and we talked for a while very pleasantly. He asked me where I was from, where I was going, etc., etc., and said that he did not know whether I was a *p'yling* or a Mongol, that he had never seen any of the former, but he did not believe that they were like me.

I thought it advisable to comply with the request to remain here; if I refused and pushed on at once, it would but confirm their suspicions and they could easily stop me. As it is, the guide who offered his services yesterday, now refuses to go with me unless the Déba says he may. I told the headman I would remain camped here until the day after to-morrow (11th), but that if his Pönbo were not here by that time, I would proceed southward and that he could overtake me if he saw fit so to do.

The Mongols are terribly frightened, they firmly believe that their last day has come. The Jalang complains of violent pains in his stomach and will not eat, Panti has passed the day listlessly blowing the bellows, and the little lama Zangbo has been reading his prayers with wild energy, a thing he had quite forgotten to do during the journey. The Chinese with their usual stolidity and

Moslem fatalism have been eating the whole day, occasionally saying the one to the other that no one can escape his fate.

The headman sent me a sheep, milk, chura and butter, enough for the day, and said he would keep me supplied until the Déba's arrival, but he would not accept pay for anything, as that was against the orders he had received.

In the afternoon a tent was put up two hundred yards from mine and about twenty men settled themselves in it as a guard. During the whole day men came riding in from every direction, but more especially from the east and southeast. They were all very polite and jolly and each one whispered to me, when he thought he was not being observed, that they were only carrying out the orders of Lh'asa.

It is an anxious moment; I will fight hard not to go to Nagch'uk'a, but I fear the whole matter will be referred to Lh'asa and that I will be delayed here for a long while.

The dress of the people is exactly like that of the K'amba of northeast Tibet, but the gowns (*ch'ubas*) are mostly of fine purple pulo, only the very poor people wearing sheepskin ones. The women wear no ornaments on their hair, which is plaited in innumerable little braids hanging over the shoulders and down to the waist where they are held together by a black ribbon. Many of the men have a half Tibetan, half Chinese coiffure, a big queue, usually of false hair and ornamented with coral and glass beads, finger rings, etc., and which hangs down their back or is twisted around the head; the rest of their hair hangs in a tangled mass about their heads, cut over the eyes in a fringe. None wear any head covering, except when riding, when they have great Korean shaped hats covered with white cotton and lined with red cloth. Physically they are of light build, men and women of about the same height, five feet four inches, to five feet eight inches—I saw one man of this latter height—with oval faces, sharp pointed chins, rather straight eyes, hair not very abundant and generally wavy. Their noses are more prominent than with the Mongols and frequently with large ends, though some have aquiline and thin ones. Their feet are small as are also the calves of their legs. Their skins are smooth, hairless and dry, the teeth strong but very uneven and none have beards; they pluck out with pincers (*chyam-ts'er*), which all carry hanging to their belts, the few hairs which grow on their faces. The complexion of the people is not much darker than that of the Mongols, but all are very much burnt by constant exposure. I noticed a great many among them pitted with smallpox marks.

The flour and tsamba the Lh'asa traders had promised to sell us are not forthcoming; they told the Hsien-sheng this evening that they were afraid to deliver them till the Déba arrived. The consequence is that we are absolutely at the mercy of these people; without food for more than a couple of days, with no guide, worn out ponies and lame mules, no possibility of buying anything or exchanging our animals for fresh ones; we can do nothing but make the best possible terms with the chief when he comes.

I picked up from the people to-day in conversation that the Namru belong to the Nyima sect,* and that, besides their own chief or Déba, they have residing among them officers sent from Lh'asa. They say that it takes five days riding to reach Lh'asa and ten or twelve to reach Shigatsé; they do all their trading at the former place. Tea is very expensive here; a brick of the *gongma chupa* kind,† worth one rupee at Ta-chien-lu, is worth 2 taels here; but very little of it is to be found, only the coarsest quality of "wood tea" is used. They drink a great deal of milk, both cold and hot, sweet and sour, in which they mix their tsamba. When tea is drunk, they put a pinch of tsamba in the pot to flavor it.

I heard that the Wang of the Torgot Mongols was stopped here the year before last when on his way to Lh'asa, and only allowed to proceed after his passport had been sent there and found to be *en règle*.‡ I believe that orders have been issued to every person living near the Tibetan frontier, under the severest penalties for disobedience (though I don't believe a word about cutting off the

* Old lamaist or red capped sect. Its principal strongholds are Sikkim, Bhutan and parts of Ulterior Tibet. See Emil Schlagintweit, *Buddhism in Tibet*, 72.

† On the different varieties of brick tea, see *Land of the Lamas*, 278.

‡ Bonvalot's advance south appears to have also been arrested in the Namru country. See H. Bower *op. cit.*, 49. Bonvalot himself makes no mention of this tribe or country in the published narrative of his journey, *De Paris au Tonkin à travers le Tibet inconnu*. Can the Torgots of whom I heard speak be those mentioned in this latter's work (p. 154 and 240)? It appears probable. The description Bonvalot gives of the Tengri nor (or whatever lake his Namtso may turn out to be, for he had it only on native authority that it was *the* Namtso, and both Bower and I were assured that *a* Namtso was in quite a different position) does not at all agree with Nain Singh's in *Journ. Roy. Geog. Soc.*, XLIV, 322 et seq. The words Namtso and Jyamts'o, the latter meaning "lake," are easily confounded.

heads of those who disregard the orders, probably a heavy fine would be the penalty), to report at once to the nearest chief the passage of any suspicious looking traveler.

July 10.—Men have been coming in all day; they are camped in four large tents. Among them are three officials from Lh'asa, in semi-Chinese dress, long brown broadcloth gowns and turned up brown felt hats with gold lace edging; they wear a very pretty long gold pendant in the left ear, in which is set a big pearl and some turquoises. These officials, Nyérpa (stewards) of the Talé lama, and now in Namru dé collecting the tithes, came to my camp and begged me to go back by the way I had come, saying that they would all be beheaded if I did not. I told them that I had no desire to travel on Lh'asan territory, that I had only come here because I had no more food. In a few days I would go westward and leave their territory. I deferred discussing the question of my movements till "the Big Chief" (*Pönbo ch'enpo*) arrived on the morrow. I added that as I knew the Tibetans were kind hearted, I felt sure they would not purposely put me to any inconvenience, delay or lengthen my journey by forcing me to take a roundabout road to Jyagar (India), where my presence was impatiently awaited.

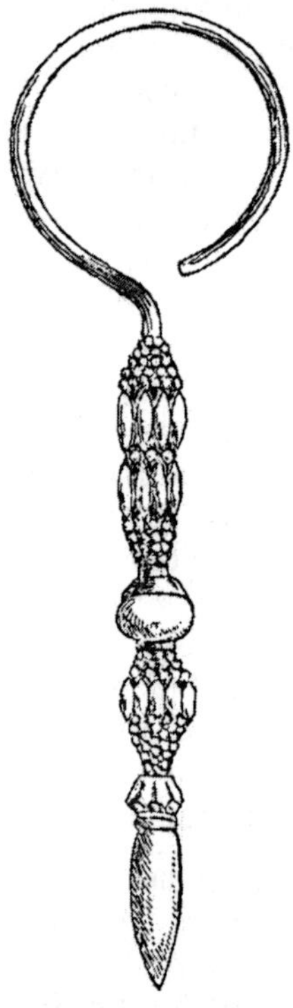

EARRING WORN BY TIBETAN OFFICERS. (Full Size.)

They said they would supply me with everything I desired, food, fresh horses and mules, etc., etc., if I would only leave their country at once. I said that under no circumstances would I go back by the way I had come. They then suggested that I should go to Nagch'uk'a and take the highroad to China and thence to India. I told them that, as I was traveling with a passport from the Chinese government, no one could control my movements but the Chinese Amban, that I would go to Lh'asa to discuss the matter with him. This threat frightened them very much. They said

Lh'asa was more than a month's journey from here, that brigands infested the road, that the Amban had gone to Ch'i-ling to discuss with the p'ylings the Sikkim business. They appeared very anxious that this business should not get into the hands of the Chinese, whom they all seemed to fear and dislike very much.

At all events we are revelling in the fleshpots of Tibet; sour milk, cream, butter, mutton, wheaten cakes (*palé*) have been given us in abundance, and we can eat, drink, sleep and bask in the sun to our heart's content. The weather is lovely though it seems rather warm. The rest is doing us good and things take a brighter aspect on a full stomach. I will insist on going south-west on leaving here, although the Nyérpa swore to-day that there was no trail leading in that direction. I fancy it will take some time to settle matters satisfactorily; Tibetans do everything "slowly, slowly" (*Kalé, kalé*).

July 11.—To-day has been a most trying one; the Pönbo ch'enpo arrived with a numerous escort. He is a good-natured looking man of the pure Drupa type, and perhaps the least well dressed of any of the chiefs I have seen, save that his purple pulo gown is of beautifully fine texture. He called on me, accompanied by the Lh'asa Nyérpa, and we discussed my plans. Seeing that I would not go back to the desert to the north, they suggested that I go to Nagch'uk'a to discuss the subject of my future movements with the high officer in command there, but they said that they must first get permission for me to go to Nagch'uk'a. They had, in anticipation of my going that way, sent a courier there yesterday and expected him back in three days. Then I proposed sending the Hsien-sheng to Lh'asa to see the Amban,* but they stoutly refused to allow him to go. As to going to Shigatsé, they refused point blank to allow me to undertake the journey, or rather, they said that, unless I went to Nagch'uk'a or awaited

*Bonvalot speaks of his conferences with the *Amban* near the shores of the Niamtso. He describes him as a blue buttoned Mandarin of pure Tibetan race, not even speaking Chinese, and who treated the travelers apparently as his superiors in rank. Bonvalot's interlocutor was most certainly not *the* Amban, who is always a high Chinese official, wearing a coral button and of Manchu origin, and who quite as certainly would not have come that far in the dead of winter to question three unknown foreigners. The official was probably an officer from one of the stations between Nagch'uk'a and Lh'asa. The "*ta amban*" and "*ta lama*" who came to his camp later on (*De Paris au Tonkin*, p. 238 et seq.) probably came from Lh'asa, but even this ta lama, whoever he was, was only a Tibetan civil official. See Bonvalot, *op. cit.*, 268 et seq.

here further orders, they would give me no supplies or fresh pack animals and that I would have to get on the best way I could, after going back to the north side of the Tsacha tsangbo ch'u, which marks the boundary of Lh'asa territory to the north. Perhaps if I were to go to Nagch'uk'a I could get permission to go back to China by the highroad *viâ* Lárego, Shobando, Ch'amdo, etc., and not have to follow the "tea road" taken by Bonvalot.

The Déba asked me to come to his tent in the afternoon, and I found there all the chiefs and people assembled, the latter squatting around the outside. Seeing my impatience to proceed, the Chief offered to have me guided to Nagch'uk'a by a little used trail, not on Lh'asa territory but running along the right bank of the Tsacha tsangbo ch'u and the foothills of the Dang la. It would take, he said, six or seven days to reach the *chang lam* at a point about a day's ride north of Nagch'uk'a. I agreed finally to this; it will take me through unexplored country. It does not make much difference after all which way I go, though it is very disappointing not to be able to carry out my original plan—but who ever does in life? I am not twenty miles from the Tengri nor; I am told it can be seen from the top of the hills to the south of this valley, but I will never see the lake.* I am ten days from Shigatsé and not more than twenty-five from British India and six or seven weeks from home, but it will be four or five months before I reach there now by the long route I shall have to travel. *T'ien ming*, "it is Heaven's decree."

Panti and the Jalang have refused to go any farther with me; they will go back to the Ts'aidam by the road by which we came. The lao-han goes back with the Mongols. I have given the old man twenty-five taels and some odds and ends in the way of

* See note p. 228. Some Tibetan works give the name of this lake as Gnam mts'o p'yag-mo, or Gnam mts'o p'yug-mo. The latter name means "Wealthy woman, heavenly lake." The name Dolmä Nam-ts'o signifies "the heavenly lake of Dolma." Dolma is the Indian goddess Aryâ Târâ; in Tibet this name is quite as common among women as Mary is with Christians. Nain Singh says that the lake is called Jáng Namcho chidmo, that it is 15,190 feet above sea level, that it took him fifteen days to travel around it, that there are a number of gombas on its shore, and that a stream called the Nai ch'u flows into it from the east. He also adds that junipers grow on its banks at Langdang, at the northeast corner of the lake. *Journ. Roy. Geo. Soc.*, XLIV, 319-322. On the fossil shells of this lake, see the same work, 327. Mr. Oldham, Superintendent of the Geological Survey of India, who examined them, thought them not older than cretaceous and probably nummilitic. The name given the lake by Nain Singh is probably, according to my system of transcription, Chang Nam-ts'o chyug-mo (p'yug-mo).

outfit, and he is filled with fear lest his *compagnons de route* should kill him for his wealth. I am truly delighted to get rid of these Mongols, but I feel sorry for the poor little lama, Zangbo, who had hoped to get to Lh'asa, and who now sees all his hopes blighted and who will probably have to go with me to Ta-chien-lu.

July 12.—The day has been well occupied amusing the Namru, who, now that the question of my movements has been satisfactorily settled, are as friendly as can be, though they will sell me nothing, refusing the most tempting offers for various ornaments, and odds and ends I want for my collections. We talked

> "Of shoes, and ships, and sealing wax,
> Of cabbages, and kings,
> And why the sea was boiling hot,
> And whether pigs have wings."

They expressed their astonishment at finding a p'yling so friendly, and not the terrible creature they say the lamas have always described them as being. They have shown me the greatest kindness and politeness, not a rough or disagreeable remark has passed their lips. They have given me every description of food they have, and all the little delicacies they delight in. Time and again they have apologized for having to stop me, "but, they said, we are not our own masters, but *Déba-djong-gi miser*" ("the serfs of Lh'asa"). They said openly that, as to themselves, they would be delighted to see foreigners visit their country, bringing curious and pretty things for them to buy, but Lh'asa would not allow it. The people of that place loved foreign money and foreign goods, but would not admit p'ylings among them. The Lh'asa people were bad and cruel, they added; should they (the Namru) disobey them, they would cut off their heads in a trice.

The Déba presented me with a nice pony, but it was with great difficulty that I persuaded him to accept a k'atag* in acknowledg-

* The use of ceremonial scarfs dates from remote antiquity in Asia; we find mention of them in old Buddhist works and persons in the act of presenting them are often figured in ancient Buddhist bas-reliefs in India. The custom appears even to have spread, for awhile, to China, thus we read in Mendoza that when he was at Fu chou in 1575, the Viceroy "commanded in his presence to put about the necks of the friars, in manner of a scarfe, to eyther of them sixe pieces of silke, and unto the souldiers, their companions, and unto Omoncou and Suisay, each of them foure pieces, and to everye one of their servants two a piece * * * so with the silke about their neckes, and with the branches in their hands, they returned out of the hall and downe the staires the way they came, and so through the court into the streetes." Mendoza, *History of China*, II, 83. (Hakluyt Soc. edit.)

ment of his gift, and the three Lh'asa Nyérpa stoutly refused the scarfs I offered them. The people are very fond of foreign curios and goods. One man had a red flowered chintz waistcoat; another a flannel border to his gown, and not a few British navy and army buttons on theirs.

I gave the two Mongols one of my tents, three ponies, sufficient tea and tsamba to last them six weeks, a kettle, etc., etc., enough to enable them to travel comfortably back to the Ts'aidam. The lao-han begged to be allowed to accompany me; he said he was afraid to go back with the Mongols who might rob him and kill him, and I agreed to take him to Ta-chien-lu whence he can reach Hsi-ning easily and at little expense. We are to leave here to-morrow; three men will escort me, and two others will see the two Mongols across the Tsacha tsangbo ch'u. We shall all part the best of friends; the three Lh'asa officials are the only ones who have been sullen and made no friendly advances.

July 13.—We broke up camp this morning and retraced our steps as far as the Tsacha tsangbo ch'u, camping near the right bank of that river on some little sand dunes, and here at about nightfall I was joined by the escort of Namru men who are to accompany me as far as the Nagch'uk'a road. There are ten men instead of three in the escort under the orders of the same head-man who requested me to stop in the Namru valley to there await the coming of the Déba.

It was with a heavy heart that I retraced my steps; it was the relinquishing of a much cherished project which I had until within a few days hoped I would have been able to accomplish. It would, however, have been sheer folly to have tried to push on to Shigatsé in the face of the opposition of the Namru, with but three Chinese to accompany me and only provisions enough for a day or two.

Before leaving this morning the Déba sent me another pony as a present; and I was able to slip into the hand of the owner of a big tent near which we had camped in the Namru valley, and who had to supply, by order of the Déba, all the mutton, tea, tsamba, etc., which had been given to me as "presents"—the value of his goods. He was of course immensely pleased, lolled out his tongue as far as he could and wished me many times "*démo p'ébs, démo p'ébs*" ("go in peace").

The lower classes here, when saluting superiors, are in the habit of bending the knee very low, putting the right hand beside the right cheek and the left hand under the elbow of the right arm, at the same time sticking out the tongue.

I know all the men in the escort, and, now that they are no longer under their chief's eyes, they are all eager to trade, and to show me any courtesy in their power. Each man has brought with him a huge pair of saddle-bags filled with cakes of sweet cream cheese (*pima*),* chura, flour, butter, dried mutton (*sha kam*), sour cream (*tarak*), wheaten cakes (*palé*), etc., etc., which he wants to exchange for buttons, thumb-rings, Japanese lacquer bowls, and such like treasures. They told me again that their lamas had always made out foreigners to be bad men, that if they should ever meet any, they were to give them what they required, take nothing from them, and make them go away; but I had talked courteously to them, paid for all I had got, and they hoped that foreigners would come this way again, if they were only all like me and their lamas did not oppose their coming.

I now learn that the big lake into which the Tsacha tsangbo ch'u empties is called Zirna ts'o and that it is a "soda lake" (*butok ts'o*). We had quite a violent hail storm to-day at 2 P. M. and at 4.30 P. M., a heavy downpour of rain.

July 14.—We crossed the river this morning during a violent thunder storm, at the ford used by the Namru; the Tsacha flows here in two branches, and the water is about four feet deep. We turned our faces northward and struck out over an undulating plain on which was here and there a pool of brackish water, and after a short ride camped at the foot of the hills, by the river bank, at a point where the river, which comes from the east-northeast, takes a bend southward as far as where we crossed it earlier in the day.

My escort looks very picturesque, the prettily shaped, though very undersized ponies nearly disappearing under the big saddles and bright saddle cloths, the riders in purple gowns and cloth-topped boots reaching to the knee, which sticks out bare above them. Their long hair falls around their faces, and their high white hats (*shara*) are cocked on one side to shade them from the sun or wind. Long matchlocks swing across their backs, the

* In Koko-nor Tibetan called *dêma*, and in Mongol *eurna*. Chinese call it *nai p'i-tzŭ*. It is brought to Peking every winter by the Mongols and sold in the Nei kuan.

stocks and locks wrapped in pieces of bright pulo or perhaps a marmot skin (*chyi pags*). At their waists hang red leather bullet bags, pouches for powder and priming-horns, needle cases and short knives, and each one has a long, straight sword passed through his belt, the right hand resting constantly on its hilt. They have already proved themselves good-hearted, obliging fellows, taking down and putting up my tent, bringing me fuel, saddling and unloading the ponies, and have, to their own inconvenience, given little Zangbo one of their own ponies to ride, and made a collection among themselves for him, supplying him, from their own small stores, with enough food for a month.

WOODEN SNUFF-BOX WITH INTERIOR SIEVE.
(Lh'asa.)

These Namru eat wonderfully little; this morning before starting they drank two cups of tea, which they made in little earthenware pots, each man having his own, and ate a little mush of chura, tsamba and butter. In preparing their tea they put a little soda in the pot, and let it boil for quite a while. This evening the first thing they did, while two or three were making the fire and the tea was cooking, was to drink a few cups of sour cream (*tarak*), and this they tell me is their invariable preliminary to a meal, their *zakuska*. This tarak they carry in little goat skin bags on which the hair has been left and which contain about half a gallon. They squeeze the bag and make the contents come out through the skin of the leg, which makes an excellent neck to this primitive bottle. Their dried mutton they soften in their tea, but they eat very little of it, a few mouthfuls at a meal suffice them.

The only thing in which these men, as well as all those we have so far met, show great suspicion is in invariably refusing to partake of any food or drink prepared by me, nor will they use any other but their own *puru* (little wooden bowl). They are afraid of being poisoned. This mode of getting rid of a person is a well known weakness of the Lh'asa people.

The Namru snuff enormous quantities of tobacco and, like the K'amba, they are not neat in taking it, smearing their noses and faces in the operation. Smoking is very rarely indulged in by them. Their snuff-horns are like those of the P'anaka, though a few own the peculiar snuff box with interior sieve made in Lh'asa.

Nearly every male I have seen in this country has curly hair, while the Lh'asa people have straight. I take the Namru and in fact all the Drupa, or tent dwelling Tibetans, to represent a much purer, if not *the* pure, Tibetan race; their language, which has retained many archaic forms, now lost in the Lh'asan dialect, or only to be found in the written language in the shape of mute or superposed letters, would seem to corroborate this opinion. "But this is another story."

July 15.—We rode all day up the right bank of the Tsacha ch'u in an east-northeasterly direction, crossing occasionally some little affluent coming down from the hills. Though we passed many old camps, we only saw one tent and that on the left bank of the river and in the Amdo ts'o-nak district, according to the escort men. The country was well covered with grass, the soil gravelly, the hills on either side of the river of limestone and slate. We rode along very rapidly, stopping only after about eighteen miles for lunch in a little valley opening on to the river where we found abundance of sweet spring water. While here the inevitable hail and rain storm swept over us, and we had to wait an hour or so before we could dry our things and load the mules.

We camped for the night on a muddy and marshy plain near a good-sized river which, coming from the west, empties into the Tsacha tsangbo ch'u a few miles to the east of us. We were compelled to come this way, which is not the trail usually followed but a roundabout one, on account of the muddy state of the ground along the river side. The constant heavy rains at this season of the year make traveling in these parts slow, wearisome and difficult, for, to add to the fatigues of the journey, fuel (dung of course) is very scarce, as nearly all is soaked by the rain. The soil is everywhere gravel and clay, and one sinks into it knee deep. Riding is out of the question, the horses have as much as they can do to pull themselves through the mud, though they carry only a few pounds of the loads of the pack mules, that are even more worn out than they.

Before we could get camped another violent rain storm overtook us, and we had to go to bed without our tea and with only a little *pima;* but we are better off than the Tibetans, we four have a tent in which we can keep pretty dry—though it is now full of holes and cannot keep out the cold—but the Namru have none, they wrap themselves in their saddle blankets and lie down shivering in the wet and mud.

July 16.—Crossing the stream near which we had camped, we followed up the course of the Tsacha tsangbo through a broad grass-covered valley. It would be more correct to say that we followed up the course of the northern branch of the Tsacha, for a few miles east-southeast of our camp of last night, a stream quite as large as the Tsacha itself, and which comes from the east, empties into it.

A mile or so beyond our camp we passed some hot springs near the bank of the stream, but I could not get to them to take the temperature of the water, as the ground was too boggy. Six miles before making camp we crossed a large clear stream flowing into the Tsacha from out the mountains on our left (north).

I learned that my guards have orders to take me to the Hsi-ning road, seven days from where we now are. Here we will be on the border of the Jya-dé (*Rgya sdé*) *i. e.*, "Chinese province." They will then point out the road to Nagch'uk'a and the direction of the nearest Drupa, but they will not venture near the tents of the Jyadé, with whom they are not on friendly terms.*

I offered the headman some money if he would consent to take me by a more direct route to Nagch'uk'a, but he said he knew of none, and even the one we are following is badly known, and hardly ever followed.

*Nain Singh speaking of the people living near the western shore of the Tengri nor says they are attacked by robbers said to come from a district called Jámaáta De, which lies to the north. Jámaáta De is said not to be under Lh'asa, and the inhabitants consequently plunder the Lh'asa districts whenever they are in want, as they often are. *Journ. Roy. Geo. Soc*, XLIV, 320. His Jámaáta De is Rgya-mi Atag Sdé, "The Chinese Atag district" on the highroad to Nagch'uk'a; it was traversed by Capt. Bower (see *Op. sup. cit.*, 51).

From where we have camped we can see to the north a snow-covered range, the Dang la, I suppose. The nearer one gets to this great chain the worse the weather becomes. These mountains arrest the moisture laden clouds coming from the southeast, hence the deluge of rain and the boggy state of this whole region during half the year. The Dang la and its continuation to the east, mark the farthest point north to which the monsoons reach. This evening, for the first time since we left the Namru valley, the sky was unclouded for a half hour, and I was able to take a few sextant observations.

July 17.—The last branch of the Tsacha* was forded a few miles beyond camp, and after crossing a low range of soft, gravelly hills, we entered the basin of the Chang t'ang ch'u, which, coming from out the mountains to the north at a point far to the east of us, flows south as far as we could make out its course. Two large streams and a number of streamlets empty into it a little to the south of our line of march. The soil was everywhere boggy, the horses sunk into the soft gravel at every step, and we had to lead them most of the way. After crossing the second large feeder of the Chang t'ang ch'u, we found the ground absolutely bare, and had to push on till dark before we could find a spot where our animals could pick up a little grass. Just as we made camp and before I could get the tent up, a terrific thunder storm came down from the mountains to the north, and again the poor Tibetans had to wrap themselves in their blankets and go supperless to sleep.

We saw to-day a herd of yaks, the first we have noticed south of the Dang la. They started on a dead run as soon as they saw us, and it was a fine sight to see them dash into the wide river and tear across it, the spray nearly hiding them from our view.

---

* From Capt. Bower's map we learn that this important river has its source in about Lat. 32° 45 Long. E. 90°, at an altitude of about 16,000 feet. · Where I left this river, not over thirty-five miles from its source, its altitude was approximately 15,400 feet above sea level. It certainly does not flow as far southeast as Capt. Bower's map shows, and the snow peak, around the east side of which it is there made to flow, is quite a distance south of the river. Capt. Bower calls this river Chang Saki Sang po. Chang means "north, northern;" the word is written *byang*. His Sang chu is, I take it, my Chang t'ang ch'u in its upper course. See H. Bower, *Op. cit.*, 47-48.

The whole country through which we have traveled to-day is but a succession of pools and streams. I never saw such a soaked and reeking region in my life.

July 18.—The storm of last night has turned the already muddy soil into a quagmire, and it took us all day to make about eight miles over a range of low hills and to ford the Chang t'ang river. At every step we took we sunk in the mud (a mixture of gravel and clay) up to our knees, and it was pitiable to see the poor mules tumbling down every few steps, unable to pull their tired legs out of the mire. Strange as it may appear the muddiest spots in this region are always to be found on the hillsides, all of which are of gravel. About eight inches below the surface is water, which, for some reason I have not as yet worked out, but probably on account of a hard substratum of clay, does not drain off. Along the river bottoms there is comparatively little mud; the ground there is sandy and firm.

After resting for a couple of hours in the river bottom, where we found good grazing and plenty of sweet, clear water, we forded the river (the east branch of the Chang t'ang ch'u), which was up to the horses' bellies, and camped on the hills beyond, on that most uncomfortable of all camping grounds, tussocks of grass and holes full of water, such a place as only a duck could enjoy. The air to-day has been redolent with the odor of onions (*allium senescens?*); the Tibetans eat them raw without even the addition of a little salt. During the day we had no rain, though very heavy clouds hung over the mountains to the north, but at 8 P. M., the heavens opened and the downpour began. Fortunately the grass is good and the horses and mules are, at least, enjoying themselves.

July 19.—Another miserable, rainy day passed picking our way over tussocks of grass and holes of water a foot or two deep and as many wide. Water an inch deep is flowing in a sheet off the ground into innumerable lakelets and pools. So bad did traveling become, that we finally took to the bed of a stream and marched in it for miles with water to the horses' bellies; here we found solid ground on which to walk. An imperceptible ascent brought us to near the divide between the basin of the Chang t'ang ch'u and some other river to the east, where we camped on a tolerably level and dry bit of ground.

Near where we have camped I noticed old fireplaces and other signs that people inhabit this country at some season of the year; it is the highest inhabited spot we have yet met with, its altitude is not less than 16,200 feet above sea level. A bear, the third seen on the journey, came near the camp but not close enough to shoot. Animals of every description appear to be very rare south of the Dang la.

I think we cannot now be more than five days' ride from Nagch'uk'a, though the Namru says it is ten. I have discovered that none of the escort have ever been over this trail before; they have heard tell that it was possible to reach the Nagch'uk'a road by this way, and are trying the experiment with me. The only object their chief had in view in sending me this way was to keep me off Lh'asa territory, which does not extend north of the Tsacha tsangbo ch'u.

No dry argols are to be had to-night, and we have had to burn one of our pack saddles; fortunately we have not two hundred pounds of luggage all told and six mules to carry it, so we do not feel the loss.

July 20.—I was glad to see to-day that our route continued in a southerly direction, for I have been fearing lest my escort should try to get me on to a road leading to the north side of the Dang la, where I know they would like to see me.* We crossed the divide about two miles beyond our camp of last night, and continued in a general east-southeasterly direction for about eighteen miles over tussocks of grass and water holes, and where these were not, there was mud a foot or more deep. To add to our misery it rained from 9 A. M. to 2 P. M.

East of the divide all the streams we have crossed flow south. They are innumerable; we crossed two large ones within a few miles of each other, each one fifty to seventy-five feet wide and from two to three feet deep; down every little valley, though possibly not over three or four miles long, flows a big brook. We made about twenty miles to-day, but it was very hard work to get the mules and ponies along. From being constantly in the water and mud, their hoofs have become very soft, and the gravel has worn them away so that they are all footsore.

* My route must have crossed Bower's here, very near his camp, 82 (November 12th, 1891).

We passed by quite a number of old camps* and pulled down some of the dung walls to get dry fuel. Yak dung is the principal substance used in domestic architecture among the Drupa Tibetans. Besides being used to make low walls around the tents, as is also customary in K'amdo, the people here build little dome-shaped structures about five feet high and six feet in diameter with a small opening in the south side. In these they keep dry sheep's droppings and yak dung for fuel; they also put away in similar storehouses, of which there are a number around each tent, such of their belongings as they do not care to keep inside their dwelling.

The Namru with me frequently whistle tunes, an unknown accomplishment among Mongols and an unusual one also in China. Their only occupation when in camp is twisting yarn or twirling their prayer wheels, but they assure me that when at home they (the men) weave the variegated stuff used for making boot tops, gun cases and such like things; they also weave their pretty garters. Weaving is, I consequently infer, not a drudgery among this people, if it were, it would be left to the women.

July 21.—Our route to-day took a slightly more southerly direction than heretofore. It led along what I suppose are the foothills (of sandstone chiefly) of the Dang la range, whose snowpeaks we have caught occasional glimpses of for the last four or five days. Two miles from camp we crossed a river flowing south-southeast.† Leaving its basin, we traveled along the flank of some hills trending southeast till we came to a pond about fifteen miles from our

* When Capt. Bower passed through this district, which he was told was part of Amdo, he found nomads' tents scattered about the valleys. He speaks of a little lake here called the Chonak Chho; I cannot believe that this is *the* Amdo ts'o-nak. My route here must have been considerably north of his; our routes were parallel all the way to the I ch'u (reached by Bower December 2d, '91, and by me on the 11th August, '92), his being a little south of mine.

† This river is the "large river," crossed by Capt. Bower lower down its course. According to information furnished him this river marks the western boundary of Jyadé (his Giate). This is not absolutely inconsistent with what I was told, as this country—and all Tibet is in the same case for that matter—is divided up in the most confusing manner, one small district belonging to Lh'asa and the next to Jyadé or some other country. Near this river Capt. Bower refers to a camp called Atak Thomar. His Atak is my Ara and Nain Singh's Jámaáta (see p. 244, note). The latter's statement that the Atag are under Chinese rule is therefore corroborated by Capt. Bower. See also on the Yagara, p. 196 (June 1st).

camp of yesterday, and here we camped. From a little hillock near our camp of this evening, I saw a good-sized river coming out of the mountains to the north and flowing due south, and my guides told me that the Hsi-ning-Lh'asa road runs along its bank. The face of the country to-day was covered with tussocks of grass, with frequent patches of mud, and old camping places were very numerous.

We stopped toward noon to-day to take tea and dry our clothes in the sun, which has at last made its appearance. The Namru, who for convenience of cooking are divided into two messes (this is a universal custom among Tibetans) of five men each, asked me to lunch with them, first with one party, then with the other. They showed themselves most excellent hosts, and were more communicative than I had heretofore found them. They told me that yesterday we had passed through the Ara district (the deserted camp we had seen belonged to people of that tribe), and that to-day we were south of the Yagara district, of which people I have previously spoken as inhabiting in times gone by, the mountains to the south of the Naichi gol.* To-morrow at an early hour we will reach a camp of the Jyadé people on the highroad to Nagch'u. They will not venture that far, but will point out the road from the hill top and give us our bearings. They begged me not to mention, when I got to Nagch'uk'a, that I had been escorted all the way from Namru by them, for it would certainly get them in trouble. They asked me many questions about my country,

* Can this tribe be a fraction of the Yegur tribe found between Lan-chou and Sa-chou (northwestern Kan-su) by Potanin—"En suivant la grande route de Lan-tcheou à Sa-tcheou, M. Potanin a découvert la peuplade appelé *Yégours*, dont une partie (les *Chara Yégours*) sont Turcs par la langue et par le type physique. Ces Chara Yégours habitent entre Kan-tcheou et Sa-tcheou." Deniker, *Bull. Soc. Anthropologie de Paris*, 3e Série, X, 207. However this may be, Potanin's Yégours are the Huang Fan or "Yellow Fan-tzŭ" of the Chinese. From the following note by Prjevalsky it would appear that the Yégurs lived in the 17th century near the Koko-nor, probably west or southwest of it, and it is possible that, after the defeat referred to by him, a portion sought refuge in Tibet. He says that "a people of Tangutan race lived on the shores of Koko-nor called Yegurs, who professed Buddhism and belonged to the red-capped sect. These Yegurs were continually plundering the caravans of pilgrims on their way from Mongolia to Tibet, until the Oliuth prince Gushi-Khan, who ruled in northwestern Mongolia, marched an army to Koko-nor to subdue them. The Yegurs were partly exterminated, but some of them escaped to northwestern Kan-su, where they mixed with the other inhabitants." *Mongolia*, I, 151. This also corroborates Potanin's statement.

how long it had taken me to get to Namru, about the sea and ships and our religion, and I managed to answer all their queries, —save, of course, the last one—quite satisfactorily.

Towards dusk all the men of the escort came to my tent and each one made me a little present, some butter, chura, pima, dried mutton, or the like, all apologizing for the smallness of their gifts. Then the headman repeated what he had told me early in the day, they would take us to where we could see the Nagch'uk'a road and there leave us and start at once for home. I thanked them for their kindness, and then gave the headman four rupees and to each of the other men I gave two. They only accepted the money when we had all given a solemn promise that we would mention it to no one. These men have been as kind and considerate as possible, and I will always remember with pleasure the friendly spirit they showed to me and my party. They have been most attentive, and have invariably done whatever they could to lighten the discomforts of the journey.

Little Zangbo has decided, after much persuasion on my part, to give us the slip as soon as we reach the highroad, and try and join the first party he sees going Lh'asaward. I gave him this evening ten rupees and filled his bag with tsamba and tea.

We thought this evening while scanning the country to the east, that we discerned tents of Drupa some miles to the south-east, but not having field glasses we could not be sure of it. The Namru, by the way, have thought all along that my prismatic compass was a *djansi*, as they call a telescope, and were greatly astonished this evening when I explained the use of the compass (*ch'yog-ta k'orlo*) in surveying.

July 22.—At day-light the Namru came to my tent and asked the Hsien-sheng to go with them a little way that they might show him the highroad, as they were in a great hurry to start for home and get far away from the Jyadé country, where they did not feel in safety. After doing a little trading with my guides, we got on our horses and turned south, while they started west-ward, after a very liberal exchange of good wishes for a safe journey.

We had not gone a mile before we saw three horsemen leading mules, and traveling south along the right bank of the river. Little Zangbo bade us a hasty good-bye and, taking his bag of food, hid himself in the hills, so as to prove an *alibi* if we ever came face to face again in Tibet, a most unlikely contingency. Riding on we joined the horseman, and I found to my horror that they were Tibetans coming from Kumbum, and that they belonged to the great caravan which leaves Tankar for Lh'asa every year in the fourth moon. Though we recognized each other—we had met at the fair at Kumbum—we all cut each other in the most approved fashion.

We begged them to sell us a few horseshoe nails, as three of our mules were so sore footed they could hardly put one foot before the other, and we were glad to pay them at the exorbitant rate of a tanka for four nails.

We learned from these men that we were on the Dang ch'u* (probably Prjevalsky's Yagra ch'u) and about a day and a half's ride north of Nagch'uk'a. The river bottom, which is covered with fine grass, is about a mile and a half broad, and beyond it rise on either side hills a hundred feet or so high of gravel, red clay and pudding stone. We rode by several sections of the caravan, some camped in nooks in the hills, others on the river bottom, but all occupying huge white cotton tents, each large enough to accommodate thirty or forty men. No one paid any attention to us, and after going about fourteen miles we camped in a sheltered spot near the river where grazing was exceptionally fine.

We had not got our tent up before two Tibetan soldiers and the man who had sold us the nails rode up, and asked us where we were going and from what place we had come. We said we had come from the Chang t'ang and were on our way to Ch'amdo. As they spoke a dialect different from any with which we were familiar, conversation proved so difficult (the man we had previously met would not act as interpreter for fear it be imagined we were acquainted) that they jumped on their horses and rode off, returning in a very short time, however, with another man who understood the Lh'asa dialect, and could thus act as a spy on the one who could, but would not, talk with us.

*A—— K——'s Yagra Chu; the stream which flows into it from the west a couple of miles south of where I was camped he calls the Saung Chu. See *Report on Explorations made by A—— K—— in 1879–'82*, 38. The Khamlung La of this explorer is probably the western shoulder of Bumza shili.

I explained my project to them, told them that I wanted a guide to Larego or Ch'amdo, also provisions, an escort and fresh pack animals and saddle ponies. I showed them my passport, although this document, written entirely in Chinese, was of no earthly value, save that the big red seal on it had an imposing aspect. I said I proposed going to Nagch'uk'a, the K'anpo at that place having been advised of my arrival by the Namru Déba. As I was "a big official" I could not, furthermore, discuss my movements or plans with them, and so I told them that, not wanting to do anything contrary to orders they might have received, I would wait where I was now camped until the 25th, so that their Déba or the Nagch'u Pönbo might have time to come and see me. I can afford to be accommodating, for I could not possibly get away from this place in less time, even if asked to continue my journey towards Lh'asa, so fatigued are the ponies and so lame are the mules. Several of the latter will probably die within a few days, or will have to be abandoned.

Two Jyadé men who came across the Dang ch'u (this river divides Lh'asa territory from Jyadé, or Chinese governed territory), said that they would bring me a sheep in the morning. They said they were willing to sell me anything I wanted. The soldiers on this side, who are of the Sang-yi clan, refused to sell me anything, saying that they would beheaded if they did. These Jyadé say there is a direct trail going from here to Ch'amdo and another to Jyäkor (Jyäkundo), where I was in 1889.

From what I can gather the boundary of Lh'asa in this direction follows the highroad from the Dang la to Nagch'u, all the country to the east of this line being under Chinese jurisdiction.*

We had a violent hailstorm from 1 to 1.30 P. M., but the rest of the day was very fine. From where we are camped we can see a dome-shaped mountain some twelve or fifteen miles south of us, and I learned that it is Mt. Bumza ; it seems to close the Dang ch'u valley in that direction, the river flowing eastward along the base of the Bumza block.

The Sang-yi soldiers accepted my proposition to remain where I am till the 25th with evident pleasure, and said that they would be back from Nagch'uk'a with the Pönbo by that time.

* This does not substantially disagree with what Capt. Bower learnt; according to him Jyadé extends some twenty miles farther west, but he was a little farther south than I (about twelve miles). See p. 248, note †.

July 23.—The whole Tankar caravan was stopped this morning by the guard until its chiefs could prove satisfactorily that I had not arrived in their company. Several of the head-traders (*tsong-pön*) came in great distress to my camp with the chief of the post, and I had to go over the whole story of my wanderings again to satisfy the soldiers that they had not assisted me in getting here. They were finally allowed to go to Nagch'uk'a to there wait until the K'anpo had seen me and heard me tell once more my story. The Tsong-pön apologized before leaving for having had me stopped, but said that had they not done so, and had we arrived together at Nagch'uk'a, their caravan would certainly have been detained there for months, or they would have had to pay a big squeeze.

Unlike the Namru, all the people of this section of the country are great tobacco smokers, whereas the former disliked extremely the odor of the smoke. The tribe living on the east side of the Dang ch'u, just opposite where we are camped, are the Jyadé Péré. Some of them came over to my camp to-day. The hats (*shara*) of several of them were low crowned, exactly the shape of our straw hats, but covered with white cotton and made of grass wrapped with woolen threads. In dress the people of this part of the country resemble the Namru, but they wear more ornaments, and most of them have more clothing, nearly all having shirts of *buré* and rather tight fitting waistcoats* of Chinese shape, and made of pulo, which they wear under their gowns. On their queues they wear sewn on a piece of red cloth, a great many ornaments, coins, small charm boxes, coral and turquoise beads, and one or more large rings of ivory. This latter ornament is nearly universally worn.

The Hsien-sheng and Kao pa-erh went to the Jyadé side of the river this morning to get the sheep we bargained for yesterday. They met over a hundred people assembled there for pony racing. The ponies were ridden bare back and singly over a course about a *li* (⅓ mile) long. The chief inquired if I had any Chinese silver or rupees to exchange for Lh'asa tankas, and said he would come over to-morrow to see me and bring me some tankas. He and

* Of the style called in Chinese *kan-chien*. The pulo usually used is of the multi-colored (*wu ts'ai* or *hua*) kind, the colors running across the piece, just as in a Roman scarf. *Buré* is a coarse, raw silk fabric made in India, and is in great demand in Tibet and the adjacent countries.

all his people were very desirous to trade for my broken down ponies and mules, or to sell me fresh ones. They said that they did not care what the Lh'asa people said about not holding intercourse with foreigners, that they were enemies of Lh'asa and not ruled by it. The Amban at Lh'asa ruled them, they said, and it is for this, I suppose, that their country is called Jyadé or "the Chinese district."*

The soldiers camped beside me apologized profusely to-day for having stopped me, saying as excuse that the Lh'asa authorities were very severe, and that they had no discretion in the matter. They thanked me very much for having consented to stop and thus prevented their getting in trouble.

July 24.—The Hsien-sheng went across the river again to trade one of my mules to the Péré Pönbo, but found him disinclined to do so until I had settled matters with the Lama Pönbo of Nagch'u. He said the Ch'amdo territory could be reached in twenty days by going through Jyadé, but that there was another road going from Nagch'uk'a to the same place, though it was a little more roundabout than the first.† Following the first mentioned road, villages were first met with ten days east of here; there were no great mountains to cross anywhere along it. He added that he supposed that since we were camped on Lh'asa territory, the Nagch'u K'anpo would supply us with guides and pack animals. as he believed he had done three years ago to some foreigners who had come to Nagch'u from Naktsang.‡

* It is not *the* Amban who rules, or rather, who has a general supervisory power over the most important acts of the chiefs of Jyadé, but the Third Amban, as he is colloquially called by the Chinese, but whose official title is I Chin-ch'ai, "Envoy to the savages." He resides at Lh'asa and has authority over Poyul, Ts'arong and a number of other districts, thirty-five in all. See under date of *October 5th.*

† This road I joined later on in the I ch'u valley. See under date of *August 11th.*

‡ He referred, of course, to Bonvalot. See Bonvalot, *op. cit.*, p. 283. The Nagch'u K'anpo was probably his *ta amban.* It would appear from Bonvalot's narrative that he was stopped at the northeast corner of the Nyamts'o, near the west side of Mt. Samden Khama of explorer A—— K—— (Bonvalot's Samda Kansain). Conf., however, p. 235, note ‡. He was here, he says (p. 293), in the country of a tribe under Chinese rule, which he calls variously Djachas, Djachong, Tatchong and Tjachong. This name must be Jya Shung or "Chinese from the Shang shung district." This district is immediately south of the Nagch'uk'a one and north of Dam (A—— K——'s Damgyastryok). Bonvalot (p. 293) says that the stream which flows into the Nyamts'o from the east, and on the banks of which he camped for quite a while, is called Samda ch'u. Nain Singh gives the name of the only eastern feeder of the lake as the Nai ch'u.

The flocks of sheep hereabout are very small, and the herds of yaks comparatively large; ponies are very undersized and dear, but more gracefully shaped than the Koko-nor ones. I learnt from my guards, who are more communicative than the Namru about things in general, that trade with China is divided between the Talé lama and the Pan-ch'en rinpoch'é of Tashil'unpo, all the caravans of the former go to Tankar, those of the latter to Ta-chien-lu, and one potentate may not send caravans to the market of the other. Of course this only refers to the great governmental caravans, and cannot possibly apply to the small private ones, of which a large number goes out every year, especially to Ta-chien-lu.

The language of the Jyadé and that of the people on this side of the river differ considerably, that of the latter being more readily understood by both the Hsien-sheng and myself. Both the pronunciation and the vocabularies of these two peoples show notable differences between them.

July 25.—The Péré Pönbo came over to see me, and I let him get the better of me, not only in trading for my lame mules, but in selling me some trinkets he wore, and which I was surprised to see were of Dérgé make*. He repeated what he had said yesterday to the Hsien-sheng about the journey to Ch'amdo through Jyadé. The road is stony but not bad (*sic*)† and there are no passes to cross, by which I understand no very high mountain ranges. There is also, he said, a much traveled road going to Jyäkundo, and it takes about as long to reach that place as it does to travel to Ch'amdo. He said, furthermore, that if I settled matters amicably with the Nagch'u people and then came over to his side of the river, he would find me a guide to go to Ch'amdo, and supply me with all the provisions I might require.

Towards evening the Sang-yi Déba (who lives near Nagch'uk'a) rode up accompanied by five or six men and came at once to my tent. A long wrangle, such as I had had in Namru, began at once. The Déba insisted on my going back the way I had come, to the north of the Dang la, where I would be free to do as I

* On Dérgé jewelry and iron work, see *Land of the Lamas*, p. 228.

† When a Tibetan says that a road is bad he means it literally. He is not, however, a very good judge of such matters as there is not a good road within the confines of Tibet.

pleased. He knew of no country outside of his own, could give me therefore no guide, nor was he willing to let me have provisions. I replied that if they did not agree by to-morrow to conduct me into Chinese governed territory and there arrange with some Pönbo to have me escorted to Ch'amdo, I would go to Nagch'uk'a and, if necessary, to Lh'asa, to see the Amban, whose Emperor's passport I had. The Déba said that I could not go to Nagch'uk'a, that it was on Déba djong territory and that they would not allow me to travel on it. I told him that he would find out if I could not go there, that two years ago three foreigners (Bonvalot and his party) had come to Nagch'uk'a without passports, and that notwithstanding this they had been escorted with all due politeness to Bat'ang. I, who had a passport, could not admit that they should show me less courtesy. In short, it was a proof of great condescension on my part to argue the question with them, what I ought to do was to go to Lh'asa to settle the question with the Amban who alone had authority to regulate my movements. Since I waived this unquestionable right, they should show their appreciation of my kindness by endeavoring to comply with all my wishes.

On this the Déba left and said he would return early to-morrow. All that I want is for these people to escort me across the river and arrange with the Péré Pönbo about guides and show to him that I am a person of some importance. I feel awfully weary of arguing with these people who, though perfectly polite, are terribly stubborn and meet all my arguments with "if you don't do so and so, off will go our heads, for this is Déba djong territory."

July 26.—Early this morning the Nyérpa of the Nagch'u K'anpo, a fine looking man of thirty, of a strongly marked Kashmiri type and very handsomely dressed in the half Tibetan, half Chinese style usual at Lh'asa, with a turban rolled around his gilt edged gray felt hat, rode up with a numerous escort of Drupa and four or five other Lh'asa men, among them two lads of between sixteen and eighteen. Two large white tents were soon pitched near mine and the Nyérpa at once called on me. He spoke the pure Lh'asa dialect, and we were soon on the best of terms, and he readily agreed to see the Péré Pönbo, tell him who I was and ask him to supply me with a guide, pack animals and all I required to travel to Ch'amdo.

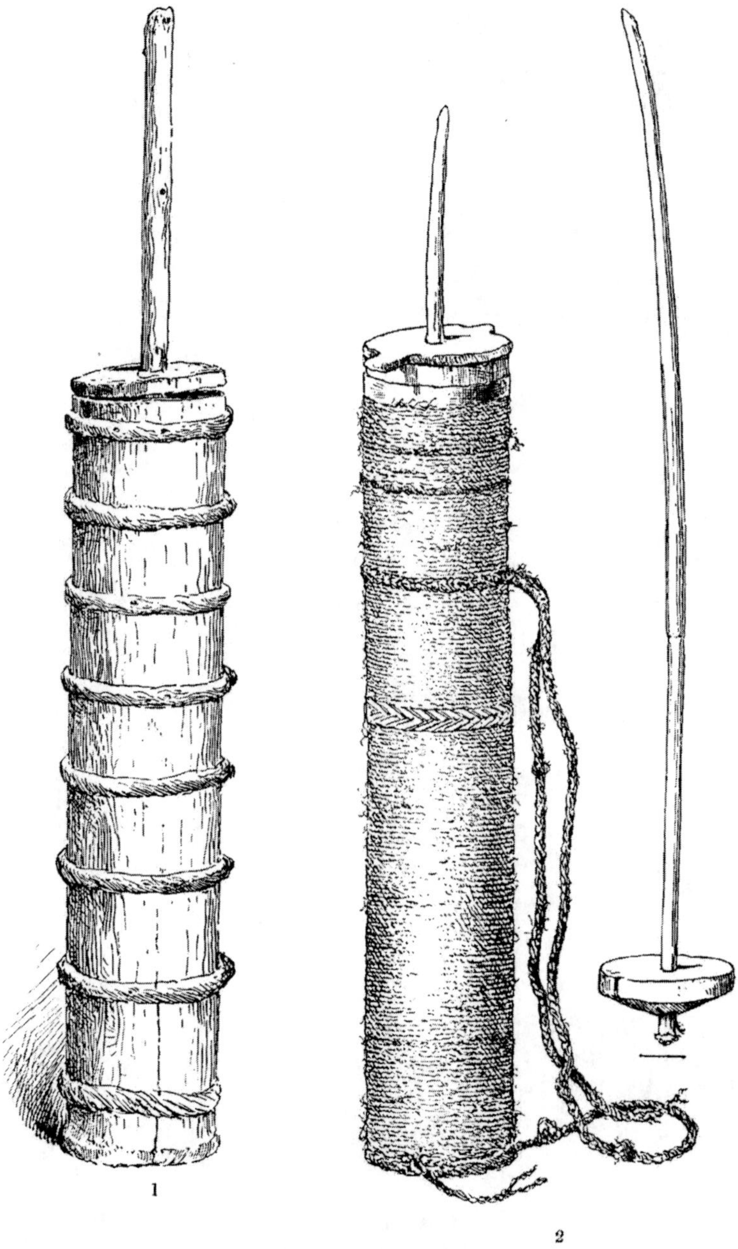

1

2

1. WOODEN TEA CHURN (Kanzé). (U. S. N. M. 131040.)
2. BAMBOO TEA CHURN, wrapped with yak-hair cord and churning-stick (Jyadé). (U. S. N. M. 167215.)

In course of conversation he said that he recognized me, though I had cut off my beard since last he saw me, and that I was one of the three foreigners who had come here three years ago, the one who spoke Chinese. He evidently took me for Mons. Dedecken who accompanied Bonvalot on his journey. He also insisted that I had been to Lh'asa and Shigatsé, for I knew all about the temples, buildings and places of interest in those cities. He himself has been to Ladak, where he had seen foreigners, and a headman who accompanied him had been to Darjeeling. Most of the day was passed amusing him and his party, and getting such information as I could from them without plying them with questions, which is a poor way to get reliable information from Asiatics. They said that the Lh'asa people are and have been for many years on bad terms (*jamdré jyab*), with the Jyadé people, and that they have nothing to do with them, and never go into their country.

He sent two old men (one a Tibetanized Chinese from Tankar) over to see the Péré Pönbo, and when they came back I was told by them that there were three routes leading hence to Ta-chien-lu, the first by Ch'amdo, the second* south of it and called the *ja-lam* or "tea road," and the third by way of Jyäkundo and the Horba country.† This latter is evidently the road I followed in 1889. It was decided among us that to-morrow the Hsien-sheng and I should accompany the Nyérpa and four of his headmen to the other side of the Dang ch'u where the Péré Pönbo will meet us and we shall then settle all questions about my further movements.

Altogether it has been a very fatiguing day for me, but my time has not been entirely lost for I do not believe that the route I am going to follow was gone over by Bonvalot; even if he did, any inhabited part of Tibet is worth careful study, and this Jyadé, of

* This second route falls into the first on reaching the I ch'u. See under date of *August 11th.*

† This route has been followed by Miss Annie R. Taylor in 1892. Miss Taylor was probably stopped at or near the point on the Hsi-ning-Lh'asa road reached by Capt. Bower and called by him Atak Memar. It may be, however, that she struck the highroad a little north of where I did (and the very vague description she has published of her travels admit of both these suppositions), in which case she must have been stopped by the same party which met me here.

which I have never heard mention in Chinese works, must prove exceptionally interesting.*

July 27.—Another very trying and anxious day is over. At daylight the Nyérpa sent me a present of a sheep and a bag of tsamba, and asked me to come drink tea with him. Taking with me some odds and ends, to give him as a return present, I went to his tent, and having drunk a few bowls of very bad tea, we got on our horses, rode across the river and stopped on a little bluff near the bank. There were in our party the Hsien-sheng and myself, the Nyérpa, the Sang-yi Déba, a Séra lama, whose official position I do not exactly understand, and two or three of the oldest men. We lit a fire, and putting the kettle on had tea, but we had scarcely drunk a bowl before the Péré Pönbo and a few men rode up and lit a fire a little way off from ours and put their kettle on. Then the Nyérpa went forward towards the Pönbo, who also advanced to meet him. The two squatted down and had a long, confidential talk, which ended by each one putting a k'atag around the neck of the other, when the Nyérpa came back to our fire in company with the Jyadé chief, and I was asked to tell the latter my story, after which more tea was drunk, and the Péré Pönbo said he would await me and my party to escort me to his camp, a couple of miles away.

I quickly rode back and struck camp, but before leaving the Nagch'u Nyérpa had the impudence to come and say that he hoped that when I returned to my country I would tell how kindly I had been treated by the Nagch'u officials and what good people they were. The Tibetanized Tankar Chinaman (who, by the way, would not speak a word of Chinese to us for fear of compromising himself, so horribly suspicious are these people) came also and begged for some *tsa-pa* tobacco,† and was given not only some tobacco but a jack knife and a pipe for the little services he had indirectly rendered us.

The Péré Pönbo's tent was in the plain about two and one-half miles east-southeast of the river, and I camped near it and on the

* I have, since writing the above, made diligent search for any mention of this Chinese province or Jyadé in Chinese official works at my disposal, but can find none.

† A very bad smelling but very popular mixture which, like all smoking mixtures, varies according to the brand, except in smell which never departs from its high standard. Bonvalot found a Kansu man (he calls the province Kensi) living at So gomba. See Bonvalot, *Op. cit.*, 340.

bank of a pool. The Pönbo brought me some tankas in exchange for sycee, and had a long talk with me about the road I should take. He at first insisted that I must go to Jyäkor (Jyäkundo),* which he said was only ten or twelve days away, but this I refused to do without, however, telling him that I had been there or knew anything of the country. Then he asked me to remain encamped where I was till he could go and see the Horgo Déba, a big chief who rules the country east of here and who is now a day's ride hence. This I again refused to do.

I said that if he would supply me with a guide at once, I would pay him at the rate of an ounce of silver for each day's march. This very tempting offer decided him, and he said he would send a man with me to-morrow so that I might move on a little, and that he, in the meantime, would go see the Horgo Déba and meet me later in the day.

Several of the Péré men who came to my tent were covered with rings and other ornaments of Dérgé make, and I bought a handsome silver-mounted belt with attached knife, needle case, etc., from one, and also several earrings of Lh'asa make, which have the additional interest of showing that the form of that ornament as usually worn by Mongol women is derived from the Tibetans, as is, in fact, most of their dress.

I heard that the number of caravans coming from the Horba country and passing through here on their way to Lh'asa is very great. Golok kafilas also take this route. The former carry tea to Lh'asa and return loaded with barley and pulo. The Jyadé are therefore enabled to do most of their trading at their tent doors. The money in general use is the Lh'asa currency, of which there are three kinds, all of the value of a *tanka*. The only variety used here (when new) is called *Gadän tanka;* there is also the kind colloquially called *Bö-gi gyalpo-gi tanka* ("the King of Tibet's tanka"), which has four numerals in the center,† and then there is the Nepalese tanka. There are many counterfeit coins, very poor imitations they are, and known as *p'ugu-tsuté*. The rupee

* Capt. Bower (*Op. cit.*, 33 and 51) is the only Tibetan traveler who gives this important locality its right name. A—— K—— and others call it Kégé, Kegudo or Kegedo, but Capt. Bower writes the name Gya Kundo and Gya Kudo.

† These numbers give the year in which the coin was struck, counted from the death of the Buddha. See on the coinage of Tibet, Terrien de Lacouperie, *Numismatic Chronicle*, 1882, which does not, however, treat the subject exhaustively.

exchanges for three tankas, although it is only worth from thirty-one to thirty-two tael cents, while three tankas are supposed to be worth forty-five. Ten rupees are given for an ounce of sycee.

July 28.—We made about six miles across a rough plain with grass-covered tussocks and pools of water, and camped at the foot of some low hills of granite about a mile east of the tent gomba of Trashiling, where there are two hundred Bönbo akas. I find out that the whole Jyadé country belongs to this persuasion, hence in all probability the enmity shown it by Lh'asa.

The Péré Pönbo left before we did, and rode to the Trashiling gomba, where the Horgo Déba is stopping, to arrange with him about my journey to Ch'amdo. About an hour after we had made camp, he and the Horgo Déba arrived, the latter a typical Drupa chief, of massive build, corpulent, with a rather thin, aquiline nose and high cheek bones, resembling on the whole very much a Sioux Indian. His hair hung down around his face in a tangled mass, and he was rather bald on the crown of his head. His already large person looked immense in his sheepskin ch'uba, over which was a purple pulo gown; a broad cloth band passed over his right shoulder and under his left arm, and on it were fastened a dozen silver charm boxes (*gawo*); a huge bunch of many colored ribbons hung also from his shoulder, and a long straight sword was passed in his belt. He wore one of the customary high crowned straw hats but covered with yellow stuff, an official badge as it were, and he rode a diminutive pony which literally disappeared under him. Behind him rode one of his men, a dirty, wild looking but smiling fellow, carrying a red cotton umbrella tied behind his back, evidently a much prized article belonging to the big chief.

Nor gyal-tsän ("The standard of wealth") is the chief's name; he is one of the thirty-six Débas appointed by the Lh'asa Amban to rule Jyadé, and who have the right to wear a coral button. These Débas receive a yearly allowance of one *yuan-pao** from the Chinese government. He proved to be a very jolly, sociable fellow, a great laugher and very amenable to reason.†

* A piece of bullion weighing 50 taels of silver. It is usually called a *yambu* (corrupt pronunciation of *yuan pao*), or *do-tsä* (*rdo-tsad*) or even *do*. *Ta-mi-ma* (*rta-rmig-ma*, "horse hoof") is also used to designate an ingot of silver, irrespective of weight.

† Bonvalot appears to have met him in Nar Pei-hu. He says of him "C'est un énorme gaillard, à l'oeil gris, qui a le tchang aimable." Bonvalot, *Op. cit.*, 367.

He agreed to have me escorted to Mér djong, the first place on Ch'amdo territory beyond Jyadé, but refused to go to the town of Ch'amdo, as he said he and his people were not on terms with that country, which professed the orthodox faith of the Gélug sect while the Jyadé were Bönbo. He said he would vouch for my safety while traveling with him, or the guides he would furnish me, or, as he put it, "if the sky falls, it shall strike me alone."

Then came the question of compensation, and it was finally agreed that I should give him a *yuan-pao*. I thereupon made him a few presents and gave him some earnest money, and also some to the Péré Pönbo, who had shown himself a good go-between.

The Horgo Déba said it would probably take from fifteen to twenty days to reach Mér djong; from what I learn the road is good and provisions abundant, so we shall at last travel in comfort and our troubles are at an end.

This chief reminds me of my former friend, Nyam-ts'o Purdung, the same frank, hearty manner, and very much the same physique. He stayed the greater part of the day with me, laughing and joking all the time, and was not over inquisitive. I bought a number of things from different men who came to my camp, and the Déba settled the price I was to pay for each object in a most satisfactory way. Quantities of silver and gold ornaments were offered me, but I unfortunately could not afford to buy many that I should much liked to have secured.

The Déba said he would be ready to start to-morrow morning, and that he would join me here at an early hour.

July 29.—The Déba, with his steward (*Nyérpa*) and a servant, joined me this morning, and we started off in high spirits. We took a general easterly course over low hills of granitic boulders covered with a thin layer of soil, with here and there patches covered with the tussocks of grass and little water holes we have got to hate so in traveling in Tibet. About twelve miles south of us was a range of hills with rounded summits and of no great height; it is called Shar-yong, and much farther away to the southeast and south-southeast rose a line of snow peaks (probably those marked on our maps as north of Larego) called Om-yong.

We made about twelve miles, and camped at a place called Chingo (or Tsinkor), where there are a few tents, and where the

Déba has to change his *ula*.* A violent hailstorm swept over us at 2 P. M., with much thunder and lightning, and about one and one-half inches of hailstones of the size of cherries fell.

The Déba has a fine white cotton tent, of the pavilion shape in general use in this country among travelers. He asked me to tea, and regaled me with dainties, such as we have not tasted for many a day, dried apricots and melons, chuoma (he pronounced the word *droma*), sweet biscuits, dried mutton, chura and milk-tea. He is a very kind man, and I touched his heart by telling him that I had not heard from my home for a year and was very anxious to get to some place where I might receive news of my people. He said he would hurry along as much as he could, that traveling with ula animals was a slow method at best, but he, being a poor man and having only one horse of his own with him, had to use ula ponies exclusively. I hardly believe we can reach Ch'amdo in less than twenty-five days.

I learnt from the Déba that the Jyäkundo road is infested by Chakba (brigands)and that the Jyadé do not often go there themselves, but travel to Lh'asa or Po-yul. He says one of the reasons which keeps him from going to Ch'amdo or Ta-chien-lu is the excessive heat of those places. The fact is that anyone who lives in this country may well fear the heat, for the thermometer marks 5° or 6° of cold every night in the hottest part of summer.

The country we have traversed since crossing the Dang ch'u is, for a grazing country, very thickly populated.† To-day we passed between thirty and forty tents, and the previous days we saw about as many. In every tent there are from four to eight persons.

The Déba's steward, Anyang by name, is also his private chaplain; this evening he read prayers in the most approved fashion, and, though he is a Bönbo, I could not notice any difference in the method of conducting the ceremony from that observed by orthodox lamas on similar occasions; he rang the bell, clapped his hands, burnt incense, etc., in exactly the same manner as they do.

* On the term *ula* and on the abuses to which it gives rise, see *Land of the Lamas*, 52, 53, 139, etc.

† A—— K——, speaking of this region, says there are 500 tents in the Shang-shung district, 3,000 in the Nagch'uk'a one, 500 in Ata, 1,000 in Yágra, etc. My experience tends to prove that A—— K—— made sometimes rather wild guesses. The country to which he thus gives a population of not less than 20,000 persons, exclusive of Akas, could barely support 5,000.

July 30.—As was to be expected in a country where the people are so fortunate as still to be able to put no value on time, the Déba's ula was not forthcoming this morning, so we have had to wait here a day. The ula supplied here will go two stages, and then we shall have to change it again, and probably make another halt of a day or so waiting for it to turn up, and so on in like fashion to the end of the journey.

I hear the Déba lives about five days east of here, and that he will leave me when we reach his home and send us on to Mér djong with other guides, and that we shall, in the latter part of the journey, be able to make up much of the time we are now losing.

I heard to-day from two men living here that towards the beginning of this year two foreigners with red beards, close fitting clothes, turbans, foreign boots and armed with rifles, revolvers and big knives, and who had come from Naktsang, had passed south of here and had gone to Ch'amdo and Ta-chien-lu. The way they followed was along the farther side of the range we see to the south of this place, and the road on which they traveled was called the Ja lam ("Tea road"). They had a Chinese interpreter (*lotsa*), a Kaché, and a number of servants, some twenty mules and horses, and their boxes were so big and heavy that it required two men to lift one. They gave the ula people a small gold coin and presented the Pönbo with two. They had a passport. The men who told me all this did not see these p'yling, only heard tell of their passage and of their strange appearance. They had also heard of the passage over this same road (*i. e.*, Ja lam) some three years ago of three other foreigners who also came from Naktsang and went towards Ta-chien-lu. This evidently refers to Bonvalot's expedition.*

The foreigners who went through this year did not reach Nagch'uk'a but were stopped some distance north of it. I cannot conceive to whom the people here refer. I have not heard of any expedition having left for Tibet since my last journey, but the details given me about these men's dress are so circumstantial that my informants cannot be lying about it. It must be a party from Kashmir or Turkestan. The gold coin they used points to India.

* Capt. Bower and Dr. Thorold passed through this country in November, 1891. See Bower, *Op. cit.*, 51, et seq.

The Déba, I was told, is a native of Nar Pai-hu (or Pei-hu as he pronounces these Chinese words).* There is also a district contiguous to his called Kar Pai-hu. All the people hereabout carry slings, called *orta* made of plaited yarn; one string has a leash and

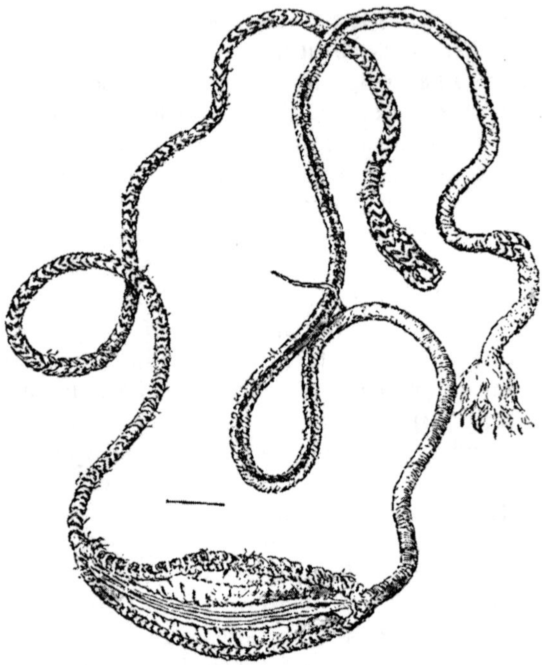

SLING (Jyadé).

is used as a whip, in driving sheep or yak. The sling is used to "round up" the herds or flocks; the herders throw bits of dry dung or small pebbles with wonderful accuracy, driving in any animal which has strayed away. I have also seen them throw large pebbles several hundred yards. I have not heard the word *yak* used by any Tibetans; in this section of the country all domestic yaks are called *nor*, this word meaning also "riches, wealth."

* Pai-hu or "Hundred families," is a Chinese administrative division used among the aboriginal tribes of China, and in Chinese dependencies generally. The chief of an Hundred is usually called Po-ch'ang.

July 31.—The ula arrived at daylight and we started by 7 A. M., but the yaks were very fresh and had hardly been loaded when they broke away and had soon scattered their loads in out of the way nooks all over the country. It took several hours to collect the Déba's property and to get it loaded again, when the same thing occurred a second time. Finally the yaks settled down to work, and we pushed on rapidly until 7 P. M., by which time we had made twenty-three miles and reached the banks of the Nashé ch'u.

About four miles from Chingo we crossed the "upper" Jyädundo road (*gong-ma lam*) to Nagch'uk'a, a well-beaten, wide trail which must be very much traveled over. A few miles farther on we passed the "middle road" or *bar-ma lam*, going also from Jyäkundo to the same place.*

We traveled in a general east by south direction over the foothills of the little range of mountains we have been skirting since crossing the Dang ch'u, but immediately after leaving Chingo we passed out of the basin of the Dang ch'u and entered one in which all the water (there were remarkably few streams in it by the way)flowed eastward to empty, in all probability, into the Nashé ch'u. The country traversed to-day showed mostly granitic rocks, the surface rock much eroded.

We saw a great many tents in clusters of three and four in every little sheltered corner. The flocks of sheep are everywhere small, we have not seen one of a thousand head. The herds of yaks vary from thirty or forty up to two hundred or three hundred. Goats are scarce, and the only dogs I have noticed are of the Chinese cur species. We have not seen any domestic fowls or cats. There are very few birds, the Mongolian lark (?) and a few wild pigeons are the only ones I have remarked.

The people in the camp near which we stopped to-day to take lunch were most polite and good-natured; the women's headdress was more ornate than any heretofore seen. I managed to photograph both men and women with little difficulty, all I had to do

* Later on we came to the lower road (*og-ma lam*) to Jyäkundo and followed it for several days, leaving it only on the Su ch'u. See under date of *August 2d.* Capt. Bower passed the upper and middle roads near or at his camps 96 and 97. He refers in his Diary (p. 54) to one of these roads, I cannot make out which, as "a broad trail leading to Lh'asa, on which we met numbers of Tibetans taking yaks laden with butter to market."

was to ask some of them to stand quite still while I showed to others their image in the finder of the camera. They took the camera for a kind of telescope.

We descended steadily all day and at our camp this evening we are at the lowest altitude reached for months, about 14,200 feet above sea level. The soil all along the route was well covered with grass, and we picked a quantity of a delicious kind of mushroom (*shara*)* with a yellow upper skin and white underneath, which we have enjoyed greatly. Fried with butter they tasted exactly like *cêpes à la Bordelaise*, perhaps they are cêpes.

The Jyadé tell me that they only occupy the high region from which we have just come, during the summer, coming down to the lower valleys, such as the Nashé ch'u, in winter. This Nashé ch'u comes from behind the range we have been following, and which terminates here, to be succeeded by another of bare limestone crags some six hundred feet high coming from the west-northwest, and continuing in a southeast by east direction as far as we can see, the Nashé ch'u running along its base. This stream empties into a "big river"† which we will come to in a few days, so says the Déba.

August 1.—We followed for a few miles the left bank of the Nashé ch'u till near where it takes a southeast direction and enters a narrow gorge, when we struck over the foothills of the rocky range on our left, and, crossing two streams flowing southwest, and which empty into the Nashé ch'u at the gorge previously referred to, we entered the basin of another little feeder of the same river.

A very heavy thunder storm overtook us at about 3 P. M., and one of the pack-horses bolted and dropped its load all over the country. We were so much delayed by this *contre temps* that we had to camp some three or four miles west of where we had intended to. The rain continued falling all the afternoon and evening.

*Jaeschke, *Tib. Engl. Dict.*, writes this word *sha-mo*, and says: "The various species of fungus receive their appellations from their color (*dkar-sha*, *nag-sha*, *smug-sha*, *ser-sha*) or from the places where they grow (*klims-sha*, *chu-sha*, *lud-sha*, *shing-sha*). The damp climate of Sikkim produces, moreover, *so-ke*, *k'a-wa* and *dé-mo sha-mo*, etc., Csoma has also *sha-mang*, a thick kind of mushroom."

†This "big river" (*ch'u ch'en-po*) is the Su ch'u.

HEADDRESS OF JYADE WOMAN.

The country to-day was covered with fine grass, and Drupa were numerous, the tents in groups of three or four. The Déba is most obliging, he sees to all my wants and sends me daily some presents, either dried meat or sweet cakes, but he will neither eat nor drink in my tent, though I daily go to his and have tea with him. He heard me say that the tinder I was using had been given me by the Nagch'u officials, and he insisted on my throwing it away, as he said it was probably poisoned. Nothing could induce him, he added, to take food or drink prepared by them, so dangerous did he consider them. This is probably all in his imagination, for, though I know of many cases of persons having been got rid of at Lh'asa by poison, I doubt very much if poison is used there in this wholesale manner.

August 2.—We changed the Déba's ula about five miles from our camp of last night and, strange to say, experienced no delay. After going about seven and a half miles in an easterly direction we struck the lower Jyäkundo road (*Og-ma lam*) and followed it in a northeast direction, crossing the range which we have been skirting since we first came to the Nashé ch'u. The road over the pass, which is called the Drajya lamo la, is very steep and runs between vertical cliffs and crags of limestone, but the pass is fortunately not at all high.

We camped about four miles northeast of the pass in a narrow valley with mountains of limestone rocks rising vertically on either side. The ground on which we have camped is one big bed of fragrant light blue flowers,* and the grass is so long that it makes a soft bed for us. Several Drupa have their tents high up the mountain sides on patches of green sward. These people showed themselves very obliging, bringing us down dry dung (*chongwa*), milk and sho (*djo*), for which I gave them a tanka. We are here in the district of Dzang ch'éré. There are so many Pönbos and such a multitude of districts that it is quite impossible to note them all. The Déba gave me the names of a dozen or more in this section of the country, but he said that he could not remember the names of all of them.

August 3.—We only made about nine miles to-day, being obliged to change the ula again. Leaving the stream which comes

* *Tretocarya sikkimensis.* See Appendix.

down from the Drajya lamo pass, we crossed another low pass and followed the valley on the northeast side till we came to a place called Song-chyang sumdo, where the brook we had been following received another stream, hence the name *Sumdo* or "three-valley-mouths"; the one through which the stream flows below this point being counted, as it would be in China, as the third. Here was the first stone structure seen since leaving the Ts'aidam. It was but a stone hut about ten feet square and five high, used as a storehouse by some people living in a black tent, of which there were three at this spot, but it was an agreeable sight.

Song-chyang sumdo, the highest spot at which we have found permanent habitations, is about 13,600 feet above sea level, and is the lowest point we have come to since leaving the Naichi gol.

One of the inhabitants brought me some musk for which he wanted five ounces of silver an ounce.* He said he went every year to Lh'asa where he got ten ounces of Lh'asa silver an ounce from the Chinese traders. He told me that musk deer were plentiful in the adjacent mountains.

Children here are very numerous,† a number of them came and played around my tent. The little girls had small bells hanging from their hair and belts; I could not learn whether they were ornaments or to drive away evil spirits. All were very dirty. The women here and elsewhere are wonderfully energetic; they carry huge buckets of water or baskets of dung on their backs up the steep hills,‡ run about after the yaks, catch and milk the cows, look after the children, load the pack animals, go on the ula, spin, weave, make clothes, cook, and are nevertheless always ready to sing and joke. I am not astonished that Chinese should have told me that they made good wives. On the whole the women are

* Capt. Bower says (*op. cit.*, p. 65) that at Tashiling he was offered musk at the rate of three pods for seven rupees. The people must have been awfully hard up or the musk of very poor quality.

† Capt. Bower (*op. cit.*, 65) speaking of this section of the country says that the number of children seen in the villages is a striking feature, and is due to the fact that polyandry is not practised. I think he assigns a wrong cause to this undoubted fact. In the lower countries the people are better protected from the weather and better fed, hence a smaller mortality among infants, but polyandry is practised by them more than by the Drupa.

‡ They rest the bottom of the long churn-shaped bucket on the thick folds of their gowns at the waist, and pass a strap around it and across their breasts.

not bad looking and not very dark skinned; soap and water would make them a light olive color and show that they have rosy cheeks.

Anyang, the Déba's steward, wears his hair short (usually he has his head shaven, he tells me); it is as curly as a mulatto's. Nearly all the men have wavy hair; the women have probably taken the curl out of theirs by plaiting and greasing it. The people all put butter on their hair and frequently rub the scalp with it, but I have not seen any one among the male population whose hair showed signs of ever having been combed.

It is very difficult to get any one of these people to part with any personal ornament or portion of his or her dress; they tell me they fear spoiling their luck if they should*; though every one is anxious to sell any thing I desire which does not come within these two categories.

Yesterday and the day before we found along the road quantities of the same delicious mushrooms first met with near the Nashé ch'u. We are now feasting upon them, and have also plenty of mutton, flour, butter and milk. We all feel ever so much stronger than when we left the Namru or the Dang ch'u, and besides that, the weather is so much better, the sun so bright, the grass so green, and the people everywhere so obliging, that we naturally see every thing in a more cheerful light.

August 4.—We had to wait until 2 P. M. before the ula arrived, and consequently only made about ten miles, camping in the valley of Ponta. About two miles after leaving camp we came to a large river, the Pon ch'u,† coming from the north-northwest and flowing, as far as I can see, a little north of east to empty into the "big river" of which we have been hearing so much of late.

* Or it may be they think they will be bewitched. In some parts of China (in Kan-su, among Mohammedans even) when a man has been shaved, he takes the hair cut off his head and conceals it. I fancy this custom has a similar origin. See p. 171, the use made of hair, etc., by the Mongols in witchcraft.

† It is difficult to follow Capt. Bower's route in all its details, but he appears to have crossed the Pon ch'u, for I find marked on his map a place called Pongra, near "a large river" flowing south. The course he assigns this river is conjectural; it flows, probably, south of where he crossed it, in an east-southeast direction, to empty into the Su ch'u a little south of where Capt. Bower crossed the latter river. He calls, by the way, the Su ch'u Sak ch'u, but on his route map it is called by mistake Ircho (I ch'u). The I ch'u empties into the Su ch'u, and the new stream bears the latter name till it becomes, if my informants were correct in their statements, the Jyamă Ngul ch'u, "the Ngul ch'u of lower Jya(dé)," which may be the Salwen.

After fording the river we crossed a mountain on its left bank, and entered a little "park" in which there were thirteen or fourteen black tents, near one of which we camped.

The limestone formation, which we first met with on reaching the Nashé ch'u, continues along the right bank of the Pon ch'u as far east as we can see. At Song-chyang sumdo a good deal of red sandstone conglomerate was also visible. This limestone range, on the north side of which we now are, is not over three or four miles in breadth.

I have been very much surprised to find throughout the Jyadé country so few ponies, here at Ponta there are not a half dozen, though yaks and sheep are plentiful.

The language spoken in Jyadé presents numerous peculiarities I have not met with elsewhere. To note only one—they use the particle *lé* and *ta* (the latter probably the Lh'asan *té* and *sté*) to indicate the present tense. Thus they say *go-lé ré*, "I (or you) want it;" *go-lé ma ré*, "I (or you) do not want it." *Rig-ta*, "I see it;" *Rig mé ta*, "I (or you) do not see it."

August 5.—The thermometer fell during the night to +22° Fahrenheit, but this morning when we left the air was quite warm. About two miles north of Ponta we crossed a low pass and descended into a narrow valley with vertical cliffs of limestone and sandstone rising a thousand feet or more on either side of it, and a good-sized brook flowing through it in an easterly direction. A good deal of brush grows in this gorge, and I noticed a few stalks of the rhubarb plant,* the first I have seen on the journey; there were also eight or nine black tents.

After riding a few miles down this gorge, we turned up a side ravine, and after a short but stiff climb reached the top of the Pon la, and "the big river" at last came in view. It is the Su ch'u (the Sok chu of our maps).† In a short valley opening on

* The altitude of the upper part of this valley is about 13,500 feet above sea level.

† This is the Souc of d'Anville, the Sac Chu of Bower, the So tchou of Bonvalot. Both these travelers crossed this river at the same place, which the first calls Tsuk Sun Dong Gong (Bower, *op. cit.*, 56), and Bonvalot, So goumba (Bonvalot, *op. cit.*, 341). The latter says the river is between one hundred and fifty and two hundred meters wide at this point. According to Chinese authors the name of this river should be written as I have done. The *Hsi-yü tung wen chih*, Bk. 22, p. 10, says it is called Su ch'u because it "leads off" (*su* in Tibetan) towards the south all the water in this country. I have never met with a word *su* with this meaning. The same work mentions, but apparently in another part of Tibet, a Sog ch'u, where the word *sog* means "the steppe" (*ts'ao ti*).

to the river and about two miles away from the Pon la was a small village of stone houses near which were several large ch'örtens. Here is the home of the Déba Nor gyal-ts'an, and the village bears the name of Ch'yi-chab. Twenty or thirty miles away to the south-southeast, and trending apparently south or southwest we saw a high range of snow-covered mountains, but the angle at which I was looking at them prevented me settling very satisfactorily their general trend.

A very steep descent of half an hour brought us to the bank of the river, where we found a few tents of Drupa with stone store-houses adjoining them and low stone walls enclosing them; no mortar or even mud being used in this rough masonry. A rawhide cable was stretched across the river between two projecting walls of rock and securely anchored at either end under large piles of stones. We unloaded and unsaddled our pack animals and ponies and drove them into the river which, below the bridge,* was about one hundred and fifty yards wide and very swift; they were soon safe on the other bank. We and our luggage were taken over later in the day when we had drunk our fill of tea and *djo*, and the old Déba had finished flirting with a buxom woman who sat with him for a long time under the shade of his gorgeous red calico umbrella. The old man was very happy at getting home, he was jollier than usual and laughed and joked with all comers. Finally, as the sun was nearing the mountain tops and as we wanted to sleep on the other shore where our tents were already pitched, we got pulled across. A traveling thimble of horn was put on the cable, and thongs attached to it passed around our waist and between our legs and lashed us securely to the thimble. By means of a guy rope attached to the thimble we were dragged across by men on the farther bank, and the thimble was drawn back by another guy rope to the nearer bank for the next passenger.

The Déba put up his tent near mine, though he was only a mile or so from his own home, but, he said, he would not leave me till he had seen me safely off to Mér djong, and I, for my part, am loth to part a minute sooner than is necessary from the good old fellow. He is going to send Anyang as my guide, and a better

* Explorer K—— P—— says that such bridges are called *bring* in Tibetan. *Report on Explor. in Sikkim, Bhutan*, etc., 12. I have never heard any other name used but *zam* or *zamba*, the usual word for bridge.

man he could not possibly furnish, he is kind, polite and energetic, a worthy servant of such a kind master.

At this point, called Tséga, we leave the "Lower Jyäkundo road" which we have been following all the way from the Drajya-lamo pass. It turns up the valley in which Ch'yi-chab is situated, while we, go naturally eastward. I hear we can certainly reach Ch'amdo within fifteen days, and everyone says the road is good.

I have inquired here about the two foreigners I heard of at Chingo, but no one had seen them though many had heard of their passage to the south of here. About two miles up the Su ch'u valley, but out of our line of vision, is a Bönbo lamasery with a hundred lamas or more. I noticed a large pile of logs by the river bank, and I learnt that they are brought here on yak-back from quite a long distance down the Su ch'u and are used in house building. Those I saw are for a new temple, or for repairing the Gomba above here. They are of pine wood and of about the size and length of railroad sleepers.

Though the morning was quite cool, the thermometer in the shade rose at 2 P. M. to 77°, but there was a pleasant breeze blowing all day, and we all enjoyed camping by this pretty river, chatting with the people, who are free and familiar without ever being obtrusive.* I have only to tell them that I want to be alone and everyone leaves my tent, and none venture near it till I call them.

August 6.—To-day has been devoted to eating, making and receiving presents and showing my various possessions to the many visitors who have called on me. My friend, Déba Nor gyal-ts'an, has overwhelmed me with presents of food for the journey, enough to carry me to Ch'amdo.

The Chief of Miri,† his son and brother and a numerous escort came down the valley, and learning that there was a foreigner

* I cannot agree with Capt. Bower who says (*Op. cit.*, 53 and 62) "It is a long time before one thoroughly understands what a mistake it is ever to be polite, or assume any affectation of friendliness, with Tibetans or Chinese. * * While by taking a high tone, civility would be insured, and as much honesty as their natures are capable of. They can be managed by fear, but not by love." I am glad to say that I have never had to regret the politeness I have shown any of these people. They, as well as all Asiatics, thoroughly appreciate politeness and courtesy, though firmness and a certain amount of reserve should never be forgotten in all one's intercourse with them.

† He lived, he said, near Pemba, on the highroad to Lh'asa.

Deba Nor gyal-tsan crossing Su ch'u by Rope Bridge.

here, they camped near by and came to see me. They were the best dressed chieftains I had seen, with gowns of black *yü-ling*, lined with lambskin and trimmed with otter fur, well combed hair falling over their shoulders and cut in a fringe over their brows, and necklaces of big coral and agate beads; they looked like nobles of the time of Louis VIII of France.

Accompanying them was their chaplain, a very clever and well read Bönbo lama, who at once asked me about the foreign alphabet and numerals. Under each letter of the alphabet that I gave him he wrote the sound in Tibetan, and seemed immensely pleased that some of the numerals used by us were identical with those of his country, and the others somewhat similar.

The Miri Pönbo surprised me by asking me if I was not in the habit of noting the names of all the rivers, mountains, villages and towns I passed by, and whether I was not looking out for deposits of the precious metals. Chinese must have told him foreigners had no other object in view when traveling than to find out the hidden treasures of a country. These chiefs expressed very freely their hatred for Déba djong, which I now feel sure is founded on the fact that they have been persecuted by it on account of their faith.

The lama asked me very embarrassing questions about our ideas of future life, and when I told him that most of us believed that the soul (*sémpa nyid*) lived eternally, he clapped his hands and said that we must then be Bönbo. I turned the conversation to another subject as I felt that we were getting on unsafe ground.

Two lama pilgrims from Labrang gomba (in Amdo) came into camp. They were on their way to Lh'asa, had left their gomba six months ago, and had come here by way of the Golok country and Jyäkundo.*

I heard also from some of my visitors that *five* foreigners had passed south of here on their way to China in January of this year. They had come from Naktsang and had tried to go to Lh'asa, but failing in that, had taken the Ja lam to Tarchendo. No foreigners, I was assured, have ever been here before me.†

---

* The road they traveled over is, in all probability, the identical one followed a year later by Miss A. R. Taylor, of the China Inland Mission.

† Bonvalot and Bower came on to the Su ch'u at or near its confluence with the I ch'u, probably fifteen to twenty miles farther down the river than Tsega.

I bought a few curios, swords, ornaments, a gun and some very pretty Dergé knives. All the people let the Pönbo fix the price of their goods, and abided without a murmur by his decision, though it was usually very much less than what they asked. A beggar woman, the first I have seen in Tibet, came to my tent, but the Pönbo would not let me give her anything and told her she ought to be ashamed of herself importuning his guest; he smacked her on the face, and then gave her a tanka himself.

When the Miri Pönbo left my tent, I heard him say to his brother "*P'yling Pönbo mi yab-bo, yab-bo ré,*" ("The foreign official is a very good man,") and turning to the Hsien-sheng, he asked him if it were likely that I would come back to Jyadé, that in case I did, I must come and stop a while with him.

August 7.—It was hardly daylight when the Horgo Déba sent and asked me to come breakfast with him. After our meal was over I paid him the 50 taels I owed him and made him a present of a handsome rug, some satin ribbons and a pair of Japanese lacquer bowls. I also bought from him a very handsome flint and steel, ornamented with gold and silver and made in Pomä, a pair of leather saddle-cloth covers from the same country, and his fine matchlock. The old man was very much pleased at my buying these things from him as he said he was more in want of money than of finery. I asked the chief to give me rupees for a *yuan-pao,* as tankas are no longer current east of here, and each time I want to pay a small sum I do not like to show large ingots of silver, it encourages thieves. While we were talking the matter over, the Miri Pönbo sent and invited me to come to his tent to drink tea.

He was seated on a pile of cushions reading out of a beautifully illuminated missal and his brother, his son and four or five servants were already drinking tea and preparing breakfast for me. The Pönbo's son cooked me a dish of hashed mutton, seasoning it with various condiments kept in little red leather bags; among these I noticed dried onions, and red pepper. They also gave me *djo* and cakes cooked in a large iron pan, which the Pönbo told me was kept exclusively for this purpose, a degree of refinement I had not been led to expect in this country.

All these people are great and loud laughers; they express astonishment or admiration by exclaiming "*Atsé*" (meaning I think, "fine, excellent"), and drawing in a very long breath.

The Miri Pönbo told me that the name Chang-t'ang applied to all the inhabited region of north Tibet including even Jyadé, but not to the desert region to the north of it. He informed me also that he had not long ago received a circular letter from the Lh'asa Amban advising him of the projected journey of four foreigners coming from Ssŭ-ch'uan, who were mapping the country.* He was directed not to molest or impede them in any way. He had also heard of the foreigners who passed south of here in January of this year.

In the necklaces these Miri men wore I noticed, besides coral and agate beads, long cylindrical beads of a black and white stone, the white forming circles or bands, both longitudinal and circular. They said these beads were of *dzä*† and were found in their country, and were very valuable, a well marked one being worth thirty or forty ounces of silver. The Chinese make imitation ones but they are easily detected, said my informants. I am inclined to think, however, that this substance is a composition, for I have never heard of agate or onyx so regularly marked. The son of the Miri Pönbo had a whole necklace made of beads of this *dzä*.

The Miri Pönbo is to supply me with rupees in exchange for my Chinese silver, Nor jyal-ts'an not having enough of them. Only Victorian rupees or *mo-go* ("female head") are everywhere current; Georgian or *p'o-go* ("male head") ones are only reluctantly taken.

I was asked to-day if this country contained any product which would be of value in foreign countries; I mentioned wool and rhubarb (*djim-ts'a*).‡ The people were very much astonished to learn that this weed had any value, or medicinal properties. They said they had never sold any and that the only use they ever made

* These travelers, I found out latter were Chinese scholars from the Peking Tung-wen kuan.

† I know of no word but *rdzas* which has the meaning of "jewel," though more usually used with that of "object, matter," etc. These beads may be of onyx, though I have never seen any marked in such a regular way.

‡ Dr. Hooker speaks of the "gigantic rhubarb of the Zemu valley in Sikkin." "This is the handsomest herbaceous plant in Sikkim: it is called 'Tchuka,' and the acid stems are eaten both raw and boiled. * * The dried leaves afford a substitute for tobacco; a smaller kind of rhubarb is, however, more commonly used in Tibet for this purpose." *Himalayan Journals*, II, 77-78. This tobacco is in great demand in those parts of Tibet which I have visited. It is brought from Lh'asa, and is called *t'ob-ch'og*.

of it was to occasionally chew the stem of the green leaves which was agreeably acid. Deer horns they sell to the Chinese traders who come to Mér (or Méru) djong and at Jyäkundo. They also sell hides and musk and a little gold dust.

The Miri Pönbo sent me in the evening a bag of beautifully white and fine wheat flour. Like all the other good things he had, it came from Pomä, a country with which the Jyadé appear to carry on a good deal of trade, traveling there by way of Shobando.

August 8.—We left Tséga at 8 A. M., the Déba Nor jyal-ts'an leading my horse, on which he insisted that I should mount, for about a quarter of a mile, while the Miri Pönbo and all the people hereabout accompanied me; some leading the horses of the rest of my party. The poor servant boy of the Déba gave me his garters and an old tea churn as parting presents, saying that we were such good friends he could not let me leave without something, and he had nothing else to offer me.

A few miles below Tséga the Su ch'u enters a narrow gorge along which travel is impossible, so we turned up a side valley less than a mile below the bridge. Here we saw the first cultivated land met with since entering Tibet; a little barley was growing near a village, or rather permanent camp, for the people were living in tents, with stone storehouses and out-buildings near by. Farther up this valley we passed a real village of eight or ten houses and a small gomba.

We followed this valley to its head and after a short descent came on to the Len ch'u, a swift and clear river, about one hundred and fifty feet wide, coming from the north-northeast and flowing south. High limestone cliffs from 1500 to 2000 feet high overhang the river, those along the right bank rising nearly vertically.

About two and a half miles down the river we forded it at a point where it was three feet deep, and then followed its left bank down to a point where, making a short but sharp bend westward, it empties into the Su ch'u, I think, in a gorge we saw a little way to the westward. There were numerous black tents in the Len ch'u gorges or high up on the mountain sides, but no signs of cultivation.

Leaving the Len ch'u we turned eastward again up a short valley called Trazé lung and camped on the mountain side about five miles from its head.

The country traversed to-day was very wild looking; occasional patches of grass, a little scrub brush, bare rocks and torrent beds piled up with débris, were the characteristic features of the landscape. We only passed one caravan, about fifty yaks loaded with logs and poles and bound for the gomba above Ch'yi-chab on the Su ch'u.

Anyang told me that the Pon ch'u, the Len ch'u and the I ch'u, which we will cross in a day or two, are the principal feeders of the Su ch'u, which lower down its course is called the Nu ch'u or Jyama Nu ch'u. The Su ch'u, he said, is held to be the main stream, though the Len ch'u and the Pon ch'u are nearly as large where we crossed them.

August 9.—It rained heavily during the night, and again this morning the rain began before we started and kept falling most of the day.

We went out of the Trazé lung by the head of the valley (called Trazé la), and, after crossing a small stream coming out of a narrow gorge of limestone rocks, its mouth marked by a great bare crag seven or eight hundred feet high, we climbed the Maja la and then turned southward along another feeder of the Su ch'u, whose name I could not learn.

We went through a short gorge on entering this valley where there is a remarkable sandstone rock. It is a pillar some fifteen to twenty feet high and not over six or seven feet in diameter and stands alone in the middle of the gorge. A small stream of water trickles from the top of the rock. I was surprised that Anyang as well as the travelers who passed us at this point did not look upon this rock as having something supernatural about it, but passed it by without even throwing down a stone at its base.

A few miles down this stream we again turned eastward and camped at a place called Gentsé, where there are two or three Drupa and where grazing is splendid. All day we have skirted mountains of limestone formation. Here at Gentsé I only notice red sandstone, but to the eastward, limestone reappears.

To-day we passed another drove of yaks carrying poles and planks westward. I suppose that very little but local traffic goes over this road, the tea caravans most likely all come from Jyäkundo or pass south of here along the ja-lam.

Rhubarb is very plentiful in all these valleys, the people use the dry stalks as a roofing for their little storehouses, putting a layer of earth on top of them. I have not seen a hare, a partridge or any other description of game, a few wild asses excepted (but they are not game), since entering the inhabited portion of Tibet. Birds are also very scarce, I have only noticed wild pigeons and they in small numbers.*

The food of the people of Tibet met with on this journey consists of mutton, fresh or dried, tea, butter, *tsamba*, *chura* (not known, however, in Jyadé), *ti* (a mixture of butter, sugar and chura, also unknown or very little used in Jyadé), *djo* or *tarak* (sour milk), *pima* or cream cheese, *chuoma* (also called *droma*),† fresh and dried mushrooms (*shara*), wheaten cakes (*palé*), *nä-chang* and arrak. Rice is occasionally used by the rich in Jyadé, who eat it sweetened and with butter, or else it is boiled in milk.

August 10.—It was raining fast when we started this morning and travel was very difficult and in many places dangerous, as the trail led along the steep flanks of the mountains and in many places on the brink of precipices three or four hundred feet deep.

We skirted the base of a limestone range (apparently the same formation we have been seeing since coming to the Nashé ch'u), the little rivulets which flow down from its flanks emptying in all probability into the I ch'u now far south of our route. The ascent of the Médo la was very gradual, but the descent on the eastern side very precipitous and slippery. It brought us to the Ch'am ch'u, another good-sized river which empties into the I ch'u. Beyond this river the hillsides facing east were everywhere covered with rhubarb plants in full bloom or going to seed. None of the plants were over five feet high including the flower, which was frequently six or eight inches long.

From the Ch'am ch'u we took a general southeasterly direction over a very rough country where we saw but few Drupa, until we finally came in sight of the I ch'u, a fine river flowing in a broad valley in a due east to west direction for about twelve miles, but taking a southerly or southwesterly bend at the point where we had come on to it.

We camped in the I ch'u valley on the bank of a little stream which issues out of the mountains to the north. A large party of Golok and Amdo pilgrims on their way home from Lh'asa met us

* On the fauna and the butterflies of Tibet, see H. Bower, *op. cit.*, 115.

† Bonvalot (*op. cit.*, 344) speaks of chuoma, but calls it *niouma*.

here, and I had to give a tanka to each to silence their incessant cries of *Suru, suru, kutsé ré, suru Pönbo la* ("Charity, Charity, sir"), a call which neither the Namru nor the Jyadé people have accustomed me to.

August 11.—We have now struck the ja-lam or "tea-route" which comes down the I ch'u valley, and parallel to which we have been traveling ever since leaving the Dang ch'u. It is a much traveled and well beaten highway, and crosses the river in front of a little Bönbo lamasery about two miles above where we camped last night.

The I ch'u was much swollen by the incessant rains and so deep at the ford that Anyang, who led the way, had to swim his horse and his little mule that always follows him about like a dog, got its load soaked. We stayed on the right bank of the river for a few miles more, and finally came to a better ford where the water was about four feet deep.

Little more than two miles beyond where we crossed the river we came to where its main branch issues out of the mountains to the north, and as far up its course as I could trace it, it flowed in a south-southwest direction. We continued up the valley of the eastern branch of the river, the road running most of the way along the slippery, steep sides of the mountains, four hundred or five hundred feet above the stream; on our left was a high range of bare, slate and red sandstone mountains, whose peaks rose 3,000 to 3,500 feet above the river.

By a hardly perceptible ascent we reached the head of the valley, and passing into that of Angé lung (or nong), camped near some tents, high up on the side of the mountains at whose base flows a brook emptying, I learnt, into the Rama ch'u, a few miles to the east of us.

Drupa are very numerous in the Angé lung; within three or four miles I counted about forty. From where we have camped I can see to the east the dark black Ramnong gangri, its upper part covered with eternal snow.* It is a striking landmark. Facing us on the south is the eastern end of the range which we

* Gang ri (*gangs ri*) means "ice mountains." Though I speak of the Ramnong ri as a separate *massif*, divided by the valley of the Rama ch'u from the mountains south of Ange lung and the I ch'u, it is really but a continuation of it, a section of one long chain.

skirted in the I ch'u valley; it here reaches to a greater height than along that valley, and a few miles east of our camp its summits are covered with snow.

Though we have been traveling constantly among Bönbos since entering Jyadé, I have not been able to detect any very marked peculiarities in their religious usages. The names of their gods, Ch'üjong and Yidam (guardian and patron divinities) are peculiar to them; they turn their prayer wheels and walk around sacred monuments from right to left. They make *tsa-tsa*, raise *mani* walls and incise prayers on stones like the lamaists, though in the case of *mani* stones they more frequently cut on them the formula *Om, matri muyê salé** *hdu* than *Om mani padmé, hum*. They make, however, pilgrimages to Lh'asa and the sacred places of Tibet, their priests shave their heads, and their gombas are architecturally like those of the orthodox church; the first, eighth, fifteenth and twenty-fourth of each moon are also their principal days of prayer.

We passed to-day several large tea caravans coming from Ch'amdo and going to Lh'asa; most of the pack animals were yaks, though there were quite a number of small mules. The caravan people looked like Horba, but I did not speak to them.

August 12.—Last night was clear and cold; the minimum thermometer fell to +20°. The sun shone brightly this morning and we spread all our belongings out to dry, and consequently started quite late. The Ramnong gangri looked most beautiful in the rays of the morning sun; this mountain appears to be the culminating point of the limestone range which we have been skirting for so many days.

Shortly before we left, a high Bönbo lama, who was stopping for a few days in one of the tents near which we were camped, came to our camp. Anyang, who is a brother (*géts-ul* or *gênyen*) of the Bönbo order, saluted him in a peculiar fashion, the like of which I have not heretofore seen. He kotowed three times, and then both of them crouched in front of each other and made their heads touch.

A few miles below camp we came to the timber line and found a number of stunted juniper trees growing on the hillsides, most of them on slopes facing eastward. Rhubarb was also very

* Bonvalot (*op. cit.*, 358) transcribes this formula "Ome ma té me ie sa le deu." On *tsa-tsa* and *mani* walls, see *Land of the Lamas*, 250, 257.

1

2

3

4

5

1. **Red earthenware teapot** (Lh'asa). (U. S. N. M. 167231 a.)

2. **Red earthenware teapot** (Lh'asa). (U. S. N. M. 167231 b.)

3. **Black earthenware teapot**, decorated with bits of chinaware, brass lid (Lit'ang). (U. S. N. M. 167231 c.)

4. **Wooden bowl** (Lit'ang). (U. S. N. M. 167230.)

5. **Copper teapot** (Dérgé). (U. S. N. M. 131038.)

abundant in spots similarly exposed. A mile or so farther on we came to the Rama ch'u which, at the ford, was three to four feet deep and one hundred and fifty feet wide. This river here enters a deep gorge for over a mile, and we skirted it high up on the mountain side, through what we all thought the most beautiful scenery we had ever seen, fresh as we were from nearly a year of desert travel. From the rocky sides of the snow-capped mountains, along the right bank of the river, the water came tumbling down in sheets of foam into the swift, clear river which dashed over the great rocks filling its bed; there were green trees and birds singing

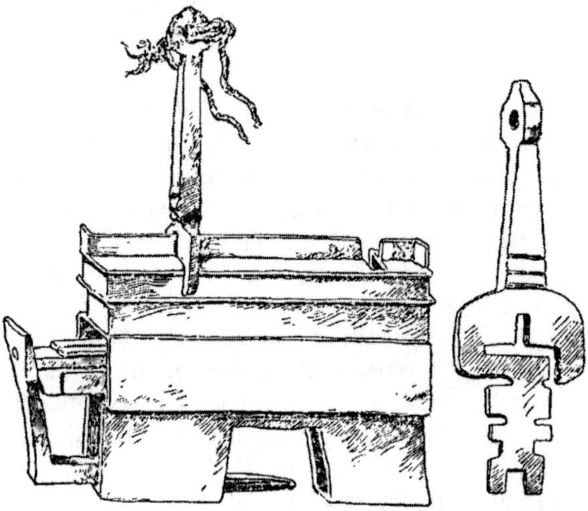

IRON PADLOCK (Lh'asa).

in their branches, and wild flowers, and beyond the end of the gorge we saw a few patches of barley enclosed within rough hedges or low walls of stone.

The valley beyond the gorge took a southeast direction around the base of the mountains and we followed it down to where the river again enters a gorge. Here the valley is called Yangamdo* (the last syllable pronounced *da*), and another stream,

* Capt. Bower calls the Rama ch'u the Lan chu. Yangamdo he calls Yangmando (camp 105). Leaving this point he followed a more roundabout way than I till our routes met again in the Batasumdo valley.

now nearly dry, coming from the western slope of the Ramnong ch'u, empties into the Rama. We camped at this spot where grazing was splendid and the river offered facilities for bathing not to be overlooked by such a way-stained traveler as I.

About half a mile from where we have camped there is a little Bönbo gomba; this and two or three little houses higher up the valley are the only permanent dwellings we have seen in the Rama lung.

Flies and mosquitoes have been quite troublesome to-day.

The people of Jyadé, when wishing to assert the truthfulness of a statement they have made, draw the thumb of the right hand down the middle of their faces and say "*Kon-ch'og sum*," "In the name of the Three Holies."

August 13.—We left the Rama ch'u a few miles below camp and crossed a very steep and rather high pass leading into the basin of the Ramnong ch'u. After going about twelve miles along a stream which has its source in the mountains we had just crossed, we came to the Ramnong ch'u itself, a large mountain torrent flowing in a general southerly direction with its sources in the Ramnong gangri.

On the sides of the mountains overlooking the Rama ch'u, we passed a number of women picking *ramba*, the seeds of which, when dried and ground, are mixed with tsamba and eaten, and this adds one more to the very small list of native dishes. These women told me that it was *jimbo, jimbo rê*, "very, very good," but they are not hard to please.*

Not far below the summit of the pass we came to little cultivated patches of ground, each surrounded with a fence of brush or of poles; a few of the latter were, by the way, spruce saplings, yet I did not notice any of this species of tree growing, but suppose they must be found in neighboring gorges. Near each little field was a small stone house, usually of two stories, a room on each floor; most of them were closed, I suppose the people at this season of the year are living higher up the valleys with their

* Ramba is *Polygonum viviparum*, Linn. See Appendix. Jaeschke, *Tib. Engl. Dict.*, s. v. *Ram-bu* says that Ram-bu or *na-ram* is *Polygonum viviparum*. *Rampa*, he says (*s. v.*) is "quick- (*quitch*) grass."

flocks and herds. We saw several small fields of turnips (*yoma*),* and we could not resist the temptation of stealing a few ; and this evening I have eaten them, tops and all, the first dish of vegetables I have tasted this year. Anyang says there is a better variety of turnips, called *la-pi* (the Chinese *lo-po*), grown in the valleys of lesser altitude, also cabbages (*pé-tsé*).

Just as we came to the confluence of the stream we have been following down from the pass with the Ramnong ch'u, we met a very large tea caravan. It belonged to Ch'amdo men and they were bound for Lh'asa; there were between six hundred and eight hundred yaks in it.

We camped on the banks of the Ramnong ch'u and received many visitors with whom I did a little trading, buying a quantity of excellent musk for twelve rupees a pod. The district in which we now are is called Géla and, together with Angnong (or lung), where we camped on the eleventh, belongs to Lh'asa. The reason for this is that the people in these two districts belong, not to the Bönbo persuasion, but to the Gélug or orthodox lamaist sect of Lh'asa, and have therefore naturally sought and obtained Lh'asan protection.

The mountain sides all along the route to-day were tolerably well covered with stunted juniper trees and the grazing was everywhere wonderfully good, considering the number of yaks and other animals constantly feeding here.

Anyang told me that throughout Jyadé and Lh'asa polyandry exists, and that it is quite common for brothers, no matter how many they may be, to have only one wife.†

August 14.—After following up the Ramnong ch'u for a couple of miles we ascended a side valley which led up to a rather high

* *Yoma* is known to the Chinese as *chieh-tsai*, which term applies also to the mustard plant. Jaeschke gives the names for turnips as *nyung-ma* and adds that "in writing and speaking this word is often confounded with *yungs*, 'mustard,' so that *e. g.*, *yungs-ma* is said for turnips instead of *nyung-ma*, *nyung-dkar* for white mustard instead of *yungs-dkar*." The confusion consequently exists in both languages.

† Conf. Bower, *op. cit.*, 65, Bonvalot, *op. cit.*, 354 et seq. I think the latter writer is wrong in assuming that several men, not brothers, have the same *wife*. The practice of having one concubine (*chyimi*) among several men is common enough, however, among traders both in Tibet and in the Ts'aidam. See also on Tibetan polyandry, *Land of the Lamas*, 211 et seq.

pass, crossing which we descended to the Batasumdo valley. This latter valley is a very wide one for this region, probably not less than half a mile in width where we crossed it. Three good-sized streams meet here and empty into the Po ch'u which comes from the east.* The river below the point where it receives these streams bears the name of Batasumdo ch'u, though Po ch'u would be a better one.

In the Batasumdo valley I saw several little hamlets ; the valley to the north is closed by a huge mass of absolutely bare rocks, rising to above the snow line, and forming an eastern extension of the Ramnong gangri. We ascended the Po ch'u for a few miles, the river flowing in a deep gorge of slate, of which rock the country hereabout is principally formed—the trail in places overhanging the river four hundred or five hundred feet high.

We camped on a steep hillside near some black tents, where we bought a quantity of delicious *djo*, a delicacy we never can get enough of. This part of the valley is called Po laga or Po latsa. All over the rocks around our camp clematis is in bloom, its large yellow flowers the finest we have seen on the journey.

The women in the Po ch'u valley have a coiffure which differs slightly from that worn anywhere else. Instead of the broad band of red, green, and black stuff covered with beads and silver ornaments attached to the plaits of hair and hanging down the middle of the back, they run all the shorter plaits from a little below their shoulders, into one big Chinese queue, reaching to the ground, and this they cover with coral and turquoise beads. They also wear earrings, an ornament not seen by me on the women to the west of this place, though they may be worn there, for I never saw any women with their finest apparel on.

August 15.—We did nothing to-day but go up and down, crossing four high passes, the Po la, Drohé la, Noshé la and Ma la, and the descent from the Ma la was very steep and rough. The valleys, or rather gorges, along which our route led were between mountains of red sandstone on our left, and of slate and schists on our right, the latter rising 2,000 or 3,000 feet above the bottom of the valleys.

* Bonvalot, *op. cit.*, 346, gives this valley its right name, Bata-Soumdo, but Bower (*op. cit.*, 60) calls it Pata Samdo and says "it is situated on the banks of the Mo chu."

From the summits of the Po la and Drohé la, on what I took for an eastern continuation of the Ramnong gangri chain and to the east of the peaks at the head of Batasumdo, I saw vast snow fields and several snow-covered peaks; the range in which they were ran a little south of east.

From the summit of the Ma la we saw green fields and fortress-like hamlets in a broad valley running southward, a wide, swift river, beating against the foot of the rocks on which these buildings stand. This is the Séremdo ch'u valley,* and the river is, according to Anyang, an affluent of the Su ch'u.

We camped near some black tents, at a placed called Churéma, several miles before reaching the cultivated part of the valley. Speaking of black tents, it is interesting to note that the people use the word *Drupa*, which properly only applies to the persons inhabiting such abodes and leading pastoral lives, to designate the dwelling, the black yak-hair tent itself, or even more correctly the word seems to have the sense of "home, dwelling." Thus they say *Na drupa-la drogi-ré*, "I am going to my tent, I am going home."

Anyang is most careful not to eat any but the food he prepares himself, he will not even use his tea churn after us until it has been well washed. I cannot believe he is afraid of our poisoning him, though he eats and drinks with other natives; it may possibly be on account of his being a Bönbo lama, yet I do not see what that has got to do with it.

For the last few days all the people from whom we have wished to buy anything have invariably asked for cotton wool in exchange for their wares. They use it for making matches for their guns and for wicks in their butter lamps, they prefer it to buttons or any of the other knickknacks we have.

In the low valleys (*i. e.*, below 13,000 feet above sea level) half breed yaks (*dzo*) and domestic cattle (*ba-lang*) are quite numerous, whereas in the country above that level I have seen none, and suppose the climate is too severe for them. Even at this lower elevation the nights are very cold, the thermometer falling every night to 8° or 10° below the freezing point. I am surprised to

* Bonvalot's Séré-Soumdo, Bower's Sari Samdo or Samdu. The latter writer calls the Séremdo ch'u the Sa ch'u. See Bower, *op. cit.*, 61. He calls the little stream which flows from the Ma la into the Séremdo ch'u the Lachu. On d'Anville's *Carte Genle du Thibet* this river is called Seri Samtou.

find that barley and turnips can stand such an amount of cold and have time to ripen at all.

I have frequently spoken to Tibetans about the great river which flows eastward, passing by Shigatsé and south of Lh'asa. They all call it the Tsang-gi tsangpo, "The river of Tsang" (*i. e.*, Ulterior Tibet). No one knows of any other name for it, and it is quite as good a one as Yaru tsangpo, by which we usually speak of it, and which only means "The river from up-country."

August 16.—Last night thieves sneaked into camp at about 10.30 P. M. It was very dark and we have no dogs—I gave them to the Namru fearing their fierceness in thickly settled districts. They stole the Lao-han's saddle from under his head. The clatter of the stirrup-irons on the ground as they dragged it along wakened me, and running out I fired off my revolver twice; I feared they had stolen the ponies, which were picketed at some distance from the tent. We finally found the horses; they had not been touched, and one of the men stumbled over the saddle which the thieves had probably dropped when I fired the revolver. We all slept with only one eye closed for the rest of the night, but we were not troubled again.

As we advance eastward, the people grow more and more importunate in begging; the best dressed among them are not ashamed to ask for charity; "*Suru kutsé-ré, Pönbo Rinpoché,*" ("Charity, please your Excellency,") is a cry we now incessantly hear. The lamas and ani who beg are less objectionable, though equally persistent. They come and squat down beside the fire, but at a respectful distance, ask for nothing, but stay there mumbling their prayers till they have received some food or money. You cannot drive them away; they stay till they shame you into giving them something, but they are content with little, while the others cannot be satisfied, the more you give, the more they want.

Following the valley down a couple of miles we came to the Séremdo ch'u, which appeared to issue out of the flanks of a great *massif* of bare and snow-covered mountains to the north, which we saw indistinctly through the clouds and mist which hung over them, filling the upper part of the valley. The valley for a few miles below where we came on it was quite broad, the hillsides dotted with numerous hamlets and the soil everywhere cultivated, barley and wheat nearly ripe, some of it already on the scaffolds on the tops of the houses where the sheaves of grain are put to dry.

We crossed the river by a rope, in the same manner as we had the Su ch'u; the horses and mules reached the farther bank very much worn out from swimming across the rapid stream. We met here a large party of Chinese traders from Lh'asa on their way back to that place; they said that they usually followed this route as it was much easier than the high road, and grazing was better along it. They said it would take me forty days to reach Ta-chien-lu. Here again I heard that two foreigners had reached Ta-chien-lu in the early part of the year after having crossed Tibet; the traders volunteered the information that they were Americans, but I think that in this particular they drew on their imaginations.

About a mile below the ferry we came to the mouth of the Ru ch'u, a good-sized stream flowing down a valley trending east-southeast. The road led up this valley, which we found to be well cultivated and thickly peopled, most of the houses standing detached in the midst of well-fenced fields. The mountains on either side of this valley rise some 2500 to 3000 feet above the river bed, and to the north, beyond the range which borders the river, is another parallel range, probably 4000 feet high. We have so far not seen a range of mountains in this country trending in any other direction than east and west.

After traveling a few miles up the Ru ch'u we camped at a place called Sagotong where there was a good-sized farm house, the people of which let us put up our tent inside their fence at the base of a big boulder. Just opposite us, high up on a bluff on the left bank of the river, is a small gomba called Trashi-ling.* It belongs to the Gélug-pa sect, and is governed by a lama sent from Lh'asa, and who is changed every two years. Probably the country south of this river belongs to Lh'asa, but I can hear nothing definite on the subject. Déba djong is in the habit of establishing its authority in a country by founding in the first place a lamasery or two in it, the abbots of which gradually gain the people over to the yellow church, and so finally the local Pönbo

* Bonvalot's Tachiline (*op. cit.*, 366). His road led along the south side of the Ru ch'u. He says that the gomba has two hundred akas. Bower also camped on the south side of the river beside the lamasery, which he calls (*op. cit.*, 64) Tashiling.

"ties his head" to Lh'asa, and the abbot becomes civil as well as religious ruler.

The women on the Ru ch'u wear earrings similar to those worn in the Ts'aidam (*i. e.*, a large hoop of silver with three stones set in heart shape on a small plate of silver and fixed on it); most of those I have seen have earrings in both ears, but not of the same pattern.

August 17.—A few miles east of where we camped last night we came to a bend in the valley and found out that the Ru ch'u comes from the north, probably from the same chain of mountains out of which the Séremdo ch'u issues. It is more than likely that both these streams, and nearly all the water courses of Tibet present the same peculiarity, have their heads on the farther sides of the mountains from which they flow.

We crossed the river by a rickety wooden bridge of the Tibetan cantilever description, and after passing a large Bönbo lamasery in which live some two hundred lamas, we crossed by a very easy ascent the Chung-nyi la,* and entered another valley trending east-southeast. Anyang told me that we were here in the valley of the Zé ch'u, or Zu ch'u, or Zom ch'u, for it has these three names.

In the upper part of the valley down which we traveled this afternoon we only saw black tents, herds of yaks and flocks of sheep and goats, while the Ru ch'u valley, which we had just left, and which cannot be more than five hundred feet lower than it, is as closely cultivated as a Swiss valley. By the way, the flat roofs, very broad for such small inside accommodation as these houses offer, the rough stone walls and pig-sty condition of these houses remind one of the farm houses in some parts of Switzerland, especially around the Italian lakes, and in the Ticino.

We camped at the mouth of a little gorge opening onto the main valley, at a place called Biwakanag, a mile or so above where the Rongwa or cultivated country begins. We have had a hard day's work, yet, notwithstanding the lameness of the mules, we have ridden twenty-three miles.

Anyang told me that the present political organization of the Jyadé dates back ever so long ago, from the time when the Great Emperor (*Gong-ma ch'en-po*) interfered in the affairs of Tibet to

* Bower's Chuni la. He calls the Zé ch'u the Kom cho. He made one march from Trashiling to Chebo tenchin.

make peace between Déba djong and the Bönbo-inhabited country. I suppose he has in mind the Chinese expedition to Tibet in 1719. Orthodox countries, Anyang and all Bönbo generally call Pen-dé or Ch'ü dé, and Bönbo countries Bön dé.* I am also told that the Bönbo have incarnate lamas. This sect interests me greatly, but it is very difficult to learn much about it, as the Tibetan people, both the Bönbo and the orthodox ones, are adverse to talking about religious questions, and they furthermore, the head lamas possibly excepted, know little about them. The great extension of the Bönbo faith, has not, I think, been fully realized heretofore; from what I have learned on this journey, it is found in all Tibetan countries, exclusive of some districts governed by Lh'asa, in which country it is, or was until recently, persecuted. Along the Chinese frontier from the Koko-nor to Ta-chien-lu, the Ts'arong and A-tun-tzŭ it is flourishing,

When on the Po ch'u I was joined by a little Amdo lama on his way back to his country from a two years' pilgrimage to Central Tibet. He asked me to put his little load, tied to his *k'ur-shing*, on one of the mules, and as he walked along beside us he made himself so pleasant that we quickly took a fancy to him, and I asked him to go to Ta-chien-lu with me. He was delighted with the offer; he can now travel swiftly on without having to beg, and will have plenty to eat and drink. We have not seen a caravan in the country without a few such pilgrims attached to it; every one thinks it will insure good luck to help them on their way.

August 18.—It rained all night, and this morning the road was so muddy and slippery that we had to go most of the way on foot, leading our worn out ponies. The valley ran in a general east-southeast direction; an immense amount of *débris* has been swept down into it from the mountains on the north side, in places reaching a depth of one hundred to one hundred and fifty feet.

* A—— K—— says "Buddhism is the religion of the country; there are two sects, one named Nangba and the other Chiba or Baimbu." *Explorations made by A—— K——*, 34. *Nangba* means "Esoteric," *Chiba* (*p'yi-ba*), "Exoteric," and *Baimbu* is Bönbo. Capt. Bower (*op. cit.*, 62) has it that "Tibet is a good deal split up amongst these rival sects of Panboo and Pindah. * * * There is a good deal of rivalry and bad feeling between these two sects." From the mode of circumambulating followed by his Panboo (*loc. cit.*), it appears that they are Bönbos. The word "Pindah" looks remarkably like Bön dé, but Bower must use it to designate the orthodox sect or Ch'ü dé, the meaning I was told it had.

Even in the more favored spots of the Rongwa the huge piles of stones heaped up in every field corner testify to its stony nature, and show the immense amount of work that farming requires in this country.

About a mile and a half below our camp of last night we came to a village which marks the upper limit of cultivation in this valley, and from this point on fields of barley and turnips, farm houses and hamlets of ten or more houses were constantly passed. We forded the Zé ch'u a little above the big village of Ten-chin (or Chyi-bo Ten chin), the chief village of Kar Pai-hu, and near which is a large Bönbo lamasery with some four hundred or five hundred akas. We were now in Nar Pai-hu,* the home of my good friend, the Déba Nor jyal-ts'an.

After passing through a number of hamlets surrounded by fields of barley, we came to a little valley at the foot of a steep cliff on the top of which is perched the village of Lah'a,† the capital of the Nar district, but a great deal smaller than Ten-chin. Anyang had reached his home. Leaving us in the care of the headman of the village, he went off to his own house, a few miles up a side valley which opens onto the Zé ch'u at this point. He will be back to-morrow with a fresh pony for himself, and possibly one or two to exchange for some of mine, which are no longer able to put one foot before the other.

The people are very friendly; men, women and children do all in their power to be of service to me, bringing me fuel, water, *sho*, and milk.‡ They tell me that I am camped on the very spot where a few months before two foreigners camped. One of these p'yling had a light beard and both were young men; they had a great many horses, an interpreter (*lotsa*), and were eight men all told.

Towards evening a man from Kar Pai-hu' dressed up in all his finest apparel, wearing a splendid earring, lots of rings and a big

* Bower places Nar (his Naru) on the north side of the river, and Kar (his Karu) on the south side. He is wrong. Bonvalot (*op. cit.*, 367) speaks of the rivalry existing between Tchimbo-Tingi and Tchimbo-Nara.

† Khemo Tinchin of Bower.

‡ Capt. Bower's experience with these people does not appear to have been as agreeable as mine. See *op. cit.*, 65. Bonvalot also had a row a little lower down the valley because the people, not being willing to sell him a sheep, he tried "de nous procurer de la viande sans permission" (*op. cit.*, 368). I cannot but think the people were justified in what they did.

Chinese straw hat, rode up, and getting off his horse came into my tent. He took out a k'atag, laid one end of it on my table the other on the ground, placed a tanka on it as a present, and then, seeing that no one was looking, handed me a very soiled piece of foolscap and asked me to read what was written on it. It was in English and said that the bearer had supplied transport, fodder and grain to Captain H. Bower, 17th Bengal Cavalry, and was dated at Tinring (Ten chin?), 17th December, 1891.

This then is the leader of the party of foreigners whom I have so frequently heard mentioned. I suppose he came from Kashgaria to near the northwest corner of the Tengri nor, thence to north of Nagch'uk'a where he took the Ja lam as far as the Séremdo ch'u, from which point he must have followed the same road I have. I heard when at Sagot'ong that foreigners had stopped at the Thrashiling gomba, so they probably did not come up the Ru ch'u valley but crossed the Séremdo ch'u some eight or ten miles below where I did.

When I had told this man, whose name was Tamé-wang-den, the meaning of the note, he asked me to write something on the same page, and I satisfied him; but I hope the next traveler who comes this way will not translate to him what I said. I then gave him a rupee as a return present, and seeing that I wanted neither horses nor any thing from him, he took his departure.

I heard that there is a rough trail leading directly from Mér djong to Bat'ang without passing through Ch'amdo, and I will endeavor to follow it, for if I keep to the highroad I will be wasting time, as I suppose Captain Bower has already surveyed it.

To-day a dwarf came to my camp; he is the first one I have seen in Tibet. He was about three feet four inches high, well shaped, with a good clear voice, not at all sharp. He would not tell his age, or rather he said he did not know it, but I took him to be between thirty and thirty-five years old. I also saw a woman near Ten-chin with a small goitre.* I have watched most carefully for evidences of this disease, but have seen none before to-day.

*In a well known Tibetan work by the famous Saskya Pandita, but originally written in Sanskrit with the title *Subhashita ratna nidhi*, occurs the following:

"They who misuse their talents,
Despise those who use them aright;
In certain countries to be without a goitre (*Lba-wa*)
Is held to be a deformity."

August 19.—I bought a number of things from Poyul, a lance, red peppers, blankets and excellent flour. The best style of workmanship I have seen in Tibet is that of Po-mä or Lower Poyul. I learned that there is a road leading there from Nar Pai-hu and passing through Shobando.* It takes about fifteen days to get there, and from what I can gather it must be a well settled, prosperous place, considerably warmer than any part of Tibet I have seen. The iron work and silverware of Po-mä are famous, as are also the horses of that country, whose hoofs, I am told, are so hard that months of constant work in the roughest country will not wear them out.† Bamboo appears to be extensively used in Po-mä; a long joint of it covered over with red and white wickerwork and used as a vessel for keeping *nä-ch'ang* in, was

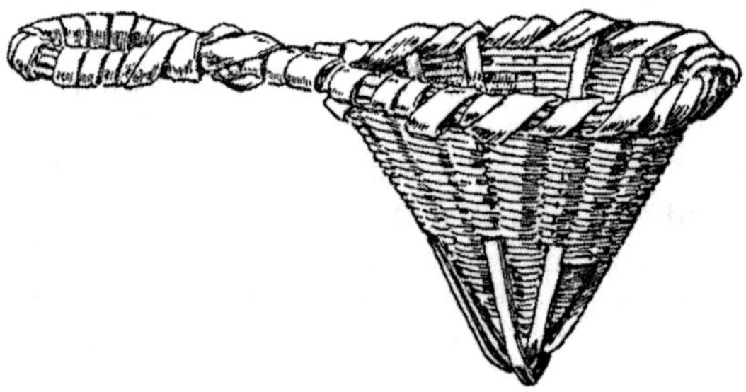

BAMBOO TEA-STRAINER.
(Ch'amdo.)

brought me for sale. The earthenware teapots used throughout the Jaydé country are nicely made and of three or four patterns. A small pot is used to infuse tea in, "to make stock" as cooks, I believe, would call it. A quantity of tea is put in it, together with a little soda, and it is allowed to simmer until all the strength of the tea is extracted. A little of this concentrated tea is added to each kettle of fresh tea when boiled.

Anyang came back early this morning, and brought me a sheep, some butter and tsamba as a present. With him came a man who had a couple of small ponies, which I finally took in exchange

*On Poyul and especially Po-mä, see under date *October 5th*.

† "The Embassy which had left Nipal in 1852 for Peking with the quinquennial tribute from the Nipalese to the Chinese government, arrived at Balaji. * * They brought back with them about one hundred China and Pumi ponies." H. A. Oldfield, *Sketches from Nipal*, I, 411.

for two of mine, though the new ones will certainly not be able to go farther than Ch'amdo. Anyang said that he heard last night that there were four foreigners in Capt. Bower's party and eight servants. One of the servants spoke Tibetan, and there was also a Mongol and a Chinaman with him.

We left at about nine o'clock and followed the right bank of the river for nearly five and one-half miles till we came to a bridge, about a mile west of the Bönbo gomba of Gunégon.* Crossing the river we took a trail along the flank of the mountains, here of red sandstone and sandstone conglomerate, and some 1500 to 2000 feet above the river. We have camped in a nook in the hills about one and one-half miles above Péné ringu. Below us and near the river bank we can see numerous villages; near each of them is a small gomba.

The country along the right bank of the Zé ch'u from the bridge at Gunégon eastward is part of the Lh'o-rong district and under Déba djong rule. A trail runs along the Lh'o-rong djong side of the river, but is very rough and being on Lh'asa soil, is not usually followed by Jyadé people.

Along the bank of the Zé ch'u I noticed to-day some men gathering from a briar bush what looked like small yellow gooseberries.† On inquiry I was told that a dye was extracted from the fruit. A little below Lah'a I saw a field of peas in flower, the first we have met with. At Gunégon all the lamas were reading prayers and drinking tea on a hilltop, while the people were ploughing the surrounding fields. The women wore a peculiar form of ornament on their hair, a disk of silver set with turquoises on the forehead, and a cap of silver of the same style just covering the crown. It resembled somewhat the ornament worn by the women in the Horba‡ and Lit'ang countries, but I have seen nothing like it on this journey.

---

* Bower (p. 65) calls this picturesque lamasery Baru, and Khembo Baru on his map. He and Bonvalot followed the bottom of the valley until near Mer djong, when they crossed the river by a bridge and took a road to Riwoché more direct, I think, than the one I followed.

† Prjevalsky *Mongolia*, II, 79, mentions a "gooseberry (*Ribes* sp.) in large bushes ten feet high, with big yellowish bitter berries," growing in the border land of Western Kan-su.

‡ See *Land of the Lamas*, 244.

Anyang says he has taken us by this little used trail so as to keep out of the way of the people who are not to be relied upon, are quarrelsome and great thieves.*

August 20.—We left at a very early hour, for we wanted to reach Mer djong gomba before night, and continued in an east-southeast direction along the flank of the mountains. Some eight miles east of our camp of last night, the Zé ch'u turns south and enters a narrow gorge, the rocks on either side rising nearly vertically 2000 or 3000 feet. I noticed that in this range south of the Zé ch'u the strata were parallel to the axis of the range (west-northwest and east-southeast) with a nearly vertical dip. They appeared to me to be of limestone formation.

We descended very gradually as we advanced and finally came in view of Mer djong, the great emporium of which we have for the last month or so heard so much. It was a great disappointment; a few low, mud buildings around a central court in which grew one good-sized poplar was all there was of this great center of trade, where we had been told time after time that we could buy everything we wanted. About fifty Akas of the Gélupa sect, an abbot, who is also governor of the district (*Djong-pön*), and a few *miser* composed the population of the place.

We camped about two hundred yards east of the gomba and near a large pool of water. The river† is at least six hundred feet lower than the Djong and is not visible from it; I hear that there is a bridge over it at the foot of the slope on which Mer djong stands. Looking southwestward I can see a zigzag trail winding up the very steep and rugged mountain side; it leads to Lh'o-rong and Shobando, while to the eastward we can distinguish another trail leading over some hills,‡ this is, I am told, the main road to Ch'amdo. As the country south of here is Lh'asa, not Ch'amdo territory, I suppose I will not be allowed to take the latter road.

I nearly omitted noting that about seven miles west of Mer djong in a little side valley down which flows a pretty brook, we

* Probably he had in mind the rows of Bonvalot and Bower when passing along this way.

† Capt. Bower calls it the Tasichu and Bonvalot Ta-tchou. The former makes no reference of Mer djong, only mentions its name (Maru). Bonvalot (*op. cit.*, 372) appears to refer to it, but calls it Tchoungo.

‡ It was followed by both Bonvalot and Bower. It crosses the Nam la.

crossed the direct Riwoché road. It goes over the hills at the eastern end of this little valley without passing by Mer djong. This valley, by the way, marks the boundary between Jyadé and Ch'amdo, between Lamaism and Bönboism.

The country all around Mer djong is well cultivated; barley, a little wheat, cabbages, onions, peas and turnips, are the principal crops. I noticed very few cattle and no sheep.

We find everything extremely dear at the gomba; we had to pay a tanka for a few sticks of cedar for fuel; there was no milk to be had, and ch'ang was as dear as firewood. Since the 14th it has rained every evening and usually during the night, and though I have been on the watch for a bit of clear sky to get a few observations, and have been up at all hours of the night, I have failed to see a patch of blue sky as big as my hat. Since reaching the inhabited parts of the country I have given up drawing, writing or taking observations in the day time, it causes too much comment, and I do not want to create undue suspicion.

August 21.—The Djong-pön called Anyang to his house early this morning and told him that I must not take the highroad, it passed on Déba djong territory and he might get in trouble if he allowed me to follow it. He said there were three or four other roads leading to Ch'amdo, and that I could follow any one of them. I sent him word that so long as I did not take the one followed by Capt. Bower I did not care, all I asked him for was a guide. He promptly sent a man who will take me a day's journey on my way, and then find me guides to Riwoché, or Roché, as the name is locally pronounced.

I gave Anyang fifty rupees and as many presents as I could spare, and we saw the good fellow get on his horse and leave us with deep regret, so much had he endeared himself to all of us. He and his master, Nor jyal-ts'an, will always be remembered by us as the best friends we ever had in Tibet, with the exception always of the good old K'amba chief Nyamts'o Purdung, who helped me on my first journey.

Just as we were leaving Mer djong three men came out of the Djong wearing the heaviest kind of cangue (*tsego*) and loaded down with chains big enough to hold an elephant, and begged us for a little tsamba. I thought they must be criminals of the worst description, but learned that they had done nothing worse than break the severe game laws which prohibit throughout many districts of Tibet, the killing of animals. These poor fellows had shot deer and were paying with three or four months of this degrading punishment for their crime. The cangue has been introduced into Tibet by the Chinese, and has become a favorite mode of punishment throughout the country, but it is a much heavier arrangement here than is usually seen in China.

Crossing a good-sized stream coming down from the north we took a general northeast course over two high mountains, the second, called the Nanyi la, especially trying, as it was one mass of broken rock over which even the mules had a very hard time picking their way. We made, however, about nineteen miles and camped in a valley called Pomundo, its head a couple of miles to our east. A small stream flows down it and, turning north at the point where we have camped, empties, I am told, into the Ké ch'u, a big river which we will reach to-morrow.

We are here again in Jyadé, and the chief of the district is known as the Huchésha Pönbo. There are ten or twelve black tents near our camp, and we can see more farther up the valley. Two men came from one of the tents and volunteered to guide us to Riwoché in two days for a rupee apiece a day. They say that the country between here and that town is uninhabited, and that Chakba (brigands) infest the Zé ch'u valley. From what they tell me I fear that the road is a very bad one, but I expect we have seen as bad before; I have still to see a good road in Tibet.

It rained a little this morning, but a northerly breeze sprang up towards evening, and for the first time since the 14th, the sky to-night is perfectly clear.

When Tibetans, whether they be lamaists or Bönbo, pass by a *labsté* on a mountain top, they usually hang a bit of rag on one of the twigs stuck up in the pile of stones, throw a stone on the pile and shout at the top of their voices, "*Lh'a jya-lo, lh'a jya-lo, oh, oh, oh!*" I have been told that this means "A hundred years, Spirit (of the mountain), a hundred years, Spirit (of the mountain)," by which "grant me a hundred years" is meant.* Bönbo, of course walk by the labsté keeping it on their left side.

August 22.—Though the Pomundo valley, which we followed up to its head this morning, is not over three miles long, I counted

* It is also interpreted by some persons as meaning "Victory to the gods" (*Lh'a rgyal lo*).

twenty-two black tents in it. Supposing four persons to a tent (usually there are six or eight), this gives a very respectable population for a grazing country. The head of this valley marks in this direction the boundary between Jyadé and Lh'asa (Riwoché). We found a few tents on the east side of the pass, but lower down the valley was deserted, though it is one of the finest grazing countries I have seen. The people fear the brigands (*chakba*) and thieves (*komang*), and abandon this rich valley to them and to the inmates of a little lamasery.

After riding about eight miles, we came to the Ké ch'u,* a clear and swift, though shallow, river coming from the west and flowing in an east-northeast direction. We camped about five miles down the stream on a grassy flat near its bank. The mountain sides begin at this point to be covered with firs, pines and junipers, but the upper part of this forest growth is dead; nothing but black trunks mark the altitude to which it extended but a short while ago, and as well as I could make out, fire has not destroyed these trees. Rhubarb again became plentiful and very luxuriant; I had not seen any since leaving the Po ch'u.

It was early when we reached camp, so we were able to take a swim in the river, though the current was so rapid that we got banged against the rocks a good deal and bruised our feet on the pebbles in its bed. This river, I hear, flows into the one which passes by Riwoché, which is frequently called Ro ch'u, though its name is the Tsé or Zé ch'u. There are Chinese traders, it appears, at Riwoché, where we will arrive to-morrow; at last we will get something to eat besides tea, tsamba and mutton, on which we have been living for so long. Chinese are fond of good eating, and wherever they live they manage to raise some vegetables or to bring some delicacy from China.

To-day has been without rain; last night we had a very heavy frost; this evening the sky is beautifully clear. The guides and men insist that brigands are lurking about; we saw three or four men up a side cañon as we came down the valley, so I and the

* Bower's Kichi and Bonvalot's Sétchou (*op. cit.*, 375). The latter writer (p. 377) makes this river, or one of the same name, to flow by Riwoché. Bower, by the way, does not mention the Ro ch'u. The *Wei Ts'ang t'u chih* (*Journ. Roy. Asiat. Soc.*, n. s. XXIII. 252) calls the Ro ch'u Tzŭ chu ho, and says that lower down it becomes the Ang chu, by which is to be understood that it empties into the Om ch'u of Ch'amdo.

Hsien-sheng have been out—the night is very dark—and have fired off our guns a number of times at some distance from the camp. If the brigands are fools they may think we are keeping guard.

My little Amdo lama told me that when at Lh'asa he had seen the *Kurtamba* of the Nä-ch'ung gomba perform most wonderful tricks, such as cutting off his fingers, eating fire, etc., etc. The gomba had only one lama who could perform these feats. My lama also said that there was now only one elephant at Lh'asa, a present of the Sikkim Rajah, and kept in a stable at the foot of Potala. He had brought back with him some of its dung as a valuable curio. He also gave me a piece of painted cardboard from the *torma* which is burnt on the 29th day of the last month of the year outside the city as a sin-offering (*Kurim*).* This was also one of his much-prized treasures.

August 23.—Last night passed quietly; neither brigands nor thieves visited us. It is true I got up several times in the night and going to some distance from the camp fired three or four shots of my revolver, but I do not believe that brigands would take much trouble to attack such a poverty-stricken looking party.

A mile below camp the valley broadened for a few miles to the very respectable width—for this country—of a quarter of a mile. The mountains on the north side were covered with juniper trees and dense shrubbery, those on the other side of the valley with fine large firs.† There are a few patches of cultivated land here, and a solitary stone house, in front of the door of which, a lot of very rough and disreputable looking men were talking. My guides left me for a while to talk to them, but we rode rapidly by, as we did not at all like their looks.

Leaving the Ké ch'u a little below this spot—it enters here a gorge with vertical walls of rock on either side, and flows in a southeasterly direction—we rode up a narrow ravine and after a rather long and very stiff climb, reached the summit of the Dré la

* On the *kurim* ceremony, see *Land of the Lamas*, 113.

† Bonvalot and Bower came on to the Ké ch'u at this point, and from here to Riwoché we all followed the same road. Conf. Bower, *op. cit.*, 68, and Bonvalot, *op. cit.*, 375. The latter calls the Dré la the Djala and gives its height as 4,500 meters (14,760 feet). Bower made it 14,720 and I, 14,735. We have not often come so close to each other as this in estimating altitudes. Bower calls this pass Dojalala La.

where we came in view of the Tsé ch'u and Riwoché with its golden spired temple.

The slope on the eastern side of the pass for some distance down is covered with rhododendrons, called by the Chinese *tung chi'ng* or "winter green" (*i. e.*, evergreen), also with a laurel-leafed shrub, and a great variety of other bushes, whose names I do not know. Lower down, the mountain sides are thickly covered with fine firs, pines and junipers. In the valley bottom grow willows, which we had seen, for the first time on the journey, along the Ké ch'u, a little above the point where we left it. On both sides we found the Dré la composed of blackish slate and fine grained limestone, sharp loose bits of which played havoc with the horses' hoofs. We had to abandon one pony on the summit of the pass as he could not be made to take another step. Of course it was one of the best I had; the poor ones have a wonderful way of hanging on, they shirk their work, while the good ones go till they drop.

On the mountain sides as we descended from the Dré la, we saw great numbers of crassoptilons, called *saga* in Tibetan, their cry closely resembling that of our guinea fowl. They ran with great rapidity uphill through the brush, and though I got very near to some of them, they never flew.

Riwoché is built on the flat bottom of the Tsé ch'u* valley on the left bank of the river. It consists primarily of a lamasery, in which the most conspicuous building is a square temple, its exterior wall painted in vertical bands of black, red and white color, so that at a distance it seems to have a row of columns around it. It has also a small gold spire. Several other temples of smaller dimensions stand against the foot of the pine clad mountains which rise precipitously behind the lamasery. A village of straggling one-storied, flat roofed houses has grown up around the lamasery, or rather on its east side, and a mud wall about ten feet high and probably built by the Chinese in 1717, surrounds the lamasery and village. There is a Hutuketu ("living Buddha") residing here, and three hundred lamas of the Nyima or "red hat"

* The *Hsi-yü tung wen chih*, XXII, says that the Rtsi ch'u (which I take to be the same as the Tsé ch'u) becomes lower down its course the Lan-tsan chiang. This lacks confirmation. The same work makes mention of an A-rtsé ch'u, but I have been unable to locate it. On this important locality, Conf., *Journ. Roy. Asiat. Soc.*, n. s. XXIII, 55 and 251. On d'Anville's *Carte Genle du Thibet* Riwoché is called Ritaché.

sect. The district belongs to Lh'asa and is known to the Chinese as Lei-wu-chi.

The Tsé ch'u valley at the town is something over a mile broad, but higher up and a little lower down it narrows to a quarter of a mile or even considerably less. A bridge of logs, of the Tibetan cantilever type and of two spans, insures means of crossing the river at all seasons.

We camped on the right bank of the river about half a mile above the town, as our road follows the right bank of the river, and we thought it prudent not to venture closer to the town and its lamas. The Hsien-sheng went into it, however, in search of the Chinese traders reported to be there, but came back much disappointed, having learned that the last of them had left for Ch'amdo a few days ago. Nothing was to be bought in the way of clothing, of which we stood principally in need, and the lamas did not show themselves very friendly to him.

Among the many visitors who came to our camp this afternoon was a man who said he had been with Captain Bower from Mer djong to Ch'amdo; he spoke in the highest terms of his kindness and liberality. He said he went from Mer djong to Ch'amdo by the Waho la, so our routes have only been the same from the Séremdo ch'u to Mer djong.* A young boy, an itinerant singer and prayer-wheel grinder, also called on me, and amused me with his songs and talk; though only eighteen, he had wandered over most of Tibet, and what he did not know about the country was not worth knowing. I had to hire yaks to carry the baggage to the confluence of the Tsé ch'u and Ké ch'u, as the mules are too much worn out to be of any further use. If only we had shoes for them they might reach Bat'ang; as it is, I fear they will not even get as far as Ch'amdo.

August 24.—Last night thieves managed to cut the hair rope by which my pony was tied to my tent, not five feet from my head, and drove him away. I heard a slight noise in the night, jumped up and ran out of my tent, but saw nothing but a lean, yellow dog looking for bones near the dying embers of the camp fire.

Some men belonging to a caravan bound for Lh'asa came to my camp and said that ten of their mules had been stolen during

* This is not true, as Capt. Bower came to Riwoché.

TEMPLE AND TOWN OF RIWOCHE (LEI-WU-CHI).

the night, so I had at least the consolation of knowing that I was not the only sufferer. I fancy my guides had a hand in this job, for they insisted on my paying them yesterday evening, and left me towards dusk, saying that they would camp at the foot of the Dré la.

We left at eight o'clock, all the luggage loaded on the seven yaks hired yesterday. The road, for about ten miles, led through a dense pine forest which covered the mountains to their summits; many of the trees were two feet in diameter at the butt. The mountain rose precipitously from the river, and the road was in many places three hundred or four hundred feet above it, a narrow trail winding among the trees, against which the yaks bumped and tore the loads as they tried to push by each other to get the lead. The country reminded me of the valley of the Nya ch'u above Kanzé down which I traveled in 1889.

Descending to the valley bottom, which in places is quite a mile broad, we traveled in a southerly direction for about seven miles, and then camped on the bank of the river, at a place, or district, called Tartung.*

Though the valley appears fertile, there is hardly any cultivation or inhabitants; a few very small hamlets on or near the left bank, and two or three hovels on the right, are all I have noticed. I hear, however, that there are a great many black tents in the lateral valleys; I suppose the people try to get as far as possible from the highroad, where exacting officials frequently pass and the grazing is comparatively poor.

The forest growth on the left bank of the river is much thinner than on the right, where it descends to the valley bottom, on which there are large black thorns (*hei-tz'u*), willows and several kinds of shrubs. The river is very swift, in places from fifty to seventy-five yards wide and between six and seven feet deep. I noticed on the rocks along its bank watermarks six or seven feet above its present level, consequently the valley bottom must at times be flooded, and so the absence of cultivation is explained.

August 25.—We continued in a general south-southeast direction along the right bank of the river, the trail running most of the way along precipitous cliffs several hundred feet above the roaring and eddying stream. For part of the way we rode through

* Very near Bower's Gaima Thong.

dense woods of pines and cedars, and over rickety bridges of logs built out from the vertical face of the rock and resting on slender poles or large boulders. Such bridges the Chinese call *pien-tzŭ.**

Here and there we saw a little cultivation, and on the opposite side of the river a place was pointed out to me where iron ore was mined. We had not ridden many miles when I noticed on the hillside on the left bank two men riding towards us, one with a red cloth hood on his head, whom we at once concluded from this well known headdress must be a Chinese soldier. He rode forward, forded the river and riding up saluted me, and said that advice having reached Nyulda, the post station on the highroad which we were now making for, that a foreigner had reached Riwoché and that the lamas wanted to prevent him proceeding as it was Déba djong territory, the Wai-wei of Nyulda had sent him, the T'ung-shih of the post, to look me up and assist me, if need be.

A mile or so farther on we came to where the Ké ch'u, which we had left on the morning of the 23d, empties into the Tsé ch'u. Here the yaks hired at Riwoché were to leave us, so we stopped at a farm near by and entered into negotiations with the people to carry the luggage on to Nyulda. As only about twelve miles separated us from the latter place, and as the ula yaks were on the mountain pastures and could not be brought in till to-morrow, the Hsien-sheng and I pushed on as rapidly as we could, leaving the two other men and the luggage to come on to-morrow, and reached En-ta (Nyulda or Nyimda)† by 2 P. M. in a heavy rain.

The valley narrowed considerably below the mouth of the Ké ch'u, the mountain sides still well timbered, but habitations rare and no black tents anywhere to be seen. We are apparently out of the Drupa region for a while.

Nyulda is a miserable little place built on a bed of *débris* at the mouth of two valleys and near the bank of the Tsé ch'u. Up one of these valleys runs the highroad to Lh'asa, Shobando being five

* Capt. Bower says of this valley (*op. cit.*, 68) "In no part of Kashmir does the beauty of the scenery exceed that in this part of Tibet."

† Bonvalot calls this station Houmda (*op. cit.*, 377), and Bower (p. 69) calls it Memda. The name is Dngul-mdah, "Silver arrow," which the Chinese transcribe En-ta. On Bower's map this place is called Logamda. Locally the name is pronounced Nyimda.

stages from this place; up the other, it is said, a trail goes to Gart'ok, but I doubt it. A half dozen Tibetan houses and a mixed population of Chinese and Tibetans, some thirty or forty all told, inhabit this unprepossessing place, which is a post station on the highroad between Ta-chien-lu and Central Tibet.

The Wai-wei or Corporal commanding the post of five soldiers had us lodged in a filthy stable dignified by the name of *Kung-kuan*, and I was obliged to make myself as comfortable as I could in it, not having a tent, and it being too bad weather to camp out. Shortly after my arrival he came, in full official dress I must do him the justice to say, to see my passport, and made me a present of onions, cabbages, turnips, *o-sung*,* a few eggs and a piece of mutton, for which I gave him a return present of 3 rupees, a lot more than the things were worth, but vegetables seemed to us worth their weight in silver, for we had not seen, let alone tasted, such delicious looking ones for an age.

When the Wai-wei had made all he could out of me, his five disreputable looking soldiers came with some more vegetables and eggs, and in turn received more money from me, then came two parties of soldiers, one *en route* for Shobando, the other going to Lh'asa, and they likewise preyed on the foreigner. Then the T'ung-shih who had discovered me, asked for a present, and I began to lose patience, and when the Wai-wei sent me word that he would like a further present, I revolted, and told them what I thought of them, and having accepted their apologies which immediately followed, we became good friends again, and nothing more was said about *li wu*.

A little above Nyulda I noticed birch trees and maples; they are the first of these species we have seen since leaving Kuei-tê in Kan-su.† I saw also some rhubarb, but nowhere along the route have I seen any as large or in such abundance as on the I ch'u and Len ch'u. I saw beside the Kung-kuan, a pile of iron ore (pyrites); it is mined a little way up the Lh'asa highroad to the southwest of here. Iron is also found, I am told, near Lagong, east of Nyulda.‡

* A kind of cabbage, I believe, of which the stalk only is eaten, after being scraped. It tastes something like boiled artichokes.

† Conf., however, p. 282, where the word 'birch' should be substituted for 'spruce.'

‡ Bonvalot (*op. cit.*, 378) describes at length the methods followed at Lagong (his Lagoun) in working iron.

It is smelted and cast into rough kettles and a few other small articles used in the country.

I was struck by hearing the Chinese soldiers here (all of them natives of Ssŭ-ch'uan and most of them from the Chien-ch'ang) speak of the (Lh'asa ?) Tibetans as Tang-ku-tu and of the Nepalese as Pei-pung-tzŭ.*

A quantity of dried red peppers was given me this evening by one of the soldiers; they came from Pomä. That region apparently supplies all eastern Tibet with delicacies; it is the land of promise of Tibet.

August 26.—The two men left behind with the luggage and mules got in to-day at noon, and I prepared to start at once for Lagong. I asked the Wai-wei to give me ula, as I found it too expensive to hire pack animals, but I intend to give the people who supply the animals good pay for them. The system of counting as a "stage" (*jya-ts'ug*), two points frequently not over a couple of miles apart and charging a rupee a stage for each yak or pony, makes hiring pack animals very expensive.

At 1 P. M. I was ready to start for Lagong, but the ula did not come, and I learnt that the yak drivers would not start for Ch'amdo before I had obtained permission of the Ta lama of that place to travel on his territory. I at once called the Wai-wei and told him that I expected him to assert his authority and to have the ula called, that I was now traveling on an imperial highroad, and being a bearer of an imperial passport, I expected every courtesy shown me. While we were talking, a number of Ch'amdo men came up and begged me not to start before they had time to inform the Ch'amdo authorities. I refused to listen to them, and said that we would all ride to Ch'amdo together.

Finally the yaks were loaded and we started out, without, however, the Wai-wei giving me an escort, as he should have done, in fact he was so overawed by the big talk of the Tibetans, that he feared to go against what he thought were their wishes in

* Tibetans call the Nepalese Pébu and Guk'ar. The first term applies to the Parbutiya, the latter to the Gorkas. These same soldiers spoke of the Ch'amdo people as Ch'amdowa, of the Lit'ang ones as Lit'angwa, etc. The term Tang-ku-tu, in English Tangut, has been erroneously applied to the Koko-nor Tibetans exclusively. It is in reality the Mongol word for Tibet or Tibetans generally.

VIEW OF MOUNTAINS NORTH OF NEDA (ERH-LANG-WAN).

BRIDGE OVER ZE CH'U OR SUNG-LO ZAMBA (CH'AMDO).

the matter. The Ch'amdo men, some ten or fifteen in number, got on their horses when I did, and rode just ahead of me along the road to Lagong.

The Tsé ch'u* below Nyulda flows as far as the Lagong or "Upper La" district, in a narrow gorge, the mountains on either side densely covered with fine pines, junipers, small birches and a variety of other kinds of trees; the ground in many places was covered with gooseberry bushes, strawberry vines and other trailing plants and ferns. In places the trail, for it is little better, though dignified with the name of highroad, is four hundred or five hundred feet above the stream, and for quite a distance after leaving Nyulda we rode over a log platform overhanging the river.

About eight miles from Nyulda the valley broadened, and we came to the village of Lagong and the Sung lo bridge, which some of the people called Tung-djung zamba, a log bridge of the cantilever style in two spans, over which runs a road leading to Riwoché and also around the city of Ch'amdo, joining the highroad to China southeast of that place and near the post station of Pao-tun (or Pungdé). The Ch'amdo men pulled up across the road when we came near the bridge, and again begged me to stop until the Ch'amdo officials could come and see me, saying that if I did not do so I would get them in serious trouble. I finally agreed to remain camped by the bridge for one day; my played out mules make it impossible for me to go on unless I leave them all behind, which I do not care to do for they are still worth a good deal of money.

We camped under some trees by the river side, where it flows at the foot of a cliff of red sandstone some four hundred feet high, and on top of which is a little lh'a-k'ang. This rock is held to be sacred, and when I wanted to fire off my gun against it, I was told that I must shoot in another direction as it would disturb the gods. There are four or five hamlets scattered along both sides of the river below here and a little lamasery around the east end of the cliff just referred to.

Bonvalot and his party were made to cross the river by the Sung-lo bridge, and I fancy that I will be requested to do the

* Bower calls it the Zichu.

same.* The Tsé ch'u valley is, so far, the most picturesque and fertile one we have seen anywhere in Tibet, and at this season of the year, when the rough, dingy stone houses are nearly hidden under the sheaves of yellow barley drying on the frameworks on the roofs, and the people are all gay and happy after plentiful harvests, we see it at its very best. The forest clad mountains, behind which rise jagged needles of rock or snow-covered peaks, form a fitting background to this alpine scene. The ground where we are camped is literally covered with edelweiss, of which there are three or four varieties.

A number of persons stopped at our camp this afternoon; each one had something to sell, a ball of butter, a pair of garters, or anything which struck our fancy. I refused to pay money for anything, and made some very good bargains with buttons as a medium of exchange. We bought, however, a fine sheep for two rupees, and gave up the day to feasting and enjoying ourselves, absolutely indifferent as to what may occur on the morrow, for we do not apprehend serious trouble, only lots of "talky-talky."

August 27.—This morning by half past five o'clock, a gorgeous lama official wearing a wide brimmed gilded and varnished hat surmounted by a coral button, came riding up with a numerous escort. His fine red silk robe and shawl of the most beautiful *tirma* had a few little patches carefully sewn on them, to conform to the rules of his

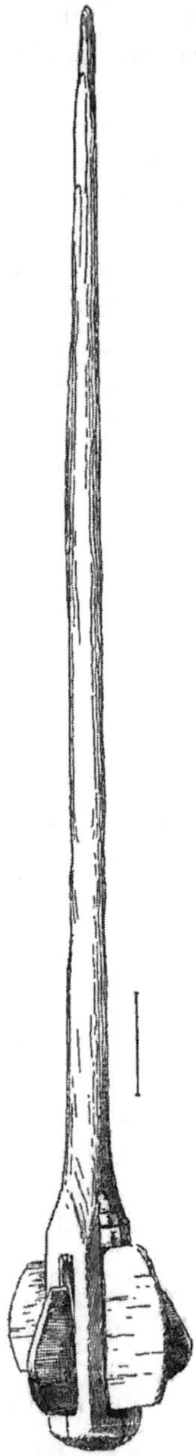

SMALL TEA DASHER (Jyadé).

* At least so I was told by the people, but Bonvalot's narrative does not bear this out, though I am fain to admit that from the time he reached Lamä until he got to Gart'ok I have no means of locating his route. It ran around Ch'amdo and then parallel to the highroad followed by Bower and myself, but to the east of it, until Gart'ok was reached. It is a great pity that the map which accompanies Mr. Bonvalot's narrative has not been more carefully prepared, it is, in fact, absolutely worthless for geographers, though it was good enough in *Le Temps* where it originally appeared a few days after Mr. Bonvalot's return to Paris.

order, which prescribe that monk's clothing must be of patched and not of new stuff; altogether he was a very fine looking fellow, and strangest of all he was remarkably clean.* This latter peculiarity, I learned later on in the day, was due to the fact that he was a Ssŭ-ch'uanese by birth, and a Tibetan by adoption. His face was distinctly Chinese, of the oval, refined type, and a black mustache hid his lip. His name was P'apa Shéré, and he had the rank of governor of a district (*djong*), and was one of the secretaries or ministers of the P'apa Lh'a, the ruler of Ch'amdo.†

I told him of my wanderings, but said that I had no account to render him of my movements, that the Chinese officer of Ch'amdo was the only person with whom I could settle the question of my further movements, adding that I was not now traveling on a road belonging exclusively to Ch'amdo or Lh'asa, but on one of the Emperor of China's highroads, along which he had guards and over which all Chinese, traders as well as officials, could travel. Finally, I said, that not speaking Tibetan well, I wanted an interpreter and that I must request of him to have one sent here from Nyulda or Ch'amdo before discussing any subject of importance with him.

He said that I was quite right in saying that I was traveling on the Emperor's highway, and that if I insisted upon it the Jyami Pönbo ("Chinese official") would unquestionably require that I be allowed to enter the town of Ch'amdo. He hoped, however, and the P'apa Lh'a had told him to tell me the same, that I would not insist on going to Ch'amdo, for it would unquestionably cause trouble there. There were in the town several thousand lamas who would not hear of foreigners entering it, and though he and the educated lamas knew that foreigners were not dangerous, still they could not impress this on the common *draba*. He would also beg me not to insist on having an interpreter, or

* Bonvalot met this same lama, see *op. cit.*, 381-382. He told me he had also seen Bower's party. See Bower's *Diary*, p. 71. I cannot imagine who Bower refers to as "the Amban of Chiamdo," it must have been the Chinese Yo-chi (Major) commanding the Chinese garrison.

† Chamdo is an ecclesiastical fief under the rule of a high dignitary of the Gélug sect, who bears the title of P'apa Lh'a. Under him are three other high dignitaries, the Djiwa Lh'a, the Jyara truku, and another whose title I could not learn. See on the subject of Ch'amdo, *Journ. Roy. Asiat. Soc.*, n. s. XXIII, 54, 125, 251, 271 and 276. Also Huc, *Souvenirs d'un voyage*, II, 460 et seq.

calling the Chinese into this affair in any way, let us settle it amicably among ourselves, for the Chinese would but make trouble.

If I would agree to it, he would have me escorted around Ch'amdo to the highroad at Pungdé by the road over the Sung-lo bridge, the same which the two other parties of foreigners who had visited this place previously had followed.* As to the various things, boots, hats, rice, etc., etc., which I said I wanted, he would purchase them in Ch'amdo for me, and meet me with them somewhere outside of the town, as he had done for the other foreigners.

I replied that having come to this country to examine it, I would not follow any road taken by other foreigners, for I would be losing time, that rather than go by the road over the bridge, I would wait here until the Chinese official at Ch'amdo could come here and talk the matter over with me.

P'apa Shéré, seeing me determined, said that there was another trail which led to Pungdé over the mountains to the south of the city and which had not been examined by any foreigners, and that if I would take it, he would meet me at a place which I would reach in three days, and besides bringing me all the things I required, he would also have for me six strong horses in exchange for my played out mules. He would also give me two guides and ula through Ch'amdo territory.

I finally accepted this suggestion and will set out to-morrow. The lama was most anxious for me to start to-day; he feared apparently the arrival of Chinese from Ch'amdo, whose interference in this matter he apprehended very much. The day has been a most trying one for me for I have talked incessantly, but I believe I have acted rightly—at least in the interests of geography—for the right of foreigners to visit Ch'amdo is not denied, and as to the town itself, we know all about it from Monseigneur Thomine Desmazure's and Pères Desgodins' and Renou's visit and sojourn there in 1861.† These missionaries' farthest point west was the village about one-quarter of a mile east of where we are now camped, and which they called Lagong, though the lama told me it was known as La-stöd or "Upper La," in contradistinction to

* He tried to deceive me here, for neither Bonvalot nor Bower went by this route.

† See C. H. Desgodins, *Le Thibet d'après la correspondence des Missionnaires*, 97 et seq.

another hamlet about five miles east of here which is called La-mä or "Lower La." The whole district is known as Lagong djong.

August 28.—We left a little before seven and rode down the valley to a bridge across the Tsé ch'u, called the Jyabo zamba, where we crossed over to the left bank of the river. The Tsé ch'u here takes a southerly bend, and the highroad leads up a valley trending east and west, the mountains on its southern side thickly covered with fine pines, those on the north side barer and terminating in high limestone peaks and needles.

A few miles up this valley we came to the hamlet of La-mä, or "Lower La,"* where I found P'apa Shéré waiting for me with a slight collation spread on the ground outside the *jya-ts'ug k'ang*, or "post station" which, he said, was too dirty for anyone to eat in—it must have been filthy indeed! I saw here some more men wearing the cangue as a punishment for killing game.

I have rarely seen such inveterate beggars as these Ch'amdo people; from the gorgeously dressed and undoubtedly wealthy P'apa Shéré down, everyone has begged for *suru*. This morning at La-mä I gave the lama about 30 taels of silver to buy things for me at Ch'amdo, the prices I was to pay for them having been settled between us. There will be a balance due me of about 2.8 rupees; this he begged me to give him with many "*Suru, suru Pönbo ch'en-po, suru kutsê rê.*" I laughed at him and tried to make him ashamed of himself, but to no effect. Then each man of his escort came and begged for a present of money, and the lama had the impudence to back their requests, but I refused to give them a cash.

What a difference between this people and the Panaka and Jyadé, who never ask for anything and are delighted with the smallest trifle one sees fit to give them. I find that wherever the Tibetan people are under direct lama rule, as in Ch'amdo, the standard of morality and self respect is very low; they are thoroughly demoralized in every respect; the lamas of Kumbum and Amdo generally, are just as bad as those of this country or Lh'asa in this respect; lamas are primarily mendicants, they never forget it.

The highroad to Ch'amdo leaves the La-mä valley a little to the east of the hamlet of that name, and ascending the steep and

* Called by Bower Lani Sacha. *Sa-ch'a* means 'land, country.'

rough limestone range which borders it here, crosses it by the Namts'o la.

We left the highroad and followed the La-mä ch'u up to its source, camping at the base of the Shi la at an altitude of about 14,700 feet above sea level. Five miles east of La-mä the valley takes, as far as its head, the name of Unda. Up to the altitude of about 13,000 feet the mountains on the south side of the valley are covered with fine timber, juniper and pine, though on the north side only a few trees and a good deal of brush are to be seen. Above this limit there are only rhododendron bushes, and they do not extend higher than the old cabin near which we have camped to-night.

One of the yak drivers has a supplementary little finger growing out of the side of his left hand. This is the first time I have noticed this deformity among the Tibetans, though it is a very common one in North China.*

The vocabulary of most Tibetans is a very limited one, this morning, for example, P'apa Shéré, who is a very well educated man, said that the only word used for "foot rule" was the Chinese *chih-tzŭ*, and *chien-tzŭ*, the Chinese term for "scissors," was also the only one known in Tibet.† He told me that Chinese copper cash were used to a limited extent at Ch'amdo, and that there were no Nepalese (Peurbu) traders living there, only Chinese, of whom there were over a hundred.

August 29.—We left at half past six and reached the top of the Shi la by eight, after a very stiff climb which we had to make on foot; in fact we walked most of the day, and it has been our practice for a long while past to get off the horses at every bit of rough or uneven road. The Shi la appears to be composed of a rather fine reddish sandstone conglomerate.

From the pass we took an east-southeast direction across the head of a little valley in which the water was flowing in a northerly direction, and then by a low col passed into another narrow and very precipitous valley whose flanks were covered with a dense and luxuriant growth of pines (or firs) and junipers, not a few of the former four feet in diameter at the ground. There was a rather

*See p. 6.

† Chinese, Mongol, Hindustani, Persian, Turkish and Sanskrit words are numerous in Tibetan, in both the written and spoken languages. Tibetan names of clothes, vegetables, household implements, etc., etc., are mostly foreign terms.

thick undergrowth of a great variety of shrubs, and rhubarb was also very plentiful. The descent of this valley was extremely steep but we very much enjoyed riding under the grand old trees from whose branches hung long threads of light yellow or bright orange colored moss (*Usnea barbata*) tinging the whole forest with their delicate hues. Here and there we caught a glimpse of far off peaks and crags and forest covered mountains all seeming to trend southeast or south-southeast, but of so nearly an even height that it was difficult to decide the question. Numerous bunches of silver pheasants (*saga*) skurried across our path, but the woods were wonderfully still; save for these *ma-chi's* cry, I do not think that I heard a sound in them but the roaring of the water in the gorge below us as it tumbled over the rocks on its way down to join the Tsé ch'u.

The yak drivers told me that throughout the forests of Ch'amdo, and I suppose in the adjacent countries to the east and especially to the south, bears, wolves, and leopards are very numerous.

We stopped for the night at the village of Gé where the road we are following branches: one trail leading up the valley goes to Draya, the other takes a northeast direction to the town of Ch'amdo, which is, a native tells me, a half day's ride from Gé.

There is a jya-ts'ug k'ang here but I preferred camping outside the village as the weather is fine and the people pleasant. Oats and turnips appear to be the only crops raised at this place, while at Lagong only a little oats is grown, and barley and wheat are the principal crops.

I must not omit to note that to-day when on the east side of the Shi la I saw two small hares, the first I have seen since entering the inhabited portion of Tibet. I suppose some animal must destroy them, for the Tibetans neither kill them nor eat their flesh. The marmots (*huang shu* in Chinese) of this section of country are so large that I am inclined to take them for a different variety from those living in the north.

Yesterday I had to abandon, a few miles beyond La-mä, the yellow pony the Namru Déba had given me; it was too worn out to take another step. I have now three saddle horses and will get six pack horses when I meet P'apa Shéré on the Om ch'u. I had to leave my mules at Lagong as they could go no farther.

I have asked a great many persons how far it was from Ch'amdo to Dergé drongcher, as I thought I might try to take that road; all have agreed in saying that it took twelve days to go there. The traffic over this road must be important, for Dergé is a very fertile district and its products are much prized and generally used all over Tibet.

August 30.—Leaving Gé we followed the Ch'amdo road up a narrow gorge covered with dense forest growth, and ascending to about eight hundred feet above the timber line by a very steep trail, we came to the summit of the Dré la. From this elevated point I was able to locate the point of junction of the two rivers which meet before the town of Ch'amdo, which as the crow flies, was not more than six or eight miles northeast of us. A large *labsté* crowns a hill which I think is immediately behind the town.

Near the summit of the pass we found two or three black tents, and stopping near one we bought a bucket of *sho* and milk and took lunch and a quiet pipe afterwards while gazing upon the beautiful scenery.

The descent from the Dré la was at first very steep and led over a few hills covered with brush, and then into a densely wooded valley. Pines, firs and junipers in the upper part, and lower down willows filled the valley, and birch, cherry, apricot, apple and plum trees were seen in great numbers.* Gooseberry and currant bushes, raspberries of apricot color and taste, and strawberries were also abundant, and I can vouch for the raspberries (*marān*) being delicious. Rose bushes were also abundant and the people, like the Ainu by the way, eat the skin of the seed-vessels.

After a most agreeable ride of about eighteen miles, we reached the mouth of the valley, and on a little bluff near the Om ch'u river,† in the hamlet of Kinda, we saw the lama P'apa Shéré standing on the roof of a house looking anxiously for us up the Djung rong tranka valley down which we were quietly making our way.

* Bonvalot found the same kind of country on the Om ch'u above Ch'amdo. See *op. cit.*, 383.

† According to the *Hsi-yü tung wen chih*, Bk. 22, 9, the name of this river is Om ch'u. Other Chinese writers (*Wei Tsang t'u chih* for example) write the name Ang ch'u. This latter work says that on account of its passing through Yün-nan it is also called Yün (nan) ho. *Journ. Roy. Asiat. Soc.*, n. s. XXIII, 251. Bonvalot (*op. cit.*, 383) calls it the Giomtchou and says it flows by Lamda on the highroad. In this he is certainly wrong. Bower calls the river the Nam chu.

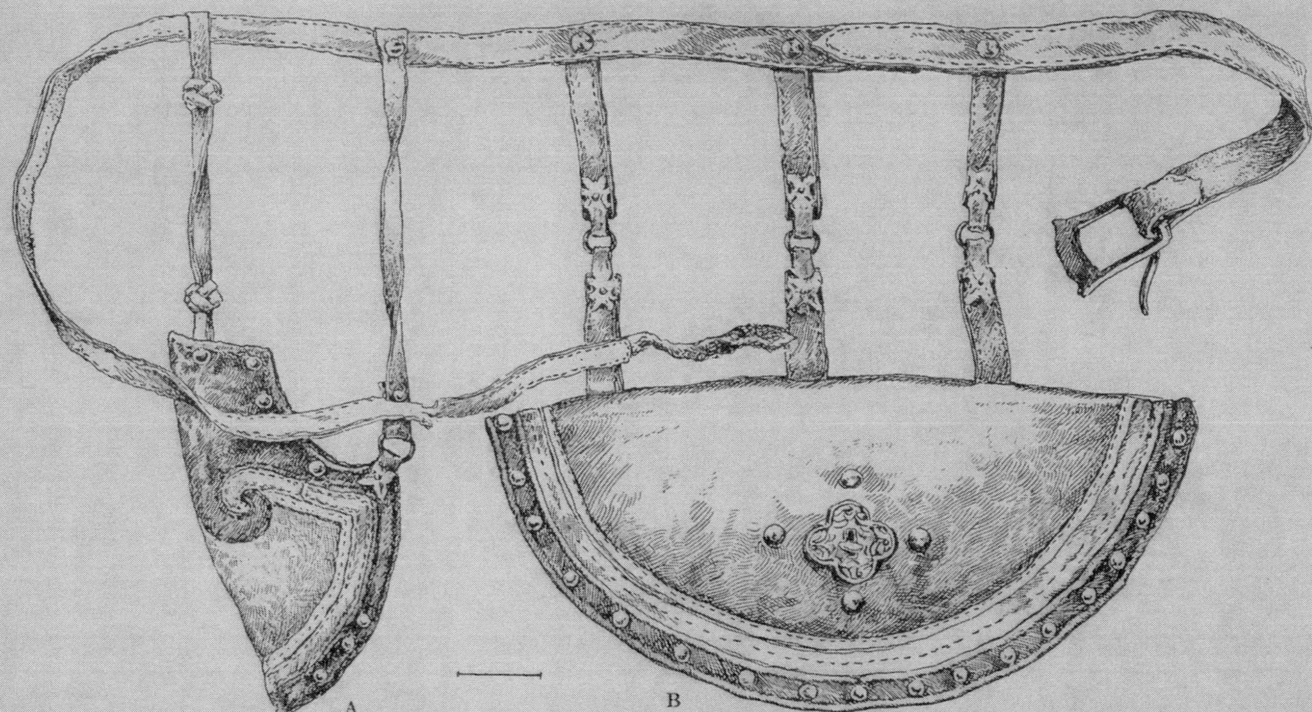

BELT, BULLET POUCH (A) AND BAG (B) of red leather, trimmed with black and green leather and brass studs. (Property of the author.)

All the things I had asked for had been brought me from Ch'amdo, and the P'apa Lh'a had sent me a lot of presents and his thanks for having waived my right to visit the town of Ch'amdo. The six pack-ponies will be here early to-morrow, when I will be able to push on down to the ferry over the Om ch'u. The lama also brought me a very good Chinese dinner of four courses and some loaves of bread which we enjoyed very much. Altogether, although he is a vile beggar, P'apa Shéré has behaved most politely, and I do not regret the journey around Ch'amdo he has made me take, it has led me through some beautiful country.

We passed the rest of the day talking with the lama, and telling him about the town of Ch'amdo and the visit made it in 1861 by the French missionaries. I also told him about the Ch'amdo mission to Peking in 1885 and of the intimacy which had sprung up between its chief and myself during the four or five months he had stayed there. I told him how foolish was the plan the Tibetans were trying to follow in keeping foreigners out of the country, how impossible it was to prevent their getting all the information they required, and I showed him the maps of the great Trigonometrical Survey, and read to him the names of all the villages around Lh'asa and other large cities of Tibet where he had been, and told him how they were made, and that, though the British had had this information for years, no harm had come of it to Tibet.

The lama readily admitted the truth of all I said, but added that his position, being a Chinese by birth, made it necessary for him to out-Herod Herod in all questions of exclusion; even where his own countrymen were concerned, he had to be anti-foreign.

Among other things he gave me the local names of the following fruits.

Currant,	*si.*
Raspberry,	*maran.**

* At Draya called *tayü*, from Gart'ok to Bat'ang known as *trésui*. In the alpine regions of west Kan-su, Prjevalsky (*Mongolia*, II, 79) met with a gooseberry with a bitter yellowish berry, a raspberry (*Rubus pungens*) with delicious fruit of pale red color, another raspberry (*Rubus Idœus ?*) similar to the European species but only two feet high, also two kinds of Barberry (*Berberis*), black currants (*Ribes*), cherry and wild strawberries (*Fragaria sp.*). Dr. Hooker, *Himalayan Journals*, I, 99 and 150, found the yellow raspberry in the Sikkim Terai at and above 4,000 feet, and Moorcroft, *Travels*, I, 56, says it grows in Kashmir near Joshimath.

Strawberry, *sa si*, (lit. "ground currant.")
Blackberry (?), *taji*.
Apricot, *kambo*.
Peach, *semkam*.

After most pressing requests, I sold the lama one of my Winchester carbines for 30 taels, and exchanged the other for the horse he was riding, a remarkably fine animal. I have no further use for rifles, and my shot gun is good enough for defense and any shooting I may want to do on the way.

August 31.—The six pack horses (pretty sorry ones, I am fain to admit) turned up early this morning, and we were soon ready to start. As far as Pungdé I have ula, so we will have only the pleasures of travel with none of the attendant trouble. I hear that one of the mules I gave the lama died two days after he got it; I am not a bit sorry, it evens up our account a little, and still he has a good balance to his credit.

Our road led down the right bank of the Om ch'u, a fine, swift river one hundred and fifty to two hundred yards wide, as large as the Dré ch'u in Dérgé. The mountains rise precipitously along the left bank, but on the right there is room for some farming and hamlets are numerous along that side. The mountains, 1,000 to 1,500 feet high, are of sandstone formation, and the road in not a few places runs along the vertical sides of cliffs overhanging the river, three hundred or four hundred feet above the stream.

At the entrance of each hamlet we found the headman, and usually a woman or two, with a jug of ch'ang (on the mouth of which is always put a little piece of butter) placed on a little table, and a rug spread on the ground for me to sit on, awaiting our passage, and I drank a cup of this harmless beverage with each one, and gave them a tanka for their pains.

A little below Kunda I saw a covey of partridges, the first I have seen in Tibet.*

About nine miles below Kinda we stopped to change ula at a good-sized hamlet. On the other side of the river nearly opposite this place and at the mouth of a gorge stands a little gomba. There is a road coming from Ch'amdo and following the left bank of the Om ch'u which goes up this gorge, and comes out on the highroad near Pungdé.

* On the game birds of Tibet, see Dr. W. G. Thorold, in Bower, *op. cit.*, 116.

At the hamlet where we stopped to change ula, the people brought us tea and ch'ang and were very friendly. There was a pretty little garden (*linga*) below the headman's house, planted with willow and poplar trees, and the whole place had quite a prosperous air about it. The people were busy harvesting their barley and oats, but the wheat was not yet ripe. The houses in this hamlet were three or four stories high—the first of this height we have seen—the walls of the ground floor made of mud and stone, those of the upper, the outside walls included, of wattle plastered over with mud. Large logs are used in great quantities in every building in a most reckless way, or rather, I suspect, where the people would like to use a bit of board, they have to use a log, not having implements, or time, or even the desire to cut the log to the desired size. In the west of the United States I have seen people put one end of a log twenty feet long in their fire-place, with the other end outside the door and keep pushing it on the fire little by little, rather than chop it up. The same praiseworthy desire to economize labor animates these poor benighted Tibetans.

We saw many women with small goitres (the first I saw were yesterday at Gé), and a few men had them also, but none, however, were very large.

About five miles before reaching the village of Nuyi, where we stopped for the night and which is near the ferry over the Om ch'u, the mountain sides became covered with fir trees and the hills sloped more gently down to the river and afforded greater space for cultivation.

The houses of Nuyi and those in the adjacent hamlets are shaded by fine poplar trees, and on many of the balconies were seen little boxes or pots of blooming flowers, a sure sign of Chinese influence. The people were vilely dirty, the women especially. The men are taller than any I have seen elsewhere in Tibet. I put up my tent on the roof of a house, and enjoyed the view of the swift, muddy river dashing down the valley; in one direction the storm clouds were gathering on the mountain tops, and the lightning was flashing, while a little beyond was a hamlet, its houses, trees and fields bathed in sunlight.

September 1.—A good part of the morning was taken up getting across the river. The Om ch'u at the ferry runs for about a mile in a straight, unbroken stream, nearly free from eddies and whirlpools, and between banks of coarse gravel and sand, rising seventy-five to a hundred feet above the water. The horses and cattle had to swim, and a hard job it was to make the poor fagged out things face the swift, broad current, but in they had to go, and all of them got across. The raft on which we crossed was made of eight big logs about ten feet long, strongly pinned and chained forward and aft to cross logs. Six half naked men armed with paddles propelled the crazy craft, two squatting on the front end and two on either side. It took five trips to get the party and our luggage across, and we only suffered a slight wetting.

On the left bank of the river were several hamlets, and nearly all the people turned out to see the foreigner and his party, bringing us ch'ang, tea and tsamba. These people I found quite as tall as those at Nuyi, the men averaging not less than five feet ten inches, and several of them six feet one or two inches.*

Leaving the Om ch'u we took a north-northeast direction, and after passing a couple of hamlets in the foothills, we ascended the steep side of the mountains and finally reached the summit of the Mité la at 2 P. M. and the little post-station of Pungdé was before us at our feet. From here I could also follow the course of the Om ch'u for some distance south of where we had crossed it. It flows in a south-southeast direction between heavily timbered mountains. About thirty miles due south of the Mité la, and probably not far from the right bank of the Om ch'u, we saw a range of snow-covered mountains trending apparently southeast by east or thereabout; but I could not connect it with any range seen farther west along our route. I also noticed that a road ran from Pungdé to Ch'amdo parallel to the Om ch'u but along the east side of the mountains on the left bank of that river.

The northern slope of the Mité la was covered with raspberry bushes and the ula people,—there were at least twenty of them, men, women, boys and girls,—who had come of their own free will for the fun of the thing, gathered a quantity for me.

Pungdé† (in Chinese, Pao-tun) is a small hamlet of eight or ten houses with a Chinese post station (*t'ang*) and a post house

* Bonvalot, *op. cit.*, 390, remarks on the height of the natives of this region: "Beaucoup d'entre eux ont plus de 1 m. 80 de hauteur."

† Bower's Pandesar. He makes it thirty-three miles from Ch'amdo. Chinese itineraries make the distance 150 li, or about 36 miles.

(*Kung-kuan*). There are four Chinese soldiers stationed here to forward the mail and government merchandise, also a station keeper, all of them with native wives. They received me most hospitably, gave me a good room, brought me some vegetables and eggs and made us all as comfortable as they could.

I gave the ula people six rupees; they had enjoyed the jaunt ever so much; it would have been too unkind to have sent them back empty handed, and so they all started off at once for home in high spirits. They will have walked, when they get back to their houses, about thirty miles in twelve hours, but they did not seem to think it was anything extraordinary.

The soldiers, Ssŭ-ch'uanese of course, told me all the gossip of the place. They said that the two foreigners who had passed here in the twelfth moon (sometime in January)* had a Nepalese interpreter whose Tibetan was so peculiar that they could not understand it and whose Chinese was worse. The foreigners themselves were very kind, they wrote and sketched a great deal, but the interpreter seems not to have made friends with the natives or the Chinese.

The soldiers' wives wear very large curious earrings studded with turquoises, such as I have not seen elsewhere. They are, I am told, peculiar to Ch'amdo.† I bought a pair from one woman who begged that I would not show them to anyone, as women were ashamed to sell their jewelry. I told her this trait was not peculiar to this part of the world, and she appeared relieved to know that others felt as she did.

These Chinese soldiers stationed along the post road between Lh'asa and Ta-chien-lu are paid 60 taels a year, but the Ta-chien-lu Chün-liang-fu and the Liang-t'ai‡ of Bat'ang, instead of giving them silver, pay them in tea which the soldiers have to accept for about double the price at which they can sell it here, or at any of the *t'ang* (post stations) along the route. The Tibetans will not

* Bower camped here on the 2d January, 1892.

† Somewhat similar ones are worn in Central and Ulterior Tibet.

‡ The Chün-liang Fu is the Commissary General for Tibet. There are Liang-t'ai, or Quartermasters, at Lit'ang, Bat'ang, Ch'amdo, Larego and Lh'asa. The soldiers are classed as "Foot soldiers" (*P'u-ping*) and "Mounted soldiers" (*Ma ping*). The salary of the latter is slightly greater than that of the former. A man is raised from P'u-ping to Ma ping for good conduct or long service, but he has to mount himself.

allow them to compete with them in trade, and so they can only exchange their tea for tsamba, flour, butter and mutton. In some of the warmer localities the soldiers raise a few vegetables, and at all the stations they keep poultry, and a pig or two. Their Tibetan wives and their numerous offspring are hostages to fortune with a vengeance, and few of them manage to get back to their native land, especially as the Chinese government does not pay their traveling expenses. They seem, however, very fond of their wives and children and have pretty easy lives; the women do all the work, and they—the men—have but to take care of the children and smoke opium, or a water pipe if they cannot afford to buy the drug. The only arms these so-called soldiers have are those they can buy themselves, for the government supplies none.

PART V.

DRAYA. MAR-K'AMS. BAT'ANG. LIT'ANG. CHALA.

September 2.—We left Pungdé accompanied by two soldiers as an escort. A few miles southeast by east from the station we crossed the Ipi la or Ku-lung shan, "Pierced mountains," as the Chinese call it, on account of the holes (*ku-lung*) in the rocks on its summit and on the eastern side of the pass. This mountain marks the boundary between Ch'amdo and Chamdun-Draya.

At the foot of the pass on the east side I found a gorgeous lama and eight or ten men of Draya awaiting my advent, seated around a fire drinking tea and smoking. The lama was a Secretary or Drung-yig of the grand lama of Draya, which district is, like Ch'amdo, an ecclesiastical principality. He begged me, in view of the disturbed state of the country, which he said was at war with Dérgé, to take a by-road leading around the north of Draya and directly to Gart'ok.* He said I could have no objection to obliging them, as I had acceded to a similar request on the part of the Ch'amdo authorities.

It was a most tempting offer, for by following the highroad which had previously been explored by Europeans I had nothing to expect in the geographical line, beyond perhaps correcting a few topographical errors or making new ones myself; whereas, if I took the road suggested by the lama I would be going over new ground and possibly reaching Dérgé drongcher, a locality I had long wanted to visit. On the other hand if I did not go to Draya, the next European who came along this way would be refused admission there and the point gained by Capt. Bower in visiting this place would be lost by me. Just as in the case of Ch'amdo, if Bonvalot had insisted on going into that town, Bower and I

* In all likelihood the route followed by Bonvalot.

could have gone there too. So very reluctantly I decided to refuse to take any other road than that leading to Draya, and having so informed the lama, I got on my horse and rode off, followed by the Drung-yig and his party who tried to take up the discussion again while riding along.

About four miles beyond the foot of the Ipi la, the Bagong ch'u, which has its source in that mountain, takes for a few miles a sharp bend eastward, coming back afterwards to its southeast course. We left the river here and crossed some forest-covered hills known as the Drama la and the Luma la.* From the summit of the latter, looking northward across the valley of the Bagong ch'u, we saw a short valley trending nearly due north. The Draya lama pointing to it said that a good road ran that way around Draya, but I rode on without heeding him. We saw ten black tents on the slopes of the Luma la, but it is poor pasture land. At the eastern base of the pass we came again to the Bagong ch'u, or Lung-tung ch'u† as it is also called, on account of the narrow cleft in the limestone rocks through which the stream here forces its way and which is said to resemble a "dragon's den" (*lung-tung*).

About two miles below this point we passed before the village of Bagong perched on the hillside some two hundred feet above the river, and stopped at the post station (*t'ang*) on the river bottom. The village is inhabited by about twenty families, and at the post station there are Chinese and Man-tzŭ kung-kuans. We stopped in the former, which is spacious and dirty. Each of the four or five soldiers stationed here brought me presents of vegetables and eggs, for which I had to give return presents of greater value, but it would never do to refuse the gifts, and these poor fellows are awfully hard up; they all told me that they never saw a rupee from one year's end to the other. The Drung-yig and his party stopped next door in the Man-tzŭ kung-kuan and amused themselves all the afternoon watching me from the roof.

The soldiers told me that large footed Chinese women are allowed by the Chinese government to go to Tibet, and only small footed ones are forbidden leaving China. This prohibition extends, or used to extend, to all countries outside of the eighteen

* Bower calls this latter pass the Shila la. For a Chinese account of the road from Pungdé to Ta-chien-lu, see *Journ. Roy. Asiat. Soc.*, n. s. XXIII, 36-53.

† Called by Bower, Socho river.

provinces, Turkestan, Mongolia, Korea, but I am under the impression that it is no longer strictly enforced except as regards Tibet.

Many of the soldiers take their native wives back with them to China, but these women soon tire of the restraint in which they have to live there and return in a year or two to their native land. Most of the soldiers I have seen are from the Chien-ch'ang* or Sung-pan T'ing.

The soldiers here have little patches of tobacco growing on the tops of their houses; they also raise in little gardens, turnips, *o-sung*, cabbages, peas and beans. So far I have not met with potatoes, either among the Tibetans or the Chinese.

September 3.—So as to escape from the Drung-yig and his importunities, I decided to make two stages to-day, *kan-chan* as the Chinese call it. The valley below Bagong remains very narrow, but we saw numerous hamlets of ten or fifteen houses every mile or so, and the soil was, wherever possible, well cultivated, wheat, barley and turnips being the staple crops.

Crossing the river by a bridge called the Zé-chi zamba (and San-tao ch'iao by the Chinese), where there is a hamlet and a small gomba in which lives a Pusa,† we rode down the left bank as far as the mouth of a valley leading to the Moto shan of the Chinese. Here we forded the river; the bridge had been carried away by a spring freshet; and passing in front of another gomba with a pretty park (*linga*) adjoining it,‡ we came after a few miles to the large village of Wangk'a, with some twenty to thirty good-sized Tibetan houses, a Chinese and a Tibetan station house (*kung-kuan*), a Chinese Sergeant (*Pa-tsung*) and six soldiers. We only stopped here long enough to take tea, and then rode on, crossing the river once more by a good bridge about a mile below the village.

*On the Chien-ch'ang district, see E. C. Baber, *Travels and Researches in Western China*, 58 et seq.

† Bower gives the name of this lamasery as Khado Gomba. A short distance before reaching the bridge we passed near a large house on a little hillock. It looked like a castle. I fancy this was once the house of the "great chief Proul Tamba," of whom Huc (*op. cit.*, II, 473, et seq.) speaks.

‡ Bower calls this gomba Tara Gomba, but on his map it is placed on the left bank of the river. He makes out the altitude of Wangk'a (Wamkha) to be 12,225 feet.

About two miles below this point we came to the mouth of a valley leading in an easterly direction; up this our road ran, and having passed two or three hamlets we came, after about four and a half miles, to the summit of the Dzo la.* The last mile of the ascent was very steep and we had to do it on foot. A few stunted juniper trees grew on the mountain sides, and from every twig and branch of those nearest the road were hung stones. Apparently, for I could not get any opinion on this weighty subject from the escort, this peculiar way of adorning the trees was in lieu of throwing the stones by the roadside to make an obo. Where these trees grew the mountain side was so steep that the stones would have rolled down into the valley below.

The descent from the Dzo la was very steep and along a narrow ledge, in places badly washed away, so that the utmost care had to be taken to get the loaded horses along. The Lao-han, the most unlucky of men—and he always does everything just as one would like him not to do—let the two pack horses he was leading fall over the cliff. Fortunately they turned over as they fell and the loads of blankets, sheepskin ch'ubas, and the like they were carrying, saved them from being hurt. We got them back on the road after a lot of trouble and a fearful expenditure of abuse on my part on the relatives, male and female, of the Lao-han to the third and fourth generations. By the time the ponies were reloaded it was night, but luckily the moon shone brightly and we could make out our way pretty plainly. The hills along the gorge on the east side of the Dzo la seemed to me in places to be of some formation looking strangely like loess, but I had not time to examine them, and I formed by opinion only from the peculiar vertical loess-like face of the hill along the bank of the little stream we were following.

We finally came to the Yung ch'u which flows due south in a quite broad and highly cultivated valley, each field in which was enclosed within high stone walls. In fact we could not find a spot to camp on except on the road, and not a blade of grass for our horses. It was too late to go to any house to buy hay, or get anything for ourselves, even wood to build a fire with. We were just opposite the hamlet of Kungsa,† but the bridge over the Yung

* Bower's Jola la.

† Probably Bower's Jindo. He calls the Yung ch'u the Charijansichu. The Bagong ch'u and the Yung ch'u empty into the Om ch'u.

ch'u having been swept away, we did not like to ford the swift and apparently deep river, and so picketed our ponies by the roadside and went supperless to sleep.

September 4.—We started early, and having passed through the hamlet of Kungsa we came after a mile to Gaga* at the mouth of the valley of Gam (called in Chinese Ang-ti). Gaga is a tumbledown, dirty hamlet of rough stone houses of two and three stories, some gutted, all dilapidated. At the four corners of the roof of the headman's house were poles with *lung-ta* fluttering on them and also large stag horns; the object of the latter is not evident; similar ornaments are frequently seen on the roofs of Chinese temples. There is a bridge over the Yung ch'u at Gaga, and the valley below this place seemed quite as carefully and extensively cultivated as higher up.

Gam or Ang-ti† is quite a large village very near the upper limit of cultivation. There is a Pa-tsung and six soldiers stationed here, but I did not stop in the village, but rode on some four or five miles to a spot where we found good grazing. Here we stopped for an hour to take tea and rest the horses before climbing the steep Gam la. We reached the summit at noon and fifteen miles to the southeast, at the mouth of a narrow valley down which the road led, we saw a grove of trees which marks the outskirts of the town of Chamdun-Draya.

On the west side of the Gam la we saw large quantities of a peculiar looking plant with large violet flowers. The guide said the leaves of this plant were used, infused in water, as an aphrodisiac. Its name is *sha-p'o gong-t'ag*,‡ the Chinese call it *hsüeh-lien* or "snow lily," and it is said to be found nowhere else than on the western side of the Gam la.

The descent from the Gam la was quite easy as long as we followed the mountain sides, but when we reached the bottom of the gorge it became very slippery, and we had to lead our horses most of the way.

When about eight miles from Draya and in front of the hamlet of Lower Yüsa‖ (Upper Yüsa is about a mile and a half

* Bower's Ghagwa.

† Bower's Gamdi and (on his map) Gamtamch'e, altitude 13,025 feet. Tamche may be *Drongcher* "hamlet" or "village."

‡ *Saussurea tangutica, Maximowitch, Mél. Biol.*, XI, 247. See Appendix.

‖ Bower's Iswa.

higher up the valley) we stopped for a while, and I sent the Hsien-sheng and the soldier who was guiding us ahead to see the Shou-pei of Draya and arrange with him for lodgings. Having waited for about an hour, we rode slowly on and after passing near a large gomba on a hill some distance south of the main valley, we came to Draya. We ascended the slope on which the town stands under a volley of stones and with much hooting from a lot of lamas and chabis (novices), who accompanied us as far as the kung-kuan, a very small building beside a Kuan-ti temple; it had good strong doors and we promptly closed them in our noisy escort's faces.

A lot of drunken lamas managed to get in the kung-kuan and tried to start a fight, but we kept our tempers and finally got them out, telling the more peaceable ones to come back later on to see us. It was told me by the old kung-kuan keeper that the Seng-kuan (lama officials) had served out lots of ch'ang to the lamas in the hope that they would get me in a row and force me to leave the town. The laity behaved very well and took no part in the hubbub, except a few girls who, I was told, were concubines of the akas.

It was quite in keeping with what I have now found out to be Chinese policy in this country for neither the Shou-pei nor any of his subordinates to turn up in this emergency. The Chinese in Tibet do not want to risk their popularity with the dominant class of the country (*i. e.*, the lamas) by befriending foreigners, to do which they would have to assert their authority without any advantage to themselves. Whenever China sees the necessity of doing so, it can effectually assert its supremacy in Tibet, for it is absurd to say that China is not the sovereign power there and that Chinese officials are only there to manage their own people and are tolerated, as it were, in the country. History, since the time of K'ang-hsi, or Ch'ien-lung at all events, and also recent events at Lh'asa and along the Indian border, prove conclusively that this is not so;* but China does not propose to hold Tibet by force of arms—the game would hardly be worth the candle; it is by diplomacy, by its superior knowledge of for-

* I refer to the negotiations between the Lh'asa Amban and the Indian authorities for the conclusion of a commercial convention between Tibet and India. See on the position of the Amban in Tibet, *Journ. Roy. Asiat. Soc.*, n. s. XXIII, 7 et seq.; *Land of the Lamas*, 291 et seq.

TOWN OF CHAMDUN-DRAYA.

TEMPLE AND MANI WALL ON OUTSKIRTS OF BAT'ANG.

eign affairs and nations, and by conciliating the lamas, that it preserves its undoubted sway.

Draya (Cha-ya the Chinese call it) or Chamdun Draya (By-ams-mdun Tag-yab is, I believe, the correct spelling of the name) is, like Ch'amdo, an ecclesiastical principality which, since 1719, has been nominally under the rule of Lh'asa. A high dignitary, a living Buddha of the Gélugpa sect, with the title of Chyab-gong Lé-pé-shé-rab, is its spiritual and temporal ruler.*

The town is built on a gentle slope and faces southeast. The upper part of the hillside is taken up by a large gomba, the Gun-t'ok gomba, and below it is a confused mass of whitewashed houses, in which live, huddled together, about a hundred and fifty families of Tibetans and some thirty or forty Chinese. On the outskirts of the lower town is a large building, an episcopal palace I suppose I may call it, where resides a living Buddha, the Jyamba truku, and a number of lamas; this building is known as the Jyam-k'ang. Altogether there are between six hundred and seven hundred lamas in the town. Below the town, on the river bottom, are two dense groves of poplars, and taking everything into consideration, Draya is a very picturesque place. Four good-sized streams meet beside the town, the largest of which is the Ombo ch'u, which comes from the north and flows south-southwest, emptying into the Om ch'u, I suppose, not very many miles south or southwest of this town. Another stream, coming from the Po-jya la, beyond Ra-djé, which is about twenty-five miles southeast of Draya, empties into the Ombo ch'u in front of the town, and the stream which comes down from the Gam la, and another of about equal size coming from the north and which empties into the Gam la stream near the town, complete the number.

The whole valley bottom around Draya is well cultivated; the crops are now ripe and the golden fields add not a little to the beauty of the scene, especially around the Jyam-k'ang, whose red walls and gilt spires look most picturesque rising up amidst broad fields of waving barley.

September 5.—To-day has been employed, as have been all other days I have passed in Tibetan towns or villages, receiving

* See *Journ. Roy. Asiat. Soc.*, n. s. XXIII, 47, 250 and 272. Draya figures on d'Anville's *Carte Genle du Thibet* as Tsüa.

dirty men and women, showing and explaining to them the various foreign things I carry with me, asking occasionally a question and endeavoring to elicit information without exciting suspicion. It is horribly tedious and a sad strain on one's patience, but a part of my work.

The interpreter for Chinese of the Ta lama came to see me early this morning and asked me in his master's name to leave the town this afternoon, as he feared that the lamas would again get drunk and might stir up a row. I naturally refused and said I did not care if they did, that I was under Chinese protection, and the Shou-pei and his men would have to take care of me as I intended immediately informing the Major of what he had just told me.

There was a big crowd of lamas and towns-people, both men and women, in the kung-kuan the whole day long, and the Hsien-sheng and I exerted ourselves to the utmost to make friends with them, and fortunately succeeded fairly well; they all went away saying that we were good friends, and that they hoped I would come back again. Trade was not brisk, for the people had nothing of any value or interest to sell me; one man brought me a couple of pecks of *yadro*,* a small bulbous root called *chih-mu yao* by the Chinese, but I had no use for it; another brought a knife, and a third some wooden cups, but no one could supply me with the things I really wanted, a kettle, a felt hat and a pair of boots. The Chinese here say that Draya is a miserable place, with no trade of any kind beyond a little musk and some peltries, mostly leopard skins. It produces nothing but barley and wheat, and even a lao-shan trader could not make a living in it. I was surprised not to find potatoes grown here nor any vegetables save turnips and *o-sung*. The soldiers complained to me of their being paid in tea; the Liang-t'ai of Bat'ang they all said was primarily and chiefly responsible for the miserable state in which they are kept. They unanimously declared that he was a great rascal.†

Goitres are very common here, but I have not seen any very large ones. Syphilitic diseases also appear to be very prevalent. I noticed two men to-day with very heavy beards, and another

* It is, I believe, the *Anemarhena asphodeloides*, and is used in China as a medicine.

† My relations with this gentleman were not of the most pleasant. See under date of *September 16th.*

man had a great deal of hair on his chest, arms and legs. He is the only one of the kind I have seen in Tibet. The women are much undersized, and the tallest man I have remarked here was only five feet, ten inches.

Most of the Chinese here know some of the French missionaries whom they have met at Bat'ang or farther east, and all speak most kindly and respectfully of them. One man told me that he had traveled some fifteen years ago with a father whom he called Hsiao-yeh. I cannot imagine what his European name can have been.

I learned that in the sixth moon of this year three scholars from the Peking Tung-wen kuan, called Hsüeh, P'in and Yi, passed through Ch'amdo on their way to Lh'asa. They were surveying the country, doing a good deal of photographing, and proposed pushing their work as far as Nielam on the British frontier. I also heard that Captain Bower crossed the Om ch'u on the ice right in front of Ch'amdo, which he was not allowed to enter and where he nearly had a fight.* He then went to Meng-pu and Pungdé, from which point he followed the same road I have been traveling along. He stopped at Draya for a day and visited the lamasery on the hill and its curiosities, among which a skull of gold especially deserved attention. I suppose it is a libation bowl.†

September 6.—The rain came down in torrents all night, but this morning the sky was beautifully clear. We left by seven o'clock accompanied by two soldiers who were to escort us as far as Ra-djong (Ra-djé it is locally called), the Lo-chia tsung of the Chinese.

Crossing the Ombo ch'u near a fine grove of poplars by a very substantial bridge, we rode up the valley of the La-sung ch'u which comes from the flanks of the Pö-jya la. We had not gone half a mile before one of the pack horses fell dead into the river, and we with difficulty recovered his load. It is a hard country on horse flesh, this makes the twenty-fourth pony I have lost since leaving Kumbum.

* This is quite correct, see Bower, *op. cit.*, 71, et seq.

† Bower does not appear to have left his lodgings while in Draya. This is another one of the senseless lies told me. I leave it in my diary for it helps one to understand how many difficulties a traveler in these countries has to contend with when he wants to get any question straightened out.

The valley is rather thickly peopled and around each little hamlet in its lower part grow patches of barley, not yet ripe for the sickle. The largest village we passed was Gumdo,* called by the Chinese O-lun-to, near which place is a bridge over the river. We passed a number of little wayside shrines, the largest near the bridge of Gumdo was remarkable for a number of yak skulls nailed against the wall, with *mantras* cut or painted in red letters on them; I counted fifteen in a single row.

I heard from one of the soldiers escorting me that the Ta Hutuketu of Draya or Chyab-gong Rinpoché Lé-pé shé-rab, as the Tibetans call him, lives at Magong (Yen-tê t'ang of the Chinese), a place two days to the south of Draya. The present incarnation is a man of about sixty. My informant also said that at Draya there were between six hundred and eight hundred lamas, one hundred and eighty odd Chinese and one thousand Tibetans. I fancy this estimate is slightly exaggerated.

We rode up the valley till we were within about half a mile of Ra-djé, when we camped on the hillside at a spot where grazing was exceptionally fine. We were all glad to be in camp instead of having to huddle together in a little room in a filthy kung-kuan.

One of the Tibetan yak drivers on the ula had a supplementary thumb growing on his right hand; this malformation appears to be as common in this country as in China. Two of the soldiers from Ra-djong came down to camp and brought me some eggs, vegetables and milk. They told us that to-morrow we would have an extra strong escort as the road over which we shall have to travel is infested by Chakba (brigands).

I forgot to note that honey is quite abundant in Draya, it is produced, I believe, to the south of that town in the villages near the Om ch'u.†

September 7.—We started out in great style this morning, for, beside the usual dirty Chinese ragamuffin of a soldier, we had six Tibetan soldiers bristling over with matchlocks, spears and swords.

---

* Probably Bower's Garing doba.

† The hives are made in hollowed out logs about four or five feet long, two being tied together and hung up under the eves of the house. The bees go in by a small hole made in one end of the log. Similar hives are in common use in many parts of the world.

About six miles south of Ra-djé we came to the head of the valley and the summit of the Po-jya la, whence we descended by a very easy declivity into a valley known as the Jya lung or "Long valley," and called by the Chinese Chia-pa k'ou or "Brigand's dale," from its being the usual haunt of bands of robbers known as the Sanghé chakba. These robber bands live along the Dré ch'u above Bat'ang and about five days' ride from this valley, and they have for the last hundred and fifty years, at least, waylaid travelers here and at two other well-known points along the highway, in the gorge south of the A-djod la (down which we will travel to-morrow) and on the Dré ch'u in front of Drubanang, a day's ride from Bat'ang, and where travelers are ferried across the river.*

It is a curious fact that these robbers should have selected for their field of operations the only road in Tibet which is patrolled by the Emperor of China's troops, and that they should have been able to carry on their business for such a length of time. At present the Chinese will take no action against these Chakba as, officially, they have ceased to exist, having been exterminated (on paper) not many years ago by an officer sent from Bat'ang or Ta-chien-lu, I do not know which, for that purpose. It is impossible to kill them off a second time, and all that can be done is to make the Tibetans fight them themselves whenever necessary.

Much against the wishes of my escort, I stopped for lunch in the Jya lung, where the grazing was, as might be expected from the valley being deserted, splendid. We saw, while drinking our tea, three or four men riding down the other side of the valley at some distance from where we were, but they did not appear to be anxious to meet us, and we on our side made no advances, so they quietly passed on.

Leaving the Long valley where it bends eastward, we crossed the Ken-jya la and entered the valley of the Lé ch'u, a good-sized stream flowing in a west-northwest direction. It is a sluggish

*See *Journ. Roy. Asiat. Soc.*, n. s. XXIII, 39, 40, 43. Cf. Bower, *op. cit.*, 81. He calls them Chukkas and Chukpas. According to a Tibetan geographical work entitled *Djamling Yéshé*, the country of these brigand tribes is called Ba-Sangan or "Sangan of Bat'ang." On Hassenstein's "*Karte des Tibelanischen und Indo-Chinesischen grenzgebieles*" in Petermann's *Geog. Mittheilungen*, 1882, Tafel 10, the home of the 'Saguen rauber" is correctly put down on the Dré ch'u above Bat'ang.

and very muddy brook of inconsiderable depth and not fifty feet broad, but it showed unmistakable signs of frequently overflowing its bank, and must often justify the term of "raging torrent" applied to it in the *Wei-Tsang t'u chih.** We followed up the right bank of the stream in a southeasterly direction for about seven miles till we came to Adjod (called A-tsu t'ang by the Chinese), where we camped in a little meadow (*ping pa-tzŭ* in Chinese) below the village.

The people, men and women, were engaged in harvesting the barley, and I noticed some very handsome girls, who in type and dress reminded me of those of Kanzé in the Horba country, though larger and taller than they. There is a Wai-wei here with six Chinese soldiers, and they and the people were very kind and friendly; unfortunately it began raining towards dusk and everyone went home, leaving us under our tent in the meadow, which was soon transformed into a pond, but it was too late to change our camping ground, and so we had to make the best of it for the night.

The only local products of Adjod are a poor variety of pottery and swords and knives of no great value or beauty. At Nyéwa (which we pass through to-morrow), swords are also manufactured, but I cannot learn where the iron ore is procured.

September 8.—We got up feeling pretty seedy and stiff, and were glad to start off and walk a few miles, as far as the top of the Adjod la. For the first time on the journey we had a Chinese soldier armed with sword and matchlock; usually the knife in their chopsticks case is their only weapon. Five Tibetan soldiers also accompanied us, to protect us against the possible attacks of Chakba on the south side of the Adjod la.

The country between Adjod and Nyéwa† (Shih-pan-kou of the Chinese) is desert, and the latter place, where there are four Chinese soldiers and about ten native families, is dirty and uninteresting. A little barley is raised around the village. Nyéwa is on the right bank of a stream flowing westward, and about a mile out of the way of the traveler going to Gart'ok, for the highroad strikes up a gorge to the east of the village.

* *Journ. Roy. Asiat. Soc.*, n. s. XXIII, 51.

† Bower's Asi.

We did not stop at Nyéwa but pushed rapidly on as the stage to Lar t'ang is a long one (about twenty-five miles). The Tang-yao shan which we had to cross on leaving the Nyéwa valley, and whose Tibetan name I could not learn*—the soldier who escorted me being a recruit and only speaking a few words of Tibetan—marks the boundary in this direction between Draya and Mar-K'ams, or "Lower K'ams," a province belonging to Lh'asa with Gart'ok, Chiang-k'a in Chinese, as its capital.†

The descent from the Tang-yao shan led down a little gorge at the lower end of which are two hamlets. Thence crossing a low col we entered the broad Lar t'ang or "Plain of Lar" (A-la t'ang of the Chinese), where we camped beside the little Trigu gomba on the bank of a stream flowing southward down a narrow valley, the lower part of which appeared to be covered with dense forest growth. About forty akas reside in this lamasery. Lar t'ang extends for about four miles in an east and west direction, and a couple of villages occupy commanding positions on the hills on its northern side. The country hereabout is very bare, not a tree to be seen anywhere, and in the plain there is hardly any ground under cultivation; it is at too great an altitude. I noticed a few domestic fowls in some of the villages; they are the first I have seen among the Tibetans.

We had not much more than made camp when there was a violent thunderstorm and a good deal of snow fell on the mountains south of us. These mountains, by the way, appear to be of considerable height and trend very nearly southeast and northwest. I fancy the Om ch'u flows along the nearer side of them, and that consequently that river cannot at this point be over six or eight miles from where we are now camped; probably it flows by the mouth of the little wooded valley below the gomba. The Om ch'u valley must here be quite wide and thickly peopled, if one may believe the descriptions given me of it by the people along the road, who spoke of it as a very rich Rongwa. One man gave me some twenty little peaches which had come from this Rongwa.

---

* Bower calls it Thongia la. Tang-yao may be the Chinese pronunciation of the native name, which perhaps is Tong jya.

† The name of this province is variously written Merlam, Merkang, Merkam, Markam, but it is certainly Mar-K'ams. There is a Bar k'ams adjacent to or forming a part of this province. Possibly there is a Teu (Stod) K'ams or "Upper K'ams." *Yar-mar, yara-mara*, are well known Tibetan terms for "upper" and "lower."

They were too green to eat, and I fancy they are from wild trees, as the Tibetans do not cultivate fruit anywhere I have been.

Some of the akas and people living around the gomba came and chatted with us; they were very jolly, and their language so closely resembled that of Lh'asa that we could converse freely with them. The language of the Draya people, on the other hand, differed so from any we had ever heard that we could hardly understand one word in ten, though they had no trouble in understanding us. All the men who came to my tent carried little bamboo flutes (*lingbu*), on which some of them played quite agreeably, and several of which I bought.

The road we have been following since Pungdé is the one described in the *Wei Tsang t'u chih*, but either the country has very much changed since 1791, when that book was written, or else its authors had very vivid imaginations. For example, it says, speaking of the Adjod la, that it is "a great snowy mountain where the cold is so intense that it blinds one." Of the Dzo la, between Gaga and Wangk'a, it says that "it is a great snowy mountain over which runs a dangerous and ice-covered trail, where the cold wrinkles up one's flesh and cracks the skin of the hands." And so on for every part of the road we have been over. This book is, however, very valuable and accurate as to most things, especially things historical and ethnographical.

September 9.—Heavy rain, as usual, fell during the night, but this morning the sky was clear. About two miles east of where we had camped we passed out of Lar-t'ang* and descended a valley densely covered with holly† and rhododendrons on its north side, and with pines on the hills along its southern face. This valley drains the country to the southeast as far as Rishod, the stream bending southward when about seven and a half miles west of that

* Bower appears to call this pass Thongia la.

† I call it holly, but it is called by the Chinese *ch'ing k'ang* or "Evergreen oak." In the dialect of Lit'ang it is known as *belo*. The French missionaries call it "chêne à feuilles de houx," though all the leaves on a given tree are not like holly leaves. Jaeschke gives the word *be-k'rod* as meaning "oak forest." He further says, s. v. *ch'a-ra* "*ch'a-ra* oak, also *mon ch'a-ra* (on account of its growing only on the southern ranges of the Himalaya mountains, inhabited mostly by Non-Tibetans) in several species, with pointed, evergreen leaves, a tree much inferior in beauty to the English oak." Dr. Hooker, *Himal. Journ.*, II, 114, mentions a species of oak (*Q. annulata ?*) growing on the outer Sikkim ranges to an altitude of 10,000 feet.

village. There are numerous small hamlets all the way to Rishod (Li-shu in Chinese) and the country is well cultivated.

We found Rishod such a dirty, muddy and unprepossessing place and the kung-kuan so uninviting, that we continued up the valley about five miles and camped at the foot of the Rishod la,* which separates us from the Shé ch'u on which stands the town of Gart'ok. Holly and pines reappeared on the hillsides about three miles above Rishod but they were not so large as those seen in the morning at the west end of the valley. We killed a few crossoptilons after camping; they were very plentiful and tame. They, together with wild pigeons, magpies, a small bird like a sparrow, and an occasional woodpecker are the only birds I have so far noticed in the country, crows, eagles and birds of that kind excepted. I am assured now that it only takes four or five days to go from Draya to Dérgé drongcher; this agrees well with what I heard in '89 in Dérgé. If no bad luck overtakes me, I think I will be able to reach Shanghai in about forty-five days, or by the 20th of October.

September 10.—Another heavy thunderstorm during the night. The ascent of the Rishod la was neither very long nor steep. There are in reality two cols to cross here, for from the Rishod la one descends a little and then one has to climb over another shoulder of the mountain before descending into the Shé ch'u valley. From this second summit we caught a glimpse of a wooded hillside about fifteen miles to the south, and some Tibetans who were traveling along with us said that Gart'ok was at the foot of that hill. The Rishod la and adjacent mountains are entirely composed of red sandstone conglomerate disposed in horizontal strata. On the top of the pass was a scaffold of three poles, on the cross one of which was the dried-up head of a Sanghé brigand, executed here in the early part of the year by the Gart'ok authorities.

Here, again, the authors of the *Wei Tsang t'u chih* are too imaginative; they described the Rishod la as "a great mountain, all the year covered with snow, and across which there blows, even in summer, a cold blast which pierces one to the bone." From this work it also appears that this second pass is properly the Rishod la; it gives the first one no name, only calls it "a little mountain."

* Bower's Khonsa La.

Four miles and a half below the pass we came to a little Chinese post station called Lu-ho t'ang where we found a Chinese soldier with his Tibetan wife and a number of children.* He and his family were the cleanest and best mannered people I think I have seen in this country. I stopped here to lunch and the soldier gave me a few dried fish—he had caught them in the stream near by—some mushrooms and eggs.

From about two miles below Lu-ho t'ang the mountain sides are covered with fine pines and junipers and this forest growth continues until near Gart'ok. We only passed a few black tents on the way down, and did not see a single hamlet until within two miles of the town. About a mile above the town we passed the mouth of a gorge running west-southwest up which runs a well beaten trail; this is probably the highroad to Southern Tibet, and the one followed by Kishen Singh when coming back from Ta-chien-lu.

Gart'ok is at the base of the hills on the west side of the valley, about a quarter of a mile from the river.† There is a small gomba behind the town in which live between two hundred and three hundred lamas (Gélupa), and along the river bank is a pretty *linga* of poplar trees. A Déba, appointed from Lh'asa, resides at Gart'ok, and there is also a Chinese Captain (*Shou-pei*), a Sergeant (*Pa-tsung*) and a garrison of one hundred and forty soldiers, from which are drawn all the detachments stationed along the highroad from here to Bat'ang territory. The Tibetan population of Gart'ok is estimated at two hundred families (nine hundred souls); there are also three Chinese firms of Shen-hsi traders and two or three Yün-nan or Ssŭ-ch'uan ones which carry on a small business in musk, the only export of any value to China from this district.

I found the kung-kuan quite a large and commodious building, and we had two good rooms assigned us with a kitchen and sufficient stable room for our poor ponies, who are all on their last legs. There is, I should remark, a small Kuan-ti miao here and the whole place is much Chinesefied. Pigs, fowls and half-breed children tumble about the muddy lanes together, and there

* Bower camped here. He calls this station Mongothong, and gives its altitude as 13,700 feet.

† The French missionaries established a station here in 1861, but after a year or so they had to withdraw to Bonga, farther south. See C. H. Desgodins, *Le Thibet*, 93, et seq. Huc, *op. cit.*, II, 498, calls it Kiang-tsa.

are a number of shops where different odds and ends are offered for sale.

In the evening the women and children sang prayers in chorus for over an hour seated in a circle before their doors; this is a custom commonly observed in most parts of Tibet, but which I had not remarked on this journey, probably because I have most of the time been among Bönbo and Drupa.

The Shou-pei was away, acting as arbitrator in a quarrel between two villages, but the Pa-tsung, a handsome young Mohammedan from Ta-chien-lu, whose people I knew, was very kind and made us as comfortable and as much at home as he could. He had been stationed for a number of years at Lh'asa and had adopted many of the customs of that locality, among others he smoked the hubble-hubble in use there among the Kashmiris; his wife was a handsome Lh'asan woman.

September 11.—The Pa-tsung sent me this morning a basket of grapes, some peaches (*semkam*) and apricots, and a big basket of vegetables. The fruit all came from the Rongmä ("Low country or farm lands") along the Dré ch'u, some two or three days south-southeast of here. The fruit, peaches and apricots, were very poor and, I think, wild.* At Gart'ok cabbages, turnips, *o-sung*, wheat, barley and oats are grown, and I am inclined to think that the oats are a wild variety,† like that which one sees in our southwestern country, New Mexico and Colorado. Pigs, fowls, cats, and Chinese dogs are also common here.

I had to ask the Pa-tsung to supply me with ula ponies and pack animals as not one of mine is fit to travel ten miles, and I have hardly any money left. I had considerable difficulty in selling to-day some musk I had bought at Song-chyang sumdo and elsewhere in Jaydé, and could only get about the same price I had originally paid for it. If I could have afforded to hold on to it until I had reached Ta-chien-lu I might have realized a considerable

* Alph. de Candolle, *Origine des Plantes Cultivées*, 177, is inclined to think that the peach tree comes originally from China. The same author (*op. cit.* p. 173) thinks that the apricot tree is a native of the region extending from the northwest of China to India.

† Moorcroft, *Travels*, II, 27, makes mention of wild oats in Ladak. De Condolle (*op. cit.*, 299) says that mention is made of oats in a Chinese historical work covering the period from 618 to 907 A. D. He thinks the plant originally came from eastern temperate Europe and Tartary (p. 302).

profit. As it is, I only got about sixty rupees, little enough for a month's journey. I will have to try and borrow some money at Bat'ang.

The Pa-tsung has acted very kindly and issued, on presentation of my passport and when I had explained how short I was of funds, an ula order good as far as Ta-chien-lu. It is a big weight off my mind for I really have no right to ula, which the Tibetans frequently refuse to Chinese officials. I am told that if we double stages—no very difficult thing—we can reach Ta-chien-lu in fifteen days. The harvest feast with lama dancing is being celebrated to-day just outside the town. All those who have tents have put them up on the meadow below the gomba, where are also camping people from all the neighboring hamlets; they are making merry, drinking and singing while the lamas are having the usual lama dance, a few of their number prancing about with hideous masks on to the accompaniment of drums, cymbals and hautboys; the Ta lama and the gomba authorities sit under a tent, drink tea and look on. The Chinese of Kumbum call such dances *t'iao-shai hou*, the Pekinese, *t'iao kuei.*

There is a Chinese here who told me that he had traveled with T. T. Cooper;* he spoke very kindly of him, and said he was a most excellent man. He went from Bat'ang to A-tun-tzŭ with him, I think he said. According to his statement Cooper had with him a Hankow Chinese who spoke and wrote foreign languages; this as I remember, is quite correct, Cooper had a Christian who spoke Latin.†

For the first time in Tibet I notice quantities of house sparrows. The people call them *cheuba.*‡

September 12.—We left Gart'ok at 7.30 with a Chinese soldier and two Tibetan ones, the latter supplied by the Mar-K'ams Déba. After fording the Shé ch'u in front of the town, we rode down

* Cooper traveled in 1868 from Ta-chien-lu to Bat'ang and thence south to Wei-hsi, whence he was forced to return to Ta-chien-lu by the way he had come. (See *Travels of a Pioneer of Commerce.*)

† His name was George Phillips. He had been educated at Macao. See T. T. Cooper, *op. cit.*, 15.

‡ Jaeschke gives the name as *chyapo* or *chyavo*, written *bya-po* and *skya-vo* respectively. Bonvalot (*op. cit.*, 339) says he heard sparrows twittering at So gomba on the Su ch'u.

the left bank of the river for about three miles, when we crossed the stream again and continued down the right bank until in front of P'ulag, when we crossed back to the left one.

The Shé ch'u valley below Gart'ok is well timbered with pine and juniper trees; in places even the valley bottom is covered with them. This valley is one of the finest I have seen; but unfortunately for the people, the highroad runs the whole length of it, and the inhabitants are ground down and interfered with in their work by the constant ula services they are called on to perform. Fortunately for them, however, the ula is changed at each village. Thus between Gart'ok and Guh'u (nineteen miles) we changed it four times, the first time when only three miles from our starting point, and a second time less than one and one-half miles farther on. At P'ulag there was not a single yak to be found when I arrived, and I feared that I would have to stop over here (it is the regular stage from Gart'ok), and the prospect was not unpleasing as the kung-kuan is large and comfortable, but after waiting an hour or so some horses came in from Gart'ok and we were able to push on.

The Shé ch'u valley is well cultivated, but villages are few; we only passed three between Gart'ok and P'ulag. This is the usual thing in Tibet; the people will not live near the highroads; they prefer more remote, though possibly poorer, localities, for there they are not interfered with by traveling officials. Leaving the Shé ch'u valley at P'ulag we turned eastward up a narrow valley leading to the Latsé la* and every where covered with pines, holly-oaks and juniper trees. Having crossed the pass we descended to Guh'u, or Ku-shu in Chinese. From the summit of the Latsé la I saw, about twenty miles to the west-southwest, a range of bare, jagged peaks here and there covered with snow. I was told that they were in Mar-K'ams.

It was dark when we reached the kung-kuan at Guh'u, and I was much surprised to find a candle burning on a table in a clean room, a big fire-bowl glowing on a stand, and a pot of tea and china cups ready on the table. The kung-kuan keeper turned out to be, not only an admirable house-keeper, but a first rate cook. He came in, made his bow, and asked if I would allow him to cook my supper, he was something of a cook he modestly said, and would like to show us what he could do. Having only stipulated with him that we should have *ching fan* ("clean food"),

* Mang shan of the Chinese. Bower's Lamba la and Dosi la. The two are only separated by a few hundred yards.

for we were Mohammedans and could eat none other, he set to work and soon served us a capital meal in six courses. Not only had he good, plump fowls and eggs, but all the condiments dear to the Chinese *cordon–bleu*, soy, *kan-fen*, ginger, red peppers, salted vegetables, etc., besides rice, vermicelli and last, but not least, good

BAMBOO JEW'S-HARP AND CASE—FULL SIZE (Bat'ang).

bread. The Hsien-sheng and I, the ula and the other two men had not yet arrived, sat long over this wonderful meal, and felt so happy when it was over that we called in a lot of the natives and had them dance to the dulcet sounds of the jew's-harp (*k'a-pi*).

This most ancient, primitive and popular instrument is brought to this part of the country (it is only used in and around Bat'ang), from the Ts'ak'a lung and the country to the south of here, and is not of Tibetan origin, nor, I think, make. It consists of three bamboo harps each of different tone, all of them played together held in the left hand, the one above the other, that with the highest note at the top. The harp with the deepest note is said to give the *p'o kä* (*p'o skad*) or "male note," the middle one gives the *ding kä* or "middle note," and the sharper note is known as *mo kä* or "female note." Three or four persons frequently play together in unison, and nearly every girl or woman carries a *k'a-pi* suspended from her girdle in a bamboo case, usually prettily decorated with chevron shaped carvings and bands of colored quills. The Chinese of Kan-su call the jew's-harp *k'ou hsien;* the Pekinese name for this instrument is *k'ou ch'i.** The Tibetan name is an exact counterpart of the Kan-su one, for *k'a* means "mouth," and *pi* stands for *pi-wang*, the three stringed banjo (*san hsien*).

At Geh'u live twenty Tibetan families and three Chinese soldiers. The village is shaded by fine poplars and is, I fancy, a rather desirable place, as far as climate goes, as it is well sheltered on every side by mountains and forests; at all events the Chinese here seemed to like it very much, and I do not hesitate to pronounce its kung-kuan the best in Tibet.

September 13.—The valley in which Guh'u stands runs nearly north and south,† so we only crossed it, ascending the Hondo la through a country covered with fine pines, and then traveling down a narrow but well cultivated valley to the important village of Lh'amdun (Nan-tun of the Chinese).‡ This point is at the junction of two roads leading, the one to Bat'ang and Ta-chien lu, the other to A-tun-tzŭ, Wei-hsi and Li-chiang Fu in Yün-nan. It is the most easterly point of Mar-K'ams in this direction, the Bat'ang boundary being on the summit of the Bam la a few miles to the northeast of it. The district is ruled by a K'anpo sent from Lh'asa and who lives in a little gomba behind the village. He

* The Pekinese jew's-harp is of iron and very like the one used among us.

† Bower calls the stream which flows by Guh'u (his Goshu) Mongothongchu river.

‡ Bonvalot's Leindünne; Bower's Lande.

and his twenty akas belong to the Sachyapa school. There are some fifteen to twenty families of Tibetans and three or four Chinese soldiers here, also a Kuan-ti miao and a fairly good kung-kuan.

We stopped for an hour at Lh'amdun while the ula was being changed, drank some tea and ate some yellow raspberries (here called *trésui*) offered me by the soldiers. I noticed in use here a good many Chinese utensils, especially of iron and copper, among which a curiously shaped cast iron teapot, cylindrical in shape and over a foot deep and five or six inches in diameter.* The copper-ware comes, I am told, from the Chien-ch'ang, from which district, by the way, comes also the best quality of the red leather so much used in Tibet. The wooden bowls, plates, round covered boxes and other similar utensils in use at Gart'ok and all through this part of the country are brought from Yün-nan.

Leaving Lh'amdun we passed over the Bam la.† We saw on the summit of the pass a large red sandstone slab half sunk in the ground. This marks the boundary between Mar-K'ams and Bat'-ang or, as the people say, between Déba djong and Jyadé, for from Bat'ang to Ta-chien-lu is also known by this latter name. I was told that there was an inscription on it, but on the part now below the surface of the ground.‡ About four miles below the pass we came to the village of Bam-ding (Pang-mu in Chinese)‖ where we had again to change the ula. While it was being got together I rested in the headman's house and his wife, a fine, well dressed and agreeable woman, gave me pomegranates (*supong*) and pears from the Rongmä, a district two days south of here, and some walnuts (*taga*), which grow in great quantities near this place.

The dress of the women at Lh'amdun and Bam-ding differs considerably from that worn farther west. It consists of a petticoat of striped pulo with heavy box plaits behind, a waistcoat (*kan-chien*), and a loose gown coming to the knee. Women

* In Shan-hsi and parts of Shen-hsi a similar kettle is in use.

† Or *laka;* this latter term is very frequently used in eastern Tibet for the former, but more correct, one.

‡ This boundary line was marked by a joint commission in 1726. See *Journ. Roy. Asiat. Soc.*, n. s., XXIII, 46.

‖ Bower's Bon. Capt. Gill, coming from Bat'ang and on his way to A-tun-tzŭ, traversed Bam-ding and passing over the eastern shoulder of the Bam la, struck the Shé ch'u (his Kiang Ka river) about eighteen miles south of that village.

wear their hair in one heavy braid with a large tassel at the end. They have no ornaments save earrings of the Bat'ang pattern, and numerous finger rings. The men's costume presents no peculiarity; it is the usual eastern Tibetan one.

It took a long time to get the ula ready, and when it came there was endless wrangling about the division of loads, each person wanting the animal belonging to him to carry a light one. The question was finally decided in the way usual in Tibet: each person on the ula gave one of his or her garters, no two pairs of which are woven in the same pattern, to the headman and he, holding them behind his back drew out first one garter, then another and placed one on each load at random, when the owner of the garter picked up the load and put it on his beast without murmuring.*

We made about five miles down the valley to a small hamlet called Djin-k'ang ding (near Mang-li† of the Chinese), where we stopped for the night in the headman's house, a portion of which is set off as a kung-kuan. It is a fine three-storied stone building, and the room given us was a very nice one. After dark the room was lit by means of chips of pitch pine burnt on a flat stone, though the usual butter lamps were not wanting. We got the women of the house to dance for us, and I awarded prizes of bits of ribbon to the best performers. While dancing they played on the jew's-harp and the step was a slow shuffle, a poor imitation I thought, of a darkey dance. We were again given pomegranates, pears and walnuts here; the first named fruit is small and flavorless, and is used more as an ornament, something like the citron called "Buddha's hand" (*Fo shou*) in China.

September 14.—Below Djin-k'ang ding‡ the valley narrows to a mere ravine covered with a dense growth of pines, holly-leaved oaks and junipers under which is a thick undergrowth of creepers and ferns; wild cherry and apricot trees are also plentiful. The road leads along the side of the hills, and the stream which flows down the valley is, after a little while, hundreds of feet below the road, dashing over rocks and fallen trees and hurrying on to the Dré ch'u which it meets a few miles to the east.

---

* Conf. Bonvalot, *op. cit.*, 363.

† Capt. Gill gives the Tibetan name of Mang-li (which is on the east side of the valley just opposite Djin-k'ang ding) as Mûng-M'heh.

‡ *Ding* in Bam ding, Djin-k'ang ding, Taga ding, etc., means "village, hamlet."

Continuing northward to the other end of this pretty valley we came to Kondjinka (Kung-tzŭ ting of the Chinese), where we changed the ula. The house of the headman is a large and commodious building, and much of the interior finish of the rooms is Chinese. I suppose Chinese carpenters from Bat'ang built it; they travel all over Tibet.* The women of the house were taking their dinner while we rested, and I noticed that they ate green peppers with their tsamba, a mixture I had not yet seen in this country. A variety of vegetables are raised around this village, but, taking them as a whole, the Tibetans are not a vegetable-eating people. Pigs, fowls, and pigeons were plentiful here.

When the *Wei Tsang t'u chih* was written (1791), the high-road between this point and Djin-k'ang ding did not apparently run up this valley, but to the west of it, for it is said that between these two localities "a big mountain, infested by brigands, has to be crossed."†

A half mile beyond Kondjink'a we reached the head of the valley,‡ and at the mouth of the one beyond it, about seven miles away, we saw the Dré ch'u flowing in a narrow valley on either side of which rise steep, bare mountains of reddish brown color, the waters of the great river dyed of the same color.

The valley leading down to the river is covered for most of its length with dense foliage and thick undergrowth. We only passed two villages, one called Taga ding or "the Walnut village," from the wide-spreading walnut trees surrounding and half hiding the village. Here we again changed the ula, to again change it a couple of miles farther down, just before reaching the river. At Taga ding I noticed for the first time some small true oak trees.||

We stopped for the night at Gura (Kung-la in Chinese), about a mile up the valley of the Dré ch'u. The valley bottom is here about a quarter of a mile wide on the right bank of the river, and the hamlet stands some two hundred feet above the river, while on the left bank, as far as I could see up and down the valley, the mountains seemed to rise precipitously from the water's side.

* See *Land of the Lamas*, 194.

† See *Journ. Roy. Asiat. Soc.*, n. s. XXIII, 49.

‡ Gill's Kong-Tze-La-Ka pass and Bower's Khonji-la pass.

|| Bower says (p. 85) that in this valley he saw squirrels on the trees. He calls Taga ding, Tangati.

Around Gura millet of two varieties (*huang mi* and *hsaio mi* the Chinese call them), squashes, peppers, wheat, etc., are grown. We camped beside a little cattle-pen, as the houses at this place were far from attractive, small, dirty and dilapidated, and overrun with vermin and children.

September 15.—A Tibetan escort of six well-armed men accompanied us to-day as far as the ferry across the Dré ch'u, which is at a point called Tsobo ch'uk'a, about two and a half miles south of Drubanang. This precaution was taken because the Sanghé chakba are said to frequently attack caravans while in the act of loading or unloading at this place.*

The road all the way to the ferry was over rocks and through sand and gravel, the mountains rising precipitously from the river bank; here and there a little brush grew along the water's edge. The only incident of the day was an encounter with the first snake I had seen in Tibet, a water snake, I think, about four feet long marked with longitudinal bands of light green and black.

We were rapidly ferried across the river in a large flat-bottomed boat made and manned by Chinese soldiers. There are two of these boats kept for this ferry, but one is usually anchored in front of Drubanang and only used in an emergency, or when the other is being repaired. There is no charge made for ferrying travelers and their cattle over, the ferry being maintained by the Chinese government.

At Drubanang (Chu-pa lung in Chinese) there are a few acres of ground under cultivation on either side of the river, and in the village live ten or twelve families of natives and four or five Chinese soldiers. The ula had to be changed here, and as all the cattle were on the right bank of the river and it required a long time to get them over to the village, I decided to push on without them, instructing the Lao-han to come on with them, while I, the Hsien-sheng and Kao pa-erh rode on to Bat'ang, still a long way off.

About eleven and a half miles farther up the river we came to the little hamlet of Shui-mo-k'ou† where we tried to get fresh ponies, but the headman refused to give me any until the ula from Druba-

* Gill came near having an encounter with some of these brigands when crossing the river at this point in 1877. See *River of Golden Sands*, II, 209.

† Probably Gill's Leh and Bower's Lah; there is here a little lh'a-k'ang between the village and the river.

nang had arrived. After a good deal of wrangling, I got one horse for Kao pa-erh and we rode off as rapidly as we could, as it was beginning to get dark and we had a steep mountain to cross and about eleven miles to make before reaching the town.

A mile or so above Shui-mo-k'ou, or rather at another little hamlet called by the Chinese Shan ken (or "Foot of the hill),* we left the Dré ch'u and crossing a steep mountain by a very rough and stony path down which we had to grope our way in the dark, we came into the valley of Bat'ang, *the* "garden spot of Tibet."

The Ba-ch'ung ch'u or Bat'ang river empties into the Dré ch'u at the base of the mountain we had just crossed. The Bat'ang valley is not over a quarter to a half mile wide and is well cultivated and thickly peopled; little hamlets and detached farm-houses, each surrounded by a grove of walnut or fruit trees, line the road from the foot of the hill to the town.

It was nine o'clock when we reached Bat'ang; the town was asleep and we had much difficulty in getting the kung-kuan keeper to open the door of that building for us, and when he did, he was very impudent and we had to wrangle for half an hour before we could get him to give us some tea and tsamba.

It was with a deep sense of relief that I closed to-night my traverse book and packed up my prismatic compass which I have constantly had in my hand since the first day of last December. Thirty-four hundred miles of surveying is no joke, and now that my traverse has joined that surveyed by Capt. Gill, whose accuracy and care we Tibetan travelers have learned to appreciate, I can safely bring my mapping to an end.

September 16.—Ba (Pa-t'ang of the Chinese) has been so frequently described † that I will say but little of the place itself. There are some two hundred families of Tibetans living here and a hundred odd Chinese, of whom, perhaps, thirty or forty are soldiers. In the great lamasery, which is on the west side of the town, live about 1,500 akas, the total population of the town,

* Gill's Niu-ku, Bower's Nougen. Gill calls the mountain Ch'a-Shu Shan or Ch'a-Keu Pass, altitude, 9,388 feet.

† See Huc, *op. cit.*, II, 502; T. T. Cooper, *op. cit,*, 245, et seq. Gill, *op. cit.*, II, 183, et seq. Bonvalot, *op. cit.*, 440. Bower, *op, cit.*, 85. *Rep. on Explor.* by A—— K——, 69, etc., etc.

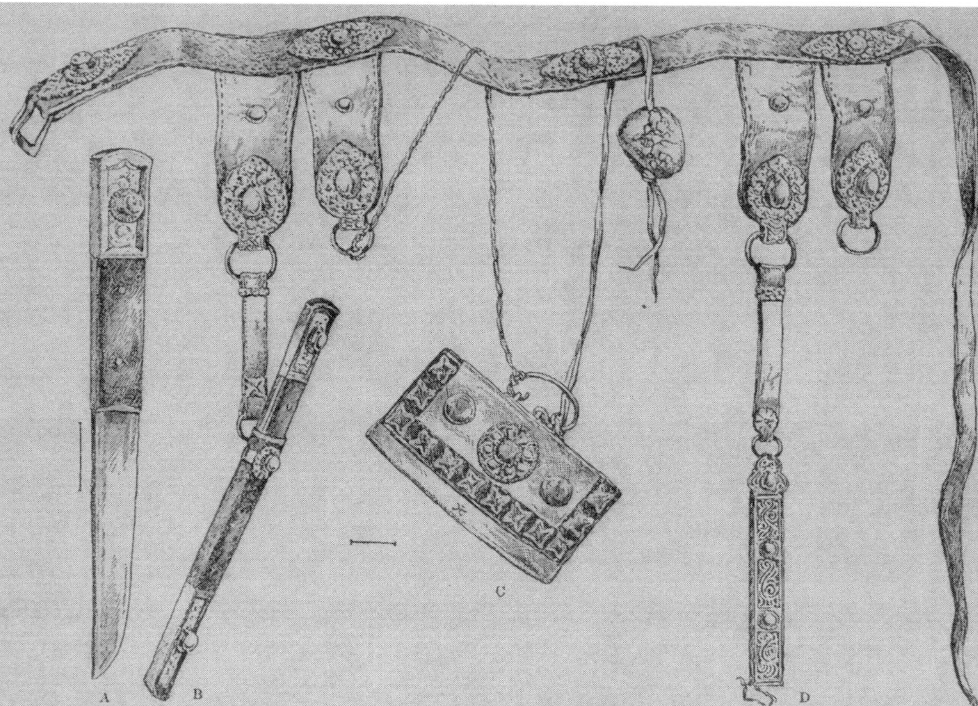

LEATHER BELT, chatelaines in silver and coral, knife and sheath (A B) silver and coral ornamentation, tinder pouch and steel (C) silver and coral ornamentation, with large turquoise hanging by thong, needle case of wrought iron and silver (D). (Dérgé.) (Property of the author.)

including the hamlets and the two or three little gombas in its immediate vicinity, may therefore be about 3,000.*

A Chinese quartermaster (*Liang-t'ai*) and a captain represent the Chinese government here, and the native authorities consist of a first and second Déba, known in Chinese as Cheng T'u-ssŭ and Fu T'u-ssŭ. The Chinese tell me that there is hardly any trade here, and there are only two small Chinese firms doing business in the town. The lamas do what trading there is and lend money to the Chinese, who are but their agents.

The climate of the Bat'ang valley is very mild, and wheat, millet, buckwheat, string beans, peas, squashes, cucumbers, peppers, cabbages, onions, peaches, pears, apricots, grapes, and watermelons (the latter known by its Chinese name of *kua-kua*), thrive here.† It is now the peach season, and quantities of small but tolerably sweet fruit were brought us. The butter sold here is very nice, I bought a quantity from a Mohammedan butcher; it was put up in little oblong prints and wrapped in poplar leaves. The rolls of bread are also delicious, but the meat is very poor, most of it yak flesh.

I had to go and see the Liang-t'ai, Wang by name, as my money was exhausted and I thought he might lend me some on a check payable to his order at Ta-chien-lu by Mgr. Biet. I put on my foreign clothes for the first time since last November, and the change was most delightful, for before dressing I managed to get a tubbing, and I actually felt clean, a nearly forgotten sensation. The Liang-t'ai was not over polite and said he had no money; I told him I would have to stay here until I could get money from Ta-chien-lu if he would not assist me, and I asked him to make inquiries at the lamasery if some one would not let me have 50 taels. All lamaseries are engaged in money lending; the question is, will they lend to a foreigner? I doubt it. The soldiers tell me the Liang-t'ai is a blackguard and treats them all very badly. I fancy this is true. I have been hearing of him ever since I came on to the highroad; he is the man who pays the soldiers in tea,

* A—— K—— (Kishen Singh) says that there are about two thousand houses, including fifty shops, at Bat'ang. *Report on Explor.*, 69. Gill, *op. cit.*, II, 189, says: "At Bat'ang, where there are only three hundred families, the lamasery contains thirteen hundred lamas." On Bat'ang and its history see *Journ. Roy. Asiat. Soc.*, n. s. XXIII, 46, 124, 249, 260 and 272.

† On the climate of Bat'ang, see Desgodins, *op. cit.*, 469.

fixing its value at twice what it is worth here, and dividing the profits of his rascality with the Commissary General at Ta-chien-lu.

The Liang-t'ai said he would let me know to-morrow if he could get the money. I don't exactly know what I will do if he does not get me any; we have two rupees between us and a few coral beads and other odds and ends of no great value, some of which we might sell, but I fear that as people know I am in a tight place, no one will buy any thing from me.

This place appears to me dull and devoid of interest; if I had some money in my purse it might look brighter and more interesting.

September 17.—The Bat'angites are very much Chinesefied and have lost many of the pleasing traits I noticed in the wilder tribes of the west. On the whole, Chinese influence in Tibet has been distinctly deleterious, for while China has introduced among this people a few of the arts and conveniences of its higher civilization, it has debased them morally. Here, and along the highroad generally, the free, open demeanor so noticeable in Jyadé and among the Panak'a and K'amba, has given place to the cringing, servile Chinese forms of politeness and duplicity. The Head Déba, for example, is a thorough Chinese,* even in dress, speaking Chinese with a broad Ssŭ-ch'uanese accent, and smoking all day long a water-pipe. The filth of the streets is quite Chinese, but the laziness of the people is not an importation from foreign parts. The men are Tibetans in dress, except that they wear their hair *à la Chinoise.* They are tall (five feet ten and over) and many of them corpulent. The dress of the women is like that of Bam-ding, previously referred to, with the exception that all wear aprons of narrow striped pulo or Pomä stuff. These are also worn at Lh'asa and over most of Tibet, except among the Drupa, where the ch'uba is the only garment of both sexes. The women are quite as much beasts of burden here as in other parts of the country, and their morals are not any better. The men do not usually carry the long sword common among Tibetans; most

* Gill, *op. cit.*, II, 196, says that "the first native chief of Bat'ang is of Chinese extraction, but as his family came from Yün-Nan ten generations since, he may fairly be considered as a native of the soil. * * * His elder brother is the second chief." Gill's chief has now retired, and his son is first chief. The second chief is the same one Gill knew.

of them have only a Chinese knife and chopsticks, though a few carry a short dirk of Shigatsé make and of decidedly Indian pattern.

Barley and walnuts are used here in lieu of subsidiary coinage. I bought a few bushels of the former to exchange for vegetables, salt, etc. Some scaleless fish, caught in the Ba-chung ch'u and about eighteen inches long, were brought to me, but I don't care for fish in this country, they eat too many corpses.

The Liang-t'ai has sent me word that he can do nothing for me, the lamas will not lend any money, and he has none, his military funds (*ping-hsiang*) have not arrived and he has no money here of his own. It is very vexatious but not desperate, for I can always travel as Chinese officials do, live on the people and give no presents. I saw him later in the day; he said he would give me ula and all I required and that I had no need for money. I told him that we foreigners would be ashamed to travel as he and the like of him did and not pay for what we got, but he did not appreciate these honorable sentiments and his reply implied that he thought me a fool.

I hear a great deal here about Gill, Mesny, Szechenyi and the other foreigners who have been through here. On the wall of the kung-kuan I found the signatures of all of them, from Szechnyi down to Bower; each with a patriotic motto under his name. The Déba spoke to me a great deal of Chi Wei-li (Gill) and Mei-Ssŭ-ni (Mesny) and of the Ching Wang (Prince d'Orleans); the two first he seemed to remember with great pleasure. Many of the soldiers, and not a few of the Tibetans, asked me about the Fathers of Ta-chien-lu and regretted that they had been forced to leave this country.

September 18.—I had a very lively interview with the Liang-t'ai; he was extremely rude, forgot all his official manners, yelled and gesticulated like a mad man, and behaved like a fool generally. I said I would report him to the Tsung-li Ya-mên, which, of course, I will not do, as I have no one at Peking to look after my interests. Having told him what I thought of him, I got up, and without a word of salutation walked out. It was very disagreeable; nearly every Chinese in town was crowded around the door of the room in which we were squabbling, and heard every word of our altercation.

The head Déba came to see me and wanted to buy my revolver. I asked him thirty taels, but he would only give ten and I refused to part with it. Knowing that I was in need of money he tried to make some good bargains, but the end of it all was that I would not sell him any thing. The Hsien-sheng sold the little remaining musk we had for twenty rupees, and we will be able to get along some way or other till Lit'ang is reached, where the Pa-tsung is an old acquaintance of '89 (he was then at Dawo), and will possibly help me on to Ta-chien-lu.

The Déba brought with him his collection of watches, of which he had between twenty and thirty of every make and metal, and wanted me to repair a dozen or so of them. The last addition to his collection was a "railway watch," which he said had been obtained from a British soldier in Sikkim last year and had been sold to him in Lh'asa.

I got the ula ordered for to-morrow; the head of the transportation service, a relative of the Déba's and a very obliging fellow, has promised me first rate ponies. It is a "long ula" and will go as far as Lamaya, which is the frontier post of Bat'ang to the east. I hear that there is a big bobbery at Lit'ang, and that the road between here and Nyach'uk'a is practically closed to trade; all the tea for Central Tibet is going by way of Kanzé to Dérgé and Ch'amdo. This explains in a degree the bad times at Bat'ang.

September 19.—We had a violent thunder storm during the night, the first we have had for some days. The ula arrived early and I was pleased to see that all the mules were good strong ones and that we would be able to make good time. We left at nine o'clock and struck up the valley of the Gun ch'u, which, coming down from the Taso pass, empties into the Ba-ch'ung ch'u at Bat'ang, where it is spanned by a good bridge.

The lower course of the Gun ch'u as far as Hsiao pa-ch'ung is through a rocky gorge, but above that point until one reaches the timber-line, the mountains on either side of the narrow valley are covered with pine, birch, oak and juniper trees and dense undergrowth. From the branches of the holly-leaved evergreen oaks or *ching k'ang*, hang long, thread-like moss of sea green or orange color.*

* *Usnea barbata.* This oak tree does not grow in this valley at a higher altitude than P'ongdramo, 12,632 feet.

About one-quarter of a mile from Bat'ang we passed a little gomba at the mouth of the Gun ch'u valley. A little farther on we came to the Hot springs (*Ts'a ch'u-k'a*) where there are a couple of low stone walls built around the springs. The springs are now nearly dry, and the reservoir over each one is not more than three or four feet square, not big enough to take much of a bath in. The people come here at certain seasons of the year (September I believe) to bathe, when they picnic by the river side and amuse themselves with singing, dancing and bathing; this is their one annual bath.

P'ongdramo (Chinese Peng-cha-mu) is a filthy hamlet with a kung-kuan, where live five or six Chinese soldiers who attend to the ula. This kung-kuan is known as a Han-Man kung-kuan or a "Chinese-Tibetan post-station;" government employés of both nationalities can stop in it. It is the second stage from Bat'ang, the first being at Hsiao pa-ch'ung.

According to Chinese itineraries P'ongdramo is 90 *li* from Bat'ang, but I only made it sixteen miles from that place. The Chinese government magnifies the distances along these remote and difficult post roads so that it appears to the home government that the couriers cover enormous distances in a very short time. In the kung-kuan here (at P'ongdramo) was posted a notice to government couriers issued by the Ping P'u (War Office) of Peking. I take the following from it: "The War Office fixes the distance from Ta-chien-lu to Nyach'uk'a (Ho-k'ou or Chung-tu) at 330 *li*, and the time allowed couriers to ride this is limited to twenty-four hours. From Nyach'uk'a to Li-t'ang the distance is 320 *li*, and couriers are allowed twenty-four hours to make it in. From Lit'ang to Bat'ang the distance is 480 *li*, and thirty-six hours is the time allowed. From Bat'ang to Lh'amdun is 220 *li*, to be ridden in sixteen hours. The penalty for being four hours late is ten blows with the heavy bamboo, for being six hours late, twenty blows, and for any longer delay, fifty blows. It is furthermore expressly forbidden to remit these punishments, they must be inflicted in every case."

Chinese itineraries agree with this order; they make the distance between Ta-chien-lu and Bat'ang about 1,200 *li*, but Captain Gill and most other European travelers who have gone over this road say it is about two hundred and twenty-five miles. In other words, the Chinese count 5 *li* to the mile when in mountainous country, whereas they only count three to the same distance when in flat country. The *li* is, therefore, in practice more a measure of time than of distance, a fact to which Baber and other travelers have, by the way, already referred.

At Bat'ang and at the various hamlets this side of it I noticed that birch bark cups and pails are largely used; they are made in the same way as those used in the Kuei-tê country.

The Hsien-sheng told me that the holly oak is found in the Han-chung Fu country;* the acorns are collected and sent to Hsi-ning Fu and other localities in Kan-su where they are used as a dye, giving the dark brown color to the felt hats worn in those parts.

September 20.—A few miles above P'ongdramo we reached the timber-line, and thence as far as the summit of the Dasho pass, the trail was over a mass of granite boulders with here and there a little patch of short grass. In the hollow near the summit of the pass are two small tarns. There was a little snow on the west side of the peaks around the pass, and on the east side a slightly larger quantity.

The descent to the hamlet of Dasho was steep, and the view from the lower part of the valley, at the mouth of which stands this unprepossessing place, very picturesque. Before us rose steep rocky peaks covered with snow, and on the sides of the valley down which we were traveling were dark pine trees, with here and there a birch or some other deciduous tree in its autumn foliage of yellow or red.

There are three or four houses at Dasho (Ta-so t'ang the Chinese call it), one of which is a kung-kuan, filthier even than its neighbor at P'ongdramo. The mud was so deep in the courtyard that we could hardly reach the door. We only stopped here to change our escort and then rode on, as Zamba t'ang was still a long way off, and a high mountain separated us from that place.

The women at Dasho wear a form of head-ornament resembling somewhat that adopted in the Horba country. It consists of a discoidal piece of amber, about two and one-half inches in diameter, with a coral bead in the center. One of these ornaments is worn on either side of the head, and the hair is arranged in three

* In northeast Shen-hsi.

plaits hanging down behind, and on these are fastened a quantity of silver plaques and bits of turquoise. The general effect is very ugly.

A good-sized rivulet, the Pa-lung-ta of the Chinese (and Ba-rong ta of the Tibetans),* flows down the Dasho valley and is crossed by a bridge a mile or so below the hamlet. From a little way beyond this point the Ba-rong ta valley, which is at least a quarter of a mile wide in places, is well timbered, but we only saw one or two houses in it. There is a trail which goes down this valley to the warm districts to the south (Ba-rong or Rongwa of Ba), but our road left the river after a few miles, and by a steep gorge (it is the Sung-lin k'ou of the Chinese) covered with fine trees, we made our way first to the top of the Mang la, and thence to the summit of the Rateu la (Ta shan or Tsan-pa shan of the Chinese).† From here we descended over a bare country, with an occasional black tent in some nook in the hills, to Rateu or Lit'ang Zamba, a small post-station which marks the boundary between Bat'ang and Lit'ang.

Rateu is a miserably dirty hole, where the kung-kuan is as big as a chicken-house and as filthy as a pig-sty. To add to the dirt of the place, it was sleeting when we arrived, and we dismounted before the door of the kung-kuan in a foot of liquid mud. To still more increase our discomfort, the ula drivers let the mule carrying our pots, pans and provisions, stray away in the dark, so we had nothing but a couple of eggs and some tea for supper.

Some twenty black tents are scattered about on the foothills of the Bamt'ang shan,‡ whose beautiful snow-clad peaks close our view to the north. Down the valley flows the Ni ch'u (Gill's Nen ch'u), and above and below this place the mountain sides are covered with dense pine woods. It is too cold here to raise anything save a few turnips; barley is brought from Bat'ang, and the soldiers trade their tea with the Drupa for the few products they can supply, but even the Drupa only stay here for three months of the year; they change their camping grounds four times annually.

---

* Bower calls it Tasu-chu river.

† Gill calls this pass (he only mentions one) Rung-Se-La. Bower calls it Lathok La.

‡ Gill calls this splendid snowpeak Mt. Kung-Rh.

September 21.—We have been obliged to pass a day at Rateu while the ula drivers went in search of the lost mule. All the people hereabout turned out to help them, and it was brought back in the afternoon minus a leather water jar, a tea churn, and a few other articles of no great value and all easily replaced. The poor boy who was in charge of this mule was terribly frightened at losing it; he said if it was not found he could never return to Bat'ang, where the Déba would have him flogged, put in the cangue, and burnt with blazing pitch-pine chips—the usual punishment for such an offense. He and the soldiers told me that the head Déba (Ying kuan the Chinese call him) is a terrible tyrant. He exercises all the *droits du seigneur* over the women folks among his subjects, and it is also said that he is in the habit, when dismounting from his horse, of using one of his kneeling subjects instead of a stepping stone. The Head Déba is not as wealthy as his uncle, the Second Déba (Erh Ying-kuan), though he owns the famous salt mines, or *ts'ak'a*, south of Bat'ang, known to us by the name of Yerkalo.* He has also an income of a thousand taels or so derived from other sources.

I asked a very bright Chinese soldier who has come with me from Bat'ang why it was that all Chinese soldiers in Tibet were unarmed. "We are here," he replied, "to talk reason (*li*) to the Man-chia, not to overawe them by force of arms. We are few and they are many. If they should rise up against us and put any of us to death, we would not resist, but would warn them, saying, we are the great Emperor's soldiers, beware of what you do. He will surely punish you." There is truth in what this poorly paid and badly cheated soldier said about their role in Tibet, but his faith in the Emperor is, I fear me, ill-placed; he would probably not trouble himself about the killing of a few poor devils in a remote corner of his vast empire.

I heard also, to my great satisfaction, that there are now two French missionaries at the Ts'ak'a (Yerkalo), an old one and a young one. This is most pleasing news; it shows the good fathers have at last got another footing in their old station, from which they had been so brutally driven a few years ago.

* The French missionaries established a station at Yerkalo in 1871. See Desgodins, *op. cit.*, 156.

VILLAGE OF RA-NANG (LAMAYA) IN LIT'ANG.

VILLAGE OF LIT'ANG GOLO (HSI OLO) IN LIT'ANG.

September 22.—Crossing the bridge over the Ni ch'u, we followed the left bank of the river to Nāda (Erh-lang-wan in Chinese), a little post station with two or three Tibetan cabins around it.

The country between Rateu and Nāda is uncultivated and the mountain sides covered with trees, mostly pines. Now and then we caught a glimpse of beautiful snow-covered mountains to the north, one of which must be at least nineteen thousand feet high.*

A mile or so before reaching Nāda we passed near a high tower built of dry stones. It stands on a rock overhanging the stream, and is similar in shape to those described by Gill, as noticed near Bakolo, to the east of Nyach'uk'a.† It is about fifty feet high and in a fairly good state of preservation. No one could tell me any thing about it, either its use or its origin.

The women at Nāda have a peculiar way of dressing their hair, it hangs down in little plaits, and a small lock, taken from the right side of the part, hangs down over the nose and reaches to the mouth. On their hair and just above the ears they wear two disks of silver, four or five inches in diameter, one on either side of the head.

About four miles below Nāda, from which place, by the way, we got a beautiful view of the snow-covered mountains to the north, and of the pine forests surrounding their base, we began to notice fields of barley and patches of turnips. At this point we left the Ni ch'u valley, which bends southward, and having crossed three low ranges of hills trending southward, we descended by a narrow gorge to Ranang ‡ (La-ma-ya of the Chinese), where we stopped in a fairly good Tibetan post station.

We had to change the ula here, but the headman seemed very unwilling to supply any in view of the unsettled state of the country. He said that Lit'ang was at war with Chung-hsi, that many men had already been killed (probably two or three are to be understood by "many"), and that the road to Lit'ang, unsafe

* This peak, called Nen-da by Gill, is apparently the center of the *massif*, of which Gill's Kung-Rh forms the western extremity and his Gombo Kung-ka the eastern. He makes Mt. Nen-da to be 20,500 feet high.

† Gill, *op. cit.*, II, 136. See under date of *September 30*.

‡ Bower's Ramo.

at all times on account of Chakba, was now extremely dangerous (we will probably not meet a living soul on it). All the people, with all their horses and a vast number of yaks were at Lit'ang, and he could not get ula ponies for me. I told him to do his best and that I felt sure we could get off to-morrow.

There are quite a number of hamlets in this valley; some barley is raised and birch trees are quite numerous on the mountain sides. I also notice a few poplars in some of the hamlets. The birch bark is used here, as elsewhere in Tibet, to make household utensils—cups and pails. I have much difficulty in reconciling the names of places along this road, as given by Capt. Gill, with those used by the natives. Many of the names used by Gill are quite unknown to all those I question on the subject. The Chinese authors of the *Wei Tsang t'u chih* give a tolerably accurate description of this road, but fall into some curious mistakes, saying, for example, "down a valley," where one would expect "up," and *vice versâ*.*

September 23.—We were detained at Ranang until 4 P. M.; the headmen of all the surrounding villages having assembled here in conclave declared they had neither men nor beasts for me, that all were at Lit'ang with the army. Finally some were found and we made a start, though we could only go a few miles.

We ascended a densely wooded valley (pines, junipers, birch, and willow trees) to a hamlet of two or three cabins, called Latsa (Lar t'ang in Chinese), about three hundred feet below the timber-line on the west side of the Gara la (or lak'a). A few turnips are grown here.

We camped on a bit of green sward near the kung-kuan, as the latter was too filthy for human beings to put up in. The two Chinese soldiers stationed here and some of the Tibetans begged me to come into the kung-kuan, as brigands and thieves were very bold and numerous in this place, but we all preferred facing any danger rather than the dirt in the dingy post station.

The filth we find in the Tibetan villages ever since entering Bat'ang territory is extraordinary, never, no not even in China, have I seen such dirty places. The mud is knee deep in all of them,

* See *Journ. Roy. Asiat. Soc.*, n. s. XXIII, 44. A similar error occurs on p. 51 (third line from bottom).

and swine, goats, chickens, dogs and cats all contribute to make the lanes and courtyards too vile smelling for even my well-seasoned nostrils. Yaks, djo, and sheep are not numerous in this part of Tibet, ponies and mules do most of the work, and meat is but little eaten, at least at this time of the year.

In the Lit'ang district the pronunciation approaches that of Lh'asa, and is, consequently, much more readily understood by us than that of Bat'ang, which we found nearly incomprehensible. To add to our trouble each locality has, of course, a large number of local idioms, with which time alone can make one acquainted.

September 24.—Last night passed peaceably, though we slept with one eye open fearing lest the much talked of robbers might visit us. We left very early, so as to be able to reach Lit'ang before dark.

The road ascended rapidly, and soon we reached the head of the Latsa valley and entered a higher one, covered with rolled granite rocks. It trended westward and was bordered to the east by a high range of rocky mountains, over which the road to Lit'ang led, and which is known to the Chinese as the Huang-t'u kang, and to Tibetans as Gara lak'a or Gara pen sum. This depression between the Latsa valley and the Huang-t'u kang has evidently been the bed of a glacier, and there are still several ponds in it. One called the "dry lakelet" (Kan hai-tzŭ by the Chinese) has a small stone cabin on its bank. This refuge-house is known to the natives as Tsung-ta. The stream flowing by Ranang has its sources in this valley.

The descent from the Gara lak'a to the post station of Jambut'ong (T'ou t'ang in Chinese) is short and very gradual, the ground covered with rocks and in a few spots with brush or grass. Jambut'ong is a dirty post station with two houses, in one of which two Chinese soldiers are stationed. There were some hundred Tibetans camped here, returning from Lit'ang, and driving home a herd of yaks and five hundred or six hundred sheep captured from the Chung-hsi people.

A couple of miles beyond Jambut'ong we came to the brow of a hill, known to the Chinese as A-la-po-sang shan, at the foot of which stretches the plain of Lit'ang, and in a nook in the hills on the north side of this broad valley we saw the town of Lit'ang, the golden spires of its Chamba ch'ü-k'or-ling temple shining in the sunlight.

After a couple of miles of continuous and rather rapid descent, we came to a bridge over the Li ch'u, where there is also an ula station. This point is called Ché zangka, possibly a corrupt form of Ch'u zamba, "river bridge"; it is known to the Chinese as Ta ch'iao, or "the big bridge."

Numerous black tents were seen scattered over the broad Lit'ang valley, and near each one herds of yaks and large flocks of sheep were grazing. The bridge over the Li ch'u had been washed away and two rickety and very springy poles, lashed to the buttresses, were all we had to walk on. The ponies and mules had to swim the river, and the luggage was carried across by the ula drivers on their backs.

We reached the town at 4.30 P. M. In the plain by the river side were camped about 5,000 men, their white cotton tents pitched in a circle inside of which the horses were picketed. Near by a herd of yaks and a very large flock of sheep, captured from the Chung-hsi people, were grazing under an escort of mounted men. I was told that in these inter-tribal wars the plunder made on the enemy is not divided among the victors, each man carries off what he himself has captured. Two days ago there was a fight in which two Lit'angites and three Chung-hsiites were killed, and another battle is anticipated in the near future.

Lit'ang stands on a hillside; on the plain at the foot of the hill are two high white-washed buildings, one the residence of the Head Déba, the other that of his brother, the Second Déba, who is a lama.* The town is much larger than Bat'ang, but the complete absence of trees makes it look very desolate. The population comprises about three hundred and fifty families and between two thousand and three thousand lamas, also one hundred and fifty Chinese.† A wall, built by the Chinese I believe,

* The first Déba's name is Derang jyamts'o, the second is Kuntun dewi (?). The chief lama official is the Drébung lama Pents'o. On Lit'ang and its history, see *Journ. Roy. Asiat. Soc.*, n. s. XXIII, 40, 124, 248 and 271.

† A—— K—— says it is "a small city, containing but two thousand five hundred houses"—*Report*, etc., 67. Gill, *op. cit.*, II, 189, says it has one thousand families and three thousand lamas. Probably the whole Lit'ang country has between one thousand five hundred and two thousand five hundred families, exclusive of lamas. Conf. p. 358. Ch'en Teng-lung in his *Lit'ang chih lüeh* (1810) says (p. 2) that there are five thousand three hundred and twenty families and three thousand two hundred and seventy lamas in the Lit'ang district.

in the eighteenth century, once inclosed the town, but is now in ruins; on a commanding point on the east side of the town stands a dilapidated Kuan-ti temple.

We had proposed stopping in a Chinese inn, of which the Chinese appeared to be quite proud, but the Liang-t'ai, fearing lest the turbulent and intoxicated soldiery might molest me there, asked me to come to his Ya-mên, where he gave me two very small rooms and a kitchen.

September 25.—My first occupation to-day was to try and get enough money to take me to Ta-chien-lu. I fortunately found a Lao-shan trader, whom I had met in 1889, and he lent me forty-five rupees to be paid to his partner at Ta-chien-lu.

The Hsien-sheng and I dined with the Liang-t'ai and had a very good dinner of sixteen courses. This official is a very stupid fellow who has bought the office he now holds. He has, however, a very bright Ssŭ-yeh (a prompter, private secretary, or whatever one chooses to call this office), who talks for him, writes his dispatches, manages all his business, and keeps him in good humor.

I heard that although the lamas do not allow the people to mine gold in the immediate vicinity of Lit'ang, a good deal of rough placer mining is carried on in remote localities. All the gold is brought here and sold for from fifteen to sixteen times its weight in silver. The Liang-ta'i said that about two thousand ounces of gold are collected annually; most of it is bought by the lamas, who send it to Ta-chien-lu. A fair day's earning for a gold washer is five *fen* * a day.

The lamas here are said to be very wealthy, and most of the twenty or thirty firms of Chinese traders of this place get their funds from them. Besides the tea trade, a large number of sheep (about ten thousand a year) are driven to Ta-chien-lu, and, besides supplying that town, help provide the Ch'eng-tu market, which city gets also much of its mutton from Sung-pan T'ing.

The people here use large quantities of gold ornaments. The women wear their hair hanging down in one large plait, and on

* A *fen* is the tenth part of a *liang* or ounce. Five *fen* of gold would be worth about 75 tael cents in silver, or 77 cents of our currency.

either side of their heads are large disks of embossed silver or gold, some of them ten inches in diameter.*

Though Lit'ang is a bare, cold place, and at a considerable altitude above sea level, and the Tibetans do not attempt to raise even barley here, some of the Chinese manage to grow a few vegetables, such as turnips, *o-sung*, greens, etc., but most of their supplies come from Nyach'uk'a or Bat'ang; even fire-wood is brought here from a day's journey to the south.

Snow falls at Lit'ang from the ninth moon to the sixth, inclusively (October to June), and rains are frequent during the months when it does not snow.

The Liang-t'ai asked the Déba to supply me with ula as soon as possible, but we learned that none could be ready before the day after to-morrow. As we will double at least one stage between here and Ta-chien-lu, I will be able to get there in five days, so I can be patient under this *contretemps*.

September 26.—To-day has passed talking with Chinese and Tibetans, asking a few questions and answering innumerable ones. All those with whom I have talked agree that the lay population of the town is between three hundred and three hundred and fifty families, and that there are several thousand families of Drupa in the Province. This I can readily believe from the presence here of the large force camped below the town. Several districts, I am assured, are not represented in the army now here.

There are in Lit'ang blacksmiths, silversmiths and coppersmiths, also a few workers in leather and saddlemakers, but none of the work I have seen is of a high order, all is very inferior to that of Dérgé. Though all the houses are of the Tibetan type (*i. e.*, two-storied), most of them have roofs covered with narrow slabs of wood, about three feet long, on which are laid sods of grass to hold them down.

* The national headdress of Tibet is that worn by the Panaka, K'amba and in Jyadé, and previously referred to. We find it first mentioned in Friar Odoric's Travels (H. Yule, *Cathay and the Way Thither*, I, 150). Athanasius Kircher (in Nieuhoff, *Embassy from the East India Company to China*, p. 39 and 44) shows that the headdresses of the eastern Tibetan women were the same in the 17th century as at present. His "Kingdom of Coin" is, I take it, K'amdo. The figures on page 39 of Nieuhoff's work are those of Koko-nor Tibetans.

The incarnate Buddha, or Truku, of Lit'ang comes from Lh'asa, and the Abbot or K'anpo, who rules the great lamasery of Chamba-ch'ü-k'or-ling, is also sent here from the same place and for a term of three years. The notes on Lit'ang in my translations, published in the Journal of the Royal Asiatic Society,* are still true at the present day, though the Chinese works from which they are taken were written over a century ago. One must not look for change or progress in this country.

September 27.—We left at 8 A. M. in company with one of the headmen of the Chala Jyabo (Ming-cheng-ssŭ) of Ta-chien-lu, who is returning from a mission to the Déba's wife, the daughter of his king. Though a Tibetan, he speaks Chinese like a native, and is a valuable addition to our party, especially as he has promised to manage things for us from Nyach'uk'a to our destination, as from that point to Ta-chien-lu all the country belongs to his master.

The road led over low hills to the top of the Dzo-mo la, which the Chinese call "the burning-hill" (Huo shao-po), why, I cannot conceive, as I saw no sign of volcanic action anywhere, either here or elsewhere in the vicinity; possibly the name means nothing more than "the hill (above) the Huo (ch'u)."

A short descent brought us to Yaokatsé on the Hor ch'u, Huo chu in Chinese, where there are ruins of a former post station. Here we met about a hundred men going to join the army at Lit'ang, all of them well armed and mounted on fine large horses, for which this section of country is justly celebrated. We followed the right bank of the river as far as Hor ch'uk'a, passing on the way numerous gold washings, in fact, all the gravel beds in and along the river have been washed for gold. The gravel is rather coarse sandstone and white quartz.

Hor ch'uk'a consists of three or four houses, one a kung-kuan, where live two soldiers, and just beyond the hamlet is a rather dilapidated Wen Hou temple. The houses are of stone, but only a story high. At this point we left the Hor ch'u and ascended a lateral valley which brought us by an easy ascent to the summit of the Wango la (Gill's Wang-gi la).

We then entered a valley in which in less than three miles we passed fifty-seven black tents. Probably several thousand yaks

* New series, XXIII, and frequently referred to in the preceding notes.

were grazing here, but I was surprised to see very few sheep. Passing out of this cattleman's paradise, at a point where it takes a southerly bend, we crossed another low range of mountains by the Ku la, and entered a rocky, narrow gorge, very appropriately called Loan-shih chiao, or "pit of boulders," the lower part of which is thickly covered with pines and oaks. We pulled up for the night at the little post station of Tsa-ma-ra dong (Tsan-ma-la-tung in Chinese), situated at its mouth, having made, without riding very hard, two stages in one day.

This little place, lost in the mountains, is one of the most picturesque spots we have seen. The steep hills around it are covered with trees, now in their many colored autumn foliage, a brook dashes down the gorge over a bed of boulders, and around the three little log houses composing the hamlet are fields of oats and vegetables. Three Chinese soldiers and their families inhabit the place; they received us with great kindness and made us as comfortable as they could. Here for the first time we ate potatoes raised in the valley, and the soldiers gave us also greens, a fowl and some eggs. The pack animals only arrived late in the night; the men had had a hard time getting them down the Loan-shih chiao in the dark; in fact, it was a wonder they got here at all, as this part of the road is very bad, even in daylight.

September 28.—I was awaked by the cries of silver pheasants on the hillside behind the house. The sun was shining brightly and the little valley looked most beautiful. I could have stayed for hours looking at the oaks, with their dark, glistening leaves, the moss-covered pines, the yellow-leaved birches and the high mountains rising all around, their summits a serrated line of reddish rocks; but we had a long ride before us, and so we rolled up our blankets and got off as soon as we had swallowed our tea and eaten a few handfuls of tsamba—our usual morning meal.

A mile or so below the station we turned up a valley leading northeast and down which flowed a little brook. All the gravel along its banks and on the lower slopes of the Zuunda la (Gill's Tang Gola), which begins here, has been worked over by gold washers. We passed two camps of some ten or twelve persons each, both men and women, busy digging and washing the gravel. Their method of mining was simple in the extreme; the gravel was shoveled into a wooden trough, about four feet long and six or eight inches broad at the lower end; through it a little stream of water was allowed to flow. Across the lower end of the trough was stretched a thick woollen rag through which the water escaped. The mud and gravel in the trough were stirred up with a stick and gently removed with the hand, while the particles of gold set free were caught in the rag. Every now and then the rag was removed, the gold collected, and put in a yak horn snuff bottle. The cabins of the gold workers were beside the diggings; they were tent-shaped and covered over with long strips of pine bark.

The descent from the Zuunda la was short but steep; at the base is the village of Lit'ang Golo (Hsi Olo of the Chinese) in a broad, fertile, well-cultivated valley, dotted over with little hamlets. Wheat, barley, potatoes, turnips, greens, etc., are cultivated here, and pigs and chickens are as plentiful as in a Chinese village. All the women we have met in the Lit'ang country wear the same horribly ugly lock of hair hanging down over the nose, which we first noticed at Năda. It is a part of the national dress and a woman is considered to be a very brazen-faced character who does not wear it. *Teuja*, the dirty black paste with which most Tibetan women smear their faces, is not much used in Bat'ang or even farther west, wherever there are Chinese, but the Drupa and the Central Tibetan women use it very generally.

We followed down the Lit'ang Golo valley for a couple of miles and then ascended the steep Mo-lung gung (Po-lang-kung shan in Chinese), which rises above the timber line some two hundred or three hundred feet.* The ascent is very steep and over loose stones which makes climbing very disagreeable. Oaks, pines and birches cover the mountain sides, and a variety of rose bush, the skin of whose seed-vessels is eaten by the natives, is also very abundant here. This mountain is famous as producing that curious worm-plant known as the *Shar-tsa gong-bu* (*tung-chung hsia-ts'ao* in Chinese), called by botanists *Cordyceps sinensis.*

Very near the summit of the mountain is a post station with two

* Gill makes this mountain to be over 15,000 feet. I think he is wrong as it only rises a few hundred feet above the timber line which I found here, as elsewhere in this latitude in Tibet, to be at about 13,500 feet. In fact while Gill's and my observations for altitude at Bat'ang, Lit'ang and Ta-chien-lu agree closely, at all other points along this route his altitudes are greatly in excess of those I found for the same places.

or three soldiers stationed in it. It is said that this spot is, or was, a famous lurking place for brigands.

We descended into a little hollow on the farther side of the mountain, and stopped for the night at the foot of another pass, which we have to cross to-morrow, and where there is another post station, called Chien-tzŭ-wan in Chinese, and Laniba in Tibetan.

At Laniba we met a party of Chinese soldiers, with their Tibetan wives and children, on their way back to their homes in Ssŭ-ch'uan, also a Salar from I-ma-mu chuang, who had been on a trading trip to Lit'ang. He dealt in shagreen (*sha-p'i*), he said, and was now on his way to Ch'eng-tu. Among the soldiers was one man who had been at Shigatsé for twenty-five years and who had only been

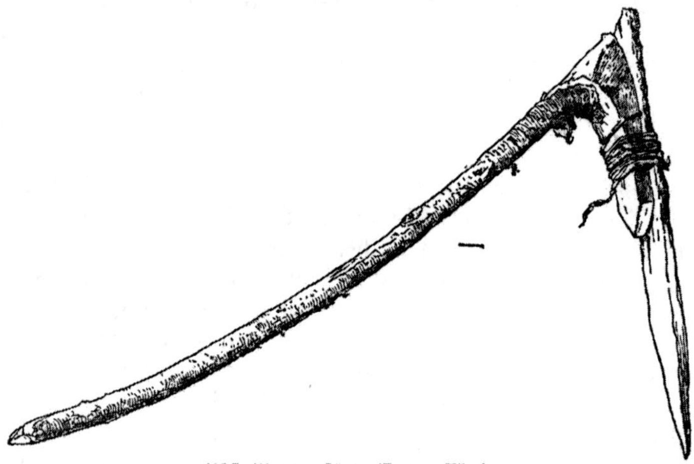

HOE, Wooden Blade (Eastern Tibet).

able after all these years to get together enough money to take him home. The Chinese government do not pay the traveling expenses of their soldiers who desire to retire from the army; that is one way of keeping men in the service. It is no easy matter for one of these poor soldiers to save up enough to pay for the journey from Lh'asa to Ta-chien-lu, as it costs from 20 to 25 taels to hire a yak from one place to the other, or rather to have a yak load carried that distance. These soldiers had left Shigatsé in February, and thought they had not been so very long on the road; four months is the time usually employed by well equipped caravans, only using mules as pack-animals, to make the journey to China.

September 29.—Last night there was a heavy frost and this morning at seven o'clock the thermometer stood at +33° Fahrenheit. After crossing the Laniba pass we followed the valley on the east side. It is everywhere well wooded with holly-leaved oaks and pines, and in the lower portion with willow, maple, birch, poplar, apple, cherry and, I think, mulberry trees. We passed on the way several small hamlets, at one, called Ma-kai-chung, there is a small Chinese inn, and around this place and also lower down the valley we saw patches of hemp and a few little fields of barley and wheat.

We reached the Nya ch'u, the Ya-lung chiang of the Chinese, by noon. The river here makes a sharp bend from north-north-west to south, and on its left bank stands the town of Nya-ch'uk'a, known by the Chinese as Chung tu, "Middle ferry," or Ho-k'ou. Another little stream coming from the east and called the Orongshé ch'u (Hsiao ho of the Chinese) empties into the Nya ch'u here. On the bluff on the right bank of the river and facing Ho-k'ou is a small village, and the steep hillsides are everywhere cultivated in terraces, buckwheat being one of the principal crops.

We made signs to the men in charge of the ferry boats (similar to the one used on the Dré ch'u below Bat'ang) to come over for us, and soon we heard a gong summoning the crew, and the big boat in a little while put off. It was rowed close along the left bank of the river till above the place where we were waiting for it, when it was steered out into the rushing, eddying river, and was soon swept over to our side. We embarked, we and our belongings, the ula not going any farther, and in a short time we reached the water-gate of the town.

Natives cross the river in little skin coracles, a number of them were bobbing about on the stream; the ferry-boat is reserved for government use and for Chinese travelers, the latter paying a small fare.*

Ho-k'ou is a thoroughly Chinese place, the houses two-storied and similar to those of Ta-chien-lu. The male population is exclusively Chinese, the women half breeds. There are forty families living here, exclusive of a Sergeant (Wai-wei) and a few soldiers. It is the extreme western point of the Chala Jyabo's possessions, and is practically the frontier post of China, as no

* In winter the river is crossed on a bridge of boats. See A—— K——'s *Report*, 66, also Bower, *op. cit.*, 91.

one is allowed to go beyond it without first showing a passport or permit from the Ta-chien-lu Chün-liang-fu. It is the lowest point we have come to in Tibet, being only a little over eight thousand feet above sea level. Barley, millet, buckwheat, maize, potatoes, cabbages, celery, peppers, onions, cucumbers and other vegetables are grown around and below the town. A variety of parroquet, with light green body and long light blue tail, is found here and taken in large numbers to Ssŭ-ch'uan. This same variety of bird is found, I am told, at Bat'ang.

The west bank of the Nya ch'u, in front of Ho-k'ou and thence northward, belongs to the Nya-rong, a dependency of Lh'asa.*

I was very comfortably installed in the home of one of our escort, a young soldier from Lit'ang, and the ula was promised for an early hour to-morrow.

Most of the women of Ho-k'ou wear one large plaque of silver on the crown of their heads, though some add another worn on the forehead. The hair is done up in one large plait hanging down the back. Their dress is a long, loose, blue cotton gown, over which is another of the same length, but sleeveless; a colored belt is worn around the waist. The earrings are of the Bat'ang pattern.

September 30.—The ula was at the door before sunrise, and we were soon on the way again. The road led up the gorge of the Orongshé ch'u, crossing and recrossing the river which dashes wildly down, eddying around or tumbling over huge boulders which fill its bed. Pine, maple, birch and holly-oak trees grow in great profusion all the way to Bagolo, where the valley broadens out a little and some land is cultivated.

Bagolo (Pa-kiao-lu in Chinese)† is a little post station beside

* Perhaps better known by its Chinese name of Chan-tui. Shortly after my first visit to Tibet, this province revolted against its Lh'asan governor. After some desultory fighting the Déba was recalled, and a new one sent in his place when peace and Lh'asan rule were restored—until the new incumbent begins to squeeze the people beyond endurance. For the Chinese official account of these disturbances and the pacification of the country, see *Peking Gazette*, 29th July, 1891, and 24th February, 1892.

† Gill says the Chinese name is Pa-kou lou or "The eight angled tower," referring to the peculiar shape of the watch tower standing here. This would be a very good name for the place, but I fancy the name is Tibetan, probably Ba golo. There is a Lit'ang golo and a Mä Nya golo. *Golo*, I believe, means "town, capital." Bower (*op. cit.*, 91) was misinformed when told that a look-out was still kept in this tower.

OLD WATCH TOWER AT BAGALO (CHALA).

which stands a very well preserved watch tower, similar to the one we passed near Näda. The people here told me that it had been built by a King of Tibet (*Tsang Wang*) to guard the highroad at a time when a Chinese invasion was feared. They may refer to Latsan̈g Khan, during whose reign (in 1719–1720) the great Chinese expedition and conquest of Tibet was undertaken.

Between Bagolo and Orongshé* (Wo-lung-shih in Chinese), about eight miles farther up the valley, we passed occasional farmhouses, all of a half-Tibetan, half-Chinese type. The district chief's residence was passed a few miles east of Bagolo; it is a finely built Tibetan house with tiled roof, the tiles made near Tungolo by Chinese who came from Ta-chien-lu and built a kiln there.

At Orongshé, where we stopped in a fairly good inn, there live nine families of Chinese, but no Tibetans. The place has a certain reputation in Tibet as producing the best maple-knot cups (*puru*). These knots are known locally as *la shing*, and in other sections of Tibet as *dzaya shing*. The Chinese frequently, in fact usually, call these knots *p'u-tao-ken mu*, which, literally translated, means "vine root." These cups sell for from 1 to 15 or 20 taels, according to the fineness of the tracings in the wood. Though a little wheat, barley and vegetables are grown at Orongshé, the inhabitants say it is a very poor place, and that they live solely on travelers.

October 1.—We left very early with the pleasing expectation of meeting an European before night, for I heard that my old friend, Father Soulié, is now living at Mä-Nya-ch'uk'a (Tungolo).† Though I have done a good deal of talking in the last nine months, it has been exclusively with Asiatics, and they have no conversation, as we understand it, so I was wild for a talk.

The valley above Orongshé is well wooded very nearly up to the summit of Kaji la, on which, by the way, we found a little snow. From its summit we saw to the east-northeast the Jara ri, around whose base I passed in 1889,‡ when going to Ta-chien-lu, and to the east-southeast its mate, the Kungka ri; between the two rises the Chédo la, over which the road to Ta-chien-lu passes.

---

* Bower's Uru Tonga.

† Bower's Mayo golok.

‡ See *Land of the Lamas*, 268.

On the east side of Kaji la there is a plateau where we noticed a few black tents, and I was told that there is a little lamasery called Kaji gomba not far off, but we could not see it.

Crossing this little plateau we descended rapidly to the Tungolo valley, only passing on the way a small farm house and the tile kiln referred to previously. This valley is quite a broad one for Tibet, and a number of lateral ones of about equal size open onto it above and below where we entered it.

I found Pére Soulié living in a little room in a Tibetan house just outside the village. He was prepared for my visit; news had been received a few days previously that I was on my way to Ta-chien-lu. We sat and chatted for a couple of hours and I drank a bottle of wine, which the good fellow insisted on sharing with me, though he had but the one to use in case of sickness. He looked aged and worn, but was the same cheerful, pleasant companion I had found him in former years.

At Tungolo is another old watch tower, but I could hear nothing of its history or original object. I left the village, which is at least half Chinese, by 2.15 P. M., and accompanied by Father Soulié, who insisted on escorting me a few miles on my way, we rode down the valley to a point where there is a little hamlet, called Watséma (Wa-ch'ieh in Chinese), beside which are the ruins of an old Chinese camp on a hill.* Here Father Soulié left me, and I turned up a lateral valley, broader even than the Tungolo one, and in which we noticed several more watch towers. We rode to Anya (A-niang-pa of the Chinese), where we lodged in the headman's house, a rather Chinesesy building, with a long line of prayer barrels around one side of the inner gallery overlooking the courtyard.

I find that the Tibetans along the highroad do not let themselves be as much imposed upon as regards supplying ula as I had supposed. A Wai-wei and three Chinese soldiers from Ch'amdo left Draya with us to go to Ta-chien-lu for money for the garrison. They had an ula order, but ever since passing Bat'ang they have had to hire horses, as the local authorities positively refused to give them ponies. They had, they said, no redress, and doubted even if they could get their expenses refunded by the Chinese authorities on their return to Ch'amdo.

* Bower's Mana Rong.

October 2.—The ula was ready by daylight and we lost no time in getting off, for Ta-chien-lu was at the end of the day's march. About three miles above Anya we came to Nashé,* where we saw yet another of the old watch towers, the last one we met with. All these towers have doors in them, and holes in the walls in which rafters for floors must once have been set; they are loop-holed and a few have windows in them near the top, which is octagonal, while the lower portion is star shaped.

Passing Nashé (Na-wa-lu in Chinese) we came to another little hamlet called Tiru (Ti-ju in Chinese), where there are three Chinese soldiers and a post station. Here we met some Chinese women on their way to Lh'asa; they were wives of small officials whom we had passed a few days before. These women were riding disguised as men, for Chinese women are not allowed in the country, wearing big red *feng-mao* to hide their headdresses and faces, and their little feet stuffed in big velvet boots. At Tiru the ascent of the Chédo la begins; it is very gradual and not over two miles long, but it was bitterly cold, a strong southeast wind blowing over the snow with which the mountain was covered. The descent on the east side is also gradual, and were it not that the road has been paved with irregular blocks of granite, it would be very good traveling, as it is, it is a veritable *loan-shih chiao*, or "pit of boulders."

The country from Tungolo to near the hamlet of Chédo, on the east side of the pass, is bare of trees or even shrubs, but at Chédo and farther down the valley of the Ché ch'u there grows a considerable quantity of brush, which supplies Ta-chien-lu with fire-wood. But what surprised me beyond measure was to see two men employed repairing the road; it was such an uncommon sight that we stopped for a few minutes to look at them work.

A few miles above Ta-chien-lu we passed the mouth of a short valley running to the southwest, in which we saw the summer residence of the King of Chala. It is a Tibeto-Chinese house of no great size, and is known as the Yü-ling Kung.

At four o'clock we reached Ta-chien-lu, and before going to my old lodgings in Yang lama's house, I stopped at the Bishop's, outside the south gate, and found my good friends, Pères Mussot and Dejean, there to welcome me, for they too had been advised that

* Bower calls Anya Amia To and Nashé Nashi.

I was coming. We passed a couple of hours talking, though it was hard work at first for me, I had not spoken a European language for so long that I was continually dropping into Chinese or Tibetan.

At Yang lama's house the *Pönbo*, as they call his wife, for she belongs to the family of the head Agia of the country, received me at the gate, and in a few minutes a crowd of my old friends were filling the courtyard to greet me. I took my old lodgings of '89, and settled down for a few days of well-earned rest before starting out for Shanghai, which I will be able to reach by the 1st of November.

October 3.—Lu Ming-yang, the lieutenant who was so kind to me at Kanzé in 1889, and who is now here on waiting orders, called on me yesterday, but I was out. He came again to-day. He told me that after my departure from Kanzé the lamas mobbed him in his Ya-mên for having given me an escort to Ta-chien-lu and otherwise befriending me. They also asked him to give up the Kanzé Horba, who had guided me from Jyäkor gomba to Kanzé, and who had taken refuge with him, as the mob wanted to put him to death. Lu kept the crowd off with the carbine I had given him, and after a long pow-wow lasting several days got them to consent to the guide's going back to Jyäkundo; but he says that he passed some very uncomfortable days before things were finally settled.

Lu also told me that the Chala King is thinking of sending troops to Lit'ang to assist the Déba, his son-in-law, and thus bringing the war there to a close, as the Ta-chien-lu trade is suffering very much by it.

The Chinese here have the following couplet :—

> "*Chiang-k'a mên chan pu-tê,*
> *Bat'ang ya-t'ou yao pu-tê,*
> *Lit'ang tsamba chih pu-tê,*
> *Ho-k'ou hsien-hua shuo pu-tê.*"

Translated this means: "At Chiang-k'a (Gart'ok), don't stand in the doorway; at Bat'ang, don't flirt with the girls; at Lit'ang, don't eat tsamba; at Ho-k'ou (Nyach'uk'a), don't talk twaddle." The explanation is said to be found in the well-established fact that the Chiang-k'a people are gossips, that the Bat'ang young women are very unreserved, that the Lit'ang tsamba is full of grit, and that the people of Hok'ou are fond of silly, empty talk.

Père Mussot showed me a map of Tibet, on which Bonvalot and Bower had roughly marked the routes they had followed. My route met theirs at Batasumdo, was more or less the same as theirs to Lagong, from which point to Gart'ok Bonvalot followed some little used trail, while Bower and I went over the highroad. Père Mussot has very obligingly lent me all the money I require to take me to Shanghai. The kindness the fathers of the Tibetan mission have shown me on both my journeys I can never forget nor sufficiently acknowledge.

October 4.—The day passed rapidly, talking first to my French friends, then to old native acquaintances, and in making arrangements to continue the journey to Ya-chou Fu. I have hired a sedan-chair to take me to the latter place in six days, a day less than is usually used for the trip. I have been told a great deal about the terrible ravages of cholera (*ma-chuo chen* or *wen*) in Ssŭ-ch'uan this year; at Ch'eng-tu people have died by thousands. The disease has spread to the Ya-chou district,* where it is still raging, but Ta-chien-lu has escaped it, though it has been visited by typhoid fever—Père Dejean has had it twice.

Lu Ming-yang called again to ask me to dine with him to-morrow. I mentioned to him the story of Punropa, so graphically told by Baber,† and asked him if he knew of any additional details of this interesting episode in Tibetan history. He said that he had known Punropa well, that he was a Chin-ch'uan man and spoke and read Chinese. This explains why, having become a Lh'asa official, he was given the government of Lit'ang. For a while he was extremely popular there among both natives and Chinese, but I fancy he worked too much in the interest of China, hence his recall to Lh'asa and his sudden death by poison.

The old king of Chala, until some twenty years ago, was a thorough-going Tibetan; he wore his hair long, carried a big sword in his belt and would suffer no interference from the Chinese. During a war with the Nya-rong (Chan-tui), in which he was hard pressed by his enemies, he had to ask the assistance of

* I found nearly half the people of Ya-chou in mourning and funeral ceremonies going on in innumerable houses, but the people told me that the scourge was abating.

† E. C. Baber, *Travels and Researches in Western China*, 98.

the Chinese Chün-liang fu and his troops. This he secured, but on the condition that he would henceforth wear a queue and dress like a Chinese; he was forced to accede to these humiliating conditions. He has, nevertheless, resisted all Chinese encroachments on his states, and frequently orders out of Chala all Chinese who have surreptitiously settled there. His sons have been brought up as true Tibetans, and live and dress as such, but they cannot escape their fate. The present king's successor will be more and more under Chinese rule, and finally this strong little state, which has resisted its powerful neighbor's encroachments for a century more than Bat'ang and other parts of Eastern Tibet, will become a part of the province of Ssŭ-ch'uan.

To the south of Chala is another large native state known as the Huang lama's country or Méli,* and south of it again live savage tribes (so say my informants, but I fancy the savages are Li-su). I have also been told that the Chin-ch'uan extends all the way from Wa-ssŭ-k'ou to Sung-pan T'ing or, in other words, to the Amdo country.†

Musk, which, when I last visited Ta-chien-lu, was a most important article of exportation, has given way to wool. The reason assigned to the fall in the price of musk (it fell to 4 *huan*, but is now at 5 or 5½) is said here to be the discovery by the British of a plant which has the same medicinal qualities and the same perfume.‡ As to the use to which the enormous quantities of elk horns || exported from here are put, I learn that they are taken to Chung-king and there ground up and are used in making a very good toilet powder (*fen*), in great demand among Chinese women.

* "Mili" and "Terres des lamas de Mong Fan" are marked on d'Anville's *Carte du Si-Fan* (Vᵉ Carte du Tibet), to the north of Li-Kiang Fu. See also Baber, *op. cit.*, 93 and 96.

† On the Chin-ch'uan, which is divided into Little and Great Chin-ch'uan, see also Baber, *op. cit.*, 94.

‡ The Customs Returns for 1893 give the export of musk from Chung-king during that year as 72,766 ounces, valued at 478,192 Haikuan taels. During the same year 8,080 ounces of musk were imported into Shanghai from foreign countries. In 1893 over 14,000,000 pounds of wool were exported from Chung-king.

|| They come principally from Lit'ang, but Ch'amdo and even the country farther west supplies a considerable quantity.

October 5.—The Hsien-sheng and I dined to-day with Lu Ming-yang at his pretty little house on the mountain side overlooking the town. Speaking of Po-yul, he told me that it was divided into Po-mä or "Lower Po" and Po-tö or "Upper Po."* The latter is inhabited by Drupa, but the former is now in the possession of people of Chinese descent. During the war between China and the Gorkas (in 1793 I think), a detachment of five hundred Chinese soldiers from Ssŭ-ch'uan and under the command of a Major (*Yo-chi*) was started for the seat of war by way of Po-yul, a country then very little known to the Chinese. The detachment lost its way, and arriving in Po-mä, was so delighted with the beauty and fertility of the country that the men decided to go no farther and to make it their home. They married women of the country and greatly prospered, and their descendants still occupy the land.

While Po-tö is under the rule of Lh'asa, Po-mä is independent in fact, it being under the nominal control of a high Manchu officer stationed at Lh'asa who is known as the I Ch'in-ch'ai, "Envoy to the savage tribes," or San Ch'in-ch'ai, "Third Amban." This official has also in his jurisdiction Jyadé, and a number of other tribes, thirty-five in all, among which is the little district of T'ai-ling (or Gata), between Ta-chien-lu and Dawo.

Po-mä is visited by Lao-shan and Yünnanese traders, and it carries on a large trade with Dérgé, Jyadé and Lh'asa. The horses of Po-mä are famous throughout Tibet, and its leather work, iron work and jewelry, as well as the products of its looms, are celebrated and in great demand. The products of the soil are varied and of excellent quality, and altogether this country would seem to be the most fertile spot of Tibet. The intimate relations existing between Po-mä and Dérgé may also account for the superior quality and style of goods made in the latter country, which resemble closely those of the former, in fact, Lu Ming-yang said that, in his belief, the Po-mä people had taught those of Dérgé to work metal and leather in the way they now do.

Lu told me also that the King of Dérgé, who is now about forty years old, is the son-in-law of one of the Ministers of State (*Kalön*)

* These words are written *Spod-smad* and *Spod stod.* On d'Anville's *Carte du Si-Fan*, previously referred to, there is a "Pays de Pomsara" on the Chin sha river just north of Li-kiang Fu, and to the west of it he places Kung-pu (Ken-Pou-Y); Pomsara is in all likelihood Po-mä.

of Lh'asa, and that he constantly calls on the latter country to assist him in squeezing his own subjects, by whom he is very much disliked. He passes much of his time at Lh'asa, where he has a residence, and is entirely under Lh'asan influence, though his people are strongly opposed to that country, and have for years resisted its attacks on their national independence.

This evening I gave the little Amdo lama, who has shared my fortunes ever since the middle of August, some money, enough to take him home to Sung-pan. I also settled my accounts with the Lao-han Ma Shuang-hsi, who will, however, travel with me as far as Ya-chou Fu, and thence go by way of Ch'iung-chou and Sung-pan to Hsi-ning. He does not look forward with much pleasure to seeing his home again; he would much prefer going directly to Shang-chia in the Ts'aidam and to his Mongol wife.

The Hsien-sheng and Kao pa-erh go with me to Shanghai, whence the latter will return to Peking. As for the good Hsien-sheng, he wants to put some of his money in foreign-made articles at Shanghai, which he will sell at a good profit at Hsi-ning. He will go home by way of Han-k'ou, Hsi-an Fu and Lan-chou, and will probably reach his home about the same time that I will mine, in December.

Four carriers (*pei-tzŭ*) left yesterday for Ya-chou with part of my luggage and two more will accompany me, carrying our bedding and cooking apparatus. I pay them at the rate of a rupee a day. My chair has eight coolies, paid at the same rate, and we will make good time. Several of these men carried me down this road in 1889.

It was with a heavy heart that I said good-bye to-night to Père Mussot and Père Dejean, they have been so kind to me and we have got to know each other so well that I felt sad at the thought that I was probably saying farewell forever to them and the mission, for which, they were good enough to say, I had done some good work in my wanderings in Tibet.

Here I close my long journal; the road over which I still have to travel is the same as that which I followed in 1889; many others have gone up and down it before and since then, and most of them have written about it, and though much remains to be said of Ssŭ-ch'uan, it is not my province, Tibet is now behind me.

APPENDIX I.

SALAR VOCABULARY.

English.	*Salar.*	*Osmanli Turkish.*
One	Pir	Bir
Two	ské	Iki
Three	Ush	Üch
Four	Tűé	Dört
Five	Pesh	Besh
Six	Alché	Alti
Seven	Yéte	Yedi
Eight	Sekése	Sekiz
Nine	Tokos	Dokuz
Ten	Un	On
Eleven	Un-pir	On-bir
Twelve	Un-iské	On-ıki
Thirteen	Un-ush	On-üch
Twenty	Igérmi	Yígirmi
Thirty	Utush	Otuz
Forty	Kéreu	Kurk
Fifty	Ellé	Elli
Sixty	Hamish	Altmish
Seventy	Yémush	Yetmish
Eighty	Siksän	Seksen
Ninety	Toksan	Doksan
Hundred	Pireus	Bir jüz
Thousand	Pirming	Bir bin
Ten thousand	Pir (or Pur?) sanza	
Ten myriad	Un sanza.	
Year	Īl	
One Year	Pir-il	Yil
Two years	Iské-il	Iki yil
First month	Pir-indyé	Bir-inji
Second "	Isk-indyé	Ikinji

English.	*Salar.*	*Osmanli Turkish.*
Third month	Ush-indyé	Üchinji
Fourth "	Tűét-indyé	Dörtinji
This year	Pilé	Bu yil
Next year	Etch'é sagon	
To-day	Pugun	Bu gum
To-morrow	Été	
Day after to-morrow	Pa-sagon	
Spring	Loyé	
Summer	Yé	Yaz
Autumn	Use names of 7th, 8th, and 9th moons, Yét-indyé, Sekése-indyé, Tokos-indyé	
Winter	Kish	Kysh
North	Ashar	
South	Uriss	
East	Ch'uyi	
West	Isht'yi	
Sky	Asman	Assman
Earth (or ground?)	Yir	Yer
Sun	Kun	
Moon	Ai	Ai
Star	Yuldus	Yildiz
Black	{ Karas Ala	Kara
White	Ah'é (or Ah'aseu)	Ak
Blue	Kuh	Güik

English.	*Salar*	*Osmanli Turkish.*
Yellow	Keuzeu	
Red	Il	
Green	Yashil	Yeshil
Mountain	T'ar	Dagh
Stone	Tash	Dash
Ground	Yir	Yer
River	Uzen	
Water	Su (or Ossu)	Su
Wind	Yel	Yel
Rain	Yarmur	Yaghmur
Snow	K'ar	Kiar
Iron	Témur	Demir
Gold	Altan (or Altun)	Altyn
Silver	Kumush	Gümush
Copper	Tuguma	
Head	Pash	Bash
Face	Jamban	
Language	Kä-cha (Tibetan)	
Nose	Purui	Burun
Lips	Aks	Agz
Teeth	T'ich	Dish
Ears	Golak (or Olosh?)	Kolak
Hand	Ell	El
Finger	Pirma	Parmak
Thumb	Pash pirma	Bash parmak.
Forefinger	Irmum	
Second finger	Otta	
Third finger	Mazum	
Little finger	Séjé	
Finger nail	Terna	Turnak
Foot	Enjé	
Eye	Kuso (or Kos)	Göz
Eyebrows	Kulu	
Eyelashes	Sukulu	
Arm	Gol	Kol
Leg	Tuz	
Throat	Porta (Portara or Pohot'eush	Boghaz
Beard	Sah'al	Sakal
Tongue	Tili	Dil
Man	Erkish (or Erké)	Erkek
Woman	Kadun (or Kadunksh)	Kyatun
Boy	Ao (Ōll or Balaksh)	Oghul

English.	*Salar.*	*Osmanli Turkish.*
Girl	Anna (or Kézeu)	Ana
Father	Ap'a (Tibetan)	Baba
Mother	Ama (or Ichia)	
Brothers	Aréné (?)	
Younger brother	Éni	
Sisters	Éhé sanyé	
Elder brother's wife (?)	Yinguo	
Friend	Nuhur séda	
House	Oyé (or Ōwê)	Ev
Wall	Tam	
Window	Terja	
Table	Shira	
Fire pan	Huo-pen (Chinese)	
Teapot	Tangun	
Candle	La (Chinese)	
Flint	Chamar tash	Chakmak dashi
Tinder	Gō	Kau
Strike-a-light	Ch'a-ma	Chakmak
Axe	Palta	Balta
Knife	Pija	
Little wooden bowl	Aih'a (Mongol)	
Spoon	Shinah'a (Mongol)	
Lamp	Chiraleu (Persian chiragh)	
Fire	Ott	At(esh)
Coal	Kuomeur	Kyümür
Wood	Arashé	Aghaj
Wine	Sorma	
Beef	Kolh'é	
Mutton	Koyé	Koyun
Milk	Sut	Süd
White salt	T'us	Tuz
Salt	Kurtus (or Kut'us)	Kuru tuz (dry salt)
Butter	Ah'er	
Chicken	T'oh	Tawuk
Eggs	Umota	Yimurta
Tsamba	Tahan	
Tea	Ch'a (Chinese)	Chai
Vinegar	La-su (Chinese)	

English.	*Salar.*	*Osmanli Turkish.*
Red pepper	La-tzŭ (Chinese)	
Garlic	Samza	Sarimsak
Onion	Ts'ohan	Soghan
Bread	Émé	
Rice	Tzut'uran	
Brown Sugar	Kara sha-tang (Chinese)	
White sugar	Aha sha-tang (Chinese)	
Potato	Yang yü (Chinese)	
Chopsticks	Ch'uko	
Porcelain bowl	Tsanza	
Tobacco	Yen (Chinese)	
Pear	Armut	Armud
Felt	Ch'éh	Keche
Winter fur gown	Ismak(or Teurdé)	
Hat	Sorok	
Belt	Bulh'a	
Trousers	Ishtan	
Socks	Lingwa (*Cf.* Chinese wa-tzŭ)	
Boots	Etu	
Queue	Sash	
Clothes	T'un	
Sandals	Häi (Chinese)	
Button	T'ügma(*Cf.* Tibetan tob-chi)	
Pillow	Yerto	
Looking glass	Kusku	
Cotton	Mamu	Pambuk
Cotton cloth	P'ost	
Stirrup	T'eng (Chinese)	
Matchlock	Yérma néchté	
Gunpowder	Em	
Gun	Kanju	
Bow	Ya	Yag
Arrow	Ush	Ok
Sword	Kilish	Kilij
Whip	Kamjo	Kamcha
Pen	Kalam (Arabic)	Kalem
Paper	Hahé	
Book	Shu (Chinese)	
Chinese cash	Hél	

English.	*Salar.*	*Osmanli Turkish.*
Horse	At	
Stallion	Erh-ma(Chinese)	
Gelding	Sha-ma(Chinese)	
Mare	Mu-ma(Chinese)	
Colt	At palas	
Ass	Ésh	
Mule	Losa (Chinese)	
Camel	Teuyé	
Ox	Kolé	
Wild yak	Haina (Mongol?)	
Domestic yak	Umuso(Mongol)	
Dog, male	Erké isht	
Dog, female	Tchist	
Goat	Esko	
Cat	Mishu	
Crow	Kalh'a	Kargha
Musk deer	Pao (Chinese)	
Musk	Yufer	
Wolf	Puri	
Bear (*k'ou hsiung*)	Isht atsé	
Bear (*jen hsiung*)	Kshat	
Tiger	Pass	
Rhubarb	Djim (Tibetan)	
Barber	Pash ilgur	
The Emperor	Huang shang (Chinese)	
Mandarin	Péch	
Soldier	Liang-tza (Chinese)	
Hsi-fan	Tur	
Mongol	Mazur	
Chinese	Kaffir	
Chinese language	Mohul kăcha	
Bayan rong T'ing	Wayen-rong (Tibetan)	
Lan Chou Fu	Ché-t'ai (Chinese colloquial designation of a Governor-general)	
Hsün-hua T'ing	Yadza (Tibetan)	
Yellow River	Muren (Mongol)	

English.	*Salar.*	*Osmanli Turkish.*
Good	Iskur	
Bad	Ishimas	Ish-imez ("itisnot good")
Rich	Parkish	
Poor	Yarkish	
Cold	Tsormo	
I	Men	Ben
You	Sen	Sen
He	Ush	O
The boy is good	Balaksh iskur	
This man is good	Kishi irshider	
That man is bad	Ukshi irshi émestér	
Those three men	Ush ischio	
To write	Pitégän	
To shave	Jamban ilgur	
To eat	Ash	Ash ("food")
To drink	Ish	Ich-mek
To ride	Min	
How old are you?	Sen nyéché éshapar (or Sen piril néché)	
I beat him	Men antugur	
The coal is burning (or Light the fire?)	Kuomeur kalabeur	
Is the food ready?	Ashwa mé yurter	

English.	*Salar.*	*Osmanli-Turkish.*
Eat, eat!	Ash, ish	
I have eaten enough	Tuito	
I do not care (or wish) to eat	Ishimus	Istemem
What is the price of this?	Ishtyé äshapar (or Néch kälébar)	
Have you eaten?	Pugun ash	
Get off your horse	Endégé	
Get on your horse	Ats-min	Ati bin
Smoke!	Yen ta (Chinese)	
Go away!	Wara, wara	
I understand	Pilé	Bil-ir-im
I do not understand	Pilmés	Bil-mem
So you have come!	Kelto	Geldin
Yes, I have come	Kelgé	Geldim
Are you well?	Sa ishitéro	
I am well	Ish	Igi-im
Where do you come from?	San kalawáhur	
Where are you going?	San katengéljir	
He is writing	Pité	
He is going to write	Pitégaro	

APPENDIX II.

San-Ch'uan T'u-jen Vocabulary.

English.	*San-Ch'uan T'u-jen.*	*English.*	*San-Ch'uan T'u-jen.*
One	Niké	North	Sorgé tala
Two	Kuer	South	Baran tala
Three	Kurban	East	?
Four	Terpien	West	?
Five	Tabun	Sky	Tengri
Six	Chirkun	Star	Hotu
Seven	Dulon	Sun	Nara
Eight	Némen	Moon	Sara
Nine	Isun	Black	Kara
Ten	Harban	White	Chékan
Eleven	Harban-niké	Blue	Koko
Twelve	Harban-kuer	Yellow	Sha
Thirteen	Harban-kurban	Green	Nohon
Twenty	Korun	Cloud	Elyé
Twenty-one	Korun-niké	Mountain	Ula
Thirty	Kuchin	River	Areu
Thirty-one	Kuchin-niké	Water	Ussu
Forty	Téchin	Stone	Tash
Year	Huan	Ground	Kadra
Month	Sara	Wind	Ké
This year	Kéto huan	Rain	Kura
Last year	Tanyé huan	Snow	Chékseu
Next year	Kuo nien (Chinese)	Iron	Timur
To-day	Nyotur	Gold	Artan
To-morrow	Magashe	Silver	Miengo
Day after to-morrow	Chenéta	Copper	Tio-she
Three days hence	No kutur	Brass	Sha tio-she
Spring	Ta ch'un (Chinese)	Road	Mor
Summer	Na chu	House	Kar (Tibetan)
Autumn	Ukur	Tent	Ch'ang-fang (Chinese)
Winter	Ukur	Cave dwelling	Yao-tung (Chinese)

English.	*San-Ch'uan T'u-jen.*
Door	Ité
Fire	Shita
Flint	Kité tash
Tinder	Hula
Gunpowder	Huo yao (Chinese)
Pine tree	Rchura
Birch tree	Hua mu (Chinese)
Willow tree	Bayen
Grass	Épéseu
Wheat	Pité
Barley	Ch'ing-k'u (Chinese)
Bean	Pitcha
Millet (Ch. *hsiao mi*)	Kuts-amo
Millet (Ch. *huang mi*)	Nara-amo
Wine	Turas
Tea	Ts'a (Chinese)
Domestic cattle	Andras okur
Domestic yak	Musun
Wild yak	Kanyer
Sheep	Konyi
Goat	Yima
Horse	Mori
Camel	Timé
Mule	Lo-sa (Chinese)
Ass	Rjigé
Dog	Nohué
Chicken	Toko
Cat	Mioré
Rat	Lotru
Wolf	Chuna
Bear	Hsiung (Chinese)
Egg	Endégé
Milk	Nä-tzŭ (Chinese)
Butter	Ch'okan tosu
Flour	Ch'okan kuru
Tsamba	Tarh'a
Tobacco	Yen (Chinese)
Felt	Sta
Leather	Koraseu
White cotton cloth	Ch'okan pus (Chinese)
Blue cotton cloth	Koko pus
Pulo (Tibetan cloth)	T'ruk (Tibetan)
Satin	Torgo
Silk	Chiu-tzŭ (Chinese)
Musk	Trakar
Fur gown	Niké

English.	*San-Ch'uan T'u-jen.*
Hat	Marka
Boot	Kutusu
Knife	Mula chitoho
Sword	Urto
Bow	Lumo
Arrow	Sumo
Ax	Seko
Hammer	Shupiké
Gun	Nu-chiang (Chinese, *Niao chiang*)
Nail	Kataseu
Tobacco pipe	Yen p'ur (Chinese, *yen;* Tibetan, *p'or*)
Man	Nun kun
Woman	Rkonör kun
Father	Ap'a (Tibetan)
Mother	Ana
Son	K'o
Daughter	Yato (Chinese, *Ya-t'ou*)
Grandchild	Sun-tzŭ (Chinese)
Elder brother	Kaka (Chinese, *Ko-ko*)
Younger brother	T'io
Boy	Bulé
Girl	Akur
Old man	Tä-kokon (Ch. *Ta ko-ko*)
Young man	Dzalu
Head	Torgé
Teeth	Shutu
Ear	Ch'iké
Nose	Kaper
Tongue	Kélé
Hand	Kar
Thumb	Rké kuru
Forefinger	Kumrké kuru
Second finger	Tunda kuru
Third finger	?
Little finger	Chuch'ta kuru
Foot	Kor
Leg	Guya
Beard	Skar
Speech (language)	Uké
Chinese man	Chung-yuan (Chinese)

English.	*San-Ch'nan T'u-jen.*
Mongol	Mongor
Fan-tzŭ	Tépé
T'u-jen	Nutan-ni kun
Yellow River	Murun
	Pi
Thou	T'a
He	Ch'i
No plural pronouns	
This	Ni
That	Ti
Far	Kolo
Near	Tatama
Here	Niento
There	Tiento

English.	*San-Ch'uan T'u-jen.*
To write	Pitcher chugenyi
To sleep	Untanyi
It blows	Ké-polan
It rains	Kura polan
Good	Shambon
Bad	Moban
This man is good	Ni niké kun shambon
That man is bad	Ti niké kun moban
Are you well?	Ch'i sambéno
Whence do you come?	Ch'i anchi sarba
Where are you going?	Ch'i anchi sini

APPENDIX III.

CENTRAL TIBET PLANTS.

BY W. BOTTING HEMSLEY, F. R. S., A. L. S.

[EXTRACT FROM THE JOURNAL OF THE LINNEAN SOCIETY—
BOTANY, VOL. XXX, PP. 131–140.]

Since the foregoing paper on Dr. Thorold's Tibet plants and Captain Picot's Kuen-lun plants was read, the Kew Herbarium has been enriched, through the kindness of Prof. C. S. Sargent, Director of the Arnold Arboretum, Harvard University, U. S. A., by the collection of dried plants made by Mr. W. W. Rockhill on his last journey in Tibet, in 1892. * * * I had prepared a brief outline of Mr. Rockhill's route from a condensed report of his account of his journey read before the Royal Geographical Society in March of the past year; but on the very day of going to press I have received a prefatory note from him, which is much more to the purpose, and may follow here:—

"The object I had in view when making the little collection of plants, which, through Professor Ch. S. Sargent's kindness, has been examined and classified by Mr. Hemsley, of the Royal Gardens at Kew, was to give some idea of the flora of the country between the Kuen-lun range to the north and the inhabited regions of Tibet adjacent to the Tengri Nor on the south. This region has an average altitude of 15,000 feet above sea level along the route followed by me in 1892, and had not, prior to my visit, been explored.

"The route followed in 1879 by Col. Prjevalsky, when traveling towards Lh'asa, which was nearly parallel to the one that I took, differed considerably as regards the configuration of the country from mine; and consequently I anticipated that notable differences in the flora along the two roads would be discovered.

"I traversed this country in the months of May, June, July, and part of August, and heavy snowstorms and nearly daily frosts occurred during this period, though the thermometer rose more than once to 70° F., and even 83° on one occasion in the shade at 2 P. M. The mean temperature from the 17th of May, when we entered the mountainous region to the south of the Ts'aidam, to the 11th of August, when we descended to below the Timber line (13,500 feet above sea-level) on the Rama ch'u, where I ceased collecting plants, except such as the natives pointed out to me as being used by them either as food or medicinally, is shown in the following table:—

1892.	7 A. M.	2 P. M.	7 P. M.
May 17 to 31 . . .	+37°.5 F.	+54°.6 F.	+37°.3 F.
June	+35°.7	+55°.9	+38°.3
July	+43°.0	+54°.6	+44°.2
August 1 to 11 . .	+40°.6	+61°.5	+47°.3

"Nearly the whole of the region traversed in this interval was of sandstone formation, the predominating color of which was bright red. The water was invariably brackish, and in many cases undrinkable; the soil everywhere sandy, or covered with a rather fine gravel, and occasionally a little clay. The grasses grew in bunches, nowhere forming a sod, except around the rare pools of pure water fed by the melting snows we occasionally passed.

"I was careful to collect all the flowering plants I saw along my route, and the barrenness of this region may be judged by the very small number I have brought home with me.

"The only edible plant we found in this country was a species of onion (*Allium senescens*), which grew in the sand in great quantities at altitudes higher than 15,000 feet above sea-level, though we looked for it in vain below this level.

"I may here remark that the rhubarb plant, which I found growing in enormous quantities on the north and northeastern slopes of mountains on the I ch'u, Len ch'u, and other feeders of the Jyama-nu ch'u, thrived at an altitude above sea-level ranging from 12,000 to 13,500 feet. I note this fact as Col. Prjevalsky (Mongolia, ii, p. 84) says that this plant rarely flourishes at an elevation of more than 10,000 feet above the level of the sea."

"W. Woodville Rockhill."

This is an exceedingly interesting collection, especially when examined in connection with Dr. Thorold's; the plants for the greater part being of the same habit and diminutive size. More than half of them, however, are different species; and most of them had previously only been collected by Prjevalsky, from whose specimens the lamented Maximowicz described them. Several, it will be seen, too, were previously only known from the extreme western part of Tibet. In all cases where the species are different from Thorold's their general distribution is given. The localities, altitudes, and geographical positions were supplied by Mr. Rockhill.

Enumeration of the Plants collected by Mr. W. Woodville Rockhill.

1. Clematis graveolens, *Lindl.*—Flowers light yellow. Po chu valley; very abundant at 14,000 ft. Lat. N. 31° 45′, long. E. 94° 45′. Aug. 14, 1892. Western Himalaya at 6,000 to 11,000 ft., Tibet and Western China. This form is the same as that named *C. orientalis* var. *tangutica* by Maximowicz, but if the two are maintained as independent species it is better referred here.

2. Anemone imbricata, *Maxim. Fl. Tangut.* i, p. 8, t. 22. ff. 1–6.—Foot-hills of Dang la mountains, N. W. extremity of range at 16,500 ft. Lat. N. 33° 40′, long. E. 90° 35′. June 27, 1892. Previously collected only by Prjevalsky on the extreme Upper Yang-tse kiang in Tibet.

3. Ranunculus tricuspis, *Maxim, Fl. Tangut.* i, p. 12; *Enum. Pl. Mongol.* i. p. 16, t. 4. ff. 17–27.—Valley of Murus, valley bottom at 15,640 ft. Lat. N. 33° 44′, long. E. 91° 18′. June 23, 1892. Mongolia.

4. Delphinium grandiflorum, *Linn.*—Ke ch'u valley at 12,700 ft. Lat. N. 31° 25', long. E. 96°, 28'. Aug. 22, 1892. On river-bottom; fine forest growth, mostly pines (?), on hillsides; fine grass.

5. Delphinium pylzowii, *Maxim. in Mél. Biol.* ix. p. 709; *Fl. Tangut.* i. p. 21, t. 3.—Dang ch'u valley, river-bottom of gravel and clay; good fodder, at 14,500 ft. Lat. N. 32° 12', long. E. 92° 12'. July 23, 1892. Mongolia.

6. Meconopsis horridula, *Hook. f. et Thoms.*—Plateau west of Dang la mountains at 16,350 ft. Lat. N. 32° 51', long. E. 89° 44'. July 3, 1892. Sandy soil, some clay.

7. Corydalis hendersonii, *Hemsl.*—Basin of Murus. Extreme head of valley on foot-hills of Dang la mountains at 16,340 ft. Lat. N. 33° 43', long. E. 90° 50'. June 25, 1892. Sandstone. See description of this species in Thorold's list at p. 109 (of present volume of Linnean Soc. Journ.).

8. Parrya exscapa, *Ledeb.*—Basin of Murus. Extreme head of valley, on foot-hills of Dang la mountains, sandstone, at 16,340 ft. Lat. N. 33° 43', long. E. 90° 50'. June 25, 1892. Altai mountains and Western Tibet.

9. Arabis, sp. ?. Insufficient for determination.—Valley of Tsacha-tsang-bo ch'u at 14,700 ft. Lat. N. 32° 13', long. E. 90° 14'. July 6, 1892.

10. Erysimum chamæphyton, *Maxim. Fl. Tangut.* i, p. 63, t. 28. ff. 1-10.—Hill-slope two miles north of Murus river (head-waters of Yang-tse-kiang); sandy soil, some clay, at 14,750 ft. Lat. N. 33° 53', long. E. 91° 31'. June 21, 1892. Basin of Murus in lateral valley, sandstone, at 15,700 ft. Lat. N. 33° 45', long. E. 91° 05'. June 24, 1892. Northeastern Tibet.

11. Eutrema prjevalskii, *Maxim. Fl. Tangut.* i, p. 68, t. 28. ff. 11–23.—Basin of Murus, in lateral valley, sandstone, at 15,700 ft. Lat. N. 33° 45', long. E. 91° 05'. June 24, 1892. Northeastern Tibet.

12. Myricaria prostrata, *Hook. f. et Thoms. in Benth. et Hook f. Gen. Pl.* i, p. 161.—Upper Naichi gol valley near river at 12,130 ft. Lat. N. 35° 52', long. E. 93° 49'. May 21, 1892. Called "aura kashim" by the Mongols. First plant in flower seen on journey. I have followed Maximowicz in restoring this form to specific rank. It is restricted to the elevated alpine regions of the Himalayas and Tibet. See Maximowicz (Fl. Tangut. p. 95, t. 31), where it is fully described and figured. In Hooker's Fl. Brit. Ind. i. p. 250, it is treated as a variety of *M. germanica.*

13. Gueldenstædtia ?, insufficient for determination.—Gela, on Ramong ch'u at 12,670 ft. Lat. N. 31° 40', long. E. 94° 36'. Aug. 13, 1892. Fine crops of barley and turnips near by.

14. Astragalus or Oxytropis, sp. ? Material insufficient to determine the genus. —Toktomai-ulan-muren at 14,340 ft. Lat. N. 34° 09', long. E. 91° 30'. June 20, 1892. Sandy soil.

15. Astragalus or Oxytropis, sp. ? Material insufficient to determine the genus with certainty.—Valley of Murus, head-waters Yang-tse kiang, at 14,900 ft. Lat. N. 33° 45', long. E. 91° 20'. June 22, 1892.

16. Potentilla fruticosa, *Linn.*, var. pumila, *Hook. f.*—Plateau west of Dang la mountains at 16,350 ft, Lat. N. 32° 51', long. E. 89° 44'. July 3, 1892. Sandy soil, some clay.

17. Potentilla anserina, *Linn.*—Plateau west of Dang la mountains; sandy, some clay, at 16,220 ft. Lat. N. 33° 09', long. E. 89° 38'. July 2, 1892. This is widely spread in the temperate and cold regions of both the northern and southern hemispheres.

18. Potentilla nivea, *Linn.*—Ke ch'u valley; on river-bottom at 12,700 ft. Lat. N. 31° 25', long. E. 96° 28'. Aug. 22, 1892. Fine forest growth, mostly pines (?), on hill-sides; fine grass. Alpine and Arctic regions of the northern hemisphere.

19. Sedum algidum, *Ledeb.*, var. tanguticum, *Maxim.*—Camp north of Tsacha-tsang-bo ch'u; sandy soil, at 15,650 ft. Lat. N. 32° 28', long. E. 90° 03'. July 5, 1892. The species is a native of the Altai regions of Siberia; the variety was described from specimens from northwestern Kan-su.

20. Aster tibeticus, *Hook. f.*—Valley of Murus, valley-bottom at 15,640 ft. Lat. N. 33° 44', long. E. 91° 18'. June 23, 1892. Western Tibet and Kashmir at altitudes of 14,000 to 16,000 ft.

21. Inula? Material insufficient for determination.—Foot-hills of Dang la mountains, northwestern extremity of range at 16,500 ft. Lat. N. 33° 40', long. E. 90° 35'. June 27, 1892.

22. Leontopodium alpinum, *Cass.*, var.—Bank Chib-ch'ang-ts'o (Lake Glenelg). Hill-side; limestone and red sandstone; lake salt, at 16,000 ft. Lat. N. 33° 27', long. E. 90° 10'. June 30, 1892. Alps of Europe, through Central Asia and North India to China, ascending in the Himalayas to nearly 18,000 ft. The variety collected by Mr. Rockhill is a very elegant little plant about three inches high with remarkably spathulate leaves.

23. Leontopodium stracheyi, *C. B. Clarke in Herb. Kew.* (L. alpinum, *Cass.*, var. Stracheyi, *Hook. f.*).—Ru ch'u valley, in river-bottom, at 12,100 ft. Lat. N. 31° 10', long. E. 95° 12'. Aug. 16, 1892. Fine crops of barley and turnips now ripe. Also a little wheat. This Western Tibet and Himalayan plant is so easily distinguished from the other forms that it may well be accorded specific rank. It ranges from Kumaon to Nepal.

24. Anaphalis mucronata, *C. B. Clarke.*—Basin of Dang ch'u, right bank affluent. Clay and sand-gravel, at 15,180 ft. Lat. N. 32° 20', long. E. 92° 08'. July 21, 1892. This form is united with *A. nubigena*, DC., in the "Flora of British India." It is only found at great altitudes in the Himalayas and Tibet.

25. Antennaria nana, *Hook. f. et Thoms.*—Valley of Murus, head-waters Yang-tse kiang, at 14,900 ft. Lat. N. 33° 45', long. E. 91° 20'. June 22, 1892. Western Tibet in the Nubra and Shayuk valleys at 12,000 to 14,000 ft.

26. Saussurea tangutica, *Maxim. in Mél. Biol.*, xi, p. 247.—Near summit of Gam (or Angti) la at 15,600 ft. Lat. N. 30° 40', long. E. 98° 13'. Sep. 4, 1892. Tangut and Northern Tibet. The leaves are infused and used by the natives as a tonic. Called in Tibetan Sha-p'o gong-t'ag. It is said to grow only on the west side of this mountain. The Chinese call it "snow lotus" (*Hsüeh lien*).

27. Taraxacum palustre, *DC.*—Valley of Murus, valley-bottom at 15,640 ft. Lat. N. 33° 44′, long. E. 91° 18′. June 23, 1892. This is usually regarded as a variety of the almost ubiquitous *T. officinale.*

28. Cyananthus incanus, *Hook. f. et Thoms.*, var. leiocalyx, *Franch. in Morot's Journ. de Bot.* i, 1887, p. 279.—Ke ch'u valley at 12,700 ft. Lat. N. 31° 25′, long. E. 96° 28′. Aug. 22, 1892. On river-bottom. Fine forest growth, mostly pines (?) on hill-sides; fine grass. A Himalayan species, of which this is a naked-calyx variety, also found in Yün-nan. The typical form inhabits alpine localities at 12,000 to 16,000 ft.

29. Androsace tapeta, *Maxim. in Mél. Biol.* xii, p. 754.—Valley of Murus, head-waters Yang-tse kiang, at 14,900 ft. Lat. N. 33° 45′, long. E. 91° 20′. June 22, 1892. Kan-su and Ssŭ ch'uan, in Western China.

30. Androsace villosa, *Linn.*, var. latifolia, *Ledeb.*—Valley of Murus, valley-bottom at 15,640 ft. Lat. N. 33° 44′, long. E. 91° 18′. June 23, 1892. This species is widely dispersed from Asia Minor through Central Asia, North Asia, and the mountains of North India.

31. Gentiana rockhilli, *Hemsl.*, n. sp. Species *G. aristatæ*, Maxim., similis sed minor strictior floribus fere cylindricis angustissimis. *Annua*, erecta, simplex vel pauciramosa, 1–2–pollicaris, glaberima. *Folia* subscariosa, lineari-subulata, vere conduplicata, 3–4 lineas longa, apice breviter aristata, basi semiamplexicaulia, sub-erecta, cauli fere appressa. *Flores* cærulei, terminales, solitarii, subsessiles, circiter 9 lineas longi; calyx subscariosus, corollæ tubum æquans, dentibus lineari-subulatis; corollæ sursum leviter dilatatæ, lobi breves, oblongi, vix acuti, erecti, conniventes, intermediis brevioribus albis tenuissimis, fauce nuda; stamina cum pistillo omnino inclusa; styli brevissimi, stigmatibus capitatis. Ke ch'u valley at 12,700 ft. Lat. N. 31° 25′, long. E. 96° 28′. Aug. 22, 1892. On river-bottom. Fine forest growth, mostly pines (?), on hill-sides; fine grass.

32. Tretocarya sikkimensis, *Oliver, in Hook. Ic. Plant.* t. 2255.—Basin of Su ch'u valley, north side, Drayalamo pass, at 14,600 ft. Lat. N. 31° 52′, long. E. 93° 17′. Aug. 2, 1892. Limestone; fine grass; flowers blue, very abundant. Sikkim Himalaya at 11,500 ft., and Western China near Ta-chien-lu. Mr. Rockhill's specimen is much smaller than the others and nearly glabrous.

33. Pedicularis oederi, *Vahl* (P. versicolor, *Wahlenb.*).—Valley of Murus, valley-bottom at 15,640 ft. Lat. N. 33° 44′, long. E. 91° 18′. June 23, 1892. Alpine and Arctic regions of Europe, Asia, and America.

34. Pedicularis prjevalskii, *Maxim. in Mél. Biol.* x, p. 84, et xii. p. 787, n. 2. fig. 2.—Large state. Basin of Su ch'u, valley north side, Drayalamo pass, at 14,000 ft. Lat. N. 31° 52′, long. E. 93° 17′. Aug. 2, 1892. Limestone; fine grass; flowers blue, very abundant. Eastern Himalaya, Tibet, and China.

35. Lagotis brachystachya, *Maxim. in Mél. Biol.* xi, p. 300.—Hill-slope two miles north of Murus river, head-waters Yangtsekiang, at 14,750 ft. Lat. N. 33° 53′, long. E. 91° 31′. June 21, 1892. Sandy soil, some clay. Kansuh.

36. Polygonum bistorta, *Linn.*—Pochu valley at 14,000 ft. Lat. N. 31° 45′, long. E. 94° 45′. Aug. 14, 1892. Temperate and cold regions of Europe, Asia, and America.

37. Polygonum viviparum, *Linn.*—Pochu valley at 14,000 ft. Lat. N. 31° 45′, long. E. 94° 45′. Aug. 14, 1892. The seeds are parched and ground and eaten

mixed with barley-meal (*tsamba*). Tibetans call it *ranpa* or *ramba*. Temperate and Arctic regions of Europe, Asia, and America.

38. POLYGONUM BISTORTIOIDES, *Boiss.*—Rama ch'u valley, hill-side, at 1,200 ft. Lat. N. 31° 48', long. E. 94° 28'. Aug. 12, 1892. Used by the natives for food like *P. viviparum*. This species or variety is found in Asia Minor and Persia. Although very distinct from ordinary *P. bistorta*, Boissier (Flora Orientalis, iv, p. 1028) subsequently united it with that species.

39. IRIS THOROLDI, *Baker, ante*, p. 118, *et Hook. Ic. Plant. ined.*—Sharakuyi-gol, hill-slope at 13,800 ft. Lat. N. 35° 50', long. E. 93° 27'. May 29, 1892. Described from specimens collected by Dr. Thorold at an altitude of 17,800 ft. Mr. Rockhill's specimens furnish better flowers.

40. TULIPA (§ORITHYIA) *sp. aff.* T. eduli, *Baker.*—Sharakuyi-gol, hill-slope at 13,800 ft. Lat. N. 35° 50', long. E. 93° 27'. May 29, 1892. *Tulipa edulis* is a native of Japan, and Mr. Rockhill's one flower is insufficient for satisfactory identification.

41. CAREX MOORCROFTII, *Boott.*—Hill-slope two miles north of Murus river, head-waters Yangtsekiang, at 14,750 ft. Lat. N. 35° 53', long. E. 91° 31'. Sandy soil, some clay. June 21, 1892. Yarkand and Western Himalaya.

42. KOBRESIA SARGENTIANA, *Hemsl.*, n. sp. *R. schœnoidei* valde affinis sed bracteis latissimis spicam fere omnino involventibus late scariosis subtruncatis simul emarginatis. Hill-slope two miles north of Murus river, head-waters Yang-tse kiang, at 14,750 ft. Lat. N. 33° 53', long. E. 91° 31'. Sandy soil, some clay. June 21, 1892.

43. MISCANTHUS SINENSIS, *Anderss.*—Near top of Fei-yueh-kuan pass, southwest of Ya-chou Fu, in West Ssŭ-ch'uan, at 3,583 ft. Oct. 11, 1892. China, from Japan and Korea to Hongkong and Canton, Luchu and Bonin Islands, Tonquin, Borneo, and Celebes.

44. STIPA, insufficient for determination.—Hill-slope two miles north of Murus river, head-waters Yang-tse kiang, at 14,750 ft. Lat. N. 33° 53', long. E. 91° 31'. Sandy soil, some clay. June 21, 1892.

45. CALAMAGROSTIS, sp.—Near top of Fei-yueh-kuan pass, southwest of Ya-chou Fu, in West Ssŭ-ch'uan, at 3,583 ft. Oct. 11, 1892.

46. FESTUCA OVINA, *Linn.*?—Hill-slope two miles north of Murus river, head-waters Yang-tse kiang, at 14,750 ft. Lat. N. 33° 53', long. E. 91° 31'. Sandy soil, some clay. June 21, 1892. Europe, North Africa, Siberia, Himalaya, North and South America, and mountains of Australasia. Mr. Rockhill's specimen is a mere fragment.

47. USNEA BARBATA, *Fries.*—Valley of Pontramo, east of Bat'ang, at 12,600 ft. Lat. N. 29° 59', long. E. 99° 42'. Sept. 19, 1892. Sometimes 30 feet long. Hangs only on the oaks called "green oaks" (*ching k'ang*) by the Chinese. This oak is called by the French missionaries "chêne à feuilles de houx." All over the world in temperate and tropical regions.

APPENDIX IV.

TABLE OF LATITUDES AND ALTITUDES.

Date.	Locality.	Latitude North.	Altitude above Sea Level by Boiling Point.	Altitude from Corrected Reading of Aneroid.	Observations.
1891.			*Feet.*	*Feet.*	
December.	Peking	39°53'00"			Fritsche, 123.
" 7	Kalgan	40°51'39"	2,555		Prjevalsky, 2,709; Fritsche, 2,706.
" 13	Tsahan obo	40°51'12"	4,824		
" 15	Pass 5¼ miles east Shih-pa-erh t'ai			4,415	
" 16	Pass 8 miles east Wu-li pa			4,741	
" 17	Shui-mo Village			3,545	
" 18	Kuei-hua Ch'eng	40°46'30"	3,665		
" 26	Ho-k'ou	40°12'12"	2,997		
" 28	Yellow River at Ho-'kou			2,842	
" 31	Chiang-pan	40°22'49"	3,153		
1892.					
January 5	Ashan	40°56'35"	3,114		
" 9	San-tao ho-tzŭ	40°18'41"	3,450		
" 12	Kuan-ti	39°51'33"	3,404		
" 16	Shih-tsui-tzŭ	39°16' 4"	3,665		
" 17	Ning-hsia Fu	38°30'12"	3,723		
" 20	Ta-p'a	37°57'58"	3,427		
" 23	Chung-wei Hsien	37°33'04"	4,005		
" 25	Pass 9.7 miles southwest Ch'ang-liu shui			4,645	
" 25	Pass 4.7 miles northeast Kan-t'ang-tzŭ			5,037	
" 26	Ying-pan shui	37°26'28"	5,326		
" 28	Chung-ch'ang-tzŭ	36°53'37"	7,373		
" 29	Col 2.3 miles southwest preceding			6,917	
" 29	Col 5.8 miles southwest preceding			7,271	

Feb.	1	Lan-chou Fu	36°04'20"	5,167		Col. Bell, 5,500; W. W. R. (1889) 5,446.
"	6	Hsin Ch'eng	36°10'23"	5,340		
"	7	Hsiang-t'ang	35°30'37"?	5,629		
"	11	Hsi-ning Fu	36°41'04"	7,509		Prjevalsky, 7,500; Kreitner, 7,559; W. W. R. (1889), 7,608.
"	12	Lusar (Lu-sha-erh)	36°30'00"	8,907		W. W. R. (1889), 9,376.
"	17	Col 8 miles south Lusar			9,733	
"	17	Sha-erh-wan		8,861		
"	18	Col 1.4 miles southeast preceding			10,146	
"	18	Pass			9,007	
"	18	Chin-t'u yahu (pass)			11,403	
"	18	Ts'a-pa	36°00'19"	9,332		
"	19	Col east-southeast preceding			10,870	
"	19	Col 7.8 miles west-northwest Bayan-rong			10,812	
"	19	Bayan-rong T'ing		9,260		
"	20	Pass 5.1 miles east-southeast preceding			10,322	
"	20	La-mo shan-ken	36°00'19"	7,004		
"	21	I-ma-mu chuang		6,582		
"	22	Pass 4.3 miles east Rdo-lung			9,864	
"	23	Yellow River			6,616	In front of Fei-tzŭ ch'uan. Probably 300 feet too high, as village is not over 150 feet above river.
"	23	Fei-tzŭ ch'uan	36°07'49"	7,112		
"	24	Pass 2.5 miles east of Ssŭ-ké			9,765	
"	25	Tsa-ma shan (pass)			9,968	
"	26	Kuei-tê T'ing	36°02'36"	7,634		Prjevalsky, 7,500.
"	29	Lajé shan (pass)			12,341	
March	15	Hung-mao pan-tao (pass)			12,866	
"	16	Sharakuto	36°23'01"	10,967		Prjevalsky (?), 11,300.
"	18	Summit Jih-yueh shan			11,171	
"	18	Wayen nor	36°24'28"	10,198		
"	19	Kaba talen	36°20'09"	9,508		
"	20	Erté ch'u-k'a	36°20'09"	10,280		
"	21	Hato		10,207		
"	22	Ts'o kadri		9,797		
"	23	Tsatsa ch'uk'a	36°21'04"	10,136		
"	25	Muri ch'uk'a	36°17'17"	11,211		

APPENDIX IV.—TABLE OF LATITUDES AND ALTITUDES—Continued.

Date.		Locality.	Latitude North.	Altitude above Sea Level by Boiling Point.	Altitude from Corrected Reading of Aneroid.	Observations.
1892.				*Feet.*	*Feet.*	
March	27	Wahon ch'uk'a		12,187		
"	28	Wahon jamkar		13,750		
"	29	Foot Wahon jamkar pass		14,865		
"	29	Summit Wahon jamkar pass			16,348	
"	29	Kukusé			15,207	
"	30	Tsahan ossu (first camp)		13,042		
"	30	Tsahan ossu (second camp)		12,279		
"	31	Tsahan ossu (third camp)	36°00'14"	12,279		
April	1	Tsahan ossu (fourth camp	36°01'14"	11,555		
"	3	Koko k'utul		12,375		
"	5	Shang, Village	36°00'35"	9,939		W. W. R. (1889), 10,552.
"	10	Yogoré gol (second camp)	35°47'12"	10,791		
"	11	Yogoré gol Kawa obo	35°31'59"	11,845		
"	12	Tosu nor	35°21'51"	13,179		
"	17	Koko k'utul of Shang			14,440	
"	17	Oim k'utul			13,195	
"	23	Oim	35°52'14"	12,533		
"	30	Baron, Village (Kuré)	36°11'10"	9,243		W. W. R. (1889), 9,809.
May	3	Shudengé		8,833		
"	4	Shara tolh'a	36°24'40"	8,799		
"	6	Tengélik	36°24'42"	8,735		A—— K——, lat. 36°24'25".
"	7	Bolang		8,631		
"	8	Toli éken	36°25'49"	8,715		
"	9	Tsahan k'ol	36°25'54"	8,525		
"	11	Naichi gol	36°26'20"	8,925		
"	17	Kano		10,720		Prjevalsky's Gono.
"	18	Kano k'utul (pass)			12,190	

"	18	Tsahan toh'a	35°55'55"	10,725		
"	19	Kokotom k'utul (pass)			11,910	Prjevalsky, 11,200 (?).
"	19	Chibeké		11,241		
"	20	Buhutai	35°52'57"	11,793		
"	21	Tator		12,133		Prjevalsky camped at about this place. He gives the altitude of his camp as 12,500.
"	22	Kuré bori	35°51'52"	12,285		
"	28	Shara-kuyi gol		13,788		
"	30	Shara-kuyi k'utul			15,559	
"	30	Ch'uwu doksai		15,152		
"	31	Ch'umarin dsun kuba	35°37'37"	14,482		
June	1	Elesu nor, camp in basin of	35°22'21"	14,442		
"	2	Elesu nor	35°13'33"	14,497		
"	4	Kokoshili éken		15,077		
"	4	Kokoshili k'utul (pass)			15,300	
"	5	Kara daban	35°05'33"	15,292		
"	7	Olon horgo		15,716		
"	8	Namchutola muren (camp 2 miles S. of Tabu tolh'a)	35°05'21"	15,471		
"	10	Shiré nor	34°55'50"	15,572		
"	14	Pass south of preceding			15,750	
"	14	North side Ulan ula		15,898		
"	15	First col in Ulan ula			16,000	
"	15	Second col in Ulan ula			16,200	
"	15	South side Ulan ula	34°55'25"	15,514		
"	16	Pass 12 miles southwest Ulan ula			15,820	
"	16	Dungburé éken	34°46'21"	15,826		
"	17	Camp		15,289		
"	18	Toktomai muren, first camp	34°32'06"	14,897		
"	19	Toktomai muren, second camp	34°19'54"	14,819		
"	20	Toktomai muren, south branch	34°09'55"	14,345		
"	21	Murus, camp 2 miles north of	33°53'33"	14,745		
"	22	Murus, camp 1.5 miles south of	33°46'32"	14,900		
"	23	Murus, camp 2 miles west of	33°45'12"	15,317		
"	24	Camp		15,729		
"	25	Camp		16,343		
"	26	Dang la éken	33°42'11"	16,479		

APPENDIX IV.—TABLE OF LATITUDES AND ALTITUDES—Continued.

Date.		Locality.	Latitude North.	Altitude above Sea Level by Boiling Point.	Altitude from Corrected Reading of Aneroid.	Observations.
1892.				Feet.	Feet.	
June	27	Camp 19 miles west-southwest preceding	33°36′23″	16,150		
"	28	Camp on Kéten gol	33°31′43″	15,891		
"	30	Chib-chang ts'o	33°27′42″	15,988		
July	1	Camp southwest of preceding		15,807		
"	2	Camp 20 miles south of preceding		16,223		
"	3	Camp south of pass	32°51′07″	16,355		
"	4	Camp on pass south-southeast		16,076		
"	5	Camp 21 miles south-southeast preceding		15,650		
"	6	Tsacha tsangpo ch'u, 2 miles south of river	32°13′37″	14,700		
"	6	Camp 8 miles south of preceding	32°08′24″	15,118		
"	8	Namru Valley	32°00′55″	15,018		
"	15	Camp near Tsacha tsangpo ch'u		15,212		
"	16	Camp Tsacha tsangpo ch'u basin	32°45′35″	15,377		
"	18	Camp 8.5 miles east-southeast preceding		15,845		
"	19	Camp 18 miles east-southeast preceding	32°35′40″	16,299		
"	20	Camp 20 miles southeast preceding		15,931		
"	21	Camp 15 miles east-southeast preceding		15,278		
"	23	Dang ch'u	32°12′49″	14,514		
"	28	Trashiling, 1.5 miles east of	32°09′06″	14,946		
"	30	Chingo	32°07′34″	15,430		
"	31	Nashé ch'u		14,176		
August	1	Camp		14,747		
"	2	Top Drajya lamo Pass			16,083	
"	3	Pass 5.5 miles southwest Song-chyang sumdo			15,769	
"	3	Song-chyang sumdo		13,364		
"	4	Ponta	32°08′22″	14,410		
"	5	Pon la			15,668	

"	5	Tséga (on Su ch'u)	32°11'31"	13,230		
"	8	Trazélung		13,377		
"	9	Maja la			15,444	
"	10	Gentsé	32°01'41"	13,345		
"	10	Medo la			15,167	
"	11	I ch'u		13,067		Here my route joins Bower's. His Ircho is my I ch'u; his Ita my I ch'u valley.
"	11	Angé-nong	31°50'56"	14,157		Approx. Bower's Camp 104; alt. 14,000.
"	12	Rama ch'u	31°48'51"	12,780		Probably Bower's Lan ch'u.
"	13	Pass 3 miles from preceding			14,919	
"	13	Ramnong ch'u	31°40'46"	12,672		
"	14	Pass 5.5 miles from preceding			15,868	
"	14	Polaga	31°37'22"	13,672		
"	15	Po la			16,032	
"	15	Drohã la			15,924	
"	15	Noshé la			15,651	
"	15	Ma la			15,797	Bower's Ma la, 15,020.
"	15	Ch'uréma		12,927		Bower's Sarisumdo and Bonvalot's Séré-Soumdo are on my Séremdo ch'u, a little below mouth of Ru ch'u.
"	16	Sagotong (on Ru ch'u)		12,096		Half a mile from Bower's Tashi ling monastery; alt. 12,820. Bonvalot's Sakoton.
"	17	Chung-nyi la			14,934	Bower's Chuni la, 14,120.
"	17	Piwa-ka-nag		13,040		
"	18	Lah'a (Nar Peihu)		12,130		Bower's Khemo Tinchin, 12,762.
"	20	Péné-ringu		14,111		
"	20	Mer-djong gomba		12,711		Bower's Maru, 12,250.
"	21	Nanyi la			16,507	Bower's Shona la (?), 15,220.
"	22	Camp on Kê ch'u	31°21'52"	12,709		Bower's Kichi; Bonvalot's Ketchaka.
"	23	Dre la			14,735	Bower's Dojala, 14,720; Bonvalot's Djala, 14,760.
"	23	Riwoché, town of	31°23'40"	12,269		Bower's Riuchi My, 12,265; Bonvalot's Routchi Djunda.
"	24	Tartung on Tsé ch'u		12,061		
"	26	Nyulda		11,942		Bower's Memda, 12,325; Bonvalot's Kintachié (Houmda).
"	27	Sung-lo zamba (Tsé ch'u)		11,722		

APPENDIX IV.—TABLE OF LATITUDES AND ALTITUDES—Continued.

Date.		Locality.	Latitude North.	Altitude above Sea Level by Boiling Point.	Altitude from Corrected Reading of Aneroid.	Observations.
1892.				*Feet.*	*Feet.*	
Aug.	29	Shi la, first col			15,909	
"	29	Shi la, second col			14,421	
"	29	Shi la, third col			15,189	
"	29	Gé, village		12,515		
"	30	Dri la			14,849	
"	30	Kinda, on Om ch'u		10,050		
Sept.	1	Mité la			13,172	
"	1	Pungdé		12,292		Bower's Pandesar, 12,900.
"	2	Ipi la			14,883	Bower's Shila la (?), 15,020.
"	2	Drama la			13,472	
"	2	Luma la			13,617	Bower, 14,100.
"	2	Bagong	30°56′21″	12,018		Bower's Bagang and Tyat Bagang, 12,400.
"	3	Dzo la			13,734	Bower's Zola la, 14,800.
"	3	Kungsa, village	30°45′08″	11,622		
"	4	Gam la			15,644	Bower, 15,020.
"	5	Chamdun-Draya		11,709		Bower, Tyat Chamdi, 12,125.
"	6	Ra-djong (1 mile below)	30°28′51″	12,560		Bower's Rajwa.
"	7	P'o-jya la			13,633	Bower's Pukchang la, 14,220.
"	7	Ken-jya la			13,073	Bower's Khonja la, 13,700.
"	8	A-djod		12,870		Bower's Achowa, 13,375 (or 13,420).
"	8	Col south of A-djod			15,000	Bower's Shafi la, 15,000.
"	8	A-djod la			14,029	
"	8	Top T'ang-yao shan			12,627	
"	10	Lar-t'ang		12,385		
"	10	Rishod Valley (4.8 miles above village)	23°55′35″	13,652		Bower gives for village Rashwa, 12,720.
"	10	Pass south of Rishod Valley			15,095	Bower's Khonsa la, 15,020.
"	10	Pass			14,610	Bower's Khonsa la, 15,020.

"	12	Gart'ok (Chiang-k'a)	29°41'39"	12,240		Bower's Monkong Garthok, 12,991; A—— K——, 11,920; lat., 29°41'07"; Bonvalot's Tchangka.
"	12	Latsé la			13,234	Bower's Lamba la.
"	12	P'u la			11,532	Bower's Doi la, 13,920.
"	12	Guhu		11,728		Bower's Goshu; Bonvalot's Kouchou.
"	13	Hondo la			13,305	Bower, 14,870.
"	13	Bam la			12,931	Bower, 14,420.
"	13	Djink'ang-ding		11,619		Gill's Kong-Tze-Ka, 11,675.
"	14	Pass at K'ong-djin-k'a			11,343	Bower, 13,420; Gill, 11,972; Bonvalot calls the village Kountsetiune.
"	14	Gura	29°42'03"	8,031		Gill, 8,660; Bower's Girathong.
"	16	Ba (Bat'ang)	30°00'53"	8,223		Desgodins, 8,065; Gill, 8,546; A—— K——, 8,160; lat., 30°00'30"; Bower, 8,500.
"	19	P'ongdramo		12,632		Gill, 13,158; Bower's Pongotomo; Bonvalot's Pendjamo.
"	20	Taso la			16,285	Gill, 16,568; Bower's Taga la.
"	20	Taso t'ang			13,261	Gill, 13,347; Bower's Tashu, 13,145; Bonvalot's Taso.
"	20	Mang la			13,940	
"	20	Rateu la			14,336	Bower's Lathok la; A—— K——, 15,340.
"	21	Rateu (Zamba t'ang)		13,083		Gill, 13,794; Bower's Rathi; Bonvalot's Sampa.
"	21	Näda (Erh-lang-wan)			11,796	Gill's Nen-Da, 13,133; Bower's Namda, 12,793.
"	23	Ranang (Lamaya)		11,777		Gill's Ra-Nung, 12,826; Bower's Ramo, 12,630; Bonvalot's Lamaïa.
"	23	Lar-t'ang	29°52'24"	12,849		Gill's Ma-Dung-La-Tza; Bower's Larothong.
"	24	Hu-p'i-k'ou			13,902	
"	24	Kan hai-tzŭ			13,996	Gill's Dzong-da; Bower's Zomda.
"	24	Garalaka			14,713	Bower's Gara la; A—— K——, 15,400.
"	24	Jambu t'ang			13,686	Gill's Jiom-Bu-T'ang, 14,718; Bower's Jambothong.
"	24	Ché zanka (bridge over Li ch'u)			12,512	Gill's Che-Zom-Ka or To-T'ang.
"	24	Li ch'u at preceding			12,351	
"	25	Lit'ang		12,914		Gill, 13,280; A—— K——, 13,400.

Appendix IV.—Table of Latitudes and Altitudes—Continued.

Date.		Locality.	Latitude North.	Altitude above Sea Level by Boiling Point.	Altitude from Corrected Reading of Aneroid.	Observations.
1892.				Feet.	Feet.	
Sept.	27	Dzomo la			13,803	Gill's Shie-Gi La, 14,425; Bower's Damado la.
"	27	Hor ch'uk'a			12,647	Gill's Ho-Chu-Ka, 13,250.
"	27	Wango la			14,307	Gill's Wang-Gi La, 15,558; Bower's Ongi la.
"	27	Ku la			13,356	Gill's Deh-Re-La, 14,584; Bower's Dera la (?)
"	27	Tsamalatung		12,469		Gill's Cha-Ma-Ra-Don; Bower's Thamo Rothang.
"	28	Zumda la			13,339	Gill's Tang Gola, 14,109; Bower's Tonga la (?)
"	28	Lit'ang golo			12,165	Gill's Lit'ang Ngoloh, 12,451; Bower's Galuh.
"	28	Timber line			13,245	
"	28	Mo-lung-gong la, first summit			13,073	Bower's Polong Gan.
"	28	Mo-lung-gong la, second summit			13,480	
"	28	Mo-lung-gong la, third summit			13,757	Gill's Ra-ma la, 15,110; Bower's Dosa la.
"	28	Laniba (Chien-tzŭ wan)	30°01′55″	13,477		Gill, 14,335; Bower's Lanipa.
"	29	Laniba Pass			14,880	Bower's Rama la.
"	29	Nya ch'u (Yalung, in front of Nya-ch'u-k'a)			9,362	
"	29	Nya-ch'u-k'a (town of Ho-k'ou)		8,518		Gill, 9,222; A—— K——, 8,410; lat., 30° 02′18″; Bower's Nagchuka; Bonvalot's Hokéou.
"	30	Orong shé		11,374		Gill, 12,048; Bower's Urong Dongu; Bonvalot's Ouonlongtche.
Oct.	1	Kaji la			14,454	Gill's Ka-Ji La, 14,454; Bower's Kashi la; A—— K——, 14,710.
"	1	Aniang-pa		11,792		Gill, 12,413; Bower's Amia To.

"	2	Tiru, village	....	....	13,150	Gill's Ti-zu; Bower's Thaju; Bonvalot's Tijou.
"	2	Chedo la	....	....	14,320	Gill's Cheh-Toh Shan, 14,515; Bower's Gi la.
"	2	Chedo, village	....	....	10,650	Gill's Chen-Toh, 10,838; Bower's Chitu.
"	5	Darchedo (town of Ta-chien-lu)	....	8,204	....	Biet, 8,207; Gill, 8,346; Baber, 8,480; A—— K——, 8.310.

N. B.—In computing altitudes, Peking has been taken as the lower station from December 1, 1891, to May 17, 1892, inclusive. From May 18, 1892, to August 1, 1892, inclusive, the lower station was Darjeeling; and from August 2, 1892, to October 5, 1892, Chung-king (Ssŭ-ch'uan).

APPENDIX V.

Mean Corrected Monthly Temperature from January to October, 1892.

	7 A. M.	2 P. M.	7 P. M.	Mean Temperature.
	F.	*F.*	*F.*	*F.*
January	+ 1°.2	+30°.4	+17°.7	+16°.4
February	+17°.5	+39°.0	+27°.0	+27°.8
March	+18°.9	+39°.0	+26°.3	+28°.1
April	+28°.1	+52°.4	+32°.5	+37°.1
May	+40°.9	+61°.5	+44°.3	+48°.9
June	+35°.7	+56°.2	+38°.3	+43°.4
July	+42°.6	+54°.6	+44°.2	+47°.1
August	+41°.7	+63°.8	+49°.5	+51°.6
September	+50°.7	+64°.0	+50°.8	+51°.1
October	+47°.3	+48°.0	+47°.5	+47°.7

INDEX.